THE DEFINITIVE PAUL SIMON SONGBOOK

THE DEFINITIVE
PAUL SIMON
SONGBOOK

Amsco Publications
New York/London/Paris/Sydney/Copenhagen/Berlin/Tokyo/Madrid

Cover photograph © 1987 Harrison Funk
Back cover and spine photograph from the Paul Simon Archives
Project editors: Inti Alejandra Viana and David Bradley

Order No. PS 11594
US International Standard Book Number: 0.8256.3323.0
UK International Standard Book Number: 1.84449.645.7

Exclusive Distributors:
Music Sales Corporation
257 Park Avenue South, New York, NY 10010 USA
Music Sales Limited
8/9 Frith Street, London W1D 3JB England
Music Sales Pty. Limited
120 Rothschild Street, Rosebery, Sydney, NSW 2018, Australia

Printed in the United States of America by
Vicks Lithograph and Printing Corporation

CONTENTS

The 59th Street Bridge Song (Feelin' Groovy)

Words and Music by Paul Simon

E♭
B♭/D
Cm7
B♭
3fr.
I've come to watch your flow - ers grow - in'. Ain't-cha got no rhymes for me?
Doot-in' doo-doo, feel-in' groov - y.
Ba da da
da da da da, feel-in' groov - y.
I got
no deeds to do, no prom-is-es to keep. I'm dap-pled and drow-sy and read-y to sleep. Let the
morn-ing-time drop all its pet-als on me. Life, I love you, All is groov-
y.
repeat and fade

7 O'Clock News/Silent Night

Narration and arrangement by Paul Simon
Words and Music by Paul Simon

Narration

(Spoken over musical background of "Silent Night")

"This is the early evening edition of the news.
The recent fight in the House of Representatives was over the open housing section of the Civil Rights Bill.
Brought traditional enemies together but it left the defenders of the measure without the votes of their strongest supporters.
President Johnson originally proposed an outright ban covering discrimination by everyone for every type of housing but it had no chance from the start and everyone in Congress knew it.
A compromise was painfully worked out in the House Judiciary Committee.
In Los Angeles today comedian Lenny Bruce died of what was believed to be an overdose of narcotics.
Bruce was forty-two years old.
Dr. Martin Luther King says he does not intend to cancel plans for an open housing march Sunday into the Chicago suburb of Cicero.
Cook County Sheriff Ogleby asked King to call off the march and the police in Cicero said they would ask the National Guard be called out if it is held.
King now in Atlanta, Georgia plans to return to Chicago Tuesday.
In Chicago Richard Speck, accused murderer of nine student nurses, was brought before a Grand Jury today for indictment.
The nurses were found stabbed and strangled in their Chicago apartment.
In Washington the atmosphere was tense today as a special sub-committee of the House Committee on Un-American activities continued its probe into anti-Viet Nam war protests.
Demonstrators were forcibly evicted from the hearings when they began chanting anti-war slogans.
Former Vice President Richard Nixon says that unless there is a substantial increase in the present war effort in Viet Nam, the U.S. should look forward to five more years of war.
In a speech before the Convention of the Veterans of Foreign Wars in New York, Nixon also said opposition to the war in this country is the greatest single weapon working against the U.S.
That's the 7 o'clock edition of the news.
Goodnight."

Ace In The Hole

Words and Music by Paul Simon

F♯m
where you been so long?
G♯m7♭5
F○7
1., 2.
A7
Don't you know me? I'm your ace in the hole."
Bm A7
3.
A/E
D♯m7♭5
ace in the hole, oh, yeah."
Dmaj7
C♯m7♭5
A♯○7
Ace in the hole, lean on me.
Bm7
to Coda
F○7
Don't you know me? I'm your guar - an -
A
Bm7/A
A7
tee.

Shuffle beat
G/D
G
F♯m
Rid-ing on this roll - ing bus,
be-neath a ston-y sky,
Bm
E7
A
A7
with a slow moon ris-ing
and the smoke-stacks drift-ing by;
G/D
G
F♯m
in the hour when the heart is weak - est, and
mem-o-ry is strong;
Bm
E7
A7
when time has stopped
and the bus just rolls a - long
D
1., 2.
A
Roll on, roll on.
Roll on roll on.
3.
A
A/G♯
F♯m
Bm
E
N.C.
Tempo I
A7
Bm
A7
D.S. (third ending) al Coda I
Bm
A7
Bm
A7
Bm
A7

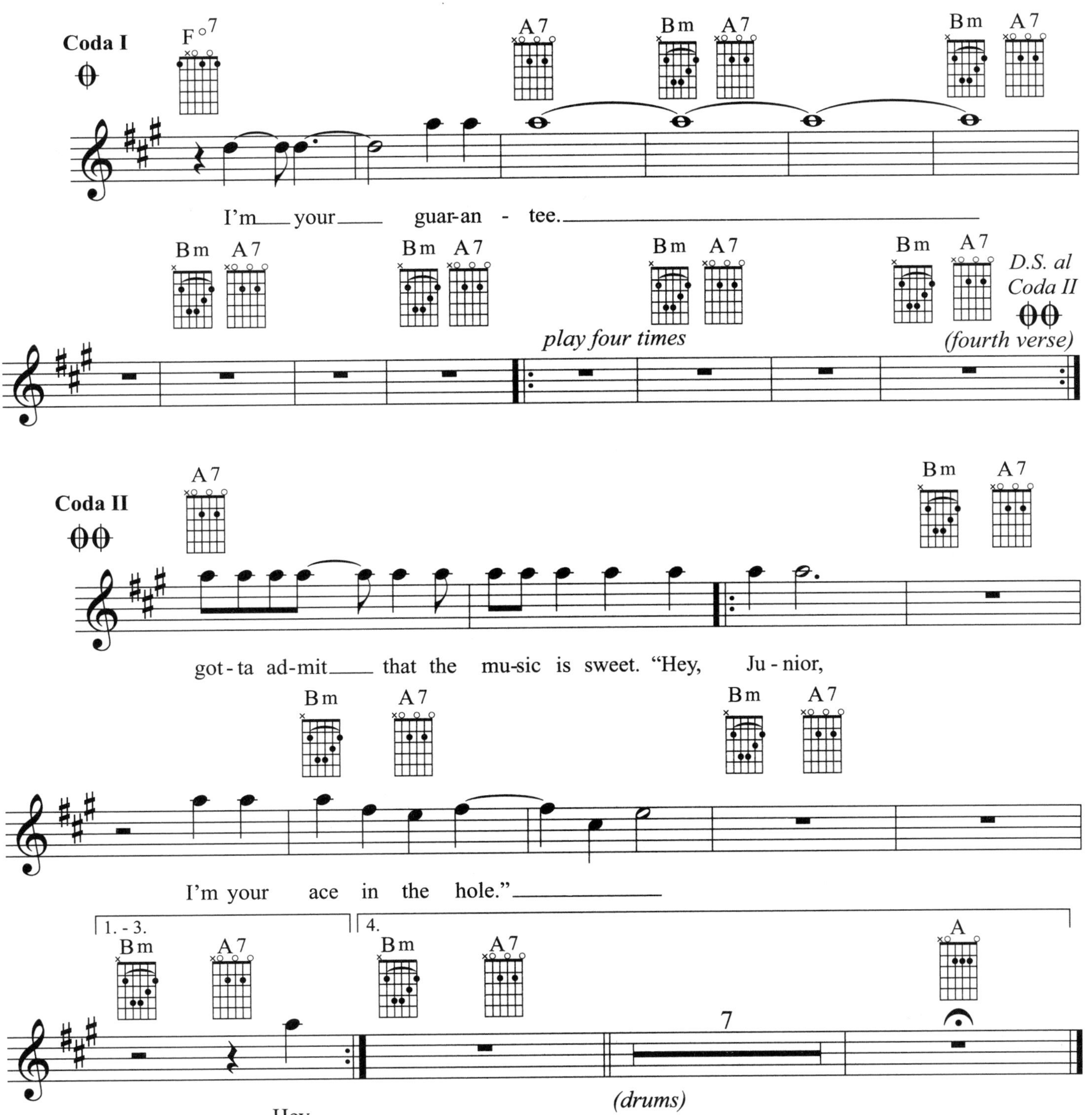
Coda I
F°7
A7
Bm
I'm your guar-an - tee.
play four times
D.S. al Coda II
(fourth verse)
Coda II
got-ta ad-mit that the mu-sic is sweet. "Hey, Ju-nior,
I'm your ace in the hole."
1. - 3.
4.
A
Hey,
7
(drums)

2. Two hundred dollars, that's my ace in the hole.
When I'm down, dirty, and desperate
That's my emergency bank roll. I got
Two hundred dollars, that's the price on the street,
If you wanna get some quality
That's the price you got to meet. And the man says,
"Hey, Junior, where you been so long?
Don't you know me?
I'm your ace in the hole."

3. Once I was crazy and my ace in the hole
Was that I knew that I was crazy,
So I never lost my self-control.
I just walk in the middle of the road,
I sleep in the middle of the bed,
I stop in the middle of a sentence,
And the voice in the middle of my head said,
"Hey, Junior, where you been so long?
Don't you know me?
I'm your ace in the hole, oh yeah."

4. Some people say music, that's their ace in the hole.
Just your ordinary rhythm and blues,
Your basic rock and roll.
You can sit on the top of the beat,
You can lean on the side of the beat,
You can hang from the bottom of the beat,
But you got to admit that the music is sweet.
"Where you been so long?
Don't you know me?
I'm your ace in the hole, oh yeah."

America

Words and Music by Paul Simon

Bright waltz tempo

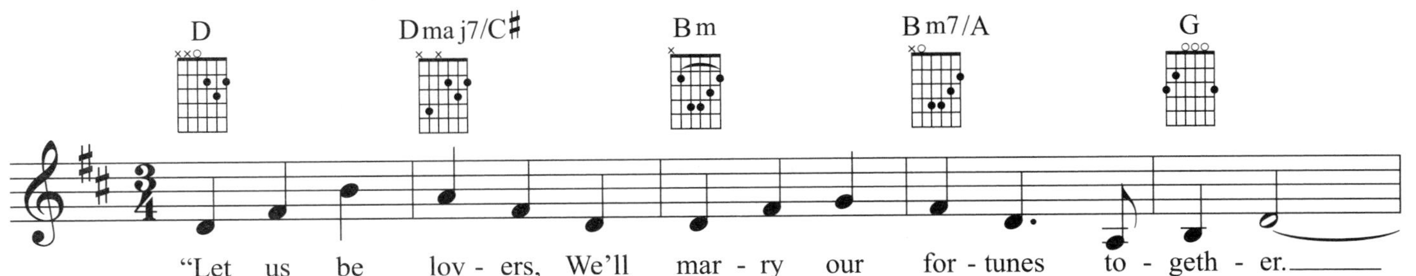

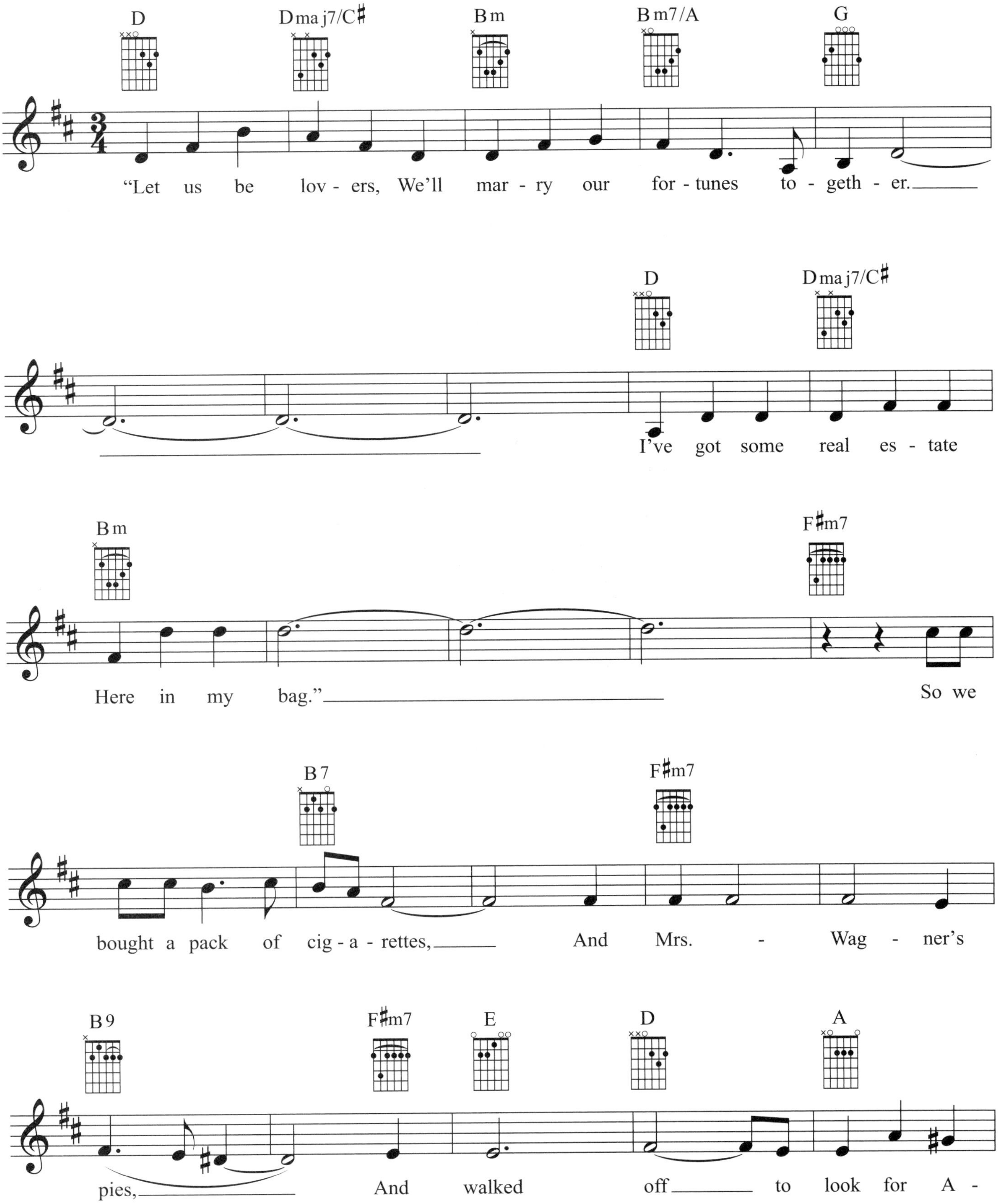

D
Dmaj7/C♯
Bm
Bm7/A
G
"Let us be lov - ers, We'll mar - ry our for - tunes to - geth - er.
D
Dmaj7/C♯
I've got some real es - tate
Bm
F♯m7
Here in my bag."
So we
B7
F♯m7
bought a pack of cig - a - rettes,
And Mrs. - Wag - ner's
B9
F♯m7
E
D
A
pies,
And walked off to look for A -

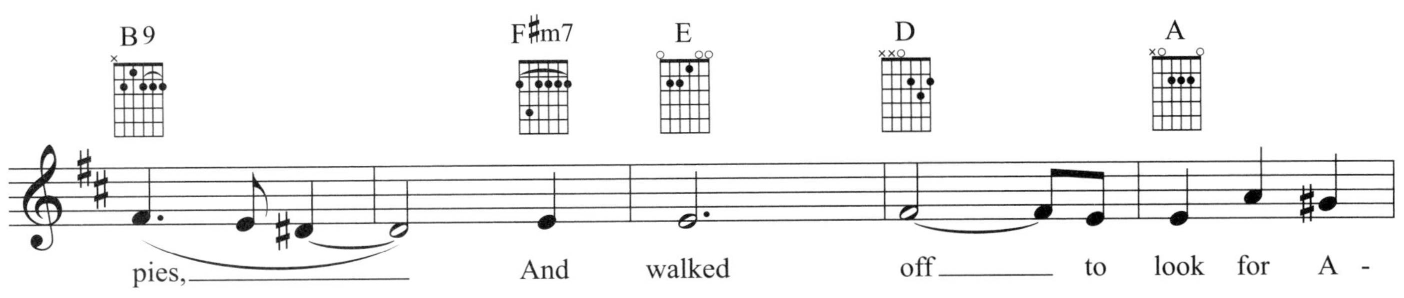

D
Dmaj7/C♯
Bm
Bm7/A
G
mer - - i - ca.
D
Dmaj7/C♯
"Kath - y," I said, As we
Bm
Bm7/A
G
board - ed a Grey-hound in Pitts - burgh,
D
Dmaj7/C♯
Bm
"Mich - i - gan seems like a dream to me now.
Bm7
A
It took me four days To hitch-hike from
E
A
E
Dmaj7
Sag - i - naw. I've come to look for A - mer -
D
- - i - ca."

Cmaj7
C
D
Laugh - ing on the bus,
Play-ing games with the fac - es,
Cmaj7
She said the man in the gab - bar-dine
D
suit Was a spy.
G
Gmaj7
D
I said, "Be care - ful, His bow - tie is real - ly a cam - 'ra."
Dmaj7/C♯
Bm
Bm7/A
G♯m7♭5
3fr.
Gmaj7
D
Dmaj7/C♯
Bm
"Toss me a cig - a - rette, I think there's
Bm7/A
G
one in my rain - coat."

D
Dmaj7/C♯
Bm
"We smoked the last one An hour a - go."
F♯m7
B9
So I looked at the scen-er - y,
F♯m7
B9
E
She read her mag-a - zine; And the moon
D
A
D
Dmaj7/C♯
Bm
rose o - ver an o - - - pen field.
Bm7/A
G
D
Dmaj7
Bm
D
G
"Kath - y, I'm lost I said, Though I knew she was sleep - ing.
Gmaj7/F♯
Em7
G
D
Dmaj7
I'm emp - ty and ach - ing and

Bm
A
I don't know why." Count- ing the
E
A
cars On the New Jer - sey Turn - pike. They've all come to
E
Dmaj7
D
look for A - mer - - i - ca,
E
A
E
Dmaj7
All come to look for A - mer - i -
D
D
Dmaj7/C♯
Bm
ca.
Bm7/A
Em7
Em7/D
A7/C♯
A7
repeat and fade

Adiós Hermanos

Music by Paul Simon
Lyrics by Paul Simon and Derek Walcott

Moderately slow

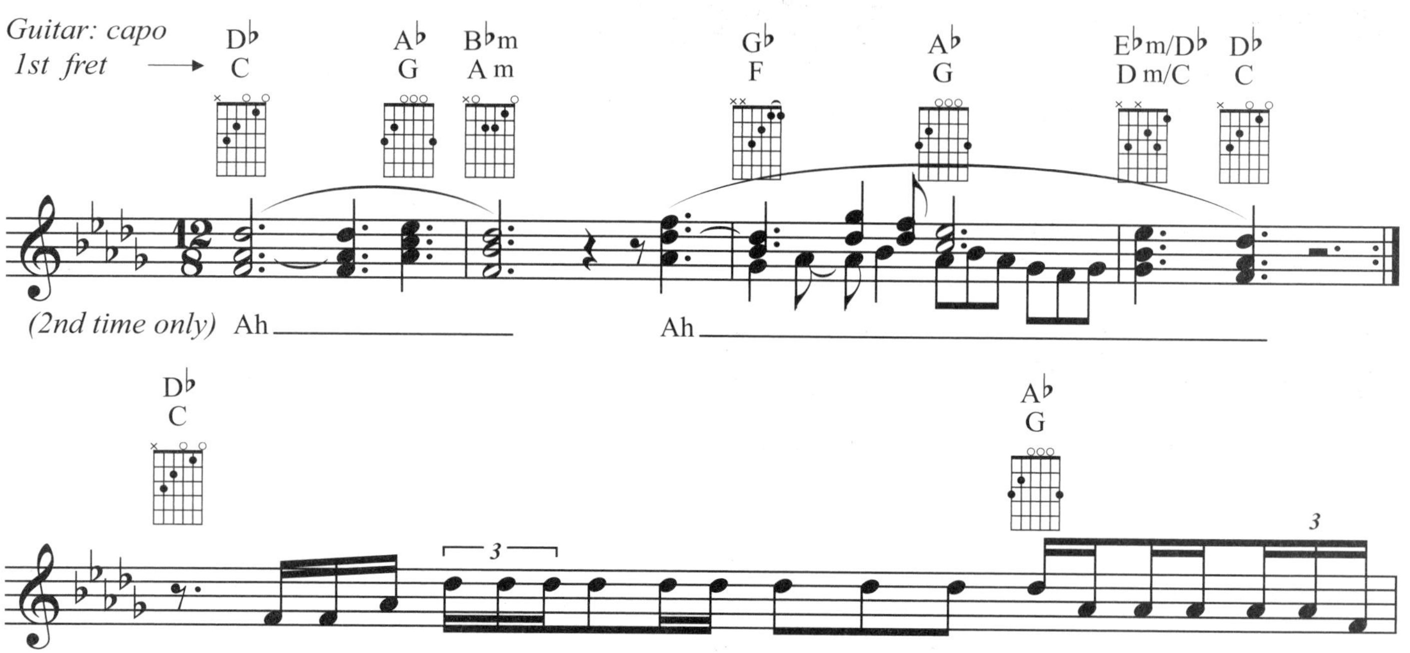

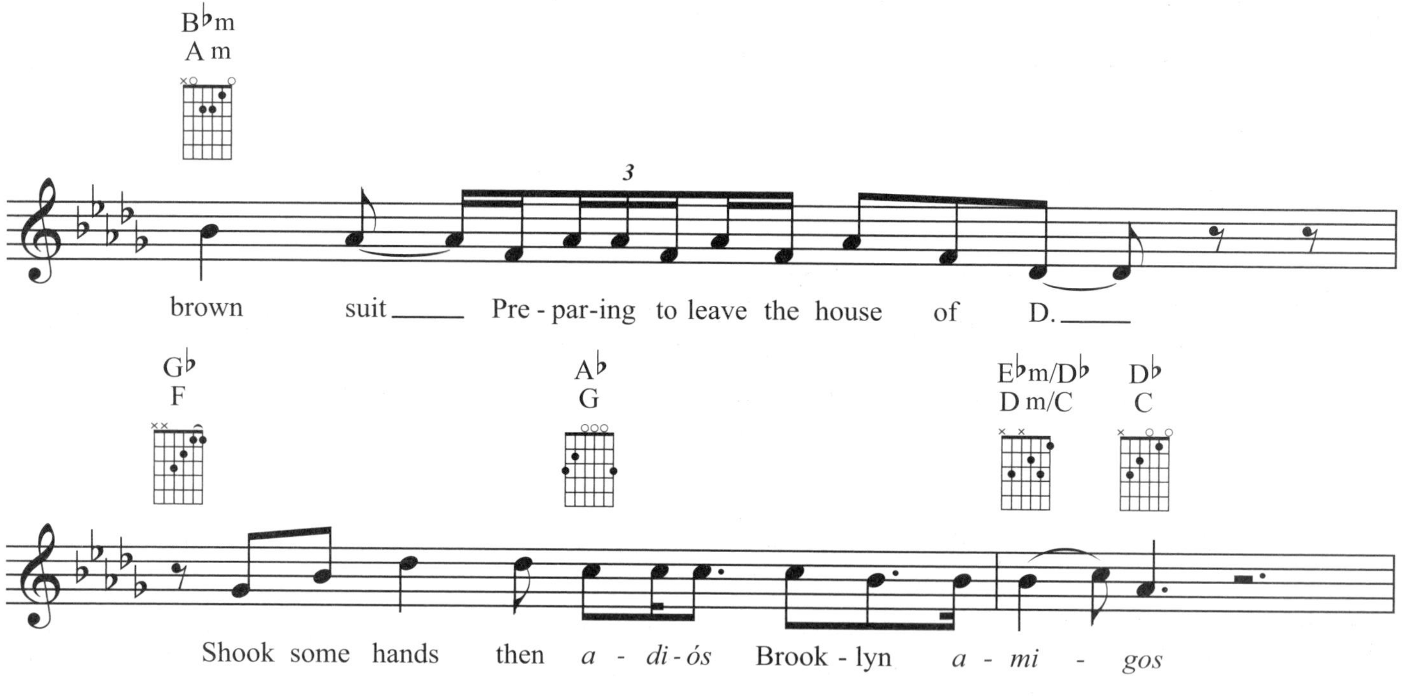

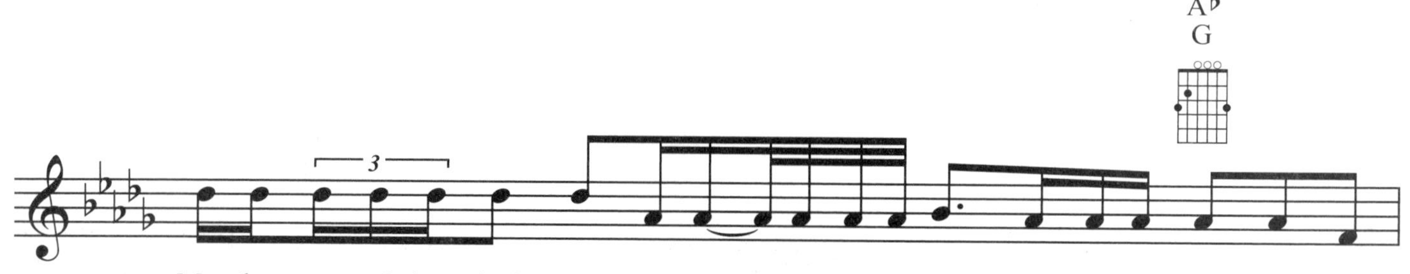

B♭m Am
G♭ F
A♭ G
judge, Judge Ger-ald Cul-kin, Would-n't play it by the book May-be let us off the hook But,
E♭m/D♭ Dm/C
D♭ C
A♭ G
Woh-oo-woh, I knew bet-ter. A-fraid to leave the pro-jects
B♭m Am
G♭ F
A♭ G
To cross in-to an-oth-er neigh-bor-hood The blan-cos and the nig-ger gangs Well,
E♭m/D♭ Dm/C
D♭ C
G♭ F
they'd kill you if they could. An-gel of Mer-cy, peo-ple are
B B♭
C° B°
D♭ C
B B♭
suff-'ring All o-ver the world
G♭ F
D♭ C
A♭ G
D♭ C
D♭7 C7
Span-ish chil-dren are taught on their knees to be-

G♭
F
G♭/B♭
F/A
B
B♭
C°
B°
D♭
C
lieve ___ An-gel of Mer-cy, peo-ple are suff-'ring All o - ver the is - land to - night, ___
B
B♭
G♭
F
D♭
C
A♭
G
D♭
C
A♭
G
A♭7
G7
___ Moth-ers weep Sis - ters grieve. ___ Well, I
D♭
C
A♭
G
3
en - tered the court - room, state of New York Coun - ty of New York,
B♭m
A m
just some spic They scrubbed off the side - walk
G♭
F
A♭
G
E♭m/D♭
D m/C
D♭
C
Guilt - y by my dress Guilt - y in the press Let The Cape - man burn for the mur-der
D♭
C
A♭
G
3
Well the "Span - ish boys" had their day in court And now it was time for some

B♭m
A m
G♭
F
A♭
G
fuck-in' law and or-der
"The e - lec-tric chair
For the greas-y pair"
Said the
E♭m/D♭
D m/C
D♭
C
A♭
G
judge to the court re-por-ter
A - fraid to leave the pro - jects
B♭m
A m
To cross in - to an - oth - er neigh - bor - hood
G♭
F
A♭
G
The news - pa - pers and the T. V. crews
Well,
E♭m/D♭
D m/C
D♭
C
G♭
F
they'd kill you if they could
An - gel of Mer-cy, peo - ple are
B
B♭
C°
B°
D♭
C
B
B♭
suff - 'ring All o - ver the world

G♭ F D♭ C A♭ G A♭7 G7 D♭ C A♭7 C7
12/8
A Span-ish boy could be killed ev-'ry night of the
G♭ F G♭/B♭ F/A
3
week But just let some white boy die And the world goes
B B♭ C° B° D♭ C G♭ F D♭ C A♭ G D♭ C
cra-zy for blood, La-tin blood. I don't lie when I
A♭ G A♭7 G7 D♭ C B♭ A
speak. Well they shack-led my
B♭m Am G♭ F A♭ G
hands A heav-y belt a-round my waist to re-
E♭m/D♭ Dm/C D♭ C
strain me And they shack-led my

B♭m A m
G♭ F
A♭ G
legs Her - nan - dez, the "Um-brel-la Man," chained be -
E♭m/D♭ D m/C
D♭ C
D♭ C
A♭ G
side me Then we rode that Black Ma - ri - ah Through the
B♭m A m
G♭ F
A♭ G
streets of Span - ish Har - lem Call-ing old friends on the cor - ners Just to
E♭m/D♭ D m/C
D♭ C
A♭ G
B♭m A m
lay our pray'rs up-on them Cry - ing A - di-ós Her-man-os, A - di - ós
G♭ F
A♭ G
E♭m/D♭ D m/C
D♭ C
A - di - ós Her-man - os, A - di-ós

All Around the World Or The Myth Of Fingerprints

Words and Music by Paul Simon

D
G
C
D
to Coda
they're all the same."
Well, the
G
C
G
sun gets wea - ry and the sun goes down, ev - er since the wa-ter-mel-on.
C
G
And the lights come up on a black pit town
C
G
Some-bod - y says, "What's a bet-ter thing to do?"
C
G
D
Well, it's just not me and it's not just you. This is all
C
G
1.
2.
D.S. al Coda
a - round the world.

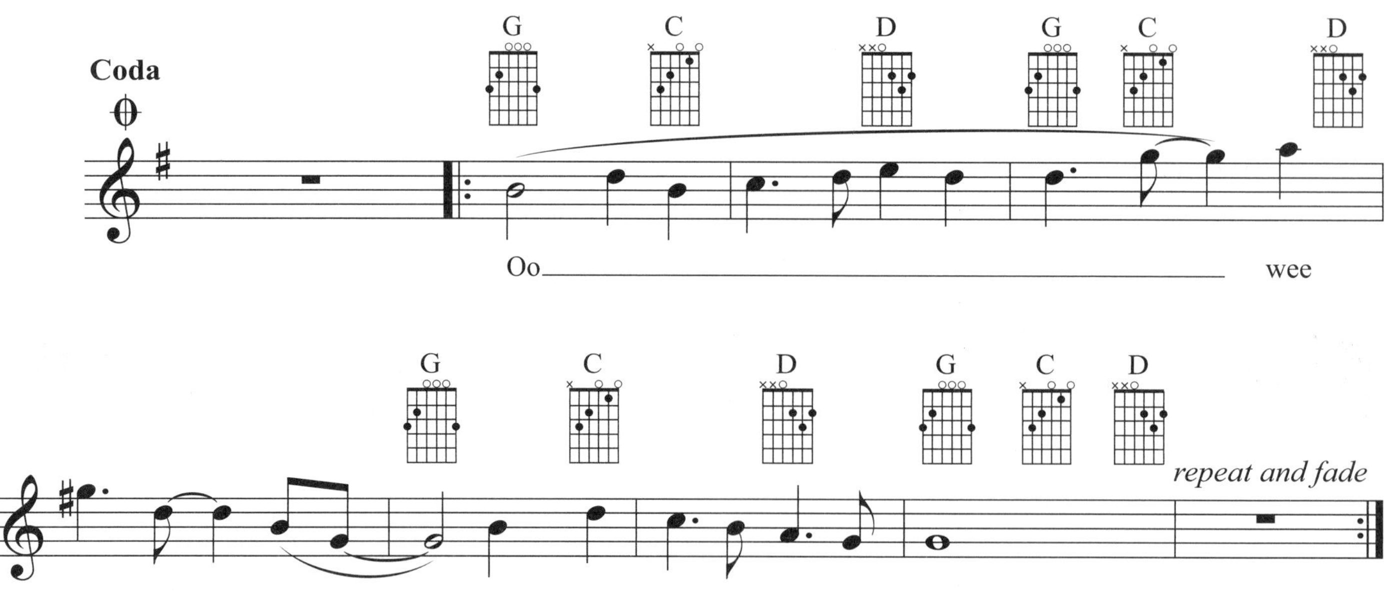

2. Out in the Indian Ocean somewhere
There's a former army post
Abandoned now just like the war
And there's no doubt about it
It was the myth of fingerprints
That's what that old army post was for

Well, the sun gets bloody
And the sun goes down
Ever since the watermelon
And the lights come up
On the black pit town
Somebody says what's a better thing to do
Well, it's not just me
And it's not just you
This is all around the world

Over the mountain
Down in the valley
Lives the former talk-show host
Far and wide his name was known
He said there's no doubt about it
It was the myth of fingerprints
That's why we must learn to live alone

Armistice Day

Words and Music by Paul Simon

D5
A5
D
Just like an eas - y chair.

D
G
F♯m
Em
Oo
Oo
Mm

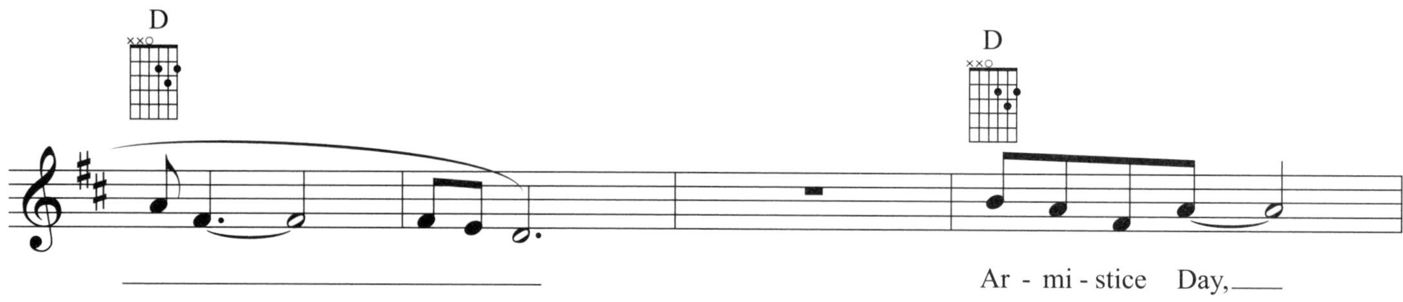
D
D
Ar - mi - stice Day,

G
F♯m
E5
Ar - mi - stice Day.
That's all I real - ly want - ed to say.

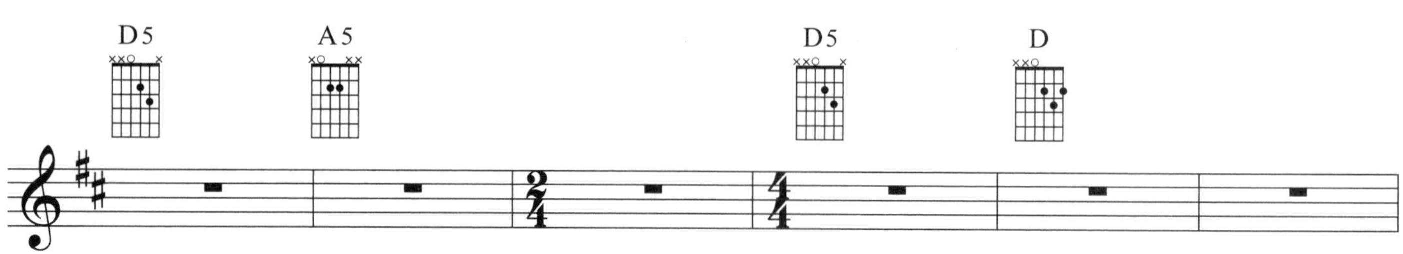
D5
A5
D5
D

2. Oh, Congresswoman,
 Won't you tell that Congressman?
 I've waited such a long time;
 I've about waited all I can.
 Oh, Congresswoman,
 Won't you tell that Congressman?

All Because Of You

Words and Music by Paul Simon

B
A
D
D♯7
5fr.
6fr.
It's all be - cause you would - n't say I do
G♯m
G♯m/F♯
G♯m/F
E 13
4fr.
3fr.
6fr.
So
I went to my drug - store I said to the drug - store man
I'm gon-na fill an old pre-scrip - tion throw the warmth
A♯○7
on down my neck He said Oh what can you
3
E
do
Well it's all be - cause of you

B
A
D
5fr.
D♯7
6fr.
You know it's all be - cause you would - n't say
A♭
4fr.
A♭/G
A♭/G♭
F m7
Ain't no - bod - y loves me no - bod - y needs my love
A○7
4fr.
B♭m7
6fr.
B♭m7♭5
5fr.
E♭7
6fr.
F m7
8fr.
This is my on - ly life Fri - see
F♯○7
8fr.
G m7
8fr.
A♭
4fr.
C m7
3fr.
D♭m7
4fr.
No nee no Love is a lone - ly girl
B♭m7♭5
5fr.
B
F♯7
G○7
G♯m
4fr.
G♯m/F♯
4fr.
Tell zoo zoo do do
G♯m/F
3fr.
E 13
6fr.
G♯m
3fr.
G♯m/F♯
4fr.
E 13
6fr.
D♯7
6fr.
to Coda
D.S. al Coda

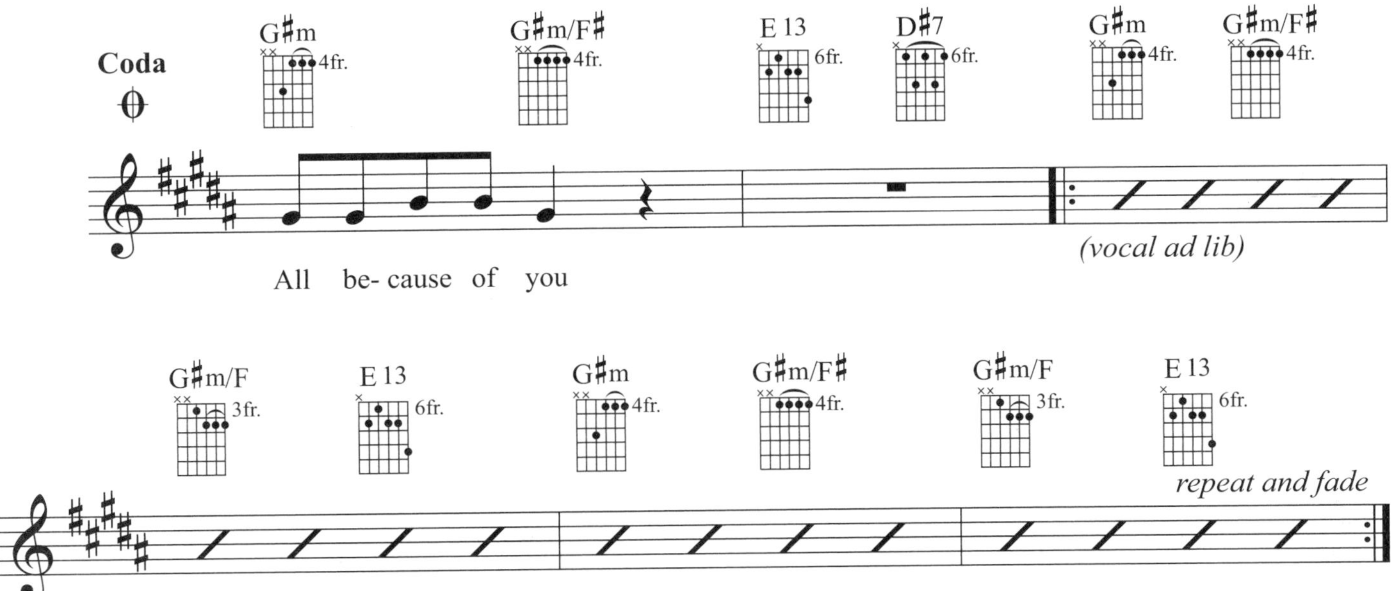

2. Holy Moses, what's this goin' on
I said
I can't believe it's true
Brain's all messed up, can't be straight
And it's all because of you
That's right, it's all because of you
Yes, it's all because of you
It's all because you would not say we're through

So I went to the gypsy woman
I said
Give me some relief
She said
I ain't got no potions and no special kind of weed
She said
I'll tell you what to do
She said, I'll tell you what to do,
She said, go away, take a week or two

I ain't got nobody
Ever since you been gone
Love is an....
Going away, another lover
Is an easy game
I won the same way too

She said it's all because of you
All because of you
All because of you, little girl
All because of you

All because of you....

Allergies

Words and Music by Paul Simon

Em(no5th) Am(no5th) F(no5th) E♭(no5th) Em(no5th)
bod - i - ly needs and my bod - y won't give it a break. My
Am(no5th) F(no5th) E♭(no5th) Em(no5th) Am(no5th) F(no5th) E♭(no5th) Em(no5th)
heart can stand a dis - as - ter. My heart can take a dis - grace. But my
Am(no5th) F(no5th) E♭(no5th) Em(no5th) Am(no5th) F(no5th) E♭(no5th)
heart is al - ler - gic to the wo-men I love and it's chang-in' the shape of my
Em(no5th) D G
face. Al-ler gies, al-ler - gies. Some-thing's liv -
F Am7/E D
- ing on my skin. Doc - tor please,
G
doc - tor please, o - pen up. It's me a - gain.

1.
C
Em7/B
Am7
to Coda
2.I
2.
C
F7
Mal - a - dies, mel - o - dies,
B♭
A♭
E♭/A♭
E♭maj7/G
F7
al - ler - gies to dust and grain.
Mal - a - dies, rem - e - dies.
B♭
Still these
E♭
Gm7
Cm
al - ler - gies re - main.

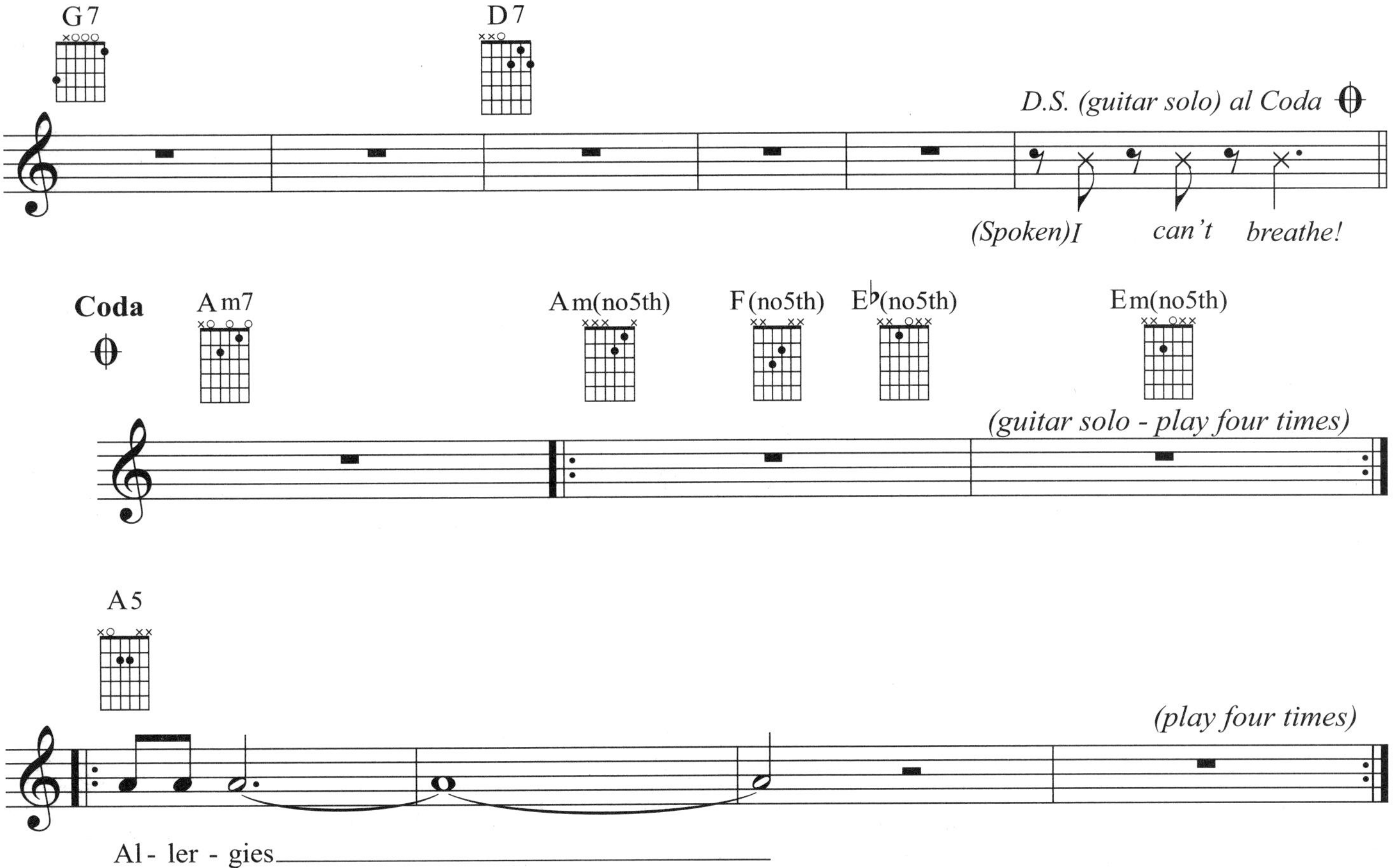

2. I go to a famous physician
   I sleep in the local hotel
   From what I can see of the people like me
   We get better
   But we never get well
   So I ask myself this question
   It's a question I often repeat
   Where do allergies go
   When it's after a show
   And they want to get something to eat?

American Tune

Words and Music by Paul Simon

C G D G C F C G
bright and bon vi - vant so far a - way from home,
1.
E E7/G♯ Am Dm C/G G C
so far a - way from home. 2.I don't know a
2.
E E7/G♯ Am Dm C/G G C
I can't help it, I won - der what's gone wrong.
C
And I dreamed I was dy - ing, I dreamed that my soul
G Am E♭°7 G/D
rose un - ex - pect - ed - ly, And look - ing back down at me,
F C G C
smiled re - as - sur - ing - ly. And I dreamed I was fly - ing.

G Am E♭dim
And high up a - bove my eyes could clear - ly see the Stat - ue of
G/D F C G
Lib - er - ty sail - ing a - way to sea, and I dreamed I was
C F C G C
fly - ing. We come on the ship they call the May -
G E E7/G♯ Am E7 Am C
flower, We come on the ship that sailed the moon. We come in the
F C G C G C B°7 Am E
ag - e's most un - cer - tain hours and sing an A - mer - i - can tune,
Am C9 F G F C G C
Oh, and it's all right, it's all right, it's all right. You can't

2. I don't know a soul who's not been battered,
I don't have a friend who feels at ease.
I don't know a dream that's not been shattered
or driven to its knees.
But it's all right, it's all right,
We've lived so well so long.
Still, when I think of the road
we're traveling on
I wonder what's gone wrong.
I can't help it, I wonder what's gone wrong.

April Come She Will

Words and Music by Paul Simon

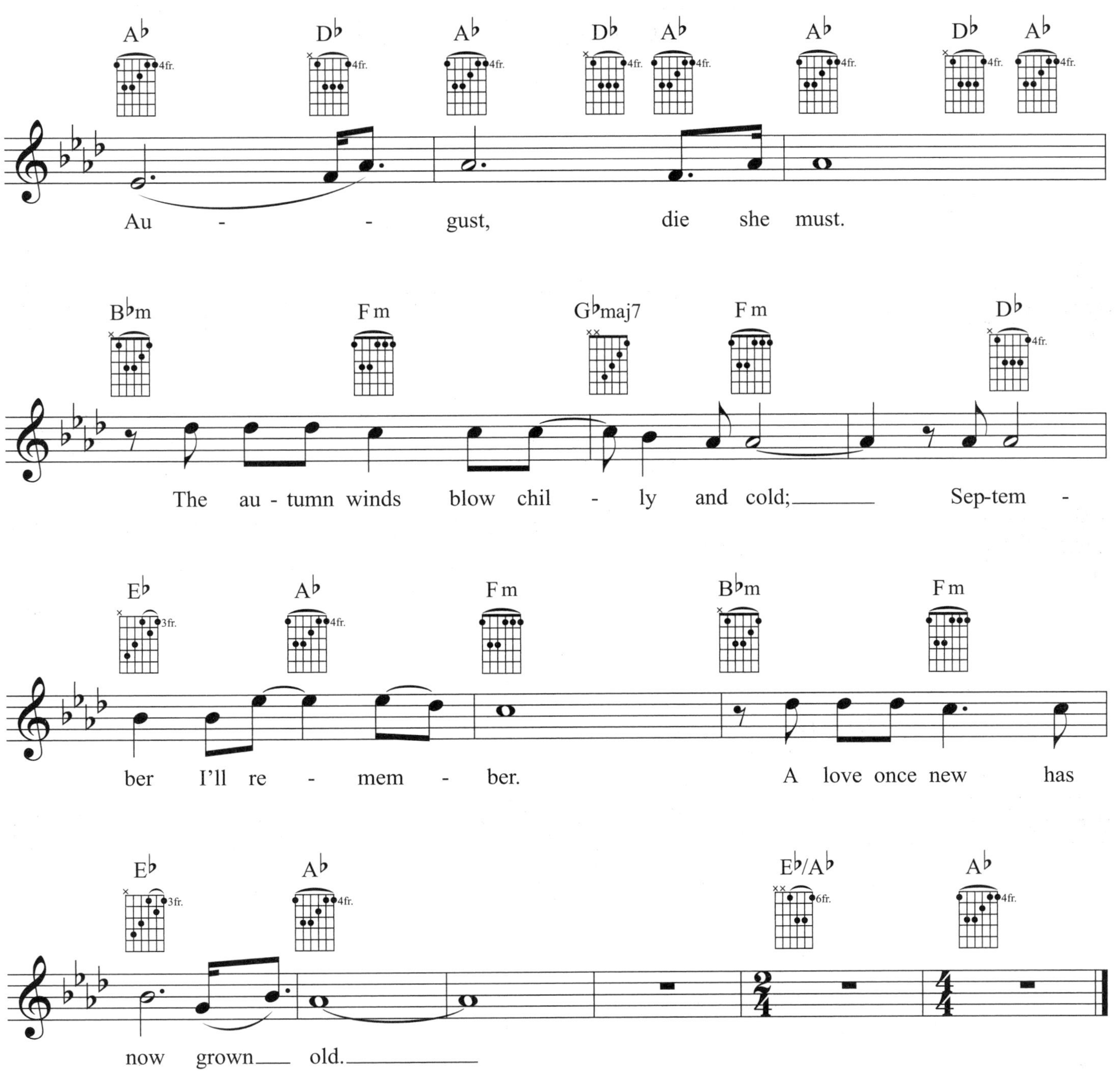

2. June, she'll change her tune.
   In restless walks she'll prowl the night.
   July, she will fly,
   And give no warning to her flight.

At The Zoo

Words and Music by Paul Simon

Moderate tempo

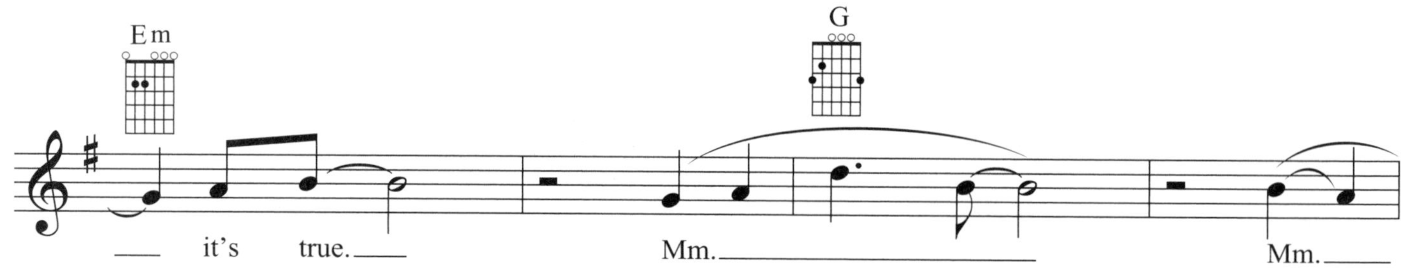

Em
G
Em
- ney From the East Side to the park; Just a
G
Em
D
D7
fine and fan - cy ram - ble To the zoo.
G
Em
G
But you can take the cross - town bus If it's rain - in' or it's
Em
G
Em
A6
cold, And the an - i - mals will love it If you do,
Em
A6
if you do, now.
Em
Amaj7
Some-thin' tells me It's all hap-pen-ing

A7
D7
at the zoo.
I do be - lieve
it,
G
Em
I do be - lieve it's true.
G
Em
Mm.
Mm.
G
Em
Whoa.
Mm.
G
Em
G
The mon-keys stand for hon - es - ty, Gi - raffes are in - sin -
Em
G
Em
D
cere, And the el - e - phants are kind - ly but they're dumb.

D7
G
Em
G
O - rang - u - tans are skep - ti - cal Of chan - ges in their
Em
G
Em
G
ca - ges, And the zoo - keep - er is ver - y fond of rum.
Em
G
Em
G
Ze - bras are re - ac - tion - ar - ies, An - te - lopes are
Em
G
Em
G
mis - sion - ar - ies, Pi - geons plot in se - cre - cy, And ham - sters turn on
Em
G
Em
fre - quent - ly. What a gas! You got - ta come and see At the
G
Em
repeat and fade
zoo. At the

Baby Driver

Words and Music by Paul Simon

D♭5
C5
B5
Em
A7
4fr.
to Coda
— my num - ber, I won - der how your en - gines feel.
D
1.
— Shine a light. — Woo, — woo,
G
— woo, — woo, — wee, —
D
3
2.
instrumental
— 2.My
G
D
G
D
D5
5fr.
D♭5
C5
B5
Em
4fr.

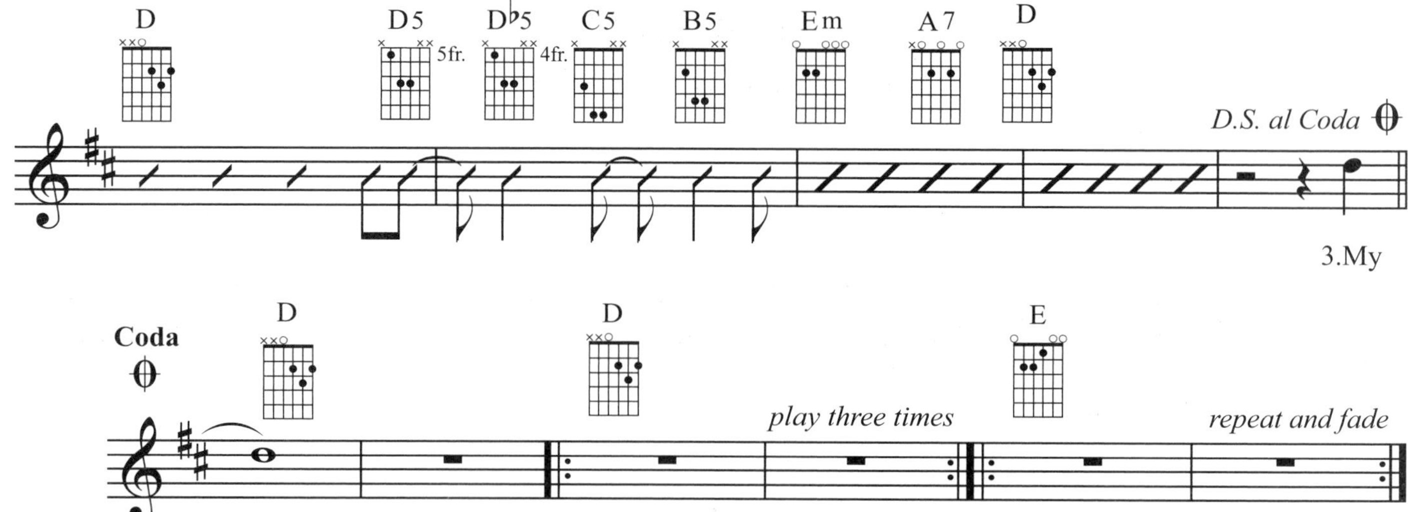

2. My daddy was a prominent frogman
   My mama's in the Naval reserve
   When I was young I carried a gun
   But I never got the chance to serve
   I did not serve.

   They call me Baby Driver
   And once upon a pair of wheels
   Hit the road and I'm gone ah
   What's my number
   I wonder how your engines feel
   Ba ba ba ba
   Scoot down the road
   What's my number
   I wonder how your engines feel.

3. My daddy got a big promotion
   My mama got a raise in pay
   There's no-one home, we're all alone
   Oh come into my room and play
   Yes we can play.

   I'm not talking about your pigtails
   But I'm talking 'bout your sex appeal
   Hit the road and I'm gone
   What's my number
   I wonder how your engines feel.
   Ba ba ba ba
   Scoot down the road
   What's my number
   I wonder how your engines feel.

Bookends

Words and Music by Paul Simon

Bernadette

Music by Paul Simon
Lyrics by Paul Simon and Derek Walcott

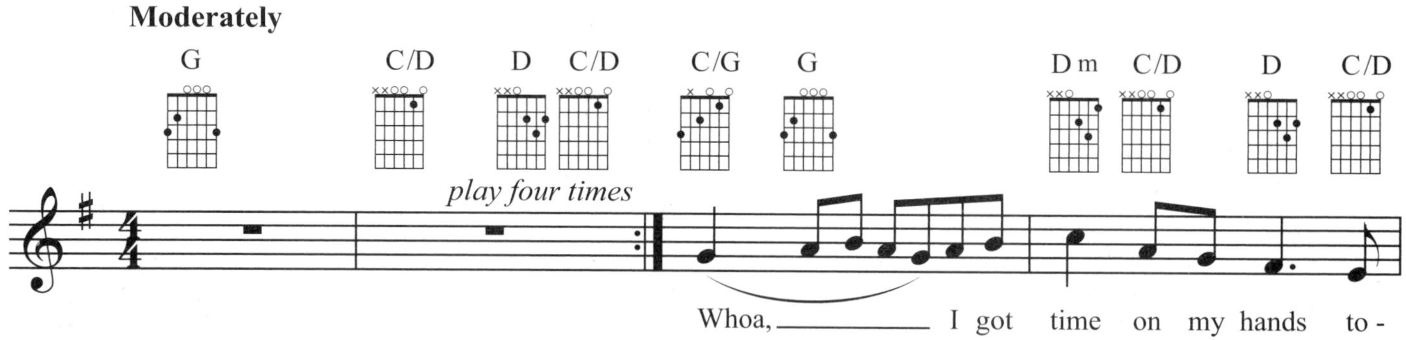

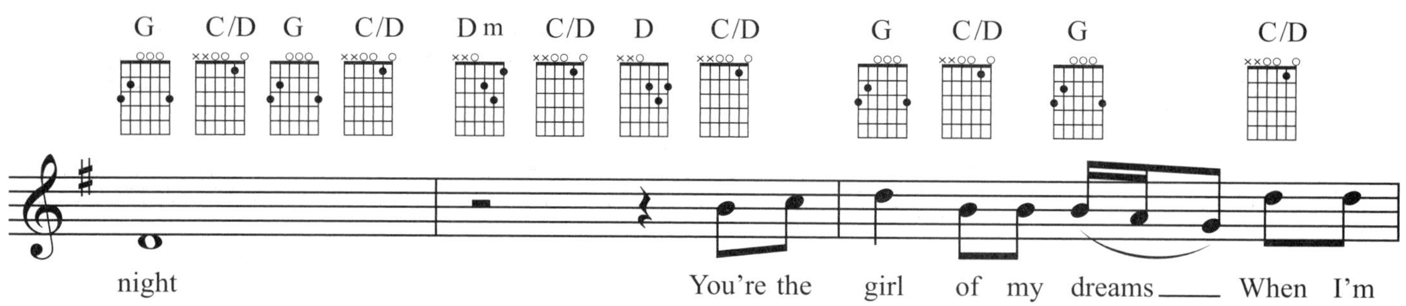

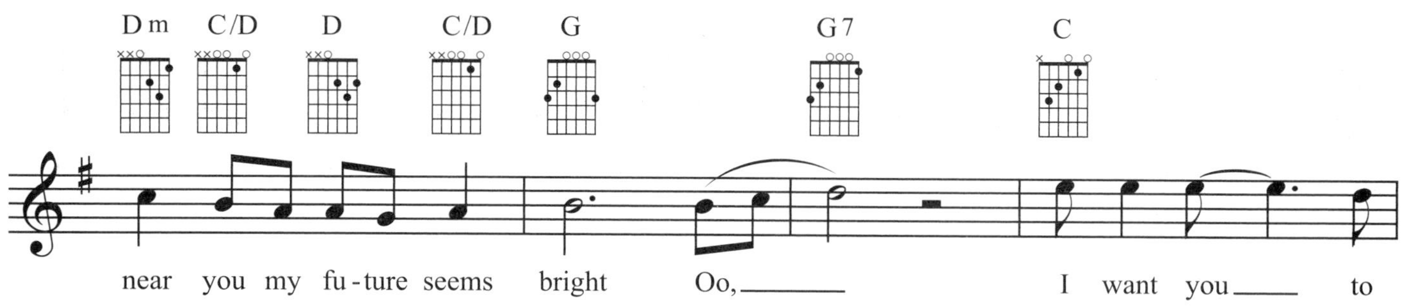

Am D7 C/G G
Sal Min-e-o and I need you so Sweet Bern-a - dette Whoa, You got
Dm C/D D C/D G C/D G C/D Dm C/D D C/D
style from your hair to your heels Though my
G C/D G C/D Dm C/D D C/D G G7
words may be jum-bled Still I'm tell-ing you just how it feels I love you
Gbass Fbass E♭bass Dbass Cmaj7 C6 Cm(maj7)
I love you And the breeze that wraps a-round
G E7/G♯ A
you Sat-in sum-mer nights
D
rit.
A girl I can't for - get

C/G
G
Dm
C/D
D
C/D
G
a tempo
1.Whoa You're the smile of the moon Bern - a - dette
2.Whoa Bern - a - dette.
C
D
C
G
C
D
C
G
Dom, dom, dom, doo Well-a well I'm home
C
D
C
G
C
D
C
G
Dom, dom, dom, doo Well-a well I'm home
C
D
C
D
to Coda
G
Wop, wop, wop, wop. Come with me.
C
D
G
C
D
G
3
There's a place I want you to see When the leaves are dark

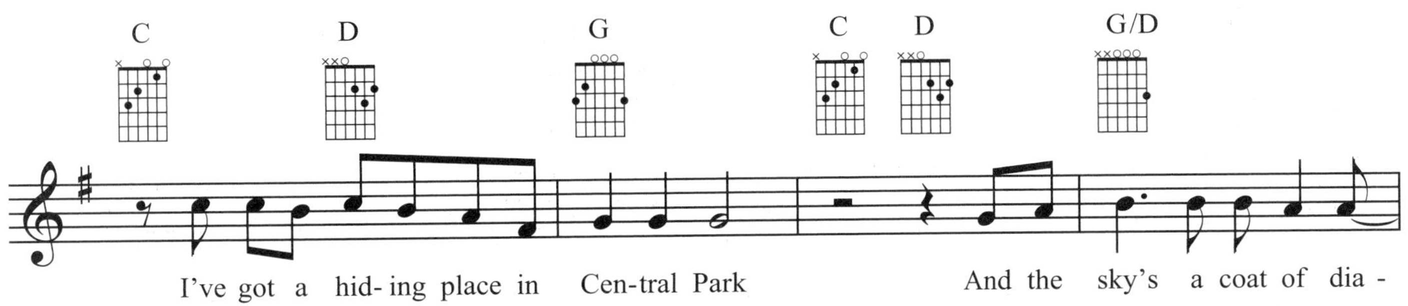
C
D
G
C
D
G/D
I've got a hid-ing place in Cen-tral Park
And the sky's a coat of dia -

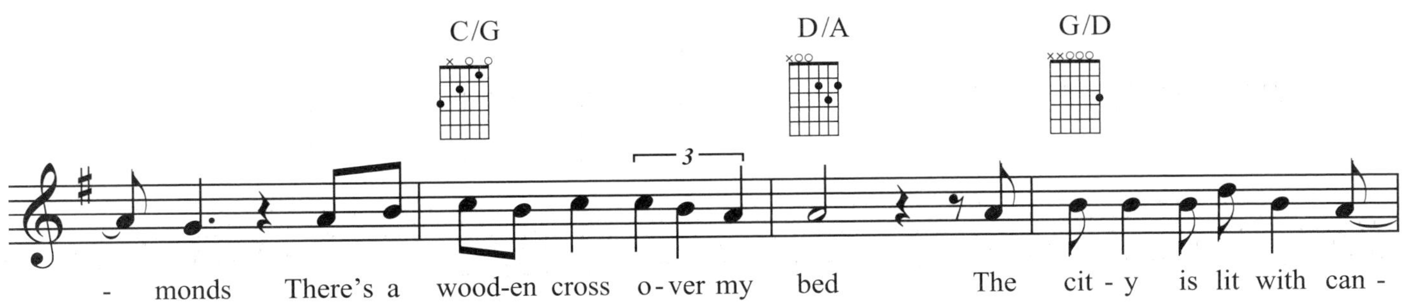
C/G
D/A
G/D
3
- monds There's a wood-en cross o-ver my bed
The cit - y is lit with can -

D/A
D
C/D
D.S. al Coda
3
- dles They're shi - ning for you, Bern - a - dette.
Whoa, Whoa,

Coda

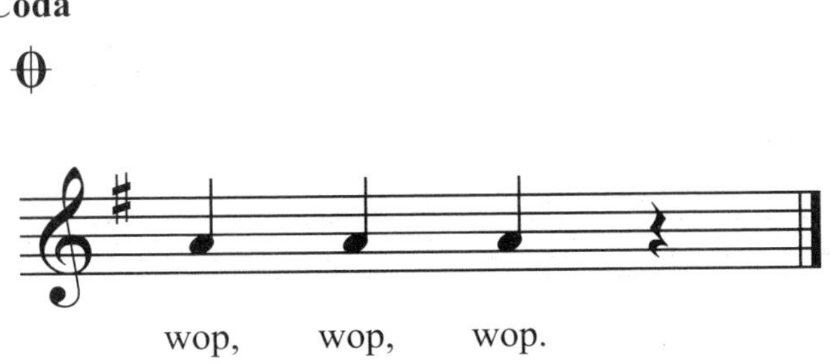
wop, wop, wop.

The Big Bright Green Pleasure Machine

Words and Music by Paul Simon

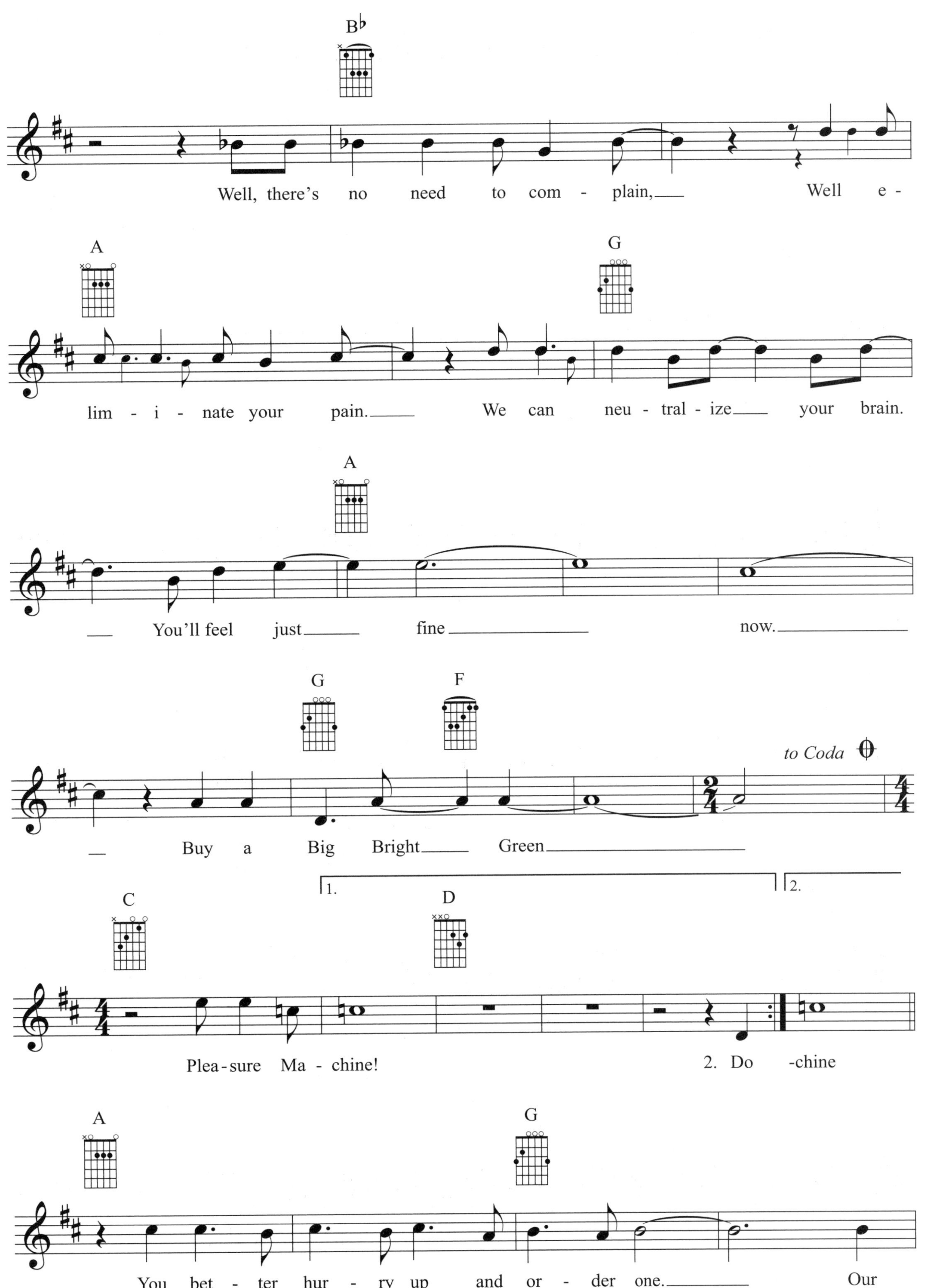
B♭
Well, there's no need to com - plain, Well e -
A
G
lim - i - nate your pain. We can neu - tral - ize your brain.
A
You'll feel just fine now.
G
F
to Coda
Buy a Big Bright Green
1.
2.
C
D
Plea - sure Ma - chine!
2. Do -chine
A
G
You bet - ter hur - ry up and or - der one. Our

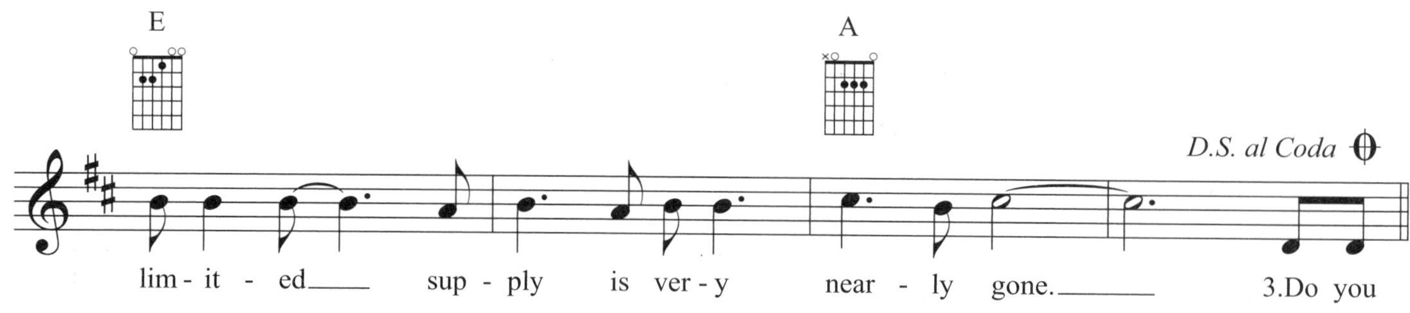

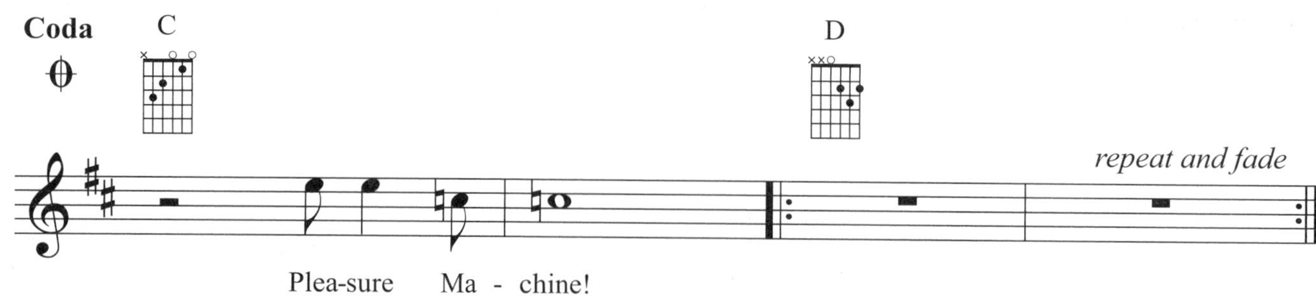

2. Do figures of authority just shoot you down?
   Is life within the business world a drag?
   Did your boss just mention that you'd better shop around
   To find yourself a more productive bag?
   Are you worried and distressed?
   Can't seem to get no rest?
   Put our product to the test.
   You'll feel just fine
   Now.
   Buy a Big Bright Green Pleasure Machine!

   You better hurry up and order one.
   Our limited supply is very nearly gone.

3. Do you nervously await the blows of cruel fate?
   Do your checks bounce higher than a rubber ball?
   Are you worried 'cause your girlfriend's just a little late?
   Are you looking for a way to chuck it all?
   We can end your daily strife
   At a reasonable price.
   You've seen it advertised in *Life*.
   You'll feel just fine
   Now.
   Buy a Big Bright Green Pleasure Machine!

Born At The Right Time

Words and Music by Paul Simon

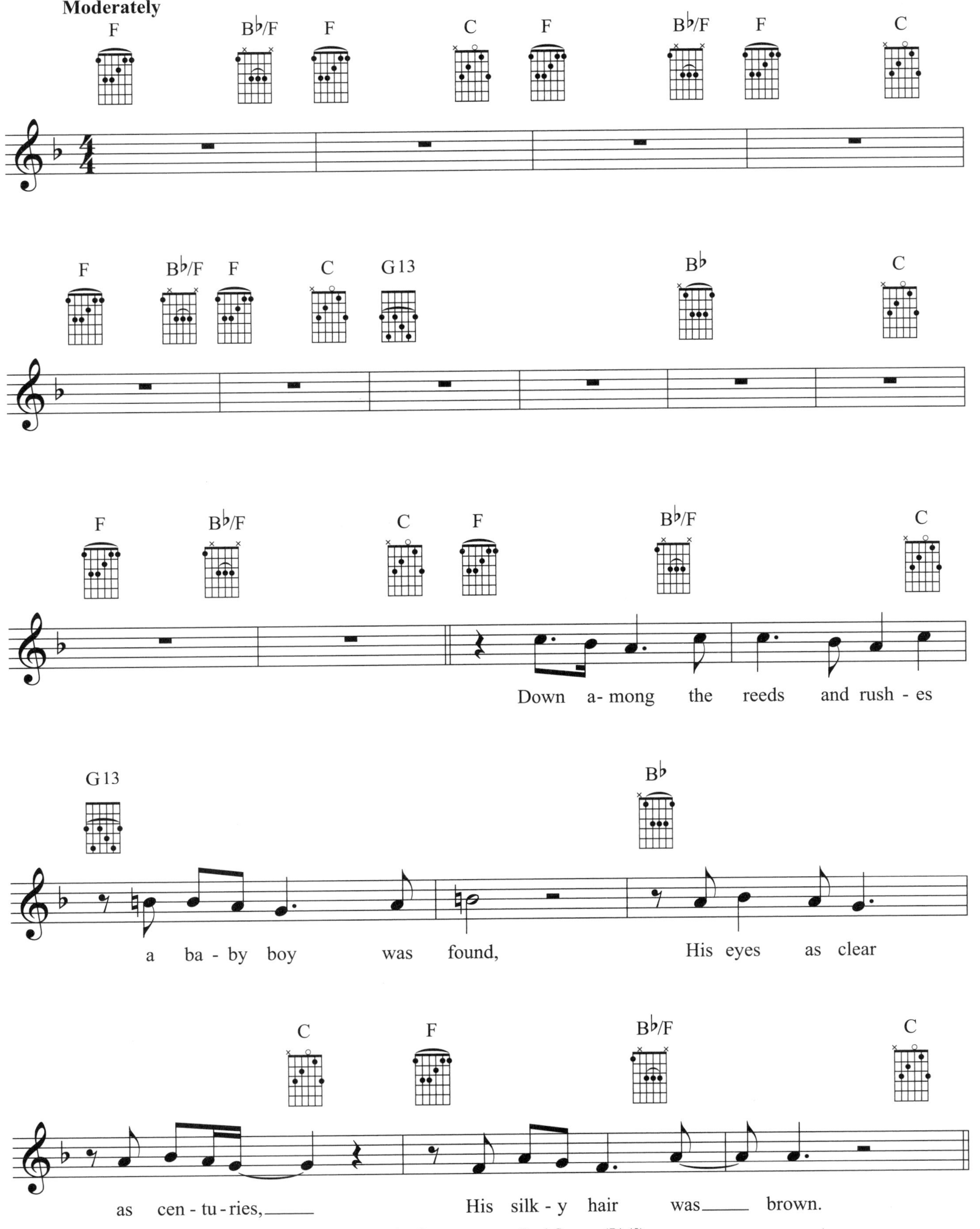

F
C
B♭
F
C
B♭
Nev- er been lone - ly
Nev- er been lied to,
Nev- er had to scuf- fle in fear,
F
B♭
F
C
B♭
F
3
Noth - ing de-nied to.
Born at the in- stant,
The church bells chime,
C
B♭
F
B♭
F
B♭/F
And the whole world whis - per - ing,
Born at the right time.
F
C
F
B♭/F
F
C
F
B♭/F
F
C
5
Me and my bud-dies we are trav - el- ing peo-ple,
We like to go down to res-tau-rant row.

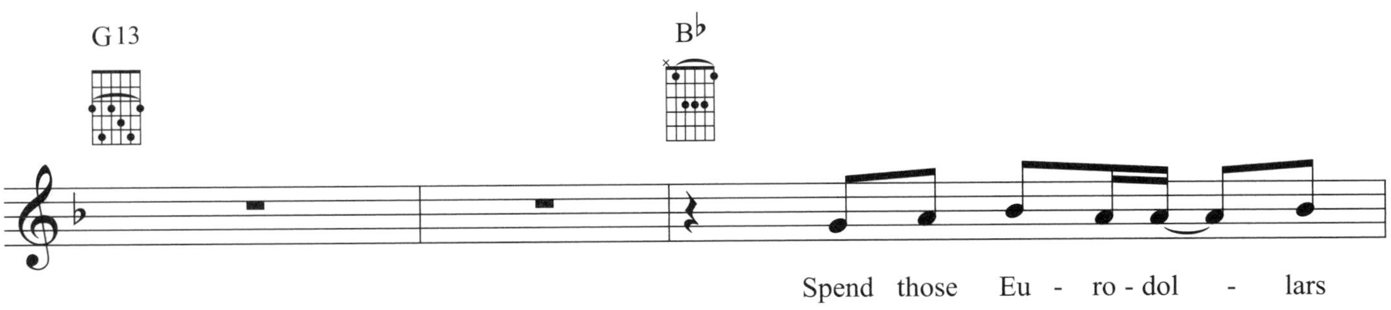
G13
B♭
Spend those Eu - ro - dol - lars

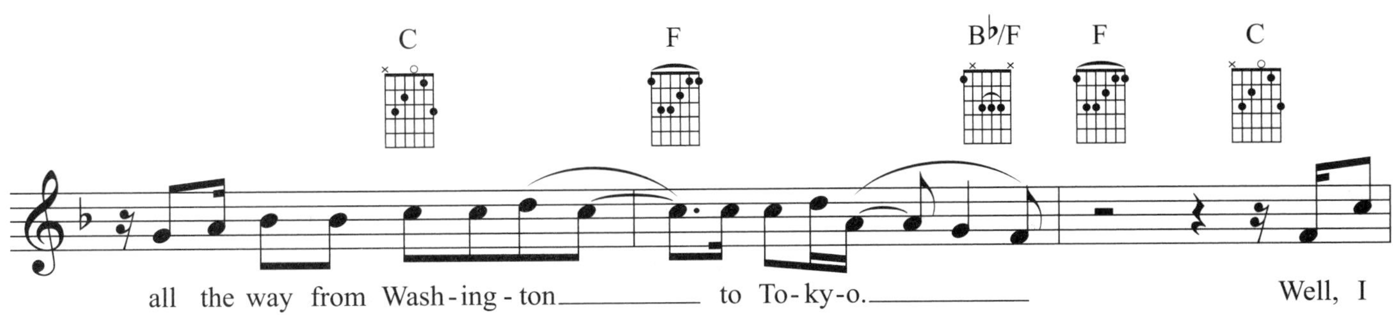
C
F
B♭/F
F
C
all the way from Wash-ing-ton to To-ky-o.
Well, I

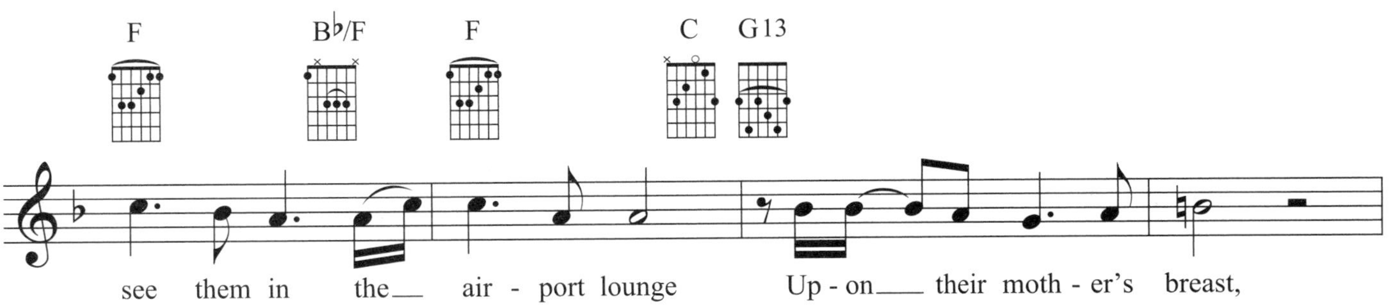
F
B♭/F
F
C
G13
see them in the air - port lounge
Up - on their moth - er's breast,

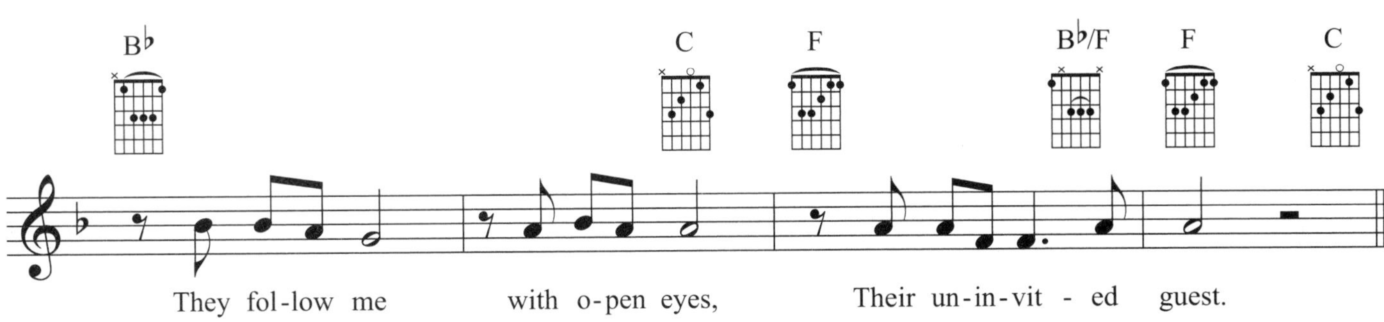
B♭
C
F
B♭/F
F
C
They fol-low me
with o-pen eyes,
Their un-in-vit - ed guest.

F
C
B♭
F
C
B♭
Nev-er been lone - ly
Nev-er been lied to
Nev-er had to scuf-fle in fear

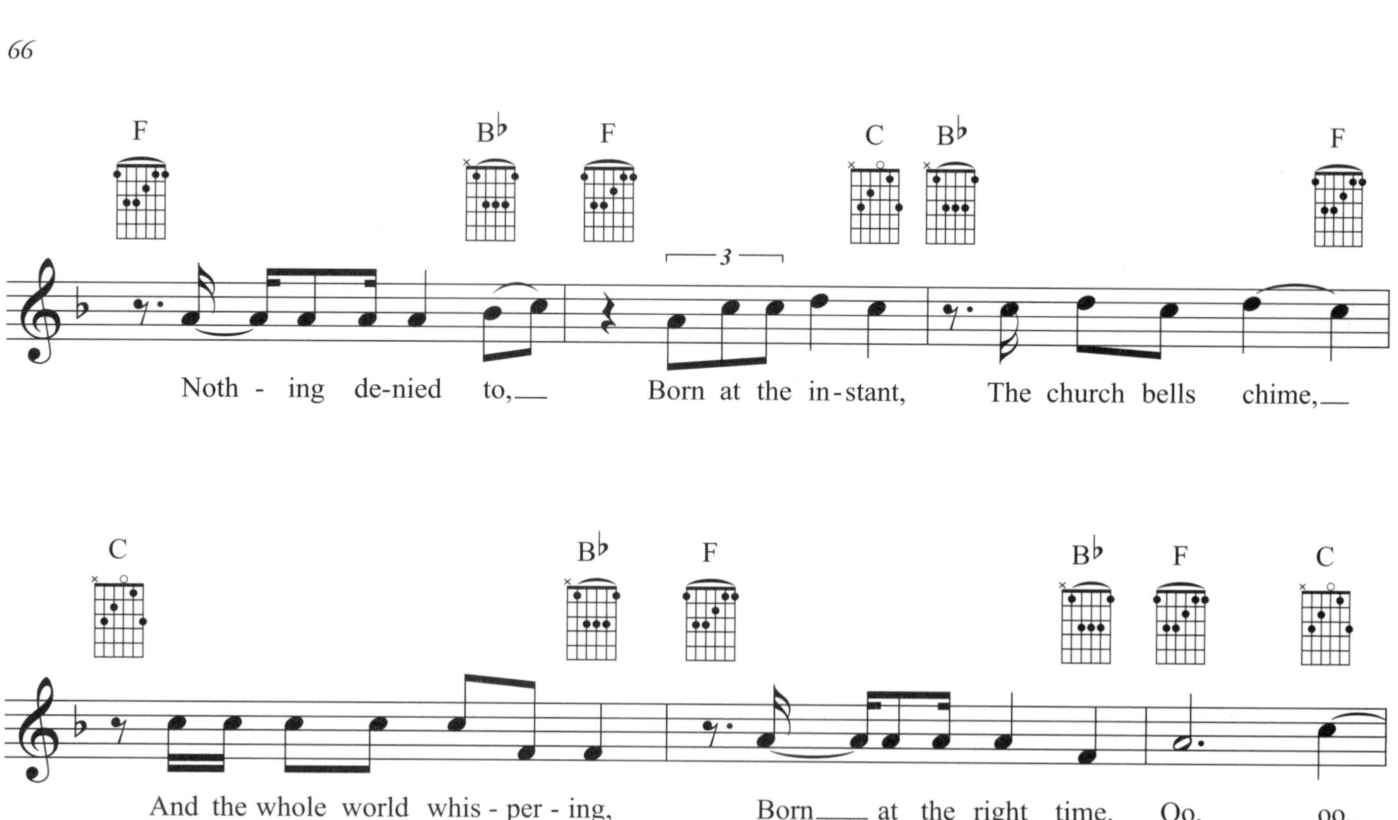
F
B♭
F
C
B♭
F
Noth - ing de-nied to,
Born at the in-stant,
The church bells chime,
C
B♭
F
B♭
F
C
And the whole world whis - per - ing,
Born at the right time. Oo, oo,

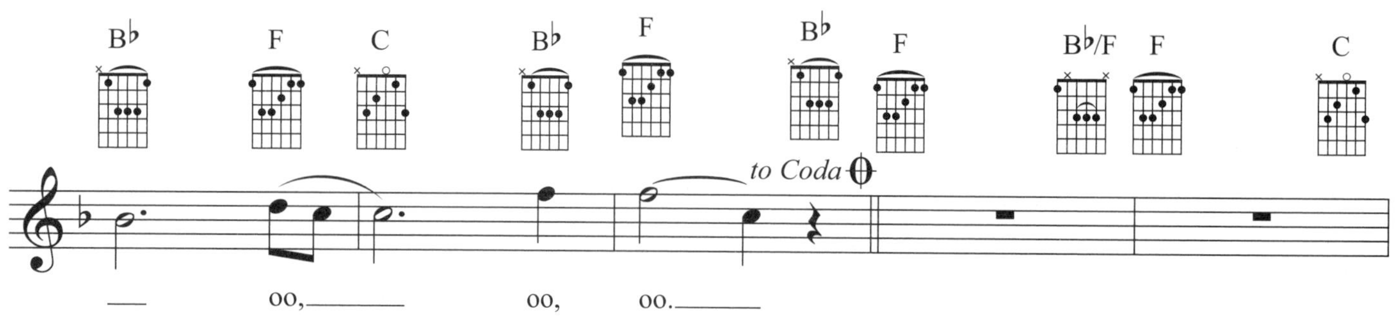
B♭
F
C
B♭
F
B♭
F
B♭/F
F
C
to Coda
oo, oo, oo.

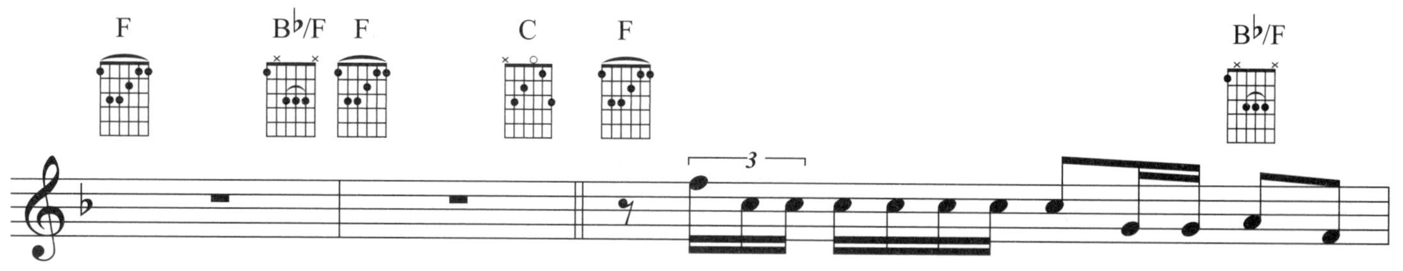
F
B♭/F
F
C
F
B♭/F
Too ma-ny peo-ple on the bus from the air - port,

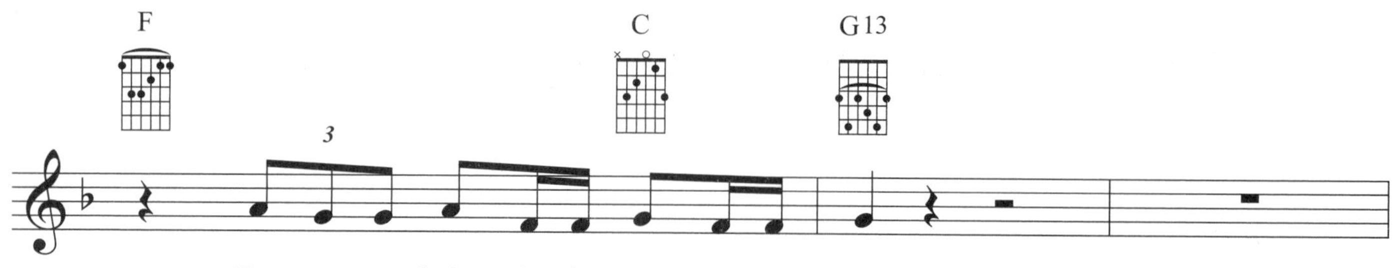
F
C
G13
Too ma - ny holes in the crust of the earth,

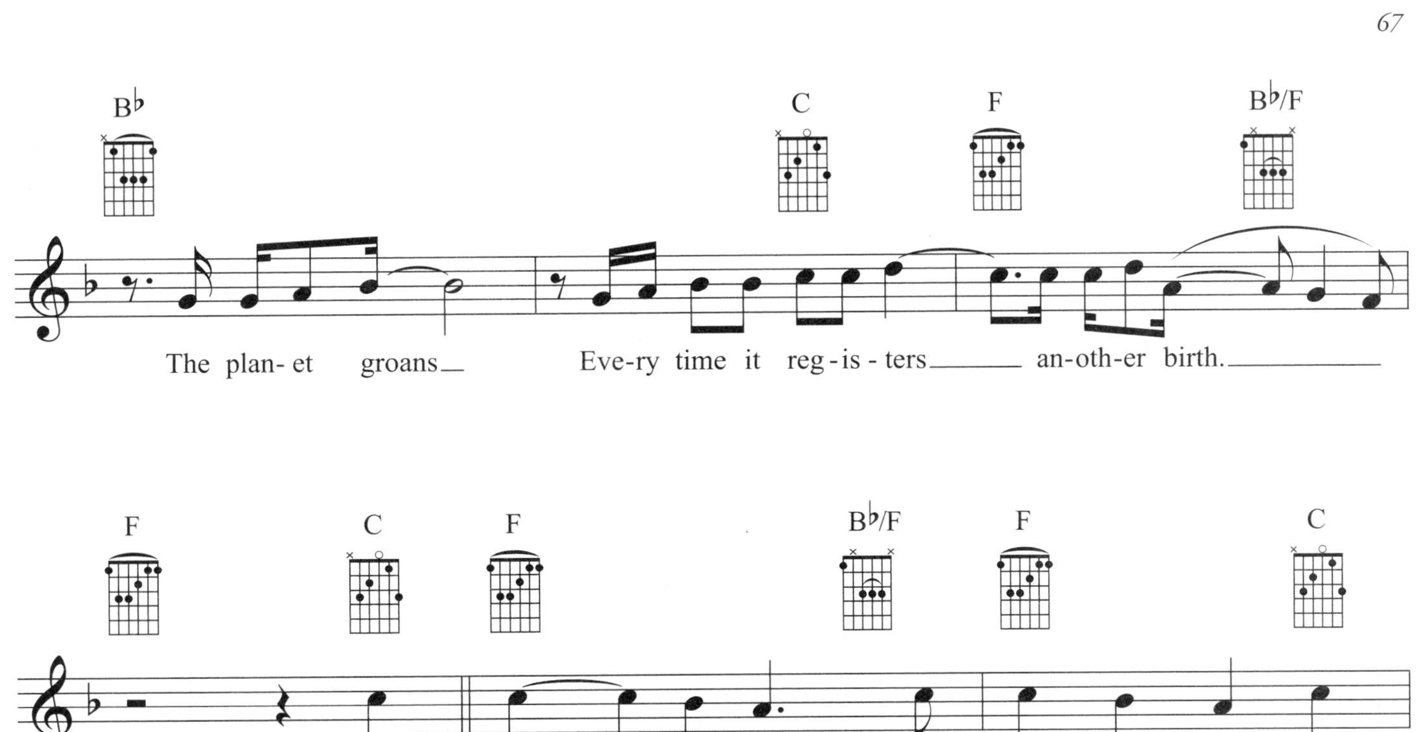
B♭
C
F
B♭/F
The plan- et groans
Eve-ry time it reg-is-ters
an-oth-er birth.
F
C
F
B♭/F
F
C
But down a-mong the reeds and rush-es

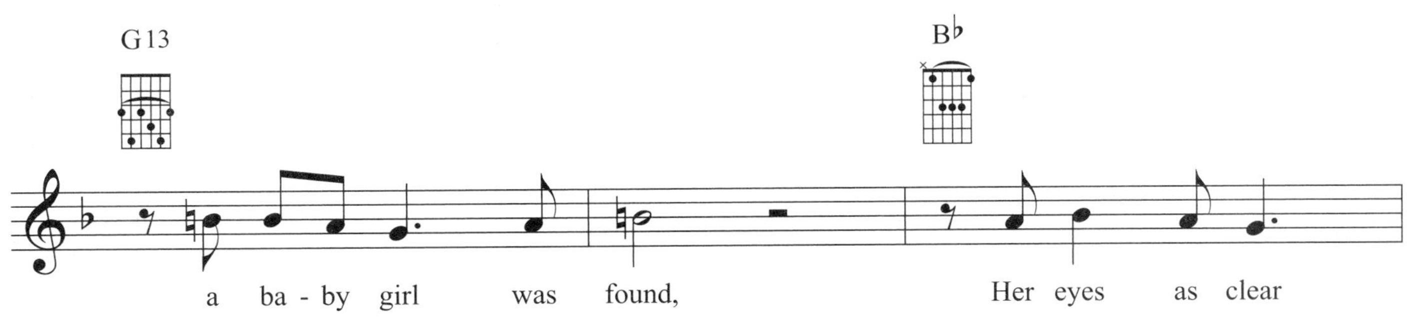
G13
B♭
a ba-by girl was found,
Her eyes as clear

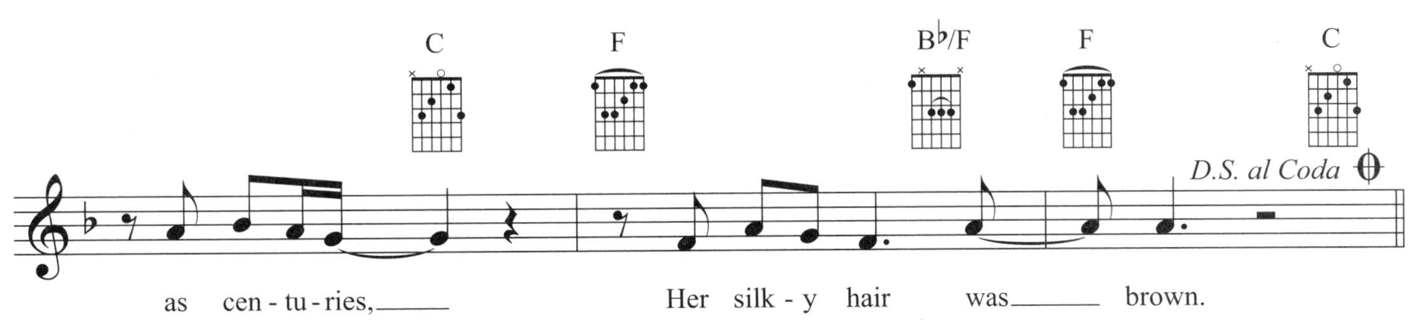
C
F
B♭/F
F
C
D.S. al Coda
as cen-tu-ries,
Her silk-y hair was brown.

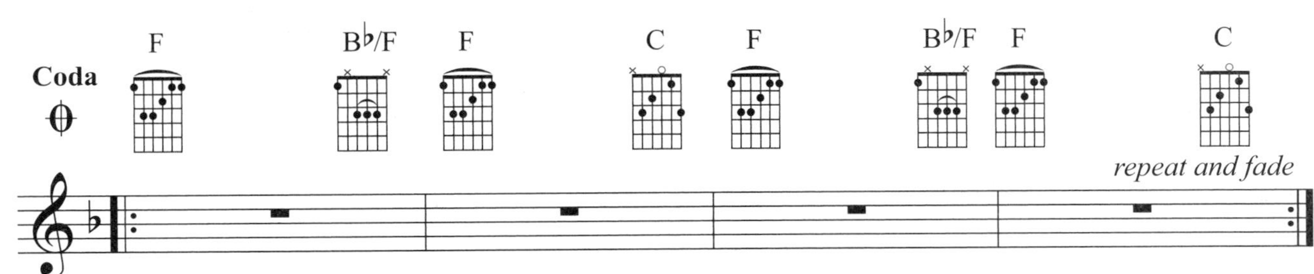
Coda
F
B♭/F
F
C
F
B♭/F
F
C
repeat and fade

Blessed

Words and Music by Paul Simon

Fairly fast

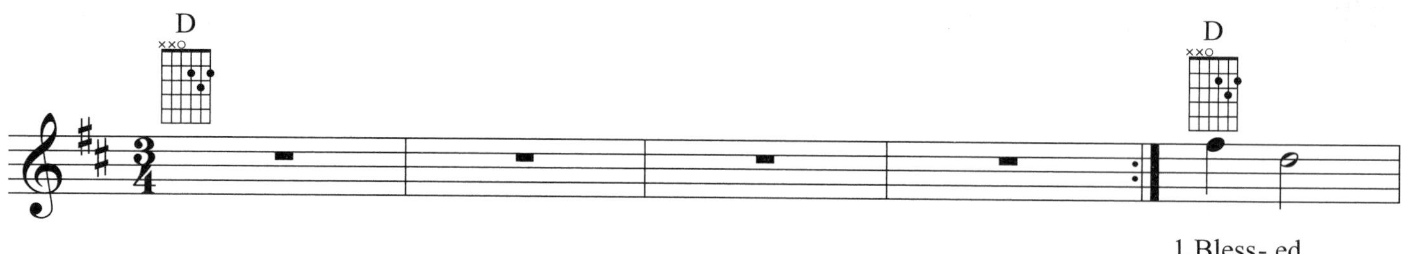

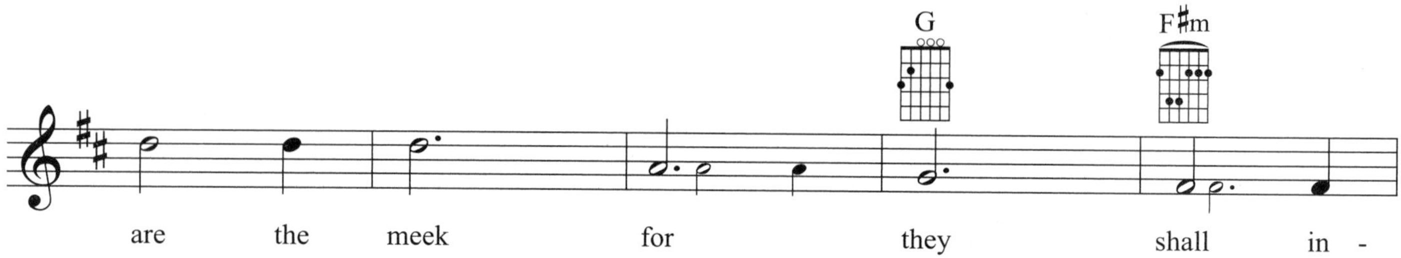

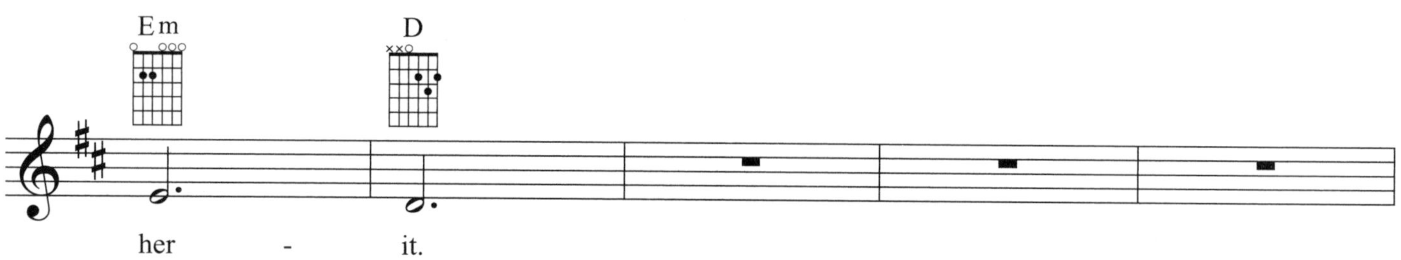

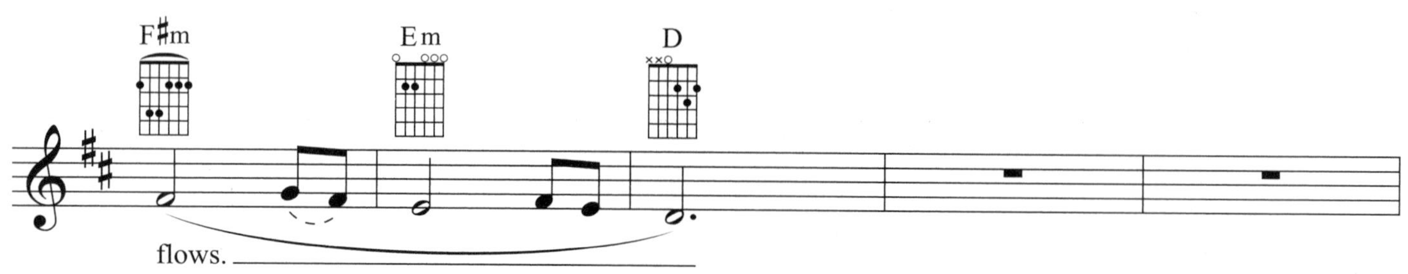

G
Bless- ed are the sat up - on,
D
C
Spat up - on,
Rat - - - - -
G
D
- ted on.
O
F♯m
Em
G
Lord,
Why have you for - sak -
D
- en me?
1.
Am/D
Bm/D
I got no place to go,

Am/D
I've walked a-round So-ho for the last night or so.
Bm/D
Ah, but it does-n't
Am/D
D
Da Capo
mat-ter, no.
2.
Am/D
Bm/D
3
My words trick-le down,
Am/D
from a wound that I have no in-ten-tion to
D
Da Capo
3.
Am/D
heal.
I

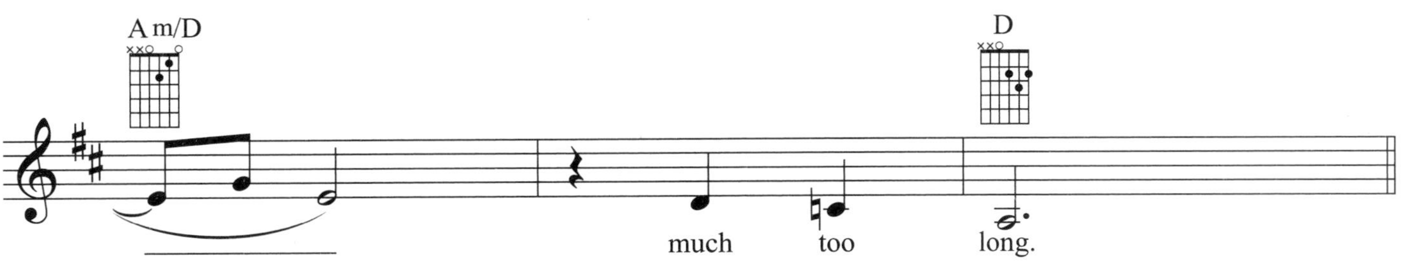

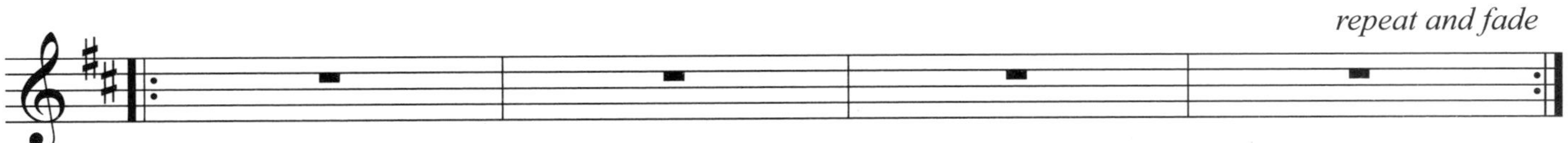

2. Blessed is the land and the kingdom.
   Blessed is the man whose soul belongs to.
   Blessed are the meth drinkers, Pot sellers, Illusion dwellers.
   O Lord, Why have you forsaken me?
   My words trickle down, from a wound
   That I have no intention to heal.

3. Blessed are the stained glass, windowpane glass.
   Blessed is the church service makes me nervous
   Blessed are the Penney rookers, Cheap hookers, Groovy lookers.
   O Lord, Why have you forsaken me?
   I have tended my own garden
   Much too long

Born In Puerto Rico

Music by Paul Simon
Lyrics by Paul Simon and Derek Walcott

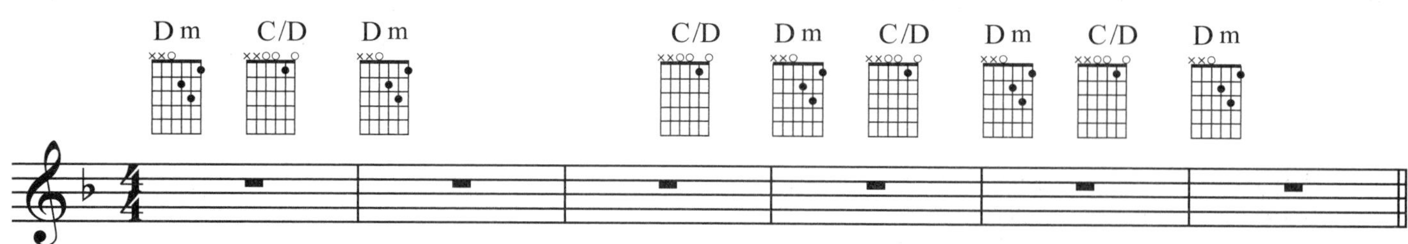

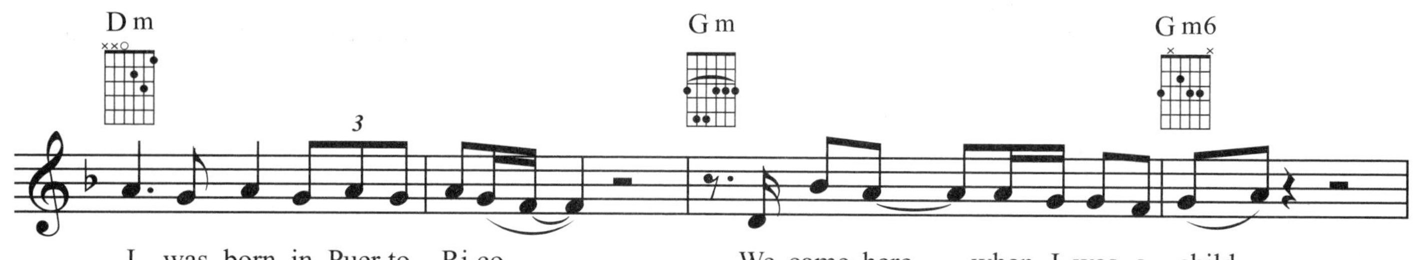

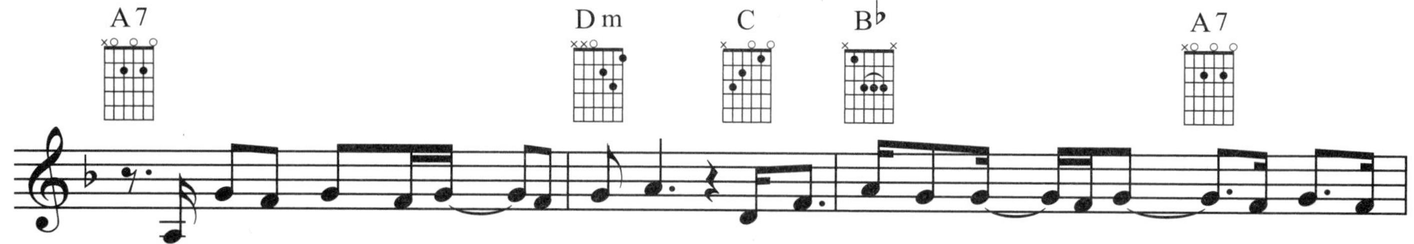

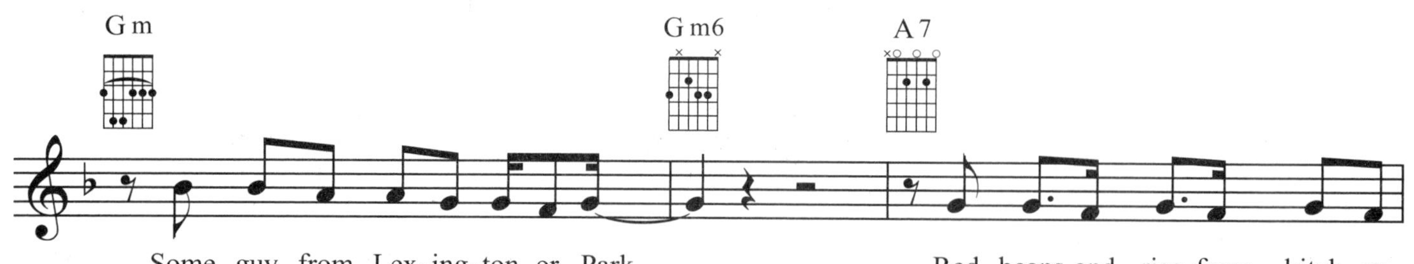

Dm
A7
Dm
C
win- dows It's sup-per time and the bar - ri - o is dark.
B♭
F
B♭
C
B♭
F
B♭
C
No one knows you like I do No-bod-y can know your heart the way I do
B♭
F
B♭
C
C♯◦7
Dm
No one can tes-ti-fy to all that you've been through But I will. I was
Gm
born in Puer-to Ri - co And my blood is Ta-i - no Span-ish Ca-rib-be-an my
Gm6
A7
Dm
soul We came here wear-ing sum-mer clothes in win-ter Hearts
A7
Dm
C
B♭
A7
Dm
C
B♭
A7
Dm
of sun - shine in the cold

B♭
F
C
B♭
C
B♭
C
Your fam-'ly rent-ed this a-part - ment
You'd watch the street lamps from your
B♭
C/B♭
F
F/A
perch
In the sac - ra - men - tal hour your
C
C♯°7
A7
Dm
C
step - fa - ther in black Preached the fire of the Pen - te - cos - tal Church
B♭
F
B♭
C
B♭
F
B♭
No one knows you like I do
No - bod - y can know your heart the way
C
B♭
F
B♭
C
C♯°7
I do
No one can tes - ti - fy to all that you've been through But
Dm
this will.
I was born in Puer - to Ri - co

Gm
Gm6
A7
Came here when I was a child. Small change and sun-light, then I
Dm
A7
Dm
left these streets for good. My days as short as they were wild.
"I'm Carlos Apache" "Angel Soto"
Gm
"Frenchy Cordero"
Gm6
"Babu Charlie Cruz"
A7
Dm
A7
Your fea-tures blurred in ev-ery grain-y pho - to And fad-ing head-line of the Dai-ly
Dm
News
"Wiltwyck School for Criminal Children,
Gm/D
Auburn, Brooklyn House of D.,
D°
Dannemora, Sing-Sing, Attica, Greenhaven.
A7/D
5fr.
Twenty years inside,
Dm
today you're free."

B♭ F C F C B♭ C
You can-not e-ven read your sto - ry
The pag-es pil-ing up in
B♭ C/B♭ F F/A
shame
Be - fore the words re-leased you, the guard
C C♯o7 A7 Dm C
would kill the light
The night you took The Cape - man for your name.
B♭ F C B♭ F C
I was born in Puer-to Ri - co
I was born in Puer-to Ri - co
B♭ F C B♭ F C C♯o7
I was born in Puer-to Ri - co
I was born in Puer-to Ri - co
Dm C/D Dm C/D Dm Dm A7 Dm

The Boxer

Words and Music by Paul Simon

Verse
1.When I left my home and my fam - i - ly, I was no more than a
2.(instrumental)
F♯/A♯
G♯m
F♯
F♯7
boy in the com - pa - ny of strang - ers in the qui - et of a
B
rail - way sta - tion run - ning scared,
Lay - ing
E
low, seek - ing out the poor - er quar - ters where the rag - ged peo - ple
go, Look - ing for the plac - es on - ly they would know.
Chorus
D♯m
Lie - la - lie,
Lie - la - lie la lie - la - lie lie - la-

G♯m
4fr.
F♯
lie
Lie - la - lie - la - la - la - la - Lie - la la la la
B
7fr.
to Coda
Verse
lie.
Ask - ing
F♯/A♯
6fr.
G♯m
4fr.
on - ly work - man's wag - es I come look - ing for a job, but I get no of -
F♯
F♯7
- fers,
Just a come - on from the whores on Sev - enth Av -
B
7fr.
F♯/A♯
6fr.
G♯m
4fr.
- e - nue.
I do de - clare, there were times
F♯
E
B
7fr.
when I was so lone - some I took some com - fort there. Ooo - la - la

F♯
B
D.S. al Coda
la- la la la.
Coda
B
Verse
Then I'm lay - ing out my win - ter clothes and
F♯/A♯
G♯m
F♯
wish - ing I was gone, go - ing home Where the
F♯
B
New York Cit - y win - ters are - n't bleed - ing me,
D♯m
G♯m
F♯
F♯7
Lead - ing me. Go - ing home.
B
Verse
In the clear - ing stands a box - er, and a

𝄋𝄋
(instrumental)
F♯/A♯
G♯m
F♯
fight - er by his trade, And he car - ries the re - mind - ers of
F♯7
B
ev - 'ry glove that laid him down Or cut him till he cried out in his
F♯/A♯
G♯m
F♯
E
an - ger and his shame, "I am leav - ing, I am leav - ing." But the fight -
B
F♯
E
B
Fine
Chorus
- er still re - mains Lie - la
G♯m
D♯m
G♯m
lie, Lie - la - le - la - lie - la - lie Lie - la - lie
F♯
B
play eight times
D.S.S. al Fine (instrumental)
Lie - la - lie - la - la - la - la - lie la la la la lie.

The Boy In The Bubble

Words by Paul Simon
Music by Paul Simon and Forere Motloheloa

G C D G C D C D
The way the cam-er-a fol - lows us in slo-mo the way we look to us all,
C D G C D
— the way we look to a dis - tant con-stel-la-tion that's
G C D C D C D G
dy-ing in a cor-ner of the sky. These are the days — of mir -
3
1., 2.
C D G C D C D C D
- a-cle and won-der and don't — cry, ba - by, don't cry, — don't cry. —
A5 C D A5 C D C D C D
A5 C D A5 C D C D C D
2.It was a

2. It was a dry wind
And it swept across the desert
And it curled into the circle of birth
And the dead sand
Falling on the children
The mothers and the fathers
And the automatic earth

These are the days of miracle and wonder
This is the long distance call
The way the camera follows us in slo-mo
The way we look to us all
The way we look to a distant constellation
That's dying in a corner of the sky
These are the days of miracle and wonder
And don't cry baby, don't cry
Don't cry

3. It's a turn-around jump shot
It's everybody jump start
It's every generation throws a hero up the pop charts
Medicine is magical and magical is art
The Boy in the Bubble
And the baby with the baboon heart

(And I believe) These are the days of lasers in the jungle
Lasers in the jungle somewhere
Staccato signals of constant information
A loose affiliation of millionaires
And billionaires and baby
These are the days of miracle and wonder
This is the long distance call
The way the camera follows us in slo-mo
The way we look to us all
The way we look to a distant constellation
That's dying in a corner of the sky
These are the days of miracle and wonder
And don't cry baby, don't cry
Don't cry

Can I Forgive Him

Music by Paul Simon
Lyrics by Paul Simon and Derek Walcott

Moderately slow

G6
A/D
A/C♯
Bm7
B/C
Please don't turn your eyes from me
Gmaj7
F♯m
Bm11
Your son, gone to God, and mine to blame
E
Em
D
My fat - ed son, He too is gone
Dm
B♭
A7
Dm
Dm/C♯
The state will see to that, I am sure,
F/C
Bm7♭5
B♭
C7
F
Señ-or - a The state will see to that, I am sure.
Fm
Fm7
A♭°7
3fr.

piu mosso
You Span - ish peo - ple, you come to this coun - try
C7♯9
E°7
Noth - ing here chang - es your lives
Fm
Fm7
Un - grate - ful im - mig - rants ask - ing for pit - y When
A♭°7
3fr.
3
B°
all of your an - swers are knives
This cit - y makes a car -
E♭7♯9
5fr.
E♭7♭9
5fr.
A♭m7
4fr.
- toon of a crime
Capes and um-brel - las the
A♭°7
3fr.
Cm
3fr.
glo - ri - fi - ca - tion of slime

B♭m
E♭
E♭+
A♭9
I have to face this hor - ror, Señ - or - a. My re-
A♭13
F m
F 7
E♭7sus4/B♭
li - gion Asks me to pray for the mur - der-er's soul
D♭/F
E♭
D♭/F
E♭
But I think you'd have to be Je-sus on the cross
D♭/F
E♭
D♭6
A♭6
To o - pen your heart af - ter such a loss
D♭/F
E♭
D♭/F
E♭
D♭6
A♭6
Can I for-give him? Can I for-give him? No, I can - not

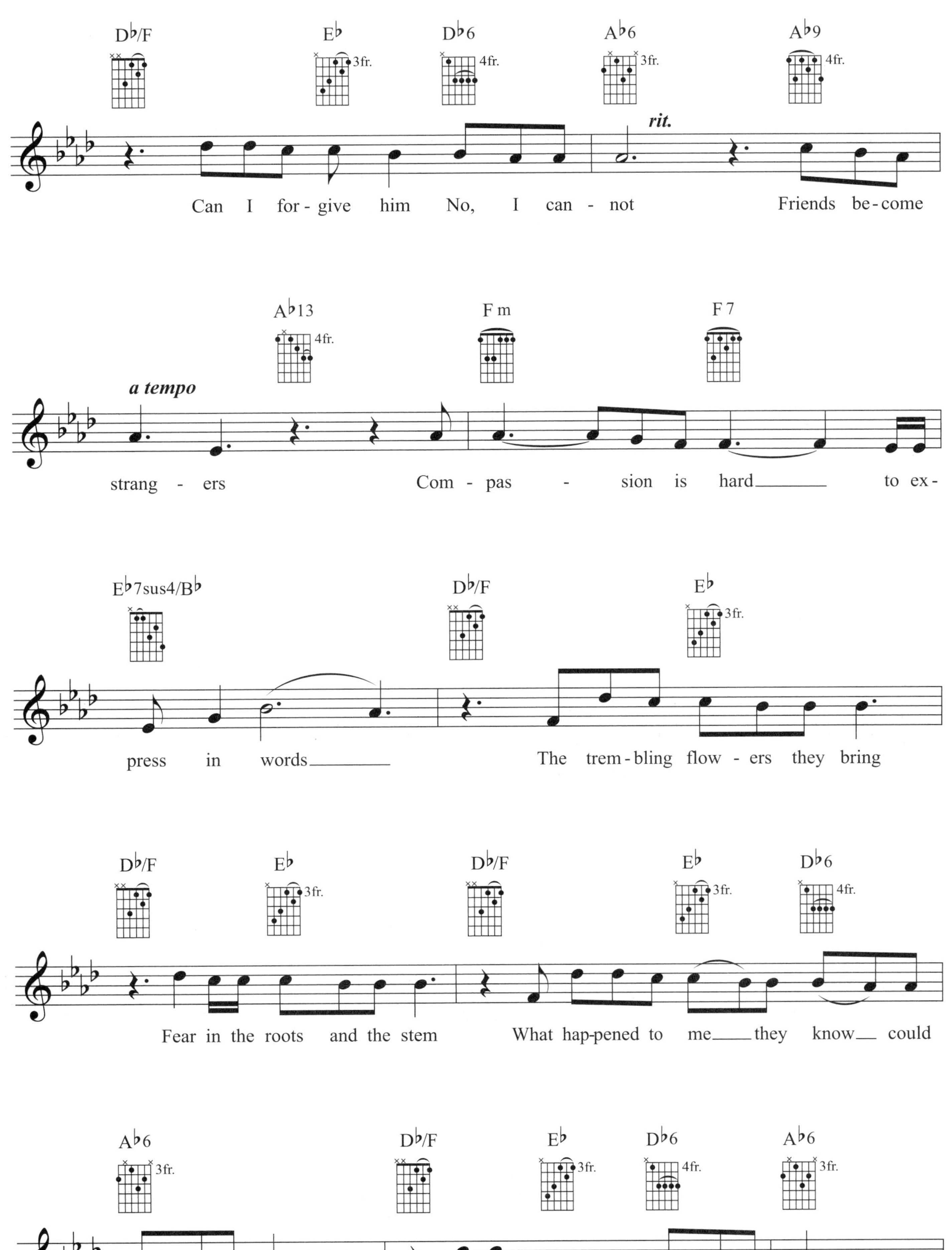
D♭/F
E♭
3fr.
D♭6
4fr.
A♭6
3fr.
A♭9
4fr.
rit.
Can I for - give him No, I can - not Friends be - come
A♭13
4fr.
F m
F 7
a tempo
strang - ers Com - pas - sion is hard to ex -
E♭7sus4/B♭
D♭/F
E♭
3fr.
press in words The trem - bling flow - ers they bring
D♭/F
E♭
3fr.
D♭/F
E♭
3fr.
D♭6
4fr.
Fear in the roots and the stem What hap-pened to me they know could
A♭6
3fr.
D♭/F
E♭
3fr.
D♭6
4fr.
A♭6
3fr.
hap - pen to them. Can I for-give him No, I can - not

D♭/F
E♭
D♭6
A♭6
Can I for - give him No
G sus4
G m
D
On - ly God can say "For - give"
G m
D
His son too re - ceived a knife
G m
E♭/B♭
But we go on, we have to live
B♭
B♭7
E♭
E♭+
A♭9
rit.
With this cross we call our life Feels like a
A♭13
F m
F 7
a tempo
bomb fell And wave af - ter wave come the

E♭7sus4/B♭
D♭/F
E♭
3fr.
af - ter - shocks
You can't be - lieve that it's true
D♭/F
E♭
D♭/F
E♭
D♭6
4fr.
There must be some mis - take
You drift through this night - mare from which you can't
A♭6
D♭/F
E♭
wake
Can I for - give him?
D♭/F
E♭
D♭6
A♭6
D♭/F
E♭
Can I for - give him, No, I can - not
Can I for - give him?
D♭
E♭
D♭6
A♭6
repeat and fade
Can I for - give him, no, I can - not

Bridge Over Troubled Water

Words and Music by Paul Simon

B♭ E♭7 E♭9/B♭ A♭ A○7 E♭/B♭ C7
— Like a bridge o - ver trou - bled wa - ter
A♭ G7 Cm E♭7 E♭9/B♭ A♭ A○7
I will lay me down. Like a bridge o - ver
1.
E♭/B♭ C7 A♭ B♭7 E♭ A♭/E♭
trou - bled wa - ter I will lay me down.
E♭ A♭/E♭ E♭ A♭/E♭
2.When you're
2.
E♭/B♭ Cm A♭ G7 Cm Cm/B Cm/B♭ F F/E F/E♭
trou - bled wa - ter I will lay me down.
E♭ A♭ Cm A♭ A♭m E♭ A♭/E♭

E♭
A♭/E♭
E♭
A♭/E♭
Rubato
Sail on
E♭
A♭/E♭
E♭
sil - ver girl,
Sail on by.
A♭
D♭
A♭
E♭
Fm
Your time has come to shine,
All your
E♭
A♭
E♭
A♭
E♭
B♭/D
Cm
dreams are on their way.
See how they
B♭
B♭7
E♭
E♭/D
shine.
Oh,
if you need a friend
E♭/D♭
E♭7
E♭9/B♭
A♭
F
B♭
E♭7
E♭9/B♭
In tempo
I'm sail - ing right be - hind.
Like a

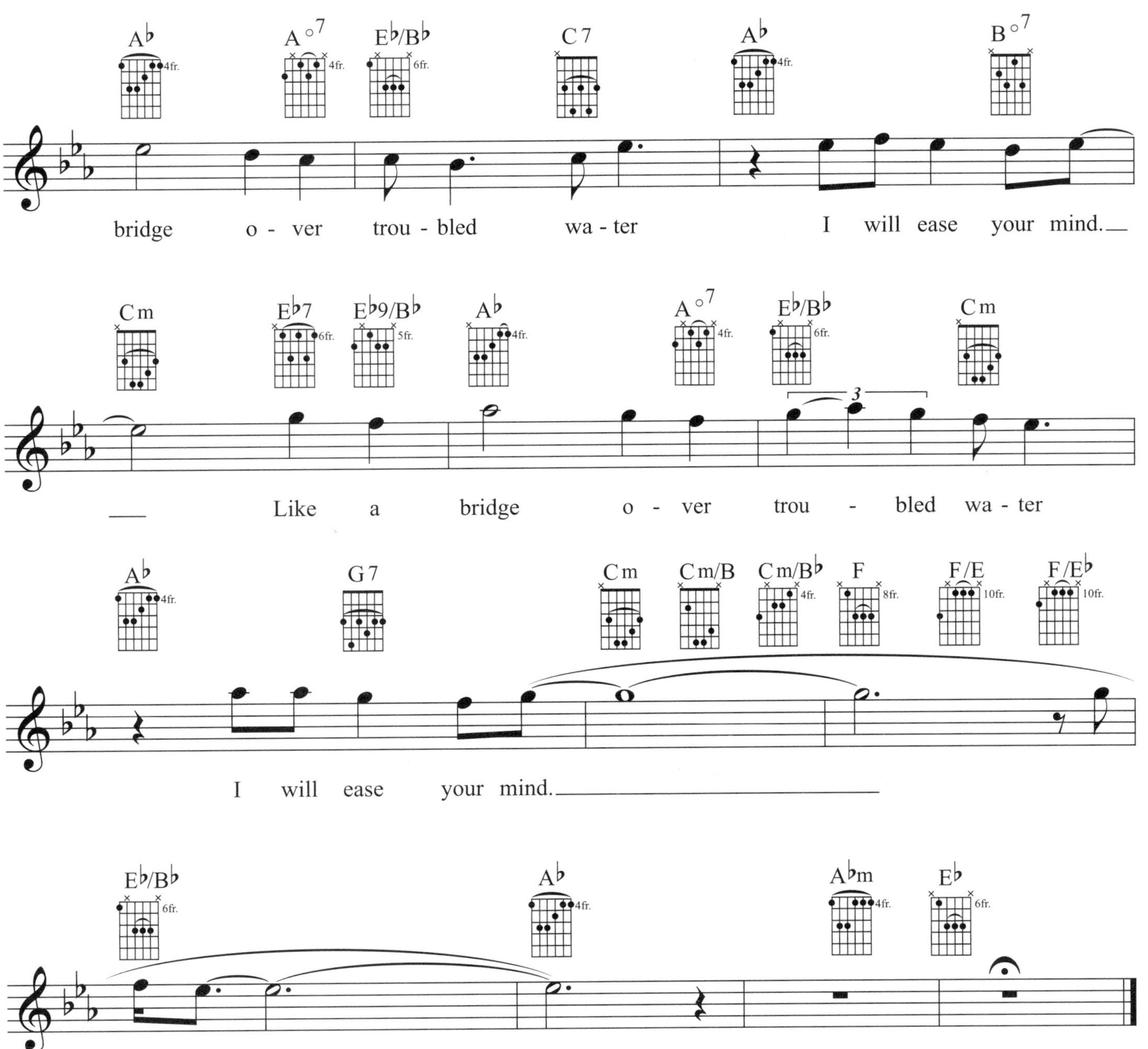

2. When you're down and out
When you're on the street
When evening falls so hard
I will comfort you (ooh)
I'll take your part,
Oh, when darkness comes
And pain is all around

Can't Run But

Words and Music by Paul Simon

Moderately bright

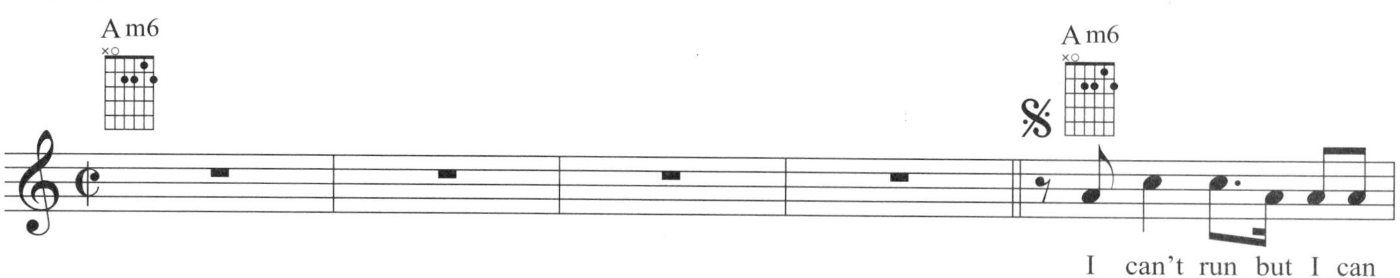

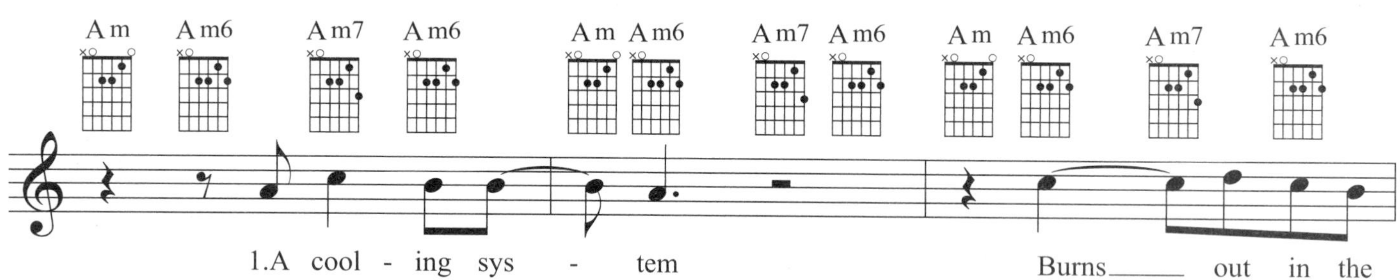

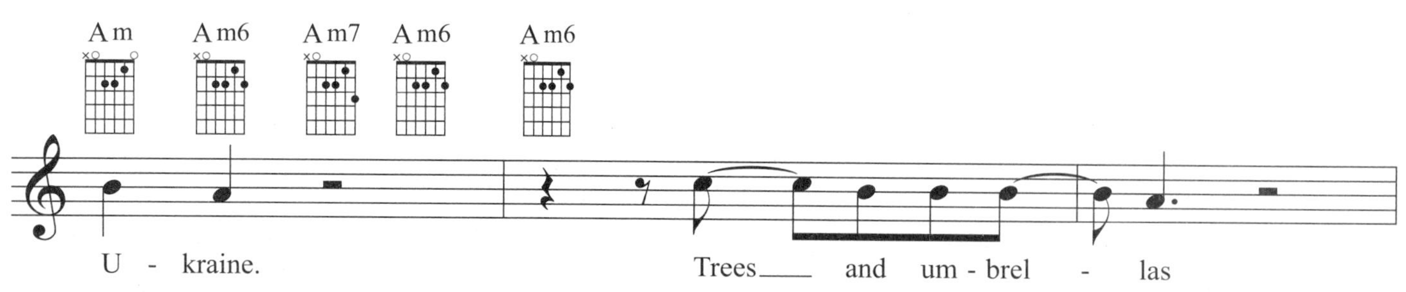

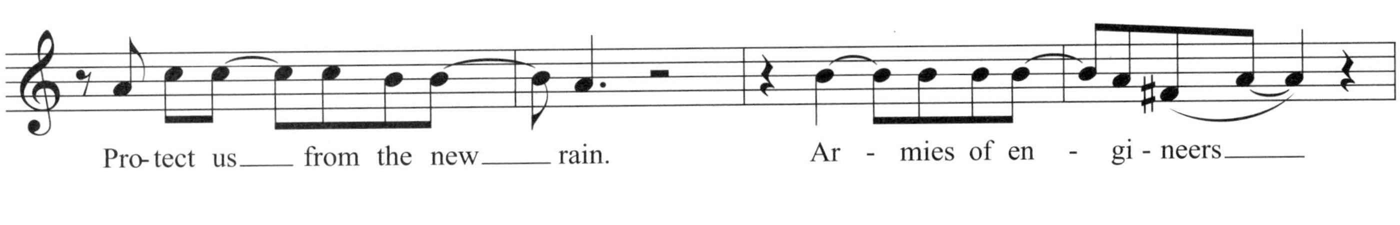
Pro-tect us from the new rain. Ar - mies of en - gi - neers

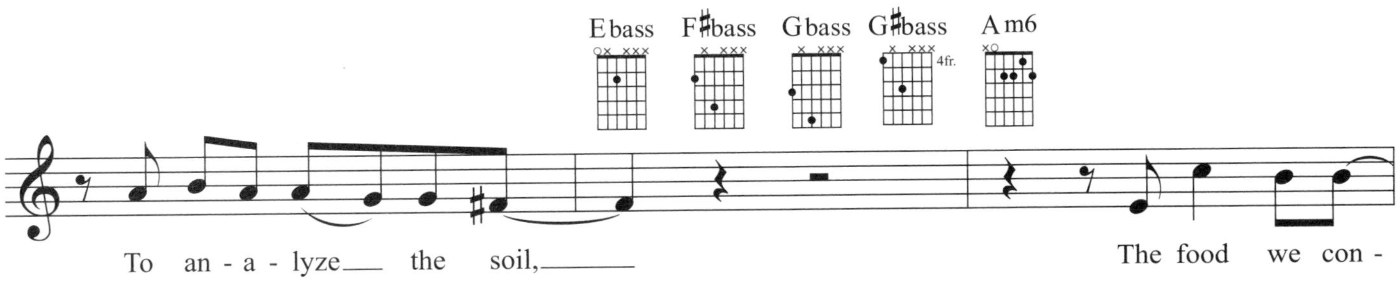
Ebass
F♯bass
Gbass
G♯bass
Am6
4fr.
To an - a - lyze the soil, The food we con -

- tem - plate, the wa-ter that we boil. I can't run but I can

walk much fas - ter than this, Can't run but I can't run but I can

Ebass
F♯bass
Gbass
G♯bass
4fr.
walk much fas - ter than this, Can't run but

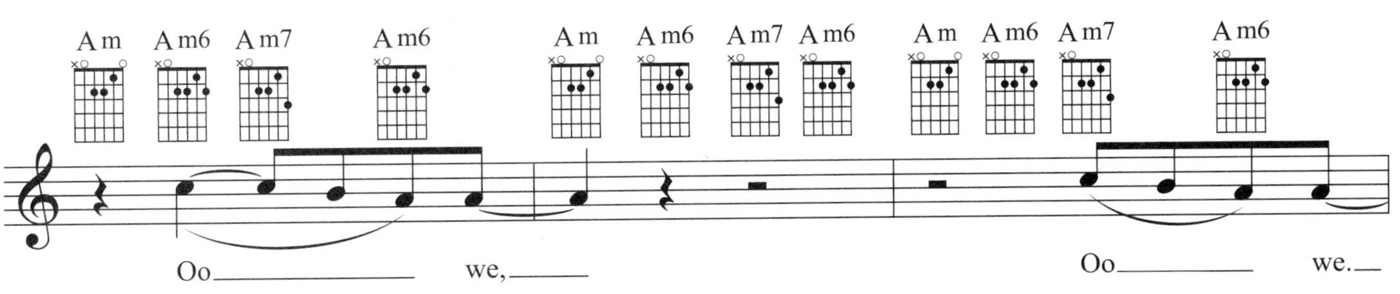
Am
Am6
Am7
Am6
Am
Am6
Am7
Am6
Am
Am6
Am7
Am6
Oo we, Oo we.

Am Am6 Am7 Am6 Am6
instrumental
(second time, fade)
Ebass F♯bass Gbass G♯bass Am Am6 Am7 Am6 Am Am6 Am7 Am6
I had a dream a-bout us in the
Am Am6 Am7 Am6 Am Am6 Am7 Am6 Am6
bot-tles and the bones of the night. I felt a pain in my shoul-
-der blade, was like a pen-cil point? A love bite? A cou-ple was rub-
Ebass F♯bass Gbass G♯bass
bing a-gainst us, Rub-bing and do-ing that new dance.

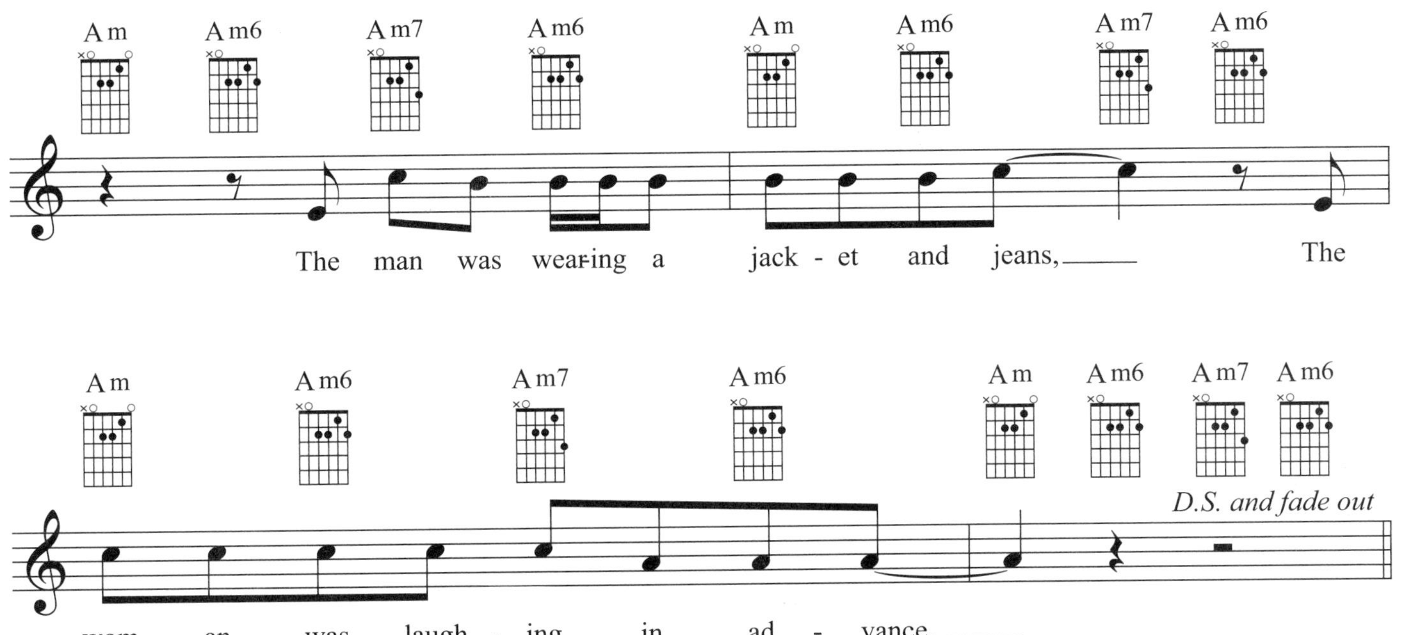

2. A winding river
   Gets wound around a heart. Pull it
   Tighter and tighter
   Until the muddy waters part
   Down by the river bank
   A blues band arrives
   The music suffers
   The music business thrives.

Cars Are Cars

Words and Music by Paul Simon

2.
C D G C D G
cars all o- ver the world. Cars are cars all o-ver the world. But
F♯m7 Bm7 C69 Bm7
peo - ple are strang - ers. They change with the curve from
Gmaj7 F♯m7 Em7 D
time zone to time zone as we can ob - serve. They
Bm7 F♯m7 C69
shut down their bor - ders and think they're im - mune.
Gmaj7 Bm7 D/C
They stand on their dif - f'renc - es and
C G
to Coda II
D.S. al Coda I
shoot at the moon. 3.Cars are

Coda I
C D G C D
cars all o-ver the world. Cars are cars all o-ver the world.
G C D G
Cars are cars all o-ver the world.
D G D G
D.S.S. al Coda II
4. I
Coda II
D
Cars are cars all o - ver the world.
G D G
Cars are cars all o-ver the world. Cars are
C D G C D
cars all o-ver the world. Cars are cars all o-ver the world.

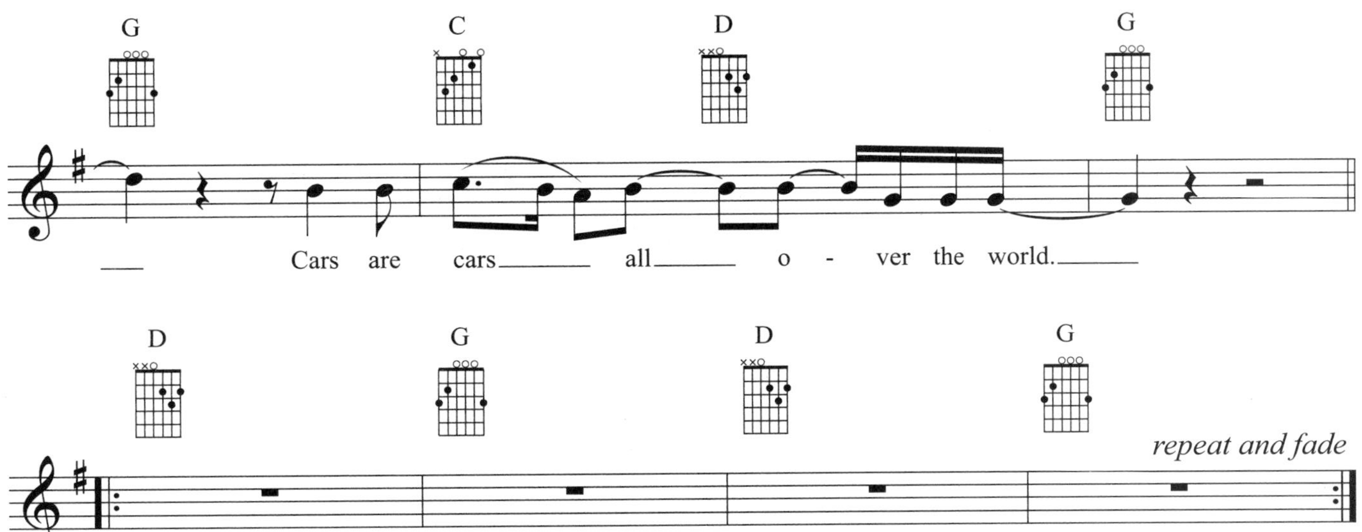

2. Cars are cars all over the world
   Cars are cars all over the world
   Engine in the front
   Jack in the back
   Wheels take the brunt
   Pinion and a rack
   Cars are cars all over the world
   Cars are cars all over the world

   But people are strangers
   They change with the curve
   From time zone to time zone
   As we can observe
   They shut down their borders
   And think they're immune
   They stand on their differences
   And shoot at the moon

3. Cars are cars all over the world
   Cars are cars all over the world
   (You could) Drive 'em on the left
   Drive 'em on the right
   Susceptible to theft
   In the middle of the night
   Cars are cars all over the world
   Cars are cars all over the world
   Cars are cars all over the world

4. I once had a car
   That was more like a home
   I lived in it, loved in it
   Polished its chrome
   If some of my homes
   Had been more like my car
   I probably wouldn't have
   Traveled this far

   Cars are cars all over the world
   Cars are cars all over the world
   Cars are cars all over the world
   Cars are cars all over the world
   Cars are cars all over the world

Congratulations

Words and Music by Paul Simon

Moderately slow

F♯m D♯m7♭5 D C♯m Bm
slip-pin' a - way, And man - y more
A A/G D/F♯ F♯aug7 G
wait-ing in the lines in the court-rooms to - day,
B E A D
oh, in the court-rooms to - day.
A A7 B7 E7
Love is not a game, love is not a toy, love's no ro -
A D/A A7
- mance.
B7 E7 A
Love will do you in, and love will wash you out, and need-less to say you
E/G♯ F♯m B7 E
won't stand a chance, and you won't stand a chance.

F♯m Gm B11 E E/D♯
I'm hun-gry for learn - in',
E7 F♯m D♯m7♭5/A D
Won't you an-swer me, please. Can a
C♯m Bm A A/G D/F♯ F♯aug7
man and a wom - an live to-geth-er in
G B E
peace, oh, live to-geth-er in peace?
A D E
A D E

Cecelia

Words and Music by Paul Simon

Moderate, not too fast, rhythmically

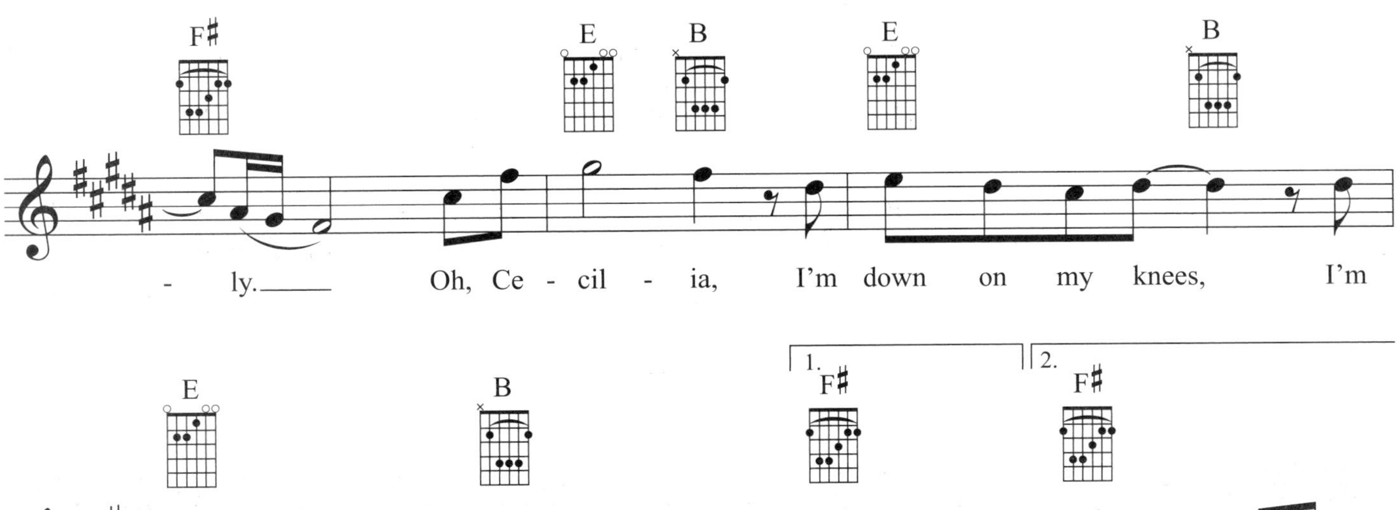

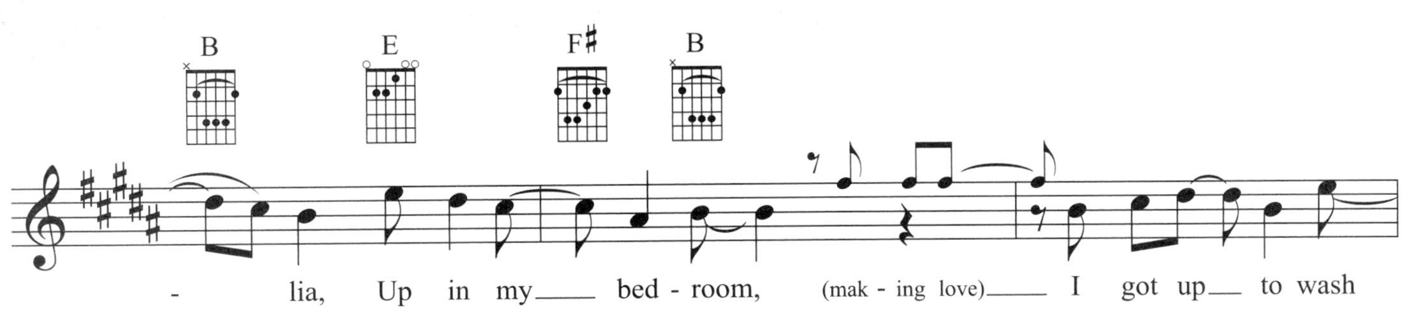

E
B
F♯
B
my face When I come back to bed, some- one's tak - en my place.

B
E
B
E
B
(instrumental on D.S.)
'Cel - ia, you're break - ing my heart, You're shak - ing my con - fi - dence dai -

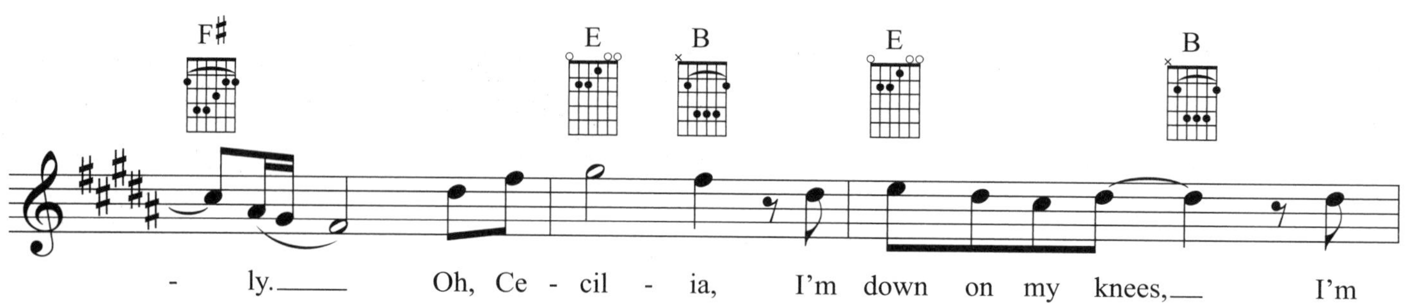
F♯
E
B
E
B
- ly. Oh, Ce - cil - ia, I'm down on my knees, I'm

E
B
F♯
B
to Coda
beg - ging you please to come home. Come on home. Poh poh

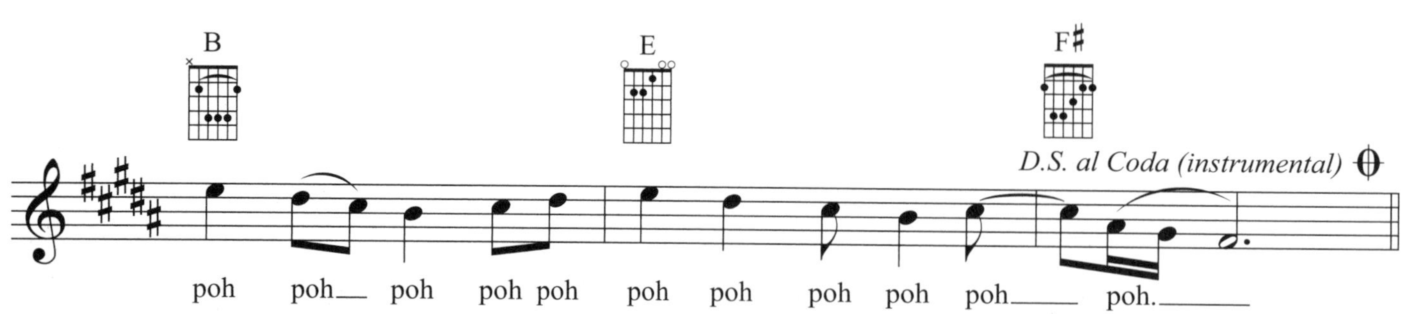
B
E
F♯
D.S. al Coda (instrumental)
poh poh poh poh poh poh poh poh poh poh poh.

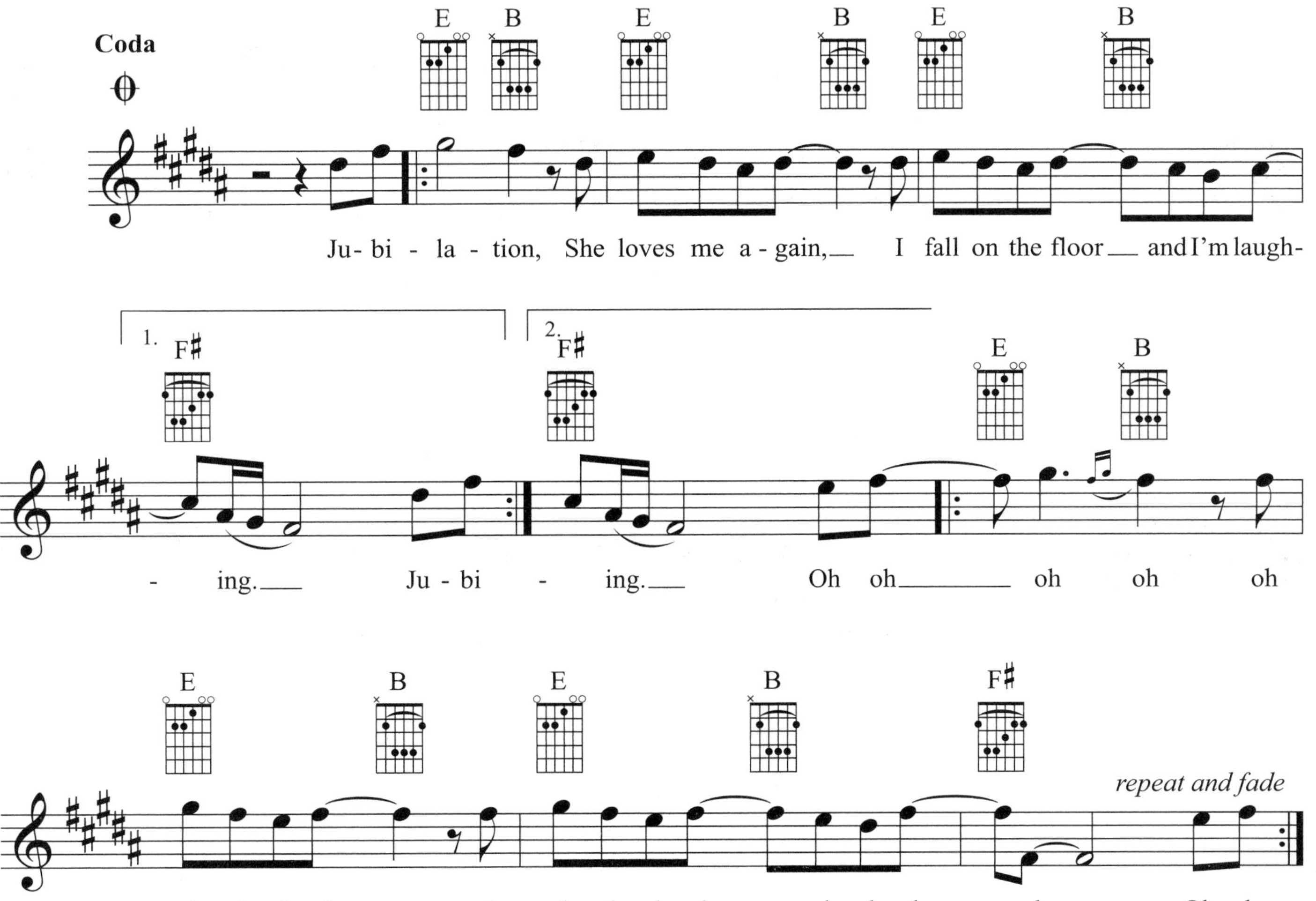
Coda
E
B
F♯
Ju - bi - la - tion, She loves me a - gain, I fall on the floor and I'm laugh-
- ing. Ju - bi - ing. Oh oh oh oh oh
oh oh oh oh oh oh oh oh oh oh oh oh oh. Oh oh
repeat and fade

A Church Is Burning

Words and Music by Paul Simon

Verse
Fm
E♭
Three hood-ed men through the back roads did creep,
torch-es in their hands while the vil-lage lies a-sleep.
A♭ Fm E♭ D♭ E♭
Down to the church where just hours be-fore
A♭ Fm E♭ A♭ Fm E♭
voic-es were sing-ing and hands were beat-ing and
A♭ B♭ E♭ B♭7 E♭
say-ing, "I won't be a slave an-y more."
Chorus
E♭ B♭ A♭ E♭
And a church is burn-ing.
A♭ B♭ E♭ B♭ E♭
The flames rise high-er, like

Gm
Fm
A♭
B♭
hands that are pray - ing, a glow in the sky.
Fm7
B♭
E♭
A♭
Gm
Fm
Like hands that are pray - ing, the fire is
E♭
A♭
E♭
B♭7
say - ing, "You can burn down my church - es, but I shall be
E♭
B♭
E♭
B♭
E♭
B♭
E♭
Fm
free."
Verse
3
1.Three hood-ed
E♭
Fm
men, their hands lit the spark. Then they fad - ed in the
E♭
A♭
Fm
night. And they van - ished in the dark. And in the cool light of
E♭
A♭
Fm
E♭
A♭
morn - ing, there's noth - ing that re - mains But the ash - es of a
4fr.
6fr.
8fr.

2. A church is more than just timber and stone,
And freedom is a dark road when you're walking it alone.
But the future is now, and it's time to take a stand
So the lost bells of freedom can ring out in my land.

Cloudy

Words and Music by Paul Simon

D
sun - shine
I have - n't seen you in a
G
long time.
Why don't you show your face and
D D/C♯ D°7 A7 F♯m
bend my mind?
These clouds stick to the sky like a
A Bm E E7
float - ing ques - tion, why?
And they lin - ger there to die.
A A7
They don't know where they're go - ing, and, my friend, nei - ther do
F♯m A7 D Dsus2 D Dsus2
I,
Cloud - y,
G
Cloud - y.

The Coast

Words by Paul Simon
Music by Paul Simon and Vincent Nguini

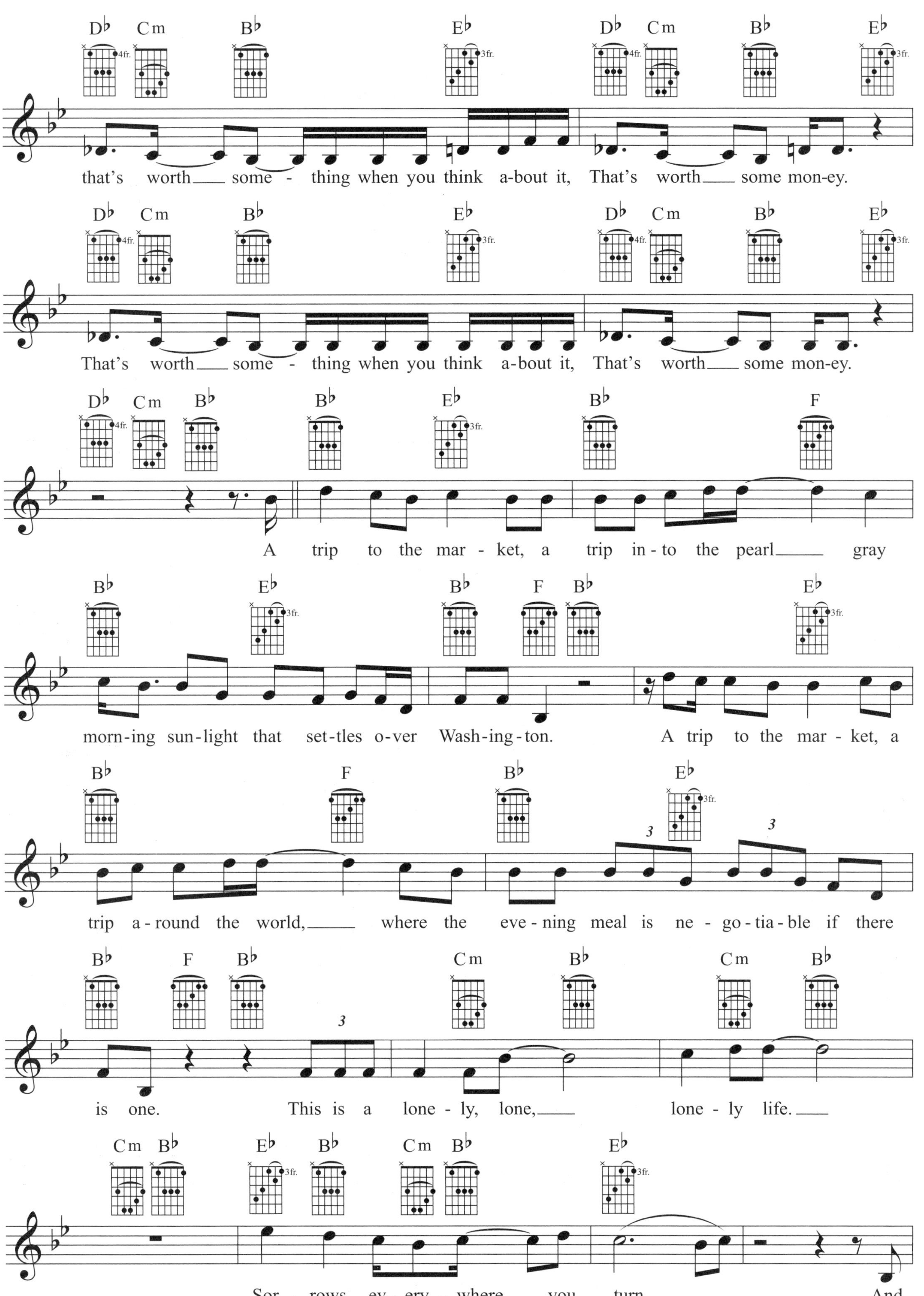
D♭ Cm B♭ E♭ D♭ Cm B♭ E♭
that's worth some - thing when you think a-bout it, That's worth some mon-ey.
D♭ Cm B♭ E♭ D♭ Cm B♭ E♭
That's worth some - thing when you think a-bout it, That's worth some mon-ey.
D♭ Cm B♭ B♭ E♭ B♭ F
A trip to the mar - ket, a trip in-to the pearl gray
B♭ E♭ B♭ F B♭ E♭
morn-ing sun-light that set-tles o-ver Wash-ing-ton. A trip to the mar - ket, a
B♭ F B♭ E♭
trip a-round the world, where the eve-ning meal is ne - go-tia-ble if there
B♭ F B♭ Cm B♭ Cm B♭
is one. This is a lone - ly, lone, lone - ly life.
Cm B♭ E♭ B♭ Cm B♭ E♭
Sor - rows ev - ery - where you turn. And

D♭ Cm B♭ E♭ D♭ Cm B♭ E♭
4fr. 3fr. 4fr. 3fr.
that's worth some - thing when you think a-bout it, That's worth some mo-ney.
D♭ Cm B♭ E♭ D♭ Cm B♭ E♭
4fr. 3fr. 4fr. 3fr.
That's worth some - thing when you think a-bout it, That's worth some mon-ey.
D♭ Cm B♭ E♭ B♭ F B♭ E♭ B♭ F B♭
4fr. 3fr. 3fr.
E♭ B♭ F B♭ E♭
3fr. 3fr.
To prove that I love you be-cause I be-lieve in you, Sum-mer skies, stars are fal-ling
B♭ F B♭ E♭ B♭ F
3fr.
all a-long the in-jured coast. And if I have mon-ey and if I have chil-dren,
B♭ E♭ B♭ F B♭
3fr.
Sum-mer skies, stars are fal-ling all a-long the in-jured coast.
E♭ B♭ F
3fr.
Oo - wah, oo - wah, Doo - wop a doo - wah.

1. B♭ E♭ B♭ F B♭
Sum-mer skies and stars are fal-ling all a-long the in-jured coast.
2. B♭ E♭ B♭ F B♭
N.C.
12
F
Sum-mer skies, the stars are fall-ing.
(percussion)
B♭ E♭ B♭ F B♭ E♭ B♭ F B♭ B♭ F B♭
We are
B♭ E♭ B♭ F
stand-ing in the sun-light, the ear-ly morn-ing sun-light, In the
B♭ E♭ B♭ F B♭ E♭
har-bor church of Saint Ce-cil-ia, To praise a soul's re-
B♭ F B♭ E♭
turn-ing to the earth, To the Rose of Jer-i-cho and the Bou-gan-
B♭ F B♭ Cm B♭ Cm B♭
vil-lea. This is the on-ly
3fr.
3

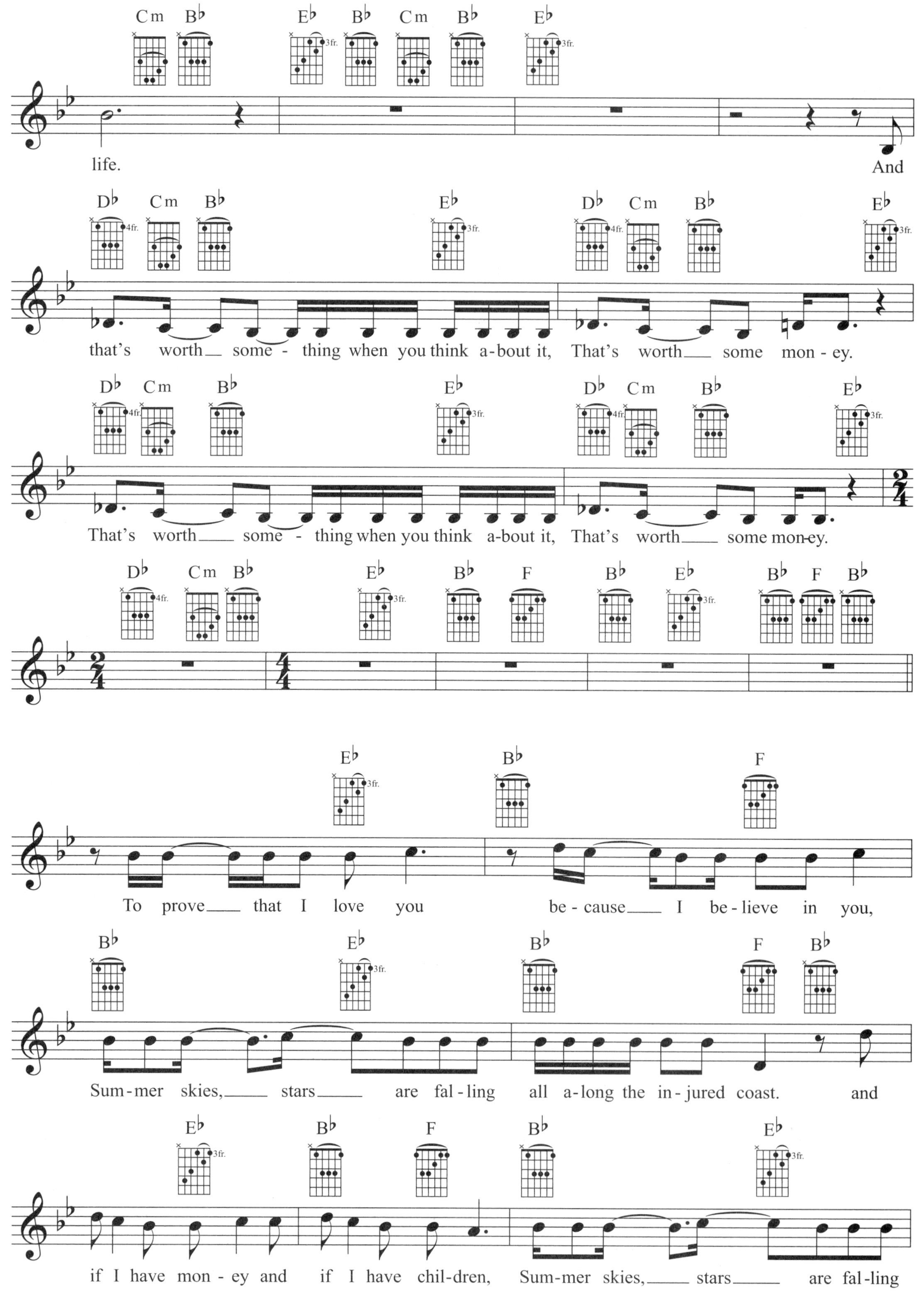
Cm
B♭
E♭
B♭
Cm
B♭
E♭
3fr.
life.
And
D♭
Cm
B♭
E♭
4fr.
that's worth some - thing when you think a-bout it, That's worth some mon - ey.
That's worth some - thing when you think a-bout it, That's worth some mon-ey.
F
To prove that I love you be - cause I be - lieve in you,
Sum-mer skies, stars are fal - ling all a-long the in - jured coast. and
if I have mon - ey and if I have chil-dren, Sum-mer skies, stars are fal-ling

B♭ F B♭ E♭
3fr.
all a-long the in-jured coast. If I have weak-ness-es,
B♭ F B♭ E♭
don't let them blind me now. Sum-mer skies, stars are fal-ling
B♭ F B♭ E♭ B♭ F
all a-long the in-jured coast. Oo-wah, oo-wah, Doo-wop a doo-wah.
B♭ E♭ B♭ F B♭ E♭
Sum-mer skies, the stars are fall-ing. Leav-ing the shad-ow
B♭ F B♭ E♭ B♭ F B♭
of the val-ley be-hind me now all a-long the in-jured coast.
E♭ B♭ F
Oo-wah, oo-wah, Doo-wop a doo-wah.
B♭ E♭ B♭ F B♭
repeat and fade
Sum-mer skies and stars are fall-ing all a-long the in-jured coast.

The Cool, Cool River

Words and Music by Paul Simon

Slowly, with a steady beat

An-ger and no one can___ heal it, Shoves a lit-tle bump___ in-to the mo-men-tum. It's

F♯m Em | G♯m F♯m | A G | G♯m F♯m

just a lit-tle lump,___ But you feel it in the... in the creas-es and the shad-

F♯m Em | G♯m F♯m | A G | G♯m F♯m | F♯m Em | G♯m F♯m | A G | G♯m F♯m

ows, With a rat - tling deep e - mo -

F♯m Em | G♯m F♯m | A G | G♯m F♯m | F♯m Em | G♯m F♯m | A G | G♯m F♯m

tion. The cool,___

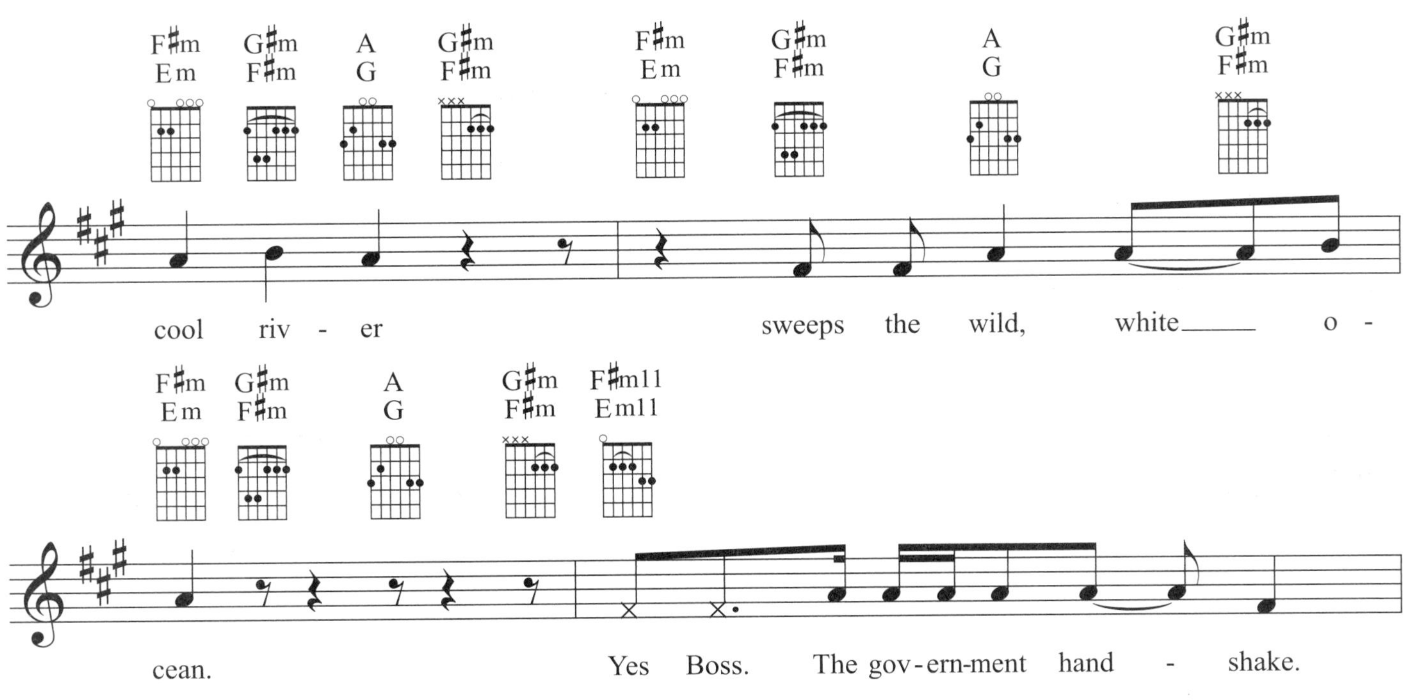

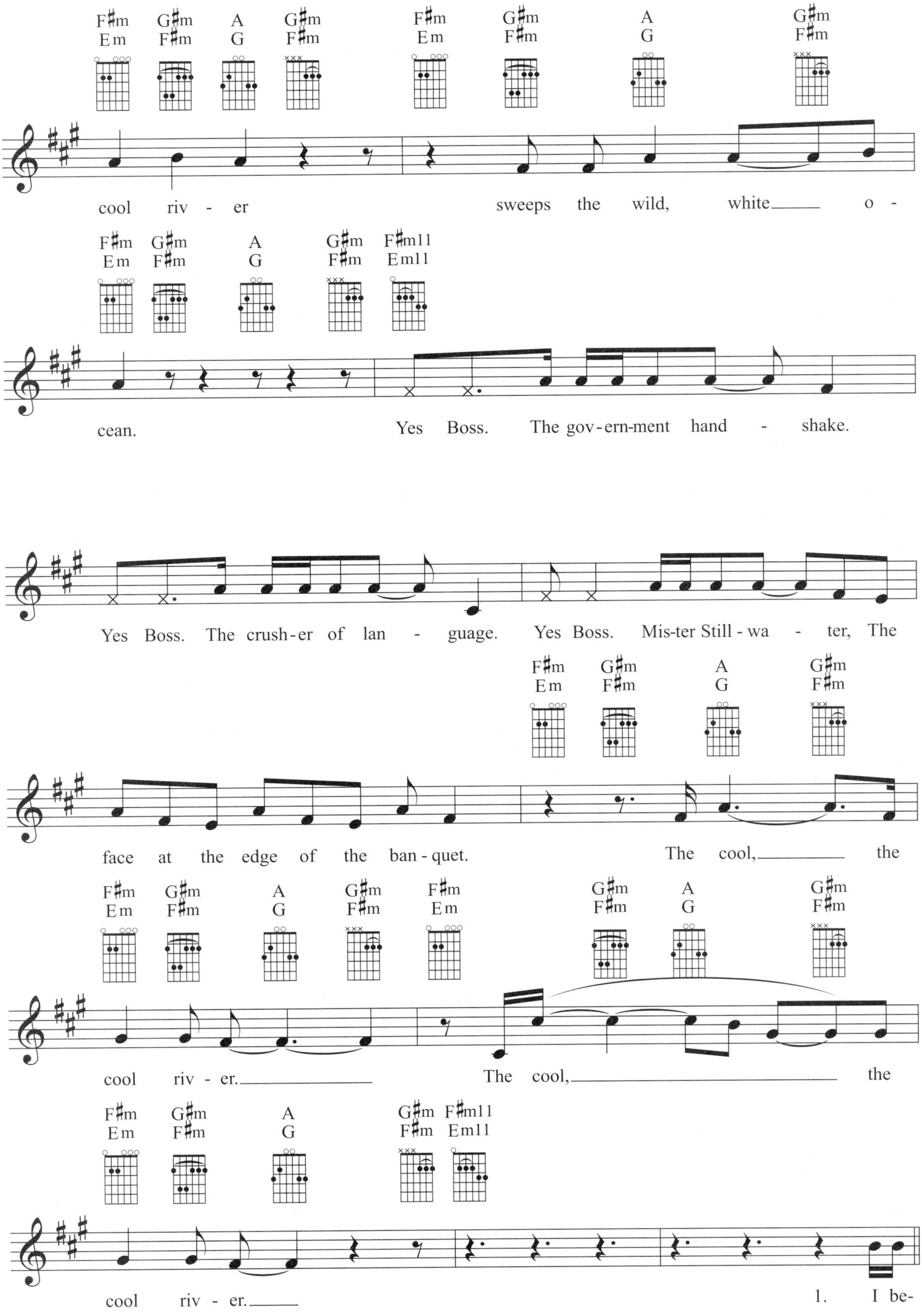

F♯m G♯m A G♯m F♯m G♯m A G♯m
Em F♯m G F♯m Em F♯m G F♯m
cool riv - er sweeps the wild, white o -
F♯m G♯m A G♯m F♯m11
Em F♯m G F♯m Em11
cean. Yes Boss. The gov-ern-ment hand - shake.
Yes Boss. The crush-er of lan - guage. Yes Boss. Mis-ter Still - wa - ter, The
F♯m G♯m A G♯m
Em F♯m G F♯m
face at the edge of the ban - quet. The cool, the
F♯m G♯m A G♯m F♯m G♯m A G♯m
Em F♯m G F♯m Em F♯m G F♯m
cool riv - er. The cool, the
F♯m G♯m A G♯m F♯m11
Em F♯m G F♯m Em11
cool riv - er. 1. I be-

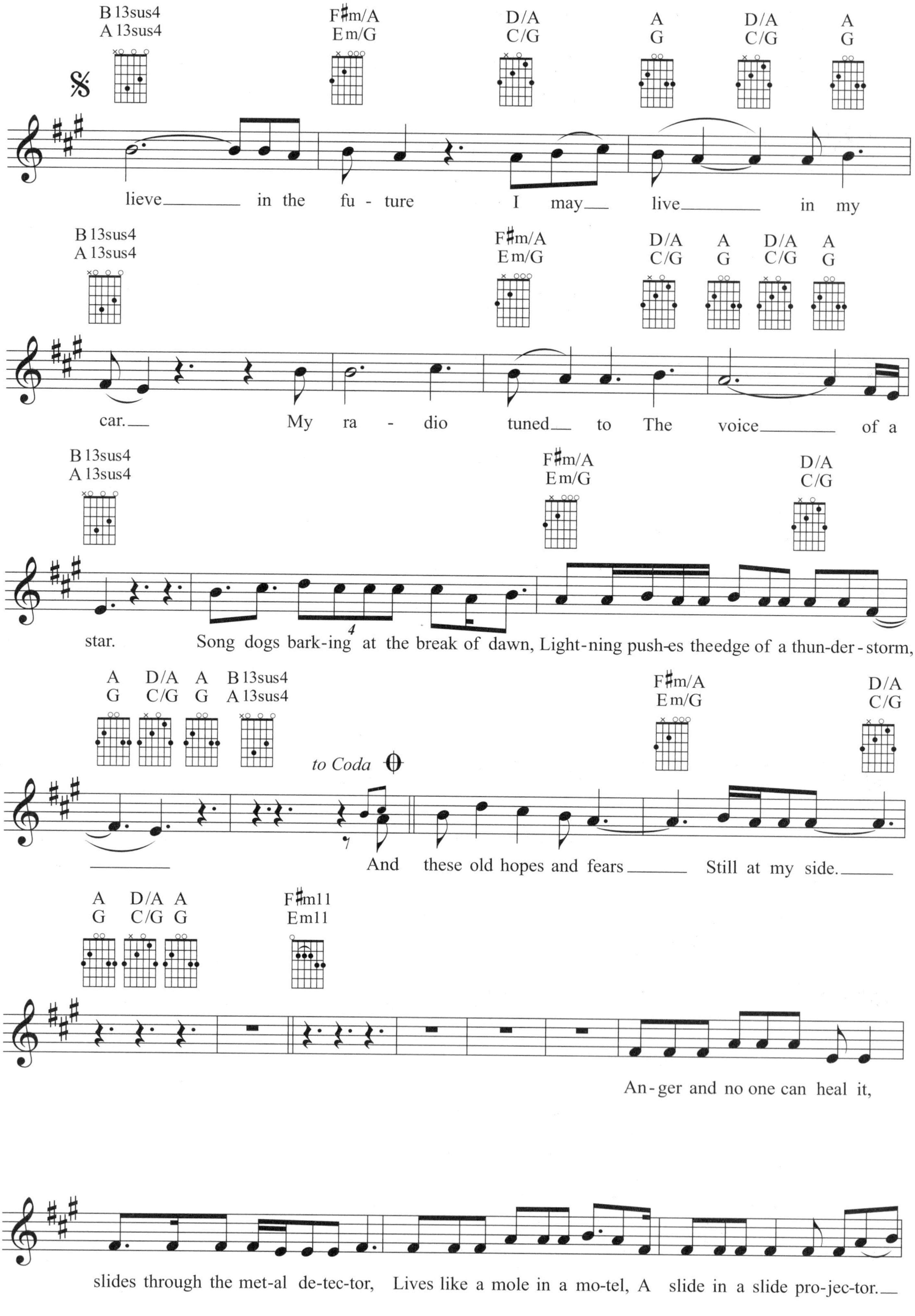

B13sus4 A13sus4 F♯m/A Em/G D/A C/G A G D/A C/G A G
lieve in the future I may live in my
B13sus4 A13sus4 F♯m/A Em/G D/A C/G A G D/A C/G A G
car. My radio tuned to The voice of a
B13sus4 A13sus4 F♯m/A Em/G D/A C/G
star. Song dogs bark-ing at the break of dawn, Light-ning push-es the edge of a thun-der-storm,
A G D/A C/G A G B13sus4 A13sus4 F♯m/A Em/G D/A C/G
to Coda
And these old hopes and fears Still at my side.
A G D/A C/G A G F♯m11 Em11
An-ger and no one can heal it,
slides through the met-al de-tec-tor, Lives like a mole in a mo-tel, A slide in a slide pro-jec-tor.

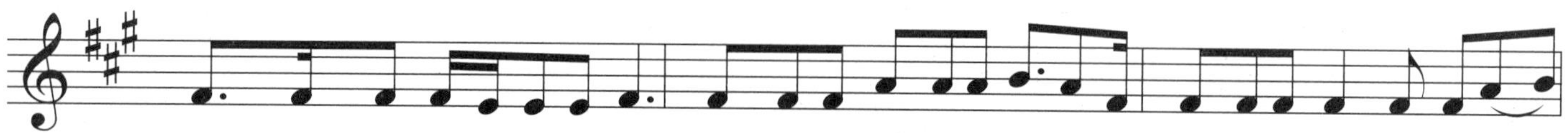

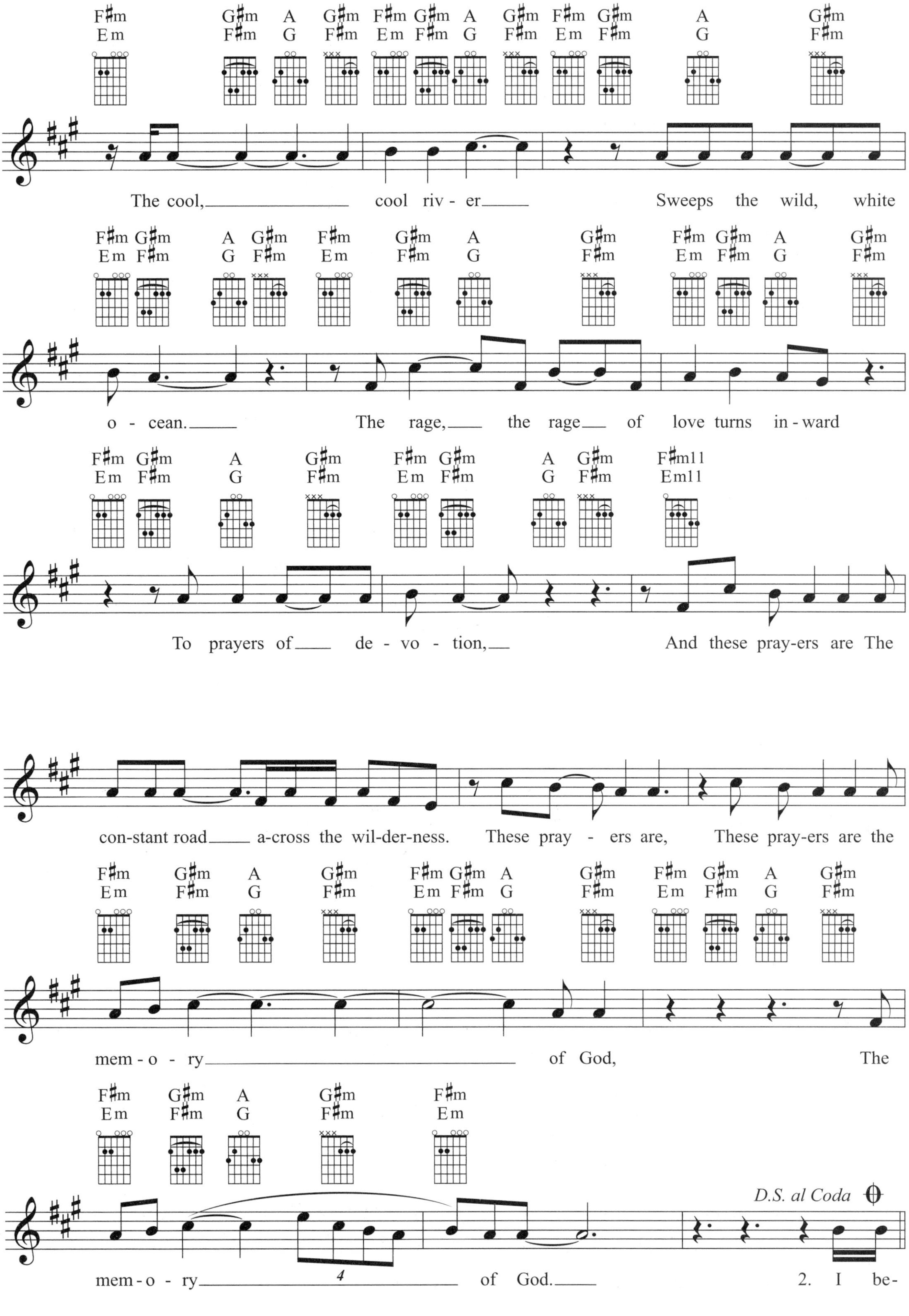

F♯m G♯m A G♯m F♯m G♯m A G♯m F♯m G♯m A G♯m
Em F♯m G F♯m Em F♯m G F♯m Em F♯m G F♯m
The cool, cool river Sweeps the wild, white
F♯m G♯m A G♯m F♯m G♯m A G♯m F♯m G♯m A G♯m
Em F♯m G F♯m Em F♯m G F♯m Em F♯m G F♯m
o - cean. The rage, the rage of love turns in - ward
F♯m G♯m A G♯m F♯m G♯m A G♯m F♯m11
Em F♯m G F♯m Em F♯m G F♯m Em11
To prayers of de - vo - tion, And these pray-ers are The
con-stant road a-cross the wil-der-ness. These pray - ers are, These pray-ers are the
F♯m G♯m A G♯m F♯m G♯m A G♯m F♯m G♯m A G♯m
Em F♯m G F♯m Em F♯m G F♯m Em F♯m G F♯m
mem - o - ry of God, The
F♯m G♯m A G♯m F♯m
Em F♯m G F♯m Em
D.S. al Coda
4
mem - o - ry of God. 2. I be-

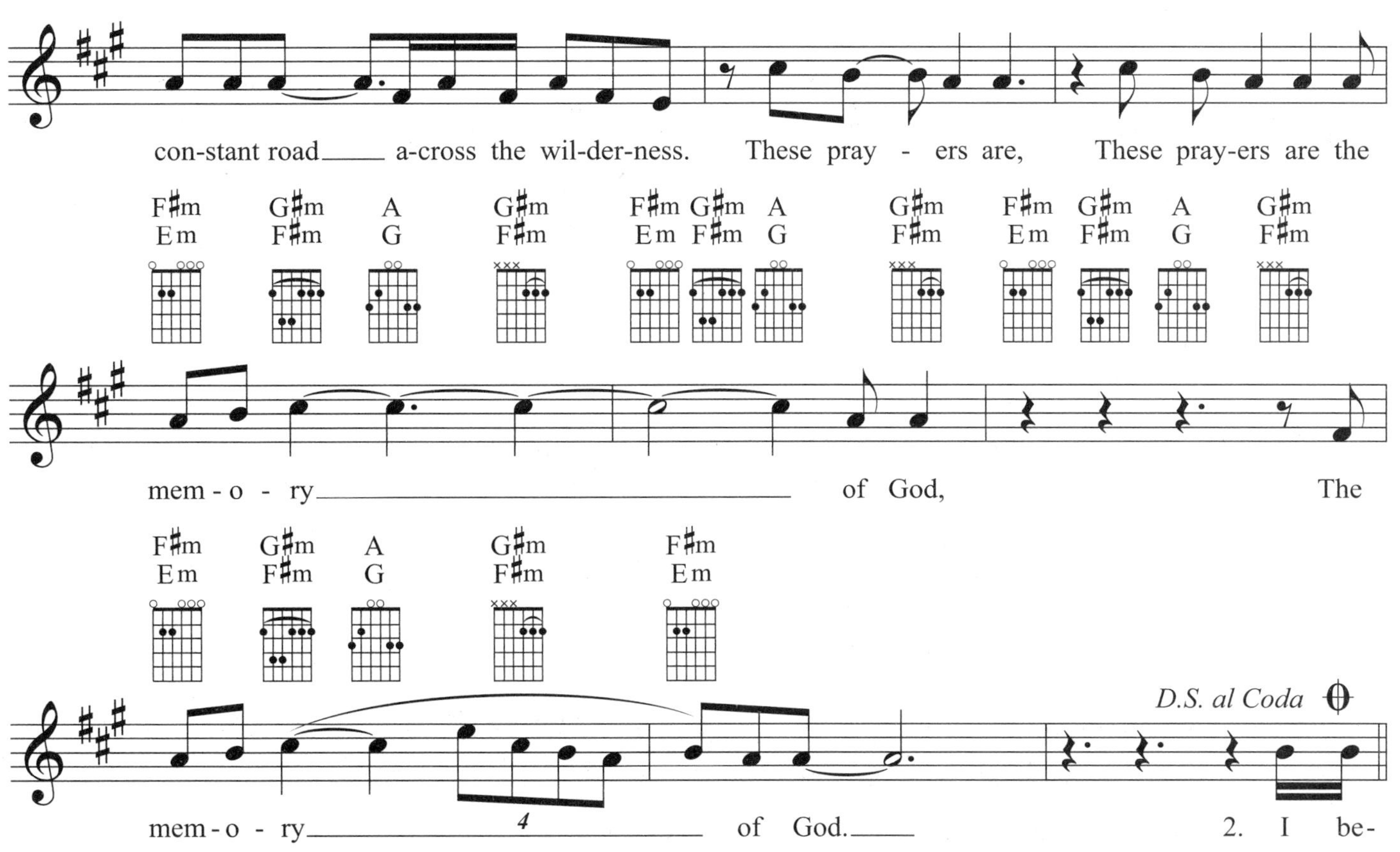

Coda
D
C
A
G
E7/G♯
D7/F♯
streets, Qui-et as a sleep-ing ar-my, Send their bat - tered dreams to
A
G
D/A
C/G
heav - en, to heav - en For the moth-er's rest - less
A
G
D/A
C/G
son Who is a wit - ness to, who is a war - ri - or
E/B
D/A
A
G
Who de - nies his urge to break and run, who says:
D/A
C/G
"Hard times? I'm used to them. The speed-ing plan-et burns, I'm used to that.
3
E/B
D/A
A
G
My life's so com-mon, it dis-ap - pears. And some - times

2. I believe in the future,
We shall suffer no more.
Maybe not in my lifetime
But in yours I feel sure.
Song dogs barking at the break of dawn,
Lightning pushes the edges of a thunderstorm,
And these streets,
Quiet as a sleeping army,
Send their battered dreams to heaven, to heaven.
For the mother's restless son
Who is a witness to, who is a warrior,
Who denies his urge to break and run.

Who says: "Hard times?
I'm used to them.
The speeding planet burns,
I'm used to that.
My life's so common, it disappears.
And sometimes even music
Cannot substitute for tears."

Diamonds On The Soles Of Her Shoes

Words and Music by Paul Simon
Beginning by Paul Simon and Joseph Shabalala

Moderately

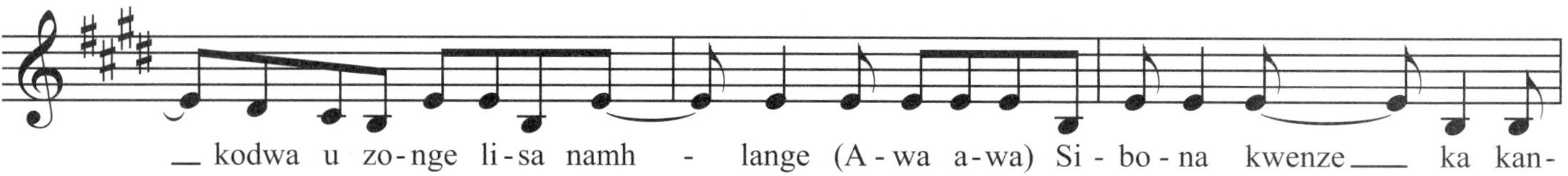

A
- ty as a pock - et with noth - ing to lose Sing Ta na na Ta
E B E
na na na She got dia - monds on the soles of her shoes Ta
A E B
na na Ta na na na She got dia - monds on the soles of her shoes
E A E
Dia - monds on the soles of her shoes Dia -
B E B
- monds on the soles of her shoes Dia - monds on the soles of her shoes
E A E
rit.
Dia - monds on the soles of her shoes

F
B♭
C
freely
a tempo
to Coda
1.Peo-ple say she's cra - zy She got
dia-monds on the soles of her shoes
Well that's one way to lose these
Walk-ing blues
Dia - monds on the soles of her shoes
She was phys - i - cal - ly for - got - ten
And then she
slipped in - to my pock-et With my car
keys
She said you've
3

B♭ C F B♭ C
tak-en me for grant-ed Be-cause I please you Wear-ing these dia - - - - -
F B♭ C F B♭ C
- monds And I could say Oo
F B♭ C F
As if ev-'ry bod-y knows What I'm talk-ing a-bout As if
B♭ C F
3
ev-'ry bod-y here would know ex-act-ly what I was talk-ing a-bout Talk-in' 'bout
B♭ C F B♭ C F F/B♭ B♭/C C F F/B♭
dia-monds on the soles of her shoes
1. 2.
B♭/C C F F/B♭ B♭/C C F F/B♭ B♭/C C B♭/C C
D.S. al Coda

2. She makes the sign of a teaspoon
He makes the sign of a wave
The poor boy changes clothes
And puts on after-shave
To compensate for his ordinary shoes

And she said honey take me dancing
But they ended up by sleeping
In a doorway
By the bodegas and the lights on
Upper Broadway
Wearing diamonds on the soles of their shoes

And I could say Oo oo oo
As if everybody here would know
What I was talking about
I mean everybody here would know exactly
What I was talking about
Talking about diamonds

Crazy Love Vol. II

Words and Music by Paul Simon

Moderately fast

C D G Am7
He said, "well, I don't claim to be hap-py a-bout this, boys,
G/D D G Am7
and I don't seem to be hap-py a-bout that."
G/D D F B♭ C F
I don't want no part of this cra-zy love
B♭ C F B♭
I don't want no part of your love. I don't want no part of this cra-
C F B♭ C
-zy love I don't want no part of your love. I don't
F B♭ C F
want no part of this cra-zy love

2 She says she knows about jokes
This time the joke is on me
Well, I have no opinion about that
And I have no opinion about me

Somebody could walk into this room
And say your life is on fire
It's all over the evening news
All about the fire in your life
On the evening news

3. Fat Charlie the Archangel
Files for divorce
He says, "Well this will eat up a year of my life,
And then there's all that weight to be lost."
She says the joke is on me
I say the joke is on her
I said, "I have no opinion about that
Well, we'll just have to wait and confer"

The Dangling Conversation

Words and Music by Paul Simon

2. And you read your Emily Dickinson,
And I my Robert Frost,
And we note our place with bookmarkers
That measure what we've lost.
Like a poem poorly written
We are verses out of rhythm,
Couplets out of rhyme,
In syncopated time
And the dangling conversation
And the superficial sighs,
Are the borders of our lives.

3. Yes, we speak of things that matter,
With words that must be said,
"Can analysis be worthwhile?"
"Is the theater really dead?"
And how the room is softly faded
And I only kiss your shadow,
I cannot feel your hand,
You're a stranger now unto me
Lost in the dangling conversation.
And the superficial sighs,
In the borders of our lives.

Darling Lorraine

Words and Music by Paul Simon

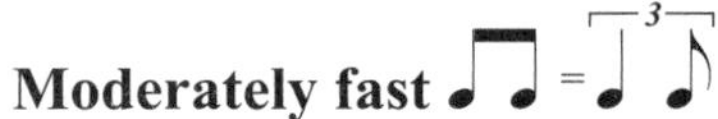

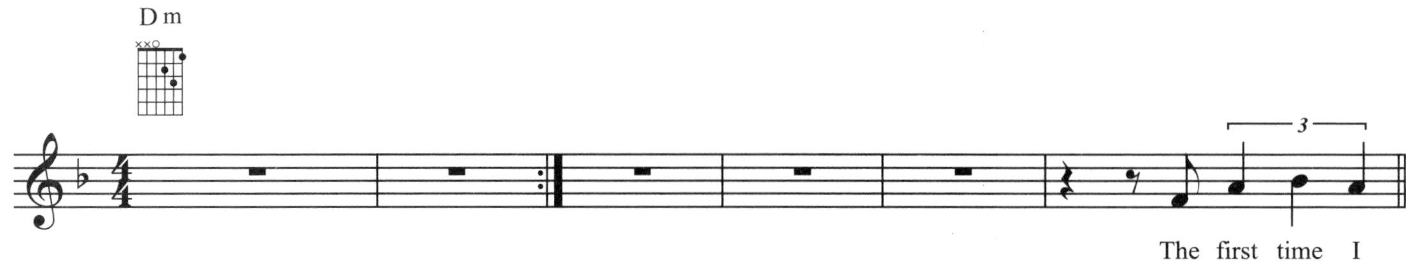

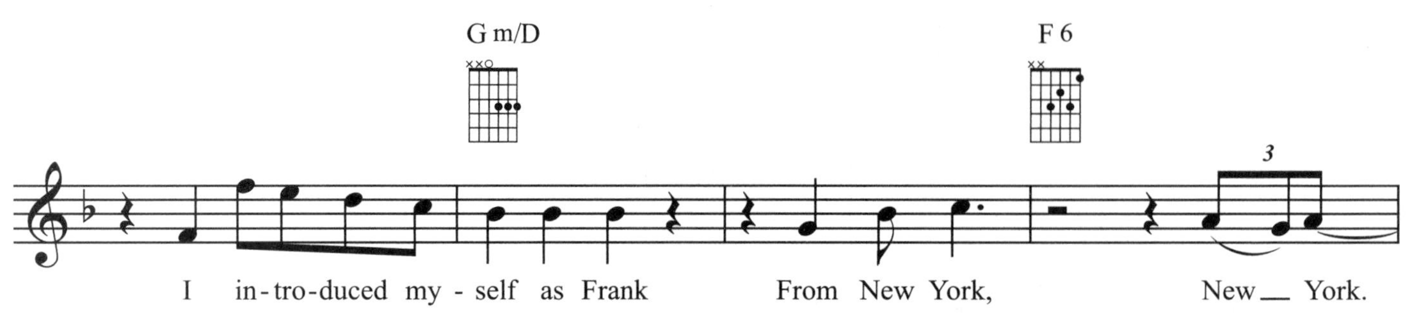

B♭
F
C
Dm
She's so hot, She's so cool, I'm not, I'm just a
fool in love with dar - ling Lor - raine.
to Coda I
1.
2.
raine.
G
What?
C/D
You don't love me an - y - more? What? You're walk - ing out the door?
G/D
What? You don't like the way I chew? Hey let me tell you,
F6
You're not the wom - an that I wed. You say you're de - pressed but you're not, You

C
F 6
C
G
D m
C
F 6
C
G/D
D m
to Coda II
just like to stay in bed.
I don't need you
dar-ling Lor - raine.
C
F 6
C/E
F
C/E
Dar-ling Lor - raine,
F 6
B♭
D m
Lor - raine,
I
long for your love.
A m
D m
D. S. al Coda I
3.Fi-nan - cial - ly
Coda I
D m
A
D
raine,
On Christ-mas morn-ing Frank a - wakes
A
D
To find Lor - raine has made a stack of pan - cakes.

G
Em
Bm7
They watch the tel - e - vi - sion, hus-band and wife.
A
A/C♯
D
Em7
D/F♯
A
All af - ter - noon, it's a won-der-ful life.
G
D. S. S. al Coda II
Coda II
C
F6
C/E
F6
Dar-ling Lor - raine, Lor - raine, Her
E sus4
F6
B♭
hands like wood. The doc - tor was
Dm
Am
smil-ing But the news was-n't good.

Dm
Dm
Dar-ling Lor-raine, Please don't leave me yet. I
know you're in pain, Pain you can't for-get. Your breath-ing is
C/D
Gm/D
like an ech-o of our love. May-be I'll go down to the
F
Gm/D
cor-ner store And buy some-thing sweet. Here's an ex-tra blan-ket hon-ey
F6
B♭
To wrap a-round your feet. All the trees
F
C
D
C
were washed with A-pril rain, And the moon in the

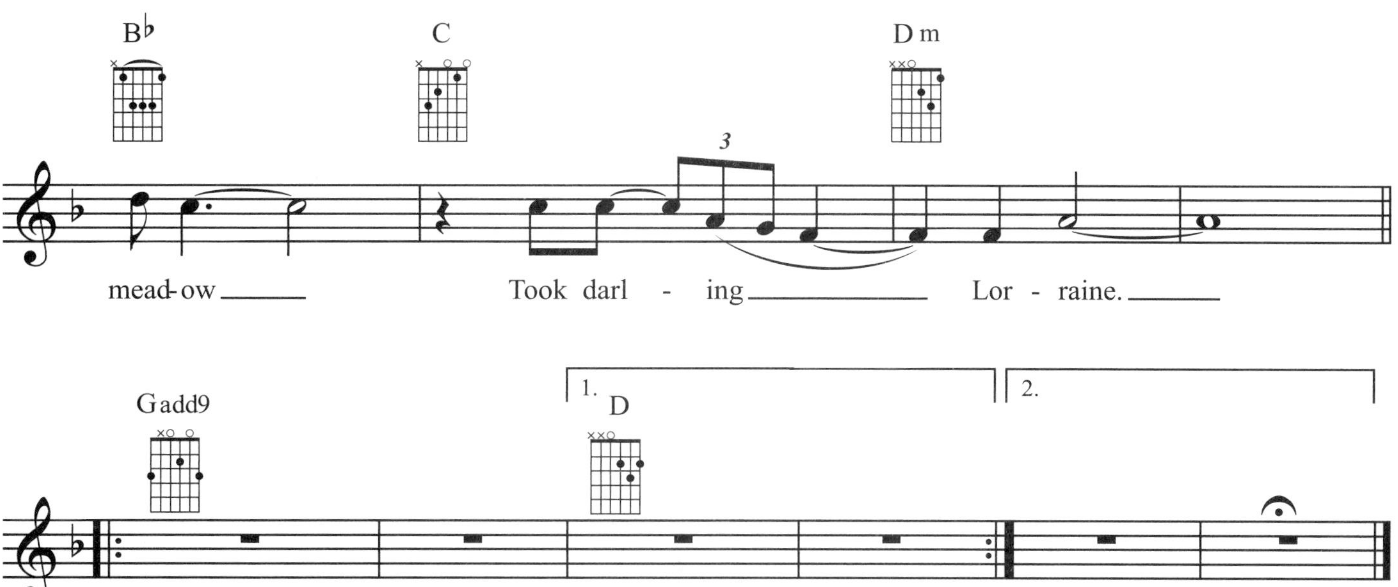

2. All my life I've been a wanderer.
Not really, I mostly lived near my parents' home.
Anyway Lorraine and I got married
And the usual marriage stuff,
Then one day she says to me
From out of the blue:
"Frank, I've had enough.
Romance is a heartbreaker,
I'm not meant to be a homemaker
And I'm tired of being darling Lorraine."

3. Financially speaking I guess I'm a washout.
Everybody's buy and sell and sell and buy and
That's what the whole thing's all about.
If it had not been for Lorraine,
I'd have left here long ago.
I should have been a musician,
I love the piano.

She's so light,
She's so free,
I'm tight, well, that's me,
But I feel so good
With darling Lorraine.

What? You don't love me anymore?
What? You're walking out the door?
What? You don't like the way I chew?
Hey let me tell you,
You're not the woman that I wed.
Gimme my robe, I'm going back to bed.
I'm sick to death of you Lorraine.

Duncan

Words and Music by Paul Simon

Moderately slow and steady

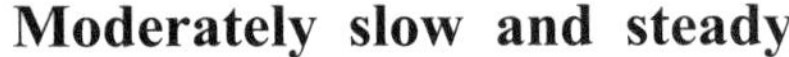

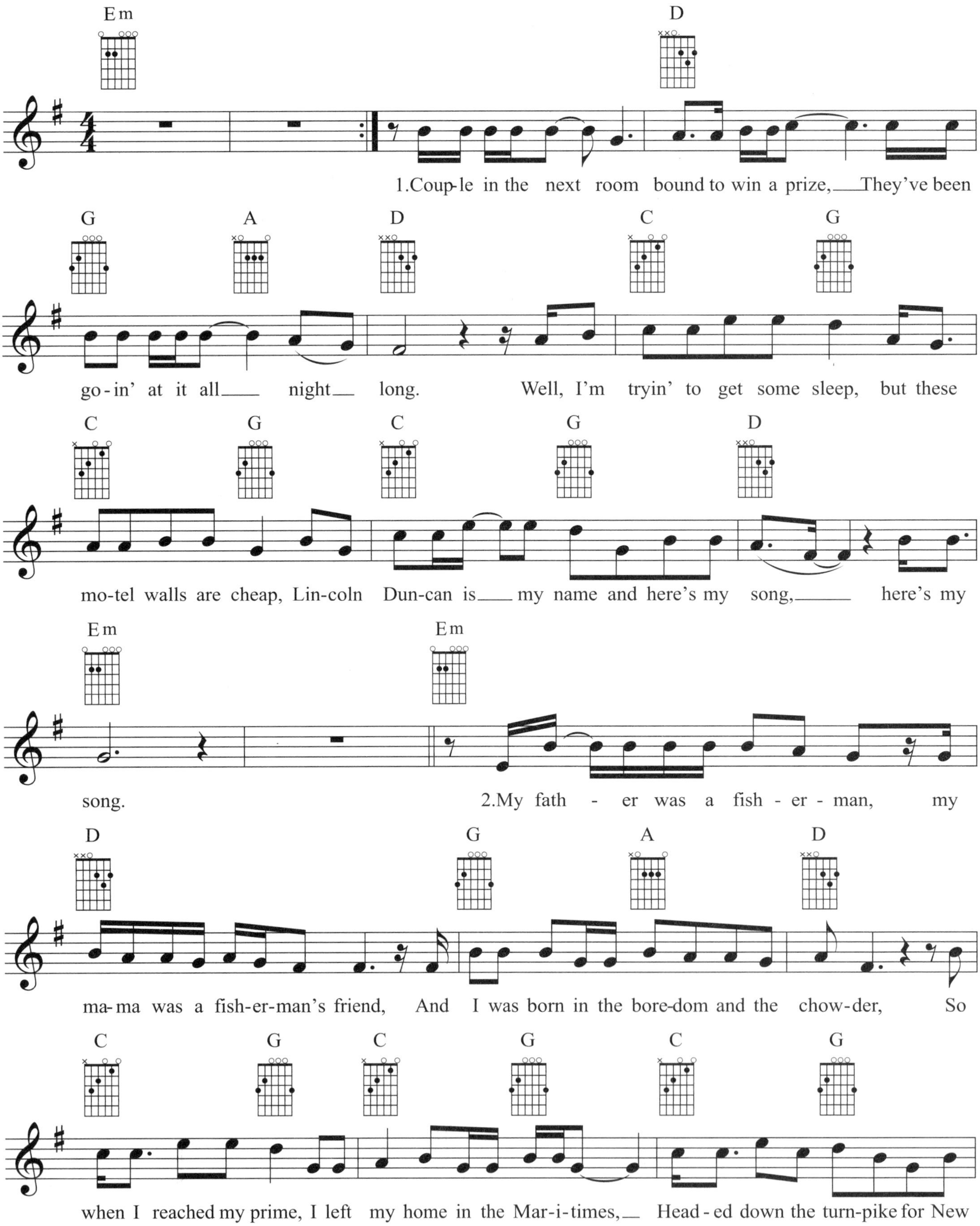

Em D
1.Coup-le in the next room bound to win a prize, They've been
G A D C G
go-in' at it all night long. Well, I'm tryin' to get some sleep, but these
C G C G D
mo-tel walls are cheap, Lin-coln Dun-can is my name and here's my song, here's my
Em Em
song. 2.My fath - er was a fish - er - man, my
D G A D
ma-ma was a fish-er-man's friend, And I was born in the bore-dom and the chow-der, So
C G C G C G
when I reached my prime, I left my home in the Mar-i-times, Head-ed down the turn-pike for New

D
Em
C
G
C
Eng-land, sweet New Eng-land.
G
C
G
Em
D
Em
Em
D
G
A
3.Holes in my con-fi - dence, holes in the knees of my jeans, I's left with-out a pen - ny in my
D
C
G
C
G
pock-et, Oo hoo hoo wee, I's a-bout des-ti-tut - ed as a kid could be, And I
C
G
D
Em
wished I wore a ring so I could hock it, I'd like to hock it.
Em
D
5
4.A young girl in a park-ing lot was preach-in' to a crowd, sing-in'

G
A
D
C
G
sa-cred songs and read-ing from the Bi - ble, Well, I told her I was lost, and she
C
G
C
G
told me all a-bout the Pen-te-cost, And I seen that girl as the road to my sur-
D
Em
C
G
C
viv - al.
G
C
G
Em
D
Em
Em
D
5.Just lat-er on the ver-y same night when I crept to her tent with a flash-light, And my
G
A
D
C
G
long years of in - no-cence end-ed, Well, she took me to the woods, say-in',

C
G
C
G
D
"Here comes some-thin' and it feels so good!" And just like a dog I was be-friend-ed, I was be-
Em
Em
D
friend-ed.
6.Oh, oh, what a night, oh, what a gar - den of de-light, Ev-en
G
A
D
C
G
now that sweet mem - o - ry ling-ers, I was play-in' my gui-tar, Ly-ing
C
G
C
G
D
Em
5
un-der-neath the stars, Just thank-in' the Lord for my fin-gers, for my fin-gers.
C
G
C
G
C
G
Em
D
Em

El Condor Pasa (If I Could)

English Lyric by Paul Simon
Musical arrangement by Jorge Milchberg and Daniel Robles

C
G
man gets tied up to the ground, He gives the world its sad-dest
D/F♯
Em
sound, its sad - dest sound.
I'd
G
D/F♯
rath - er be a for-est than a street. Yes I would. If I could, I sure - ly
Em
G
would. I'd rath - er feel the earth be-neath my feet. Yes I
Em
3
would. If I on - ly could, I sure - ly would.

Everything Put Together Falls Apart

Words and Music by Paul Simon

E
E7
A
Am
Em
F♯m
your style,
Mm
I see it hap-pen-in' ev-'ry day.
Dm7
Cmaj7
Em7
D/F♯
Uh huh,
spare your heart.
ev-'ry-thing
Dm/C
G7
C7
put to-geth-er
soon-er or lat-er falls a-part, there's noth-in'
Fm7
C
to it, noth-in' to it. You can cry and you can lie,
For
F7
Cm7/F
B♭
B
all the good it-'ll do you, you can die,
Oh, but when it's
done and the po-lice come, and they're lay-in' you down for dead,
Oo,
just re-
F♯m7
mem-ber what I said!

Fakin' It

Words and Music by Paul Simon

Moderate tempo, with a beat

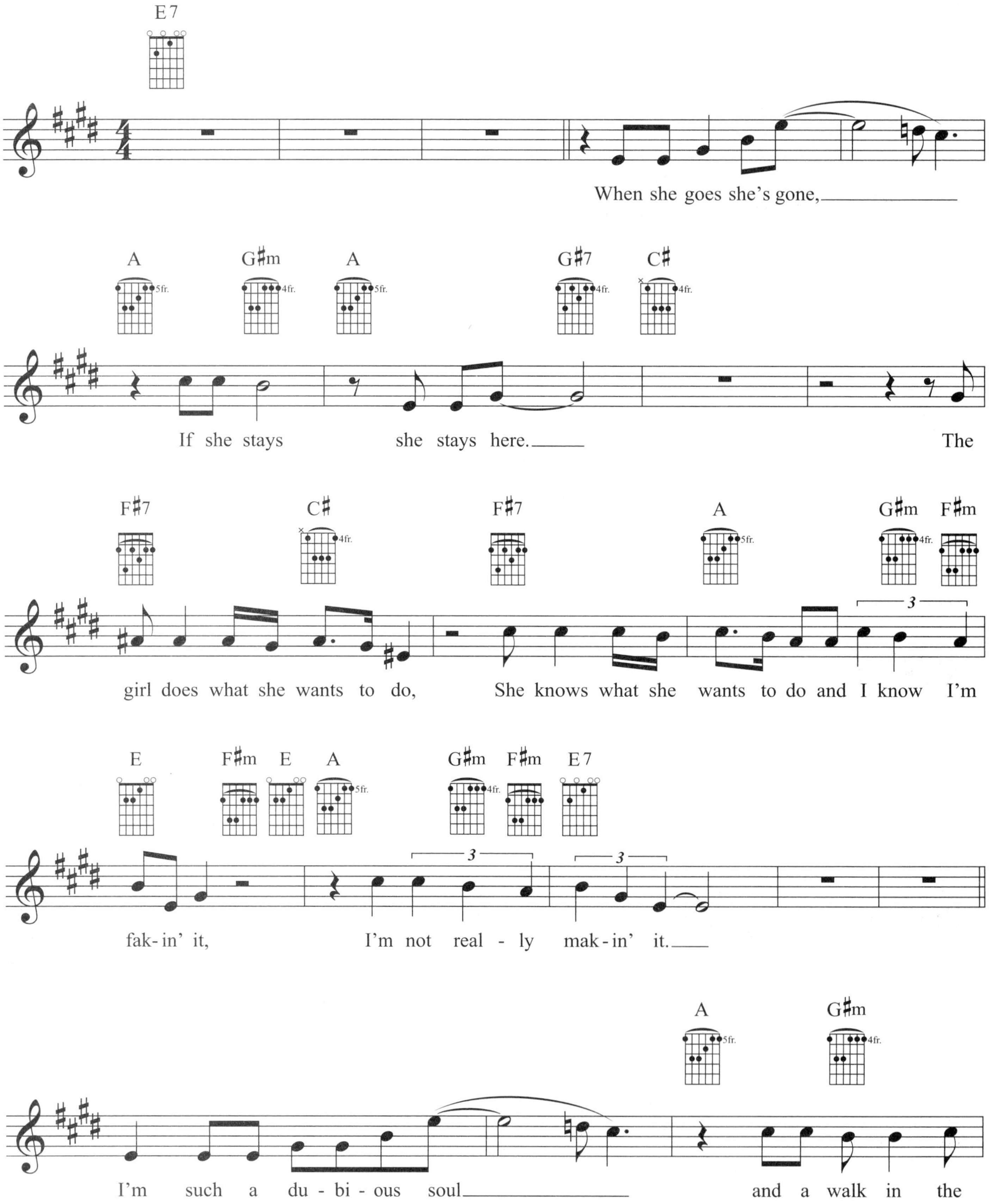

E7

When she goes she's gone, ___

A G♯m A G♯7 C♯

If she stays she stays here. ___ The

F♯7 C♯ F♯7 A G♯m F♯m

girl does what she wants to do, She knows what she wants to do and I know I'm

E F♯m E A G♯m F♯m E7

fak-in' it, I'm not real - ly mak-in' it. ___

A G♯m

I'm such a du - bi - ous soul ___ and a walk in the

A
G♯7
C♯
F♯7
C♯
gar - den wears me down.
Tang-led in the fall-en vines,
F♯7
A
G♯m
F♯m
E
F♯m
E
Pick-in' up the punch lines,
I've just been fak-in' it,
A
G♯m
F♯m
E7
Not real - ly mak-in' it.
(Spoken): No, no, no, no.
A
G♯m
A
G♯7
Is there an-y dan - ger?
No, no, not real - ly,
Just
C♯
F♯7
C♯
lean on me.
Take the time to
F♯7
A
G♯m
F♯m
E
F♯m
E
treat your friend-ly neigh-bors hon-est - ly,
I've just been fak-in' it. Fak - in' it,

A G♯m F♯m E F♯m E A G♯m F♯m
Not rea - ly mak - in' it; This feel - in' of
E F♯m E A G♯m F♯m E7
fak - in' it, I still have - n't shak-en it.
A G♯m A G♯7
Pri-or to this life - time I sure - ly was a tai - lor, Look at
C♯ G♯7 C♯
me.
(Spoken): Good morning, Mr. Leach. Have you had a busy day?
I
F♯7 C♯ F♯7 A
own a tai-lor's face and hands, I am the tai-lor's face and hands.
A G♯m F♯m A G♯m F♯m E F♯m E
I know I'm fak - in' it. Fak - in' it,

A
G♯m
F♯m
E
F♯m
E
A
G♯m
F♯m
I'm not real - ly mak - in' it.
This feel - in' of
E
F♯m
E
A
G♯m
F♯m
E
F♯m
E
fak - in' it
I still have - n't shak - en it, shak - en it.
A
G♯m
F♯m
E
F♯m
E
A
G♯m
F♯m
I know I'm fak - in' it,
I'm not real - ly
E
F♯m
E
A
G♯m
F♯m
E
F♯m
E
repeat and fade
mak - in' it.

Father And Daughter

Words and Music by Paul Simon

F♯7
E6
E/D♯
B
To the mead-ow in the moun-tain Where we count-ed ev-ery fall - ing
C♯m
4fr.
A
E
F♯m7
B 9sus4
star I be-lieve the light that shines on you Will shine on you for-ev -
E
F♯7
E6
- er And though I can't guar - an - tee There's noth - ing
E/D♯
B
C♯m
4fr.
scar - y hid - ing un - der your bed I'm gon - na
A
E
F♯m7
B 9sus4
E
stand guard Like a post-card of a Gold-en Re - triev - er And nev-er
F♯7
E6
E/D♯
B 9sus4
C♯m
4fr.
leave till I leave you With a sweet dream in your head

Eadd9
Aadd9
Eadd9
I'm gon-na watch you shine Gon-na watch you grow Gon-na paint a
Aadd9
Eadd9
Aadd9
sign So you'll always know As long as one and one is two
Eadd9
Aadd9
E6
E/D♯
There could nev - er be a fa - ther Loved his
C♯m7
B9sus4
to Coda I
to Coda II
C♯m
4fr.
daugh - ter more than I love you
A
E/G♯
F♯m7
B9sus4
E
Trust your in-tu-i - tion It's just like go-in' fish-in' You
F♯7
E6
E/D♯
B9sus4
C♯m
4fr.
cast your line And hope you get a bite

A
E/G♯
F♯m7
B 9sus4
But you don't need to waste your time
E
Wor-ry-ing a-bout the mar-ket place
Try to help the hu-man race
F♯7
E 6
E/D♯
B
C♯m
4fr.
D.S. al Coda I
Strug-gling to sur-vive its harsh-est night
Coda I
C♯m
A 6
B 7
play four times
D.S. al Coda II
you
(instrumental solo)
Coda II
E sus2
1.
2.
E
you

God Bless the Absentee

Words and Music by Paul Simon

1.
B♭7
Fm7
E♭
B♭7
2.
B♭7
E♭m7
E♭m6
Bm/D
G♭/D♭
I miss my wom - an so
I miss my bed
Cm7♭5
C♭maj7
B♭/C
D.S. (guitar solo) al Coda
I miss those soft plac - es I used to lay my head
Coda
B♭9
Fm7
E♭
B♭7
Fm7
E♭
B♭7
(end guitar solo)
E♭m7
E♭m6
Bm/D
G♭/D♭
My son don't need me yet
His bones are soft
He
Cm7♭5
C♭maj7
B♭/C
flies a sil - ver air - plane He wears a gold - en cross
God

2. Lord, I am a surgeon
And music is my knife
It cuts away my sorrow
And purifies my life
But if I could release my heart
And veins and arteries
I'd say God bless the absentee

Fifty Ways To Leave Your Lover

Words and Music by Paul Simon

Moderately

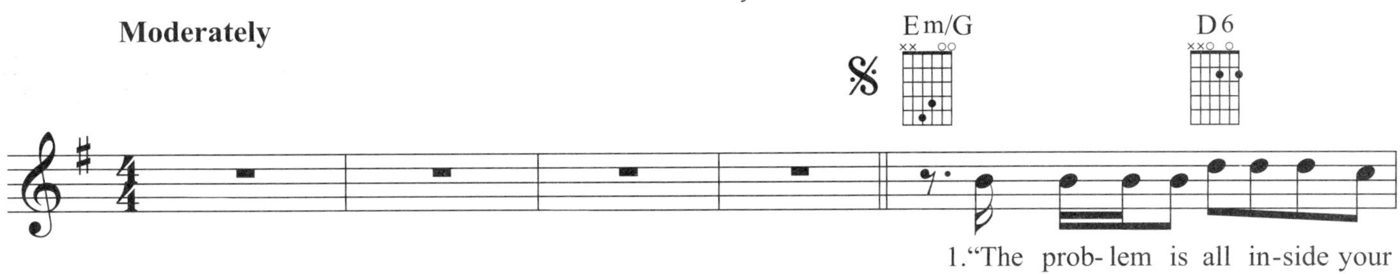

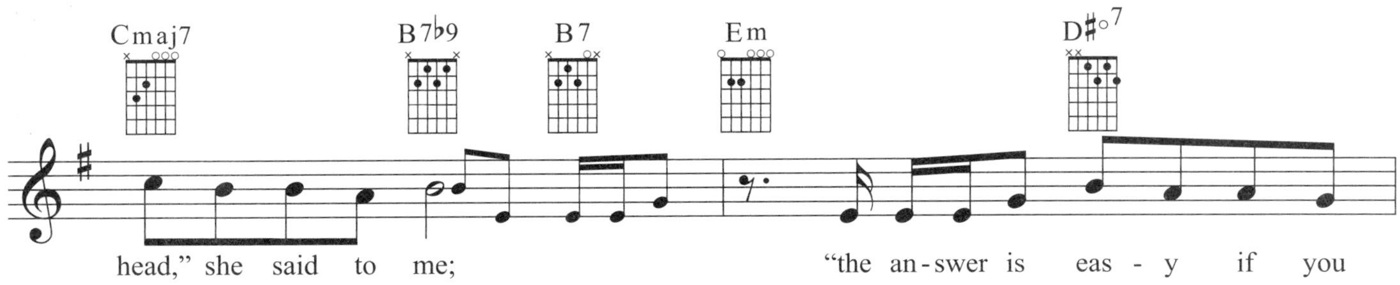

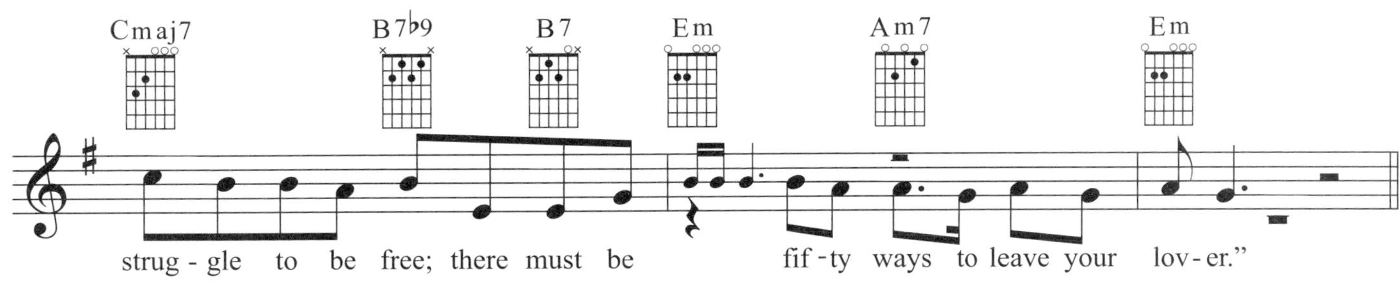

Em
D♯°7
Gmaj7♯5
B+
I hope my mean - ing won't be lost or mis - con - strued. But
Em
D6
Cmaj7
B7♭9
B7
Em
Am7
I'll re - peat my - self at the risk of be - ing crude; there must be fif - ty ways to leave your
Em
Am7
Em
lov - er, fif - ty ways to leave your lov - er." Just slip out the
G
B♭6
back, Jack; make a new plan, Stan;
C7
G
you don't need to be coy, Roy; just list - en to me.
B♭6
Hop on the bus, Gus; you don't need to dis - cuss much;

2. She said, "It grieves me so to see you in such pain;
I wish there was something I could do to make you smile again."
I said, "I appreciate that, and would you please explain
About the fifty ways?"

She said, "Why don't we both just sleep on it tonight;
And I believe in the morning you'll begin to see the light."
And then she kissed me and I realized she probably was right;
There must be fifty ways to leave your lover,
Fifty ways to leave your lover.

Flowers Never Bend With The Rainfall

Words and Music by Paul Simon

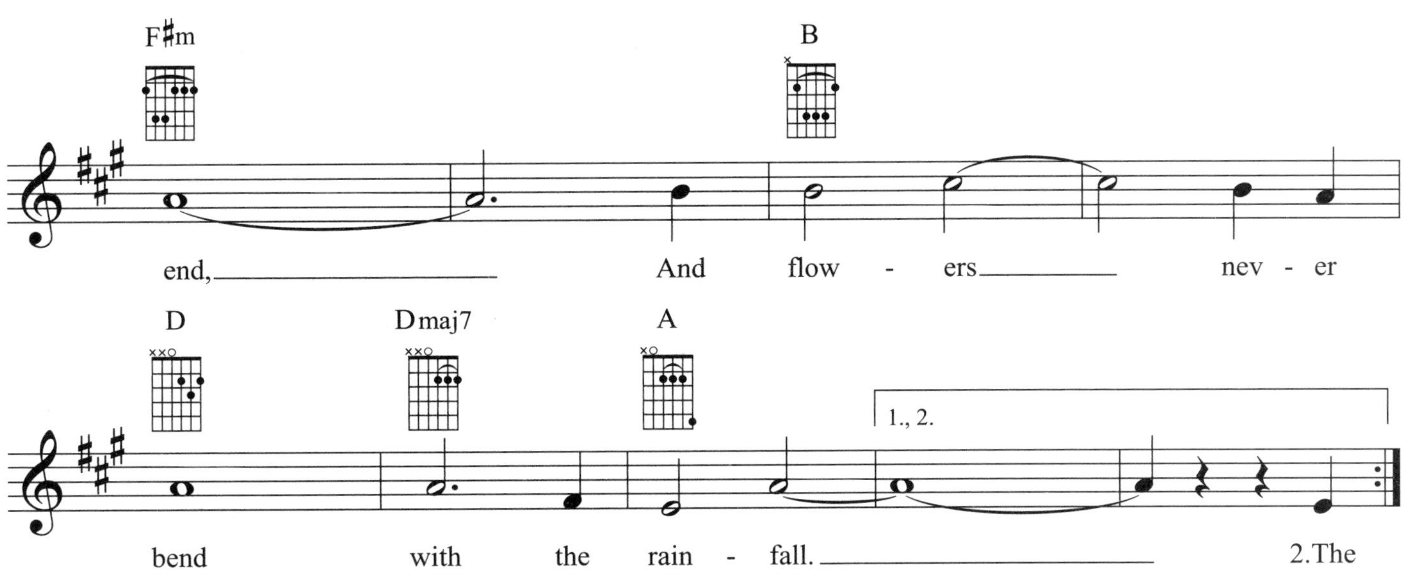

2. The mirror on my wall
Casts an image dark and small
But I'm not sure at all it's my reflection.
I am blinded by the light
Of God and truth and right
And I wander in the night without direction.

3. It's no matter if you're born
To play the King or pawn
For the line is thinly drawn 'tween joy and sorrow,
So my fantasy
Becomes reality,
And I must be what I must be and face tomorrow.

For Emily, Whenever I May Find Her

Words and Music by Paul Simon

Coda
F
B♭
Gm
And when you ran to me your cheeks flushed with the night.
F
E♭maj7
3fr.
We walked on frost - ed fields __ of ju - ni - per and lamp - light,
B♭
C
F
I __ held your hand. __ And when
B♭
Gm
F
I a - woke and felt you warm and near, I __ kissed your
E♭maj7
3fr.
B♭
hon - ey hair __ with my grate - ful tears. Oh __ I
C
E♭
3fr.
B♭/D
love you, girl. __ Oh, I __
B♭sus2
B♭sus2/A
__ love __ you. __

Gone At Last

Words and Music by Paul Simon

C
G7
C
C
pray-in' it's gone at last. Gone, gone at last, gone at
F
C
last, gone at last, gone at last. I've had a
C7
F
to Coda
C
G7
long streak of that bad luck but I'm pray-in' it's gone at
1., 2.
C
F
C
G
last.
C
3.
C
D.S. al Coda
2.I ain't last. Gone, gone at
Coda
C
G7
C
pray - in' it's gone at last.

2. I ain't dumb
I kicked around some
I don't fall too easily
But that boy looked so dejected
He just grabbed my sympathy
Sweet little soul now, what's your problem?
Tell me why you're so downcast
I've had a long streak of bad luck
But I'm praying it's gone at last

Gone, gone at last, gone at last
Gone at last, gone at last
I had a long streak of that bad luck
But I'm prayin' it's gone at last
Oo, oo, oo

3. Once in a while from out of nowhere
When you don't expect it, and you're unprepared
Somebody will come and lift you higher
And your burdens will be shared
Yes I do believe, if I hadn't met you
I might still be sinking fast
I've had a long streak of bad luck
But I'm praying it's gone at last

Gone, gone at last, gone at last
Gone at last, gone at last
I had a long streak of that bad luck
But I'm prayin' it's gone at last
Oo, oo, oo

Further To Fly

Words and Music by Paul Simon

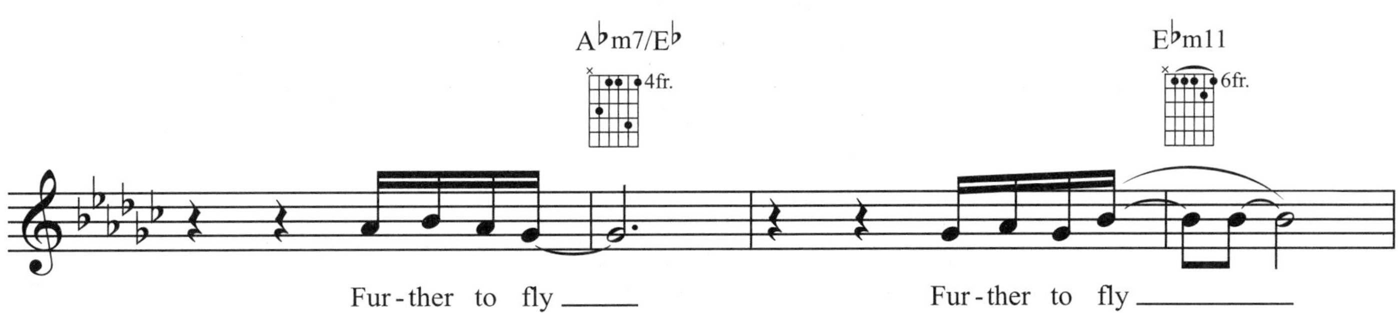

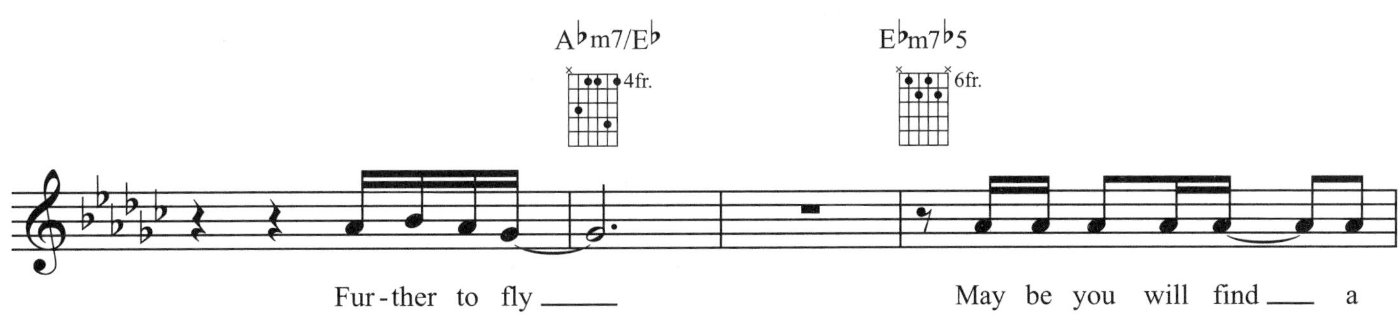

E♭○7
5fr.
E♭m7
6fr.
gen-tly As a pick - pock-et Brush-es your thigh Fur-ther to fly
3
E 6
5fr.
E♭7
6fr.
A♭m
4fr.
Ef-fort-less mu-sic from the Cam-e-roons
G♭
A♭m
4fr.
The spin-ning dark-ness of her hair A con-ver-sa - tion in a
B♭7
6fr.
E♭
6fr.
E♭7
6fr.
A♭m
4fr.
crowd-ed room go - ing no - where The o-pen palm of de-
G♭
A♭m
4fr.
B♭7
sire Wants eve-ry-thing It wants eve-ry-thing It wants eve - ry-thing
E♭m7
6fr.
A♭
4fr.
E♭m7
6fr.
A♭
4fr.

E♭m11
6fr.
Some- times I'll be walk-ing down The street and I'll be think-ing "Am I cra - zy Or
B○7
6fr.
E♭m11
6fr.
is this some mor - bid lit - tle lie?" Fur-ther to fly
A♭m7/E♭
4fr.
E♭m11
6fr.
Fur-ther to fly Fur-ther to fly
A♭m7/E♭
4fr.
E♭m7♭5
6fr.
A re-cent loss of mem-o-ry A shad-ow in the fam - i - ly
E♭○7
5fr.
E♭m7
6fr.
The ba-by waves bye-bye I'm try - ing, I'm
E 6
5fr.
E♭7
6fr.
A♭m
4fr.
G♭
3
fly - ing There may come a time When I will lose

A♭m B♭7 E♭
4fr. 6fr.

you Lose ___ you as I lose my light Days fall-ing back-ward in the

E♭7 A♭m G♭
6fr. 4fr.

vel-vet night. Oh, ___ the o-pen palm of de-sire Wants ev-ery-thing It wants

A♭m B♭7
4fr.

ev - ery-thing It wants soil as soft as sum-mer And the

E♭m7 A♭ E♭m7 A♭ E♭m11
6fr. 4fr. 6fr. 4fr. 6fr.

(instrumental) *play four times*

strength to push like spring

E6
5fr.
E♭7
6fr.
A♭m
4fr.
Fur-ther to fly
There may come a
G♭
A♭m
4fr.
time
When I will lose
you
Lose
you as I lose
B♭7
6fr.
E♭
6fr.
E♭7
6fr.
A♭m
4fr.
my sight
Days fall-ing back-ward in-to vel-vet night
The o-pen palm of de-
G♭
A♭m
4fr.
B♭7
6fr.
sire
The Rose of Jer-i-cho
Soil as soft as sum-mer
E♭m7
6fr.
A♭m
4fr.
E♭m7
6fr.
A♭
4fr.
E♭m11
6fr.
repeat and fade
The strength to let you go

Graceland

Words and Music by Paul Simon

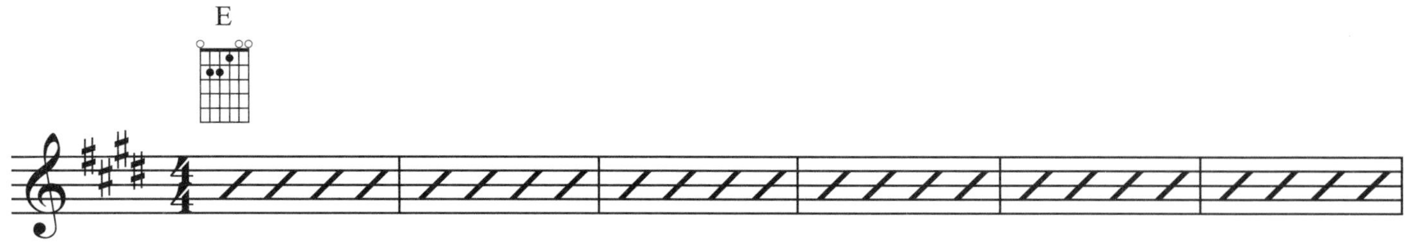

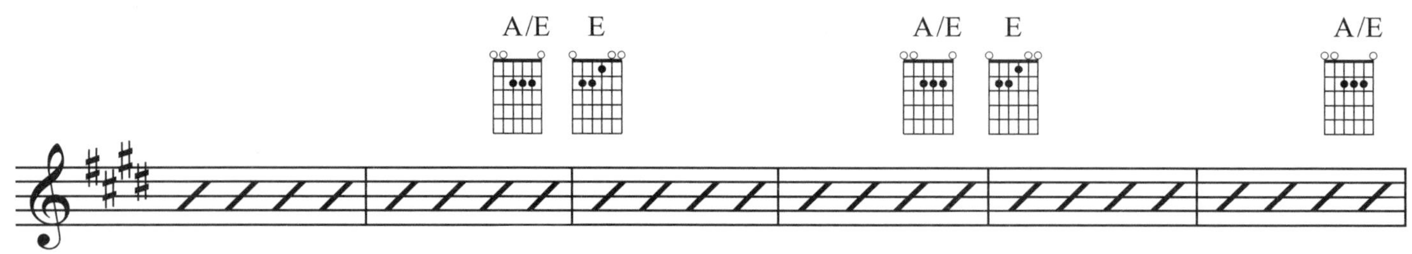

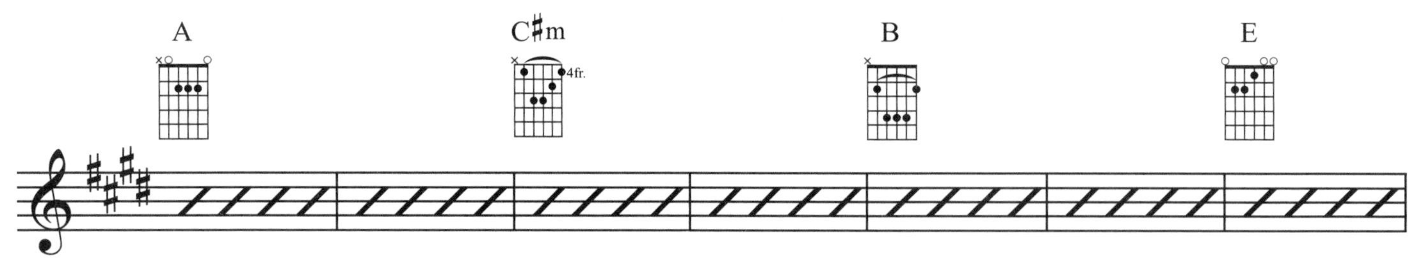

A E
1.I'm going to Grace - land, Grace-land in
A E D A
Mem-phis, Ten-nes-see. I'm go-ing to Grace - land.
E A E
Poor boys and pil-grims with fam-i-lies and we are go-ing to Grace - land.
D A E A
My trav-'ling com-pan-ion is nine years old, He is the
E D A E
child of my first mar-riage. But I've rea-son to be-lieve we both
A E D A
will be re-ceived in Grace - land.
to Coda

E
A/E
E
She comes back to tell me she's gone, as
A
C♯m
4fr.
if I did-n't know that, as if I did-n't know my own bed,
B
as if I'd ne-ver no-ticed the way she brushed her hair
E
from her fore-head. And she said los-ing love is like a win-dow in your
A
C♯m
4fr.
heart, Ev-'ry-bod-y sees you're blown a part, ev-'ry-bod-y sees the
1.
2.
B
A
A
D.S. al Coda
wind blow. 2.I'm go-ing to Grace - Oh, in Grace

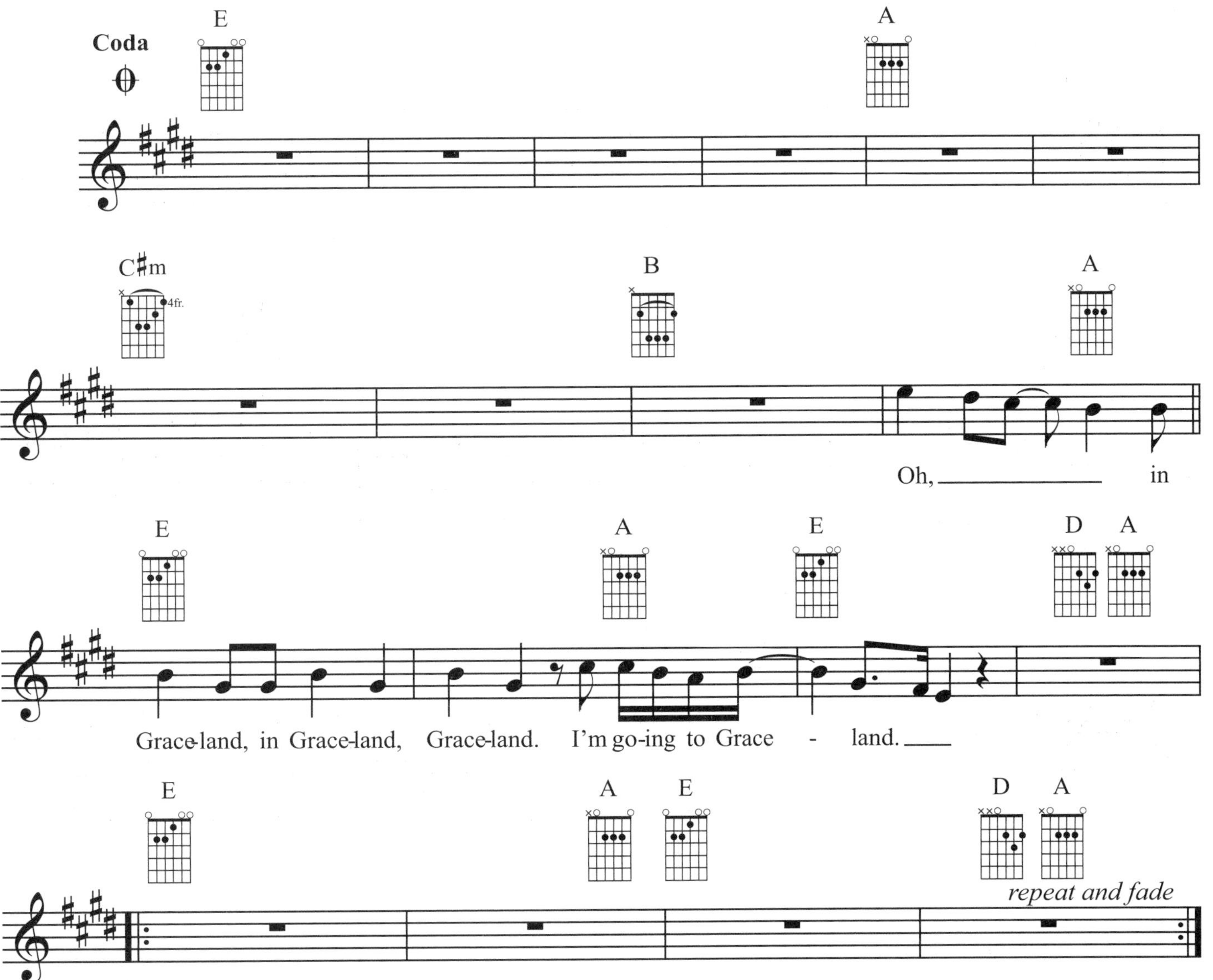

2. I'm going to Graceland
   Memphis Tennessee
   I'm going to Graceland
   Poor boys and pilgrims with families
   And we are going to Graceland

   And my traveling companions
   Are ghosts and empty sockets
   I'm looking at ghosts and empties
   But I've reason to believe
   We all will be received
   In Graceland

   There is a girl in New York City
   Who calls herself the human trampoline
   And sometimes when I'm falling, flying
   Or tumbling in turmoil I say
   Oh, so this is what she means
   She means we're bouncing into Graceland
   And I see losing love
   Is like a window in your heart
   Everybody sees you're blown apart
   Everybody feels the wind blow

3. In Graceland, in Graceland
   I'm going to Graceland
   For reasons I cannot explain
   There's some part of me wants to see
   Graceland
   And I may be obliged to defend
   Every love, every ending
   Or maybe there's no obligations now
   Maybe I've a reason to believe
   We all will be received
   In Graceland

Gumboots

Words by Paul Simon
Music by Paul Simon and Johnson Mkhalali

2. It was in the early morning hours
When I fell into a phone call
Believing I had supernatural powers
I slammed into a brick wall
I said hey, is this my problem?
Is this my fault?
If that's the way its going to be
I'm going to call the whole thing to a halt

You don't feel you could love me
But I feel you could
You don't feel you could love me
But I feel you could

3. I was walking down the street
When I thought I heard this voice say
Say, ain't we walking down the same street together
On the very same day
I said hey Señorita that's astute
I said why don't we get together
And call ourselves an institute

You don't feel you could love me
But I feel you could
You don't feel you could love me
But I feel you could

Have A Good Time

Words and Music by Paul Simon

Moderately, with a blues feeling

B♭
E♭9
lov - ing and lov - ing and lov - ing; I'm ex -
B♭
F7
B♭
E♭9
haust - ed from lov - ing so well.
I should go to bed, but a
E°7
B♭/F
F
to Coda
voice in my head says, "Aw, what the hell!" Have a good time,
B♭
E♭
B♭
F
B♭
have a good time, have a good time,
E♭
B♭
1.
F
2.
F
D.S. al Coda
have a good time.
2.Par-a
3.May be I'm
Coda
B♭/F
F
keep it that way, and we'll all have a good time,

2. Paranoia strikes deep in the heartland
But I think it's all overdone
Exaggerating this and exaggerating that
They don't have no fun

I don't believe what I read in the papers
They're just out to capture my dime
I ain't worrying
And I ain't scurrying
I'm having a good time

Chorus:
Have a good time

3. Maybe I'm laughing my way to disaster
Maybe my race has been run
Maybe I'm blind to the fate of mankind
But what can be done?

So God bless the goods we was given
And God bless the U. S. of A.
And God bless our standard of livin'
Let's keep it that way
And we'll all have a good time

Chorus:
Have a good time

A Hazy Shade Of Winter

Words and Music by Paul Simon

Moderate rock beat

Dm C

Time, time, time, See what's be - come of me, while I

B♭ Am

looked a - round for my pos - si - bil - i - ties, I was so

C Dm C

hard to please, But look a-round, leaves are brown, And the sky

B♭ A7 Dm

is a ha - zy shade of win - ter. Hear the Sal-va-tion

C B♭

Ar-my Band, Down by the riv-er side, It's bound to be a bet-ter ride, than

Am C

what you've got planned, Car-ry your cup in your hand, And look a - round,

Dm
C
B♭7
A7
leaves are brown now, And the sky is a ha - zy shade of win -
Dm
C
- ter. Hang on - to your hopes, my friend,
B♭
Am
That's an eas-y thing to say, but if your hopes should pass a-way, Simp-ly pre-tend that you can
C
Dm
C7
build them a - gain. Look a-round; The grass is high, the fields are
B♭7
A7
Dm
ripe: It's the spring - time of my life.
B♭
F
Fmaj7
Sea-sons change with the scen - er - y, Weav-ing time in a
C9
Dm
A7
Dm
tap - es - try. Won't you stop and re - mem - ber me,

C
B♭
At an - y con - ve - nient time? Fun-ny how my mem-'ry skips, while
Am
C
3
3
look-in' o-ver man-u-scripts of un - pub-lished rhyme, Drink-ing my vod - ka and lime.
Dm
C7
B♭7
I look a - round Leaves are brown now, And the sky is a ha -
A7
Dm
C
B♭7
- zy shade of win - ter. Look a - round; Leaves are brown, There's a patch
1. A7
Dm
2. A7
Dm
of snow on the ground. Look a - round of snow on the ground.

Hearts And Bones

Words and Music by Paul Simon

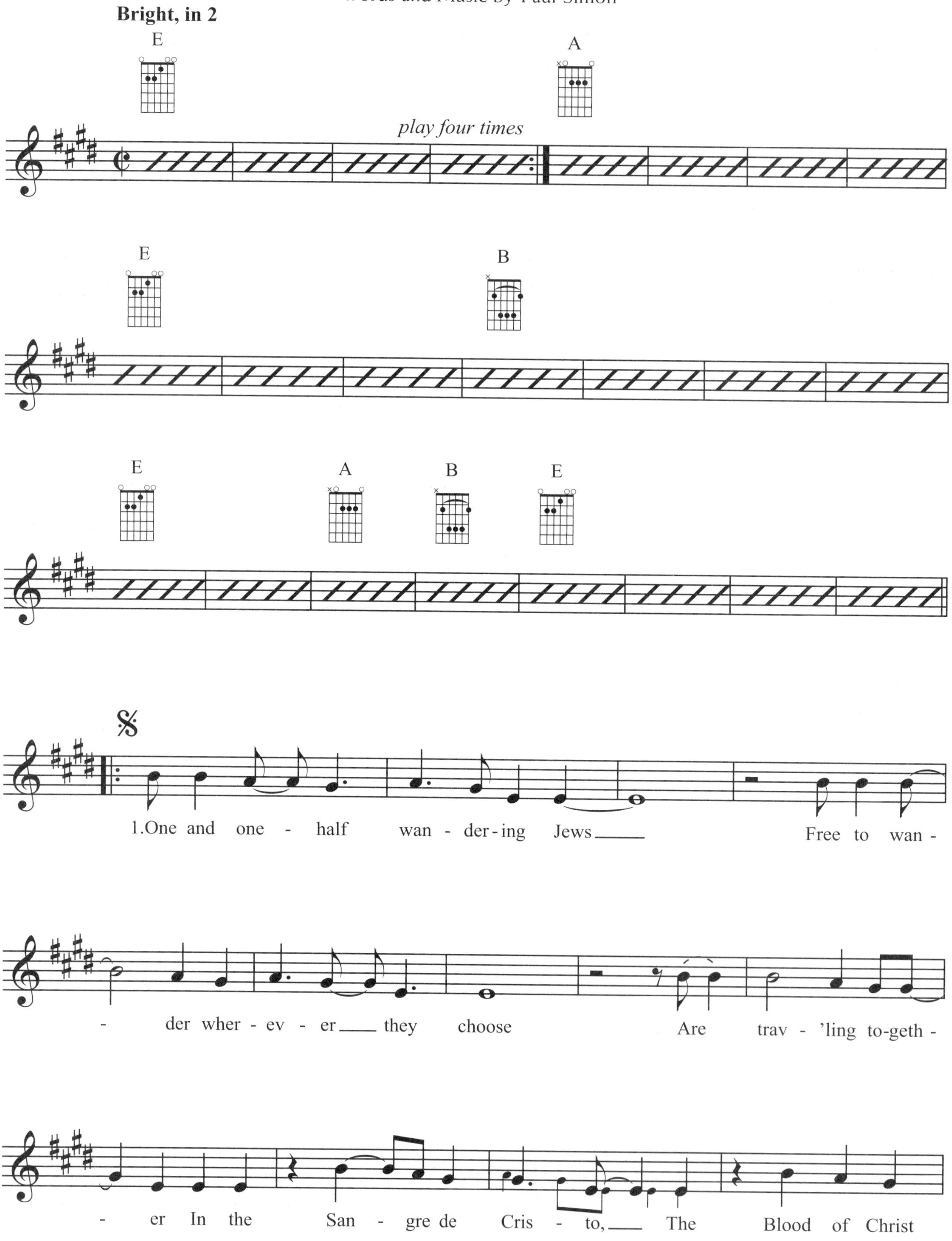

Bright, in 2
E
A
play four times
E
B
E
A
B
E
1.One and one - half wan - der-ing Jews
Free to wan - der wher - ev - er they choose
Are trav - 'ling to-geth - er In the San - gre de Cris - to, The Blood of Christ

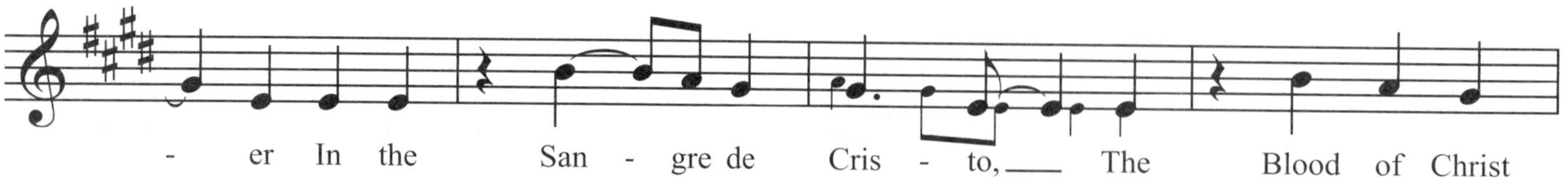

B
Moun - tains Of New Mex - i - co
Bm7 C♯m7 D♯m7♭5 D♯◦7
4fr.
On the last leg of a jour - ney They
C♯m7 C♯m6
4fr. 3fr.
start - ed along time a - go The arc of a
Bmaj7
love af - fair Rain - bows in the
Amaj9 E
high des - ert air Moun - tain
A
to Coda
pass - es slip - ping in - to stones

B
B/C♯
E
Hearts and bones
G♯m7/D♯
4fr.
C♯m
4fr.
Hearts and bones
Hearts and
1.
E
(4)
(8)
bones
2.Think-ing
2.
Aadd9
A
Aadd9
A
bones
Hearts and
E
(4)
(8)
bones
3.And
E
F♯m
E/G♯
A
E
whoa whoa whoa She said Why?

N.C.
Why don't we drive through the night and we'll
A
E
wake up down in Mex-i-co
Oh I
N.C.
I don't know noth-in' a-bout
A
noth-in' a-bout no Mex-i-co
E
N.C.
Tell me why
Why won't you love me For
A
who I am Where I am

A m
He said: 'Cause that's not the way the world is ba - by
E/G♯
This is how I love you, ba - by
E m/G
This is how I love you, ba - by
E
D.S. al Coda
(4)
(8)
Coda
E
Their hearts and their bones
A
And they won't come un - done

E G♯m7/D♯

Hearts ___ and bones ______ Hearts and bones __

C♯m Aadd9

______ Hearts and bones ______

E

Hearts ___ and bones ___

2. Thinking back to the season before
Looking back through the cracks in the door
Two people were married
The act was outrageous
The bride was contagious
She burned like a bride
These events may have had some effect
On the man with the girl by his side
The arc of a love affair
His hands rolling down her hair
Love like lightning shaking till it moans
Hearts and bones
Hearts and bones
Hearts and bones

4. One and one-half wandering Jews
Return to their natural courses
To resume old acquaintances
Step out occasionally
And speculate who had been damaged the most
Easy time will determine if these consolations
Will be their reward
The arc of a love affair
Waiting to be restored
You take two bodies and you twirl them into one

Their hearts and their bones
And they won't come undone
Hearts and bones
Hearts and bones
Hearts and bones
Hearts and bones

Hey, Schoolgirl

Words and Music by Paul Simon and Arthur Garfunkel

2. She said, "Hey, babe, I gotta lot to do,
It takes me hours till my homework's through,
Someday we'll go steady, so don't you fret.
Oh, not yet!"

Hobo's Blues

Words and Music by Paul Simon and Stephane Grappelli

B♭7 6fr.
A7 5fr.
A♭7 4fr.
G7 3fr.
3
F
D7 3fr.
B♭7 6fr.
B♭m7 6fr.
3
3
3
3
3
3
F
D7 3fr.
G7 3fr.
C7
F
B♭7
F
C7
F
F7
B♭7 6fr.
A7 5fr.
A♭7 4fr.
G7 3fr.
F
D7 3fr.
B♭7 6fr.
B♭m7 6fr.
F
D7 3fr.
G7 3fr.
C7
F
B♭7
F

Homeless

Words and Music by Paul Simon and Joseph Shabalala

home - less, we are home - less The moon-light sleep - ing on a

mid-night lake And we are home - less, home-less, home - less The

moon-light sleep - ing on a mid-night lake Zi - o ya-mi, zi - o ya - mi, n-hli-

zi - yo ya - mi N - hli - zi - yo ya - mi a - ma - kha - za asengi bu - le - le N - hli -

zi-yo ya - mi, n-hli - zi-yo ya - mi N-hli - zi-yo ya - mi, angi-bu - le-le a-ma-kha-za N-hli-

zi - yo ya - mi, n - hli - zi - yo ya - mi N - hli - zi - yo ya - mi so-mand -

- la angi-bu-le-le ma-ma Zi-o ya - mi, nhli - zi-yo ya - mi Nhli - zi-yo ya - mi, n-hli-

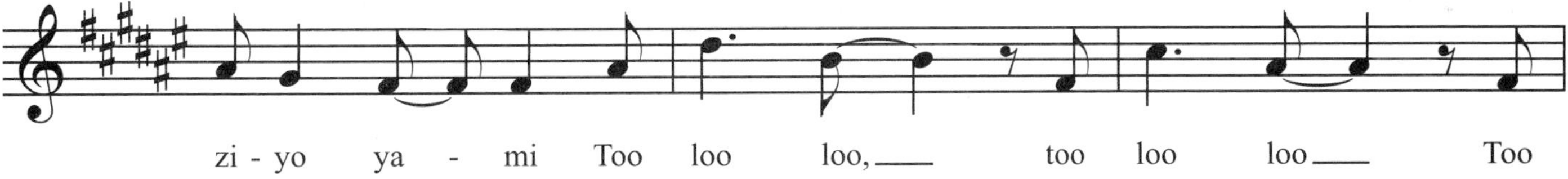
zi - yo ya - mi Too loo loo, too loo loo Too

loo loo loo loo loo loo loo loo loo Too loo loo, too
loo loo Too loo loo loo loo loo loo loo loo loo
Strong wind de - stroy our home Man-y dead, to-night it
could be you Strong wind, de - stroy our home
Ma-ny dead, to-night it could be you And we are home-less,
home - less Moon-light sleeping on a mid - night lake And we are
home - less, home - less Moon-light sleeping on a
mid-night lake Home - less, home - less The

Slightly faster
moon-light sleep - ing on a mid-night lake
Some-bod-y say

ih hih ih hih ih Some-bod-y sing hel-lo, hel-lo, hel-lo Some-bod-y say

ih hih ih hih ih Some-bod-y cry why, why, why? Some-bod-y say

ih hih ih hih ih Some-bod-y sing hel-lo, hel-lo, hel-lo Some-bod-y say

ih hih ih hih ih Some-bod-y cry why, why, why? Ku-lu-

ma - ni Ku-lu - mani, Ku-lu-ma-ni siz - we Sin - gen-ze njani

Ba - ya ja - bu - la a - basi-thanda - yo Ho

Homeward Bound

Words and Music by Paul Simon

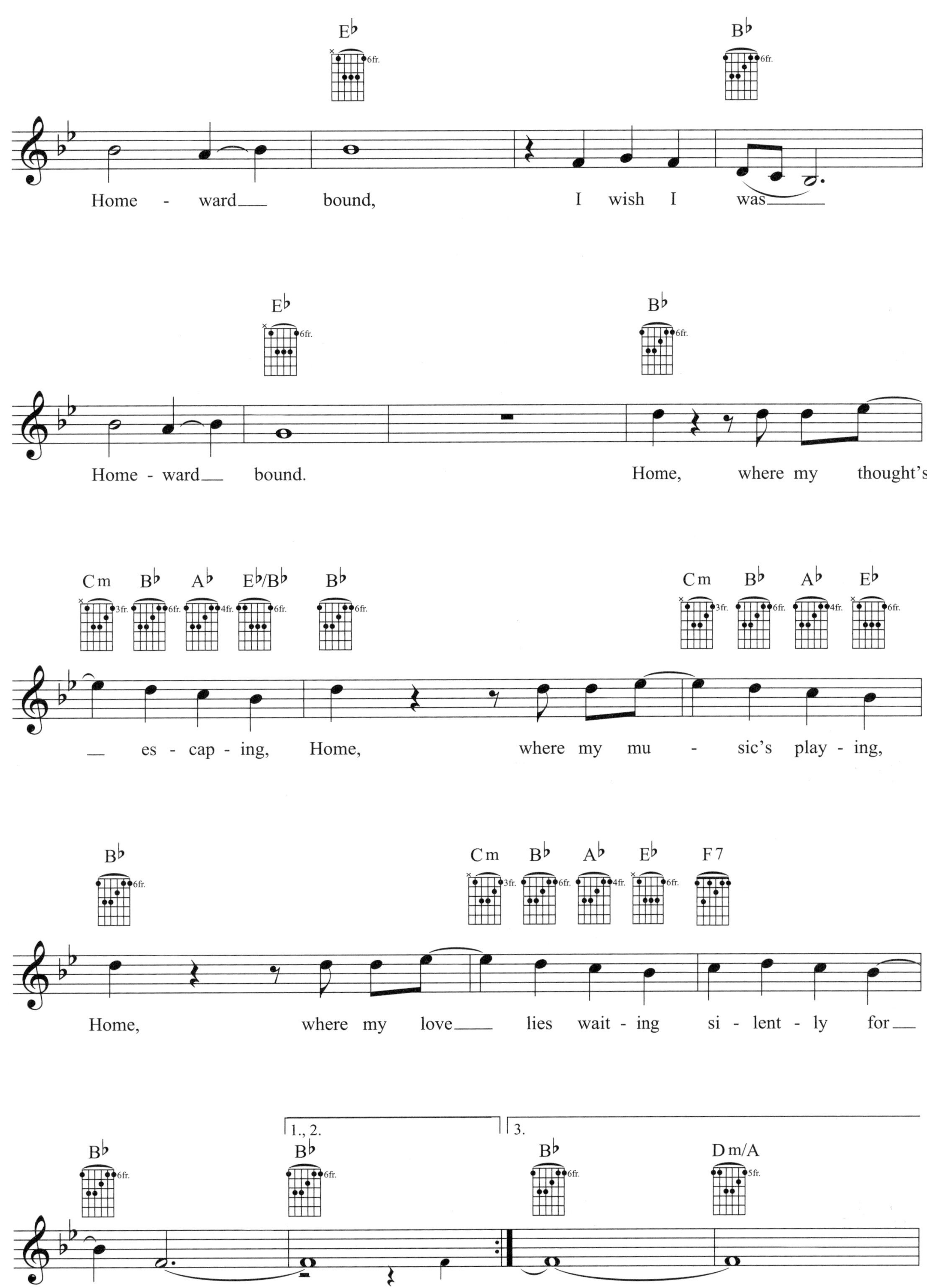
E♭
6fr.
B♭
6fr.
Home - ward bound, I wish I was
E♭
6fr.
B♭
6fr.
Home - ward bound. Home, where my thought's
Cm
3fr.
B♭
6fr.
A♭
4fr.
E♭/B♭
6fr.
B♭
6fr.
Cm
3fr.
B♭
6fr.
A♭
4fr.
E♭
6fr.
es - cap - ing, Home, where my mu - sic's play - ing,
B♭
6fr.
Cm
3fr.
B♭
6fr.
A♭
4fr.
E♭
6fr.
F7
Home, where my love lies wait - ing si - lent - ly for
1., 2.
3.
B♭
6fr.
B♭
6fr.
B♭
6fr.
Dm/A
5fr.
me. 3.To -

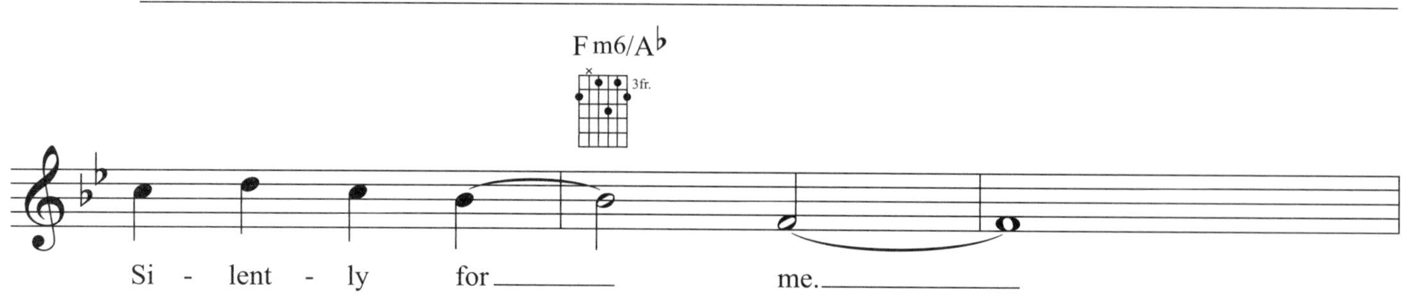

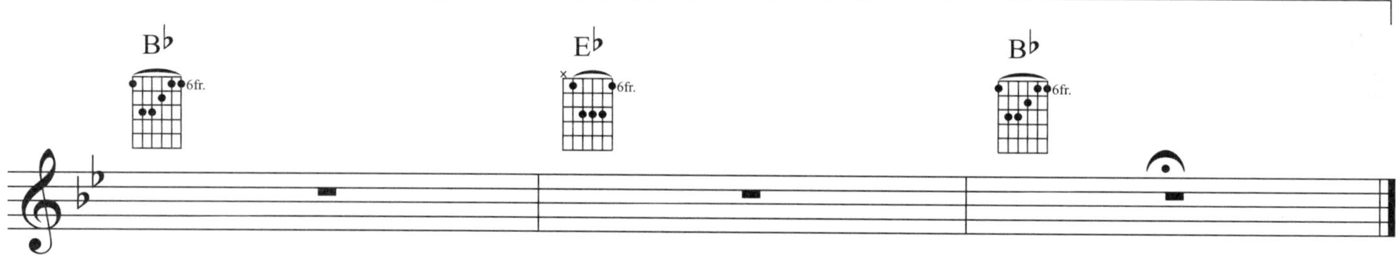

2. Everyday's an endless stream
Of cigarettes and magazines.
And each town looks the same to me,
The movies and the factories,
And every stranger's face I see
Reminds me that I long to be

3. Tonight I'll sing my songs again,
I'll play the game and pretend.
But all my words come back to me
In shades of mediocrity,
Like emptiness in harmony.
I need someone to comfort me.

I Do It For Your Love

Words and Music by Paul Simon

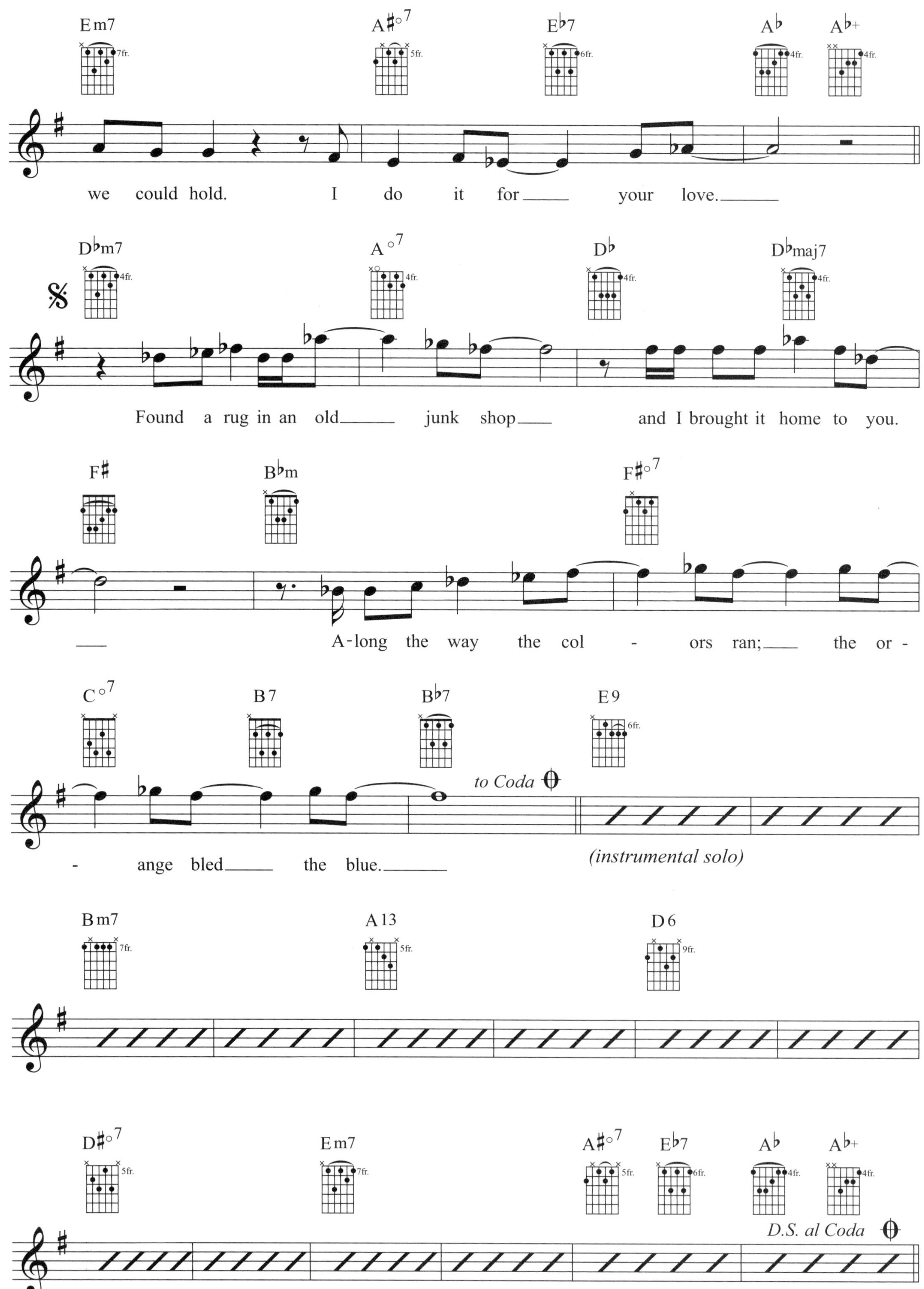
Em7
A♯°7
E♭7
A♭
A♭+
we could hold. I do it for ___ your love. ___
D♭m7
A°7
D♭
D♭maj7
Found a rug in an old ___ junk shop ___ and I brought it home to you.
F♯
B♭m
F♯°7
___ A-long the way the col - ors ran; ___ the or -
C°7
B7
B♭7
E9
to Coda
- ange bled ___ the blue. ___
(instrumental solo)
Bm7
A13
D6
D♯°7
Em7
A♯°7
E♭7
A♭
A♭+
D.S. al Coda

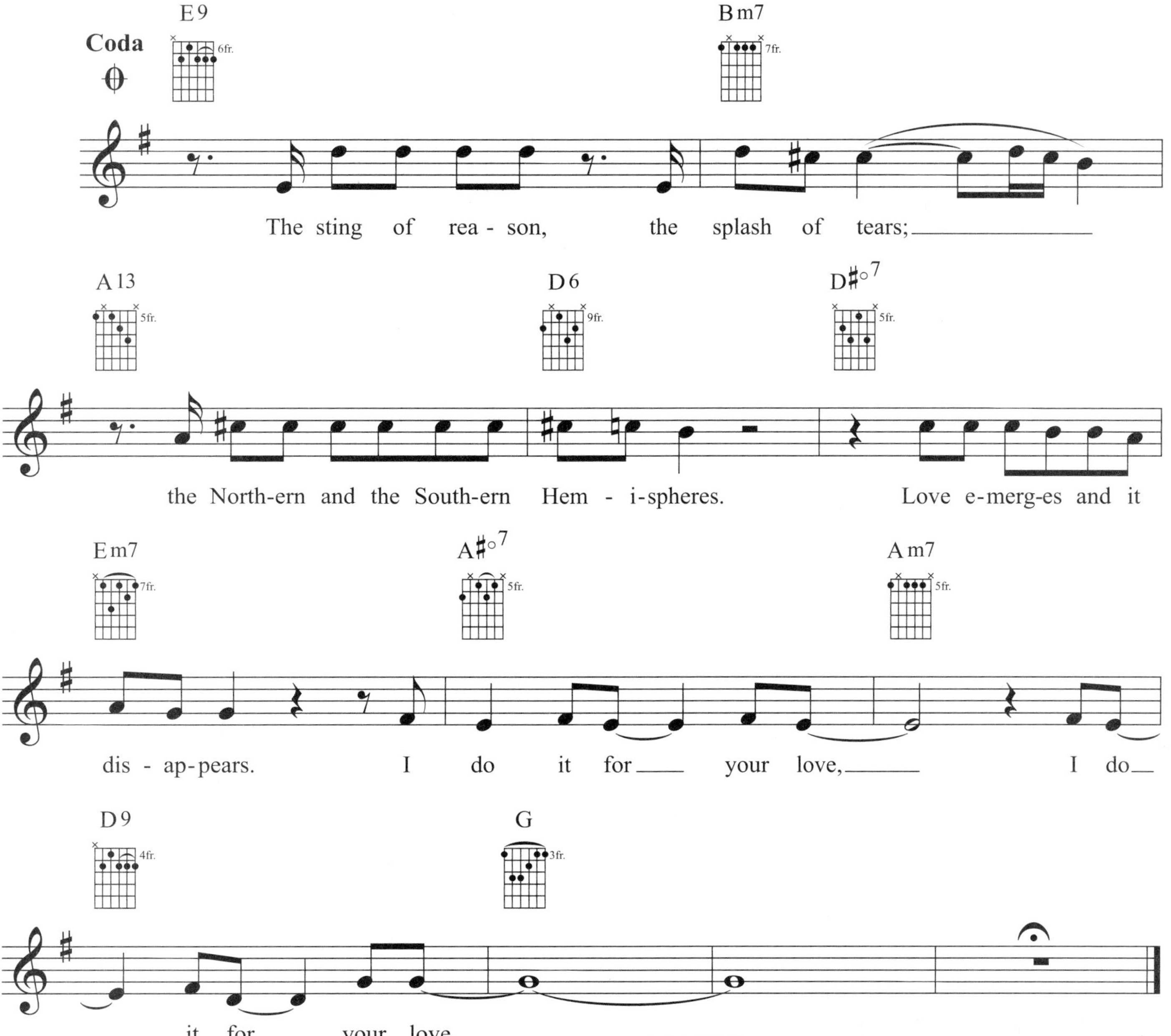
Coda
E9
6fr.
Bm7
7fr.
The sting of rea - son, the splash of tears;
A13
5fr.
D6
9fr.
D♯°7
5fr.
the North-ern and the South-ern Hem - i-spheres. Love e-merg-es and it
Em7
7fr.
A♯°7
5fr.
Am7
5fr.
dis - ap-pears. I do it for your love, I do
D9
4fr.
G
3fr.
it for your love.

How The Heart Approaches What It Yearns

Words and Music by Paul Simon

2. *(guitar solo)*
In a dream we are lying on the top of a hill
And headlights slide past the moon
I roll in your arms
And your voice is the heat of the night
I'm on fire

3. In a phone booth
In some local bar and grill
Rehearsing what I'll say, my coin returns
How the heart approaches what it yearns
How the heart approaches what it yearns

Hurricane Eye

Words and Music by Paul Simon

Moderately bright

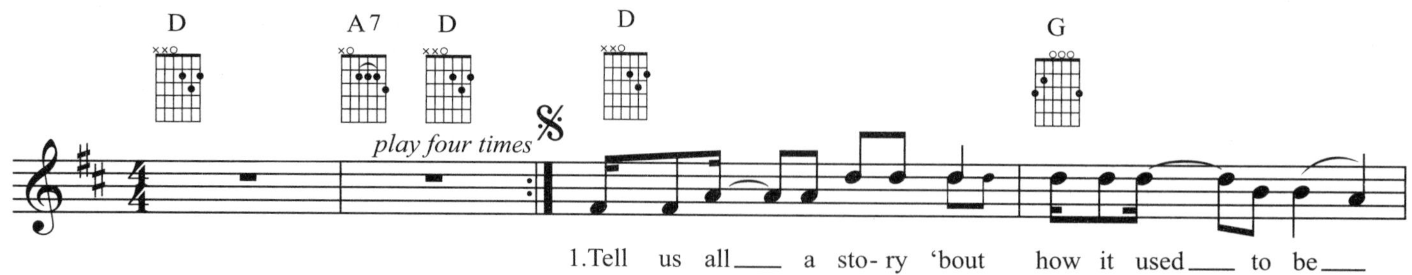

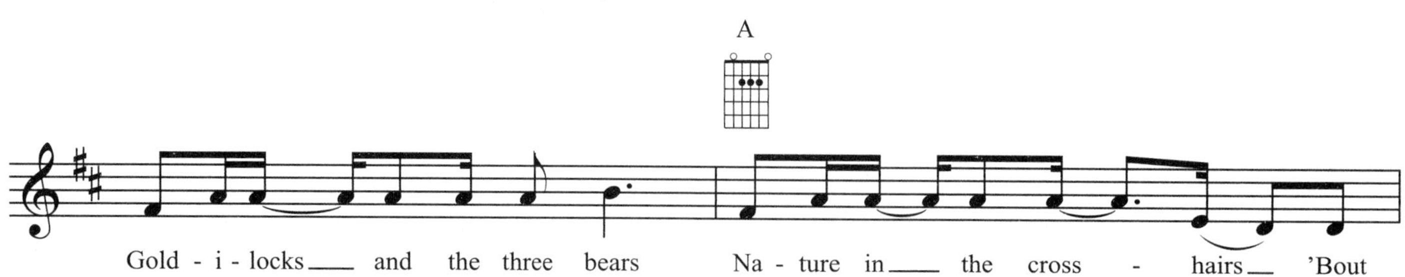

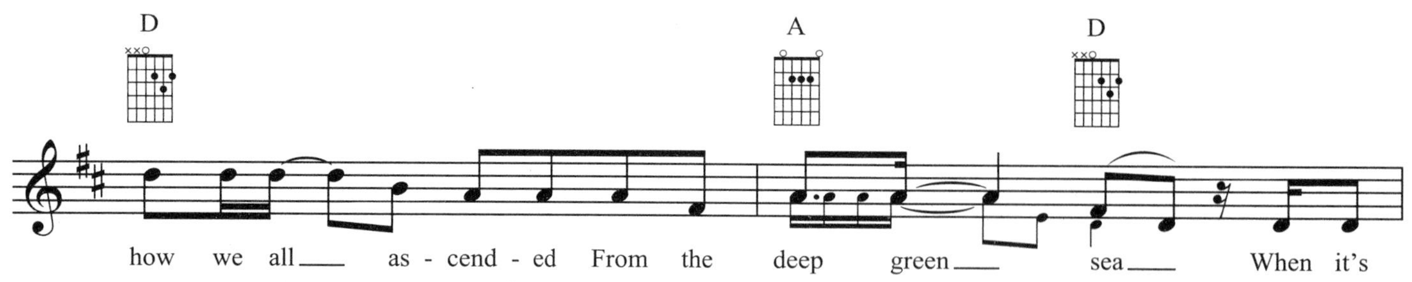

D
A
D
just right and there's sun-light Then we're home,
Em
A7
G
D
Em
Fin - ally home Home in the land of the home-less
A7
G
D
to Coda
Fin - ally home Oh
G
A
D
what are we gon - na do? I nev-er did a thing to you
G
A
D
Bm
G
Time peace-ful as a hur-ri-cane eye Peace-ful
A
D
A7
D
A7
D
D.S. al Coda
as a hur-ri-cane eye
A

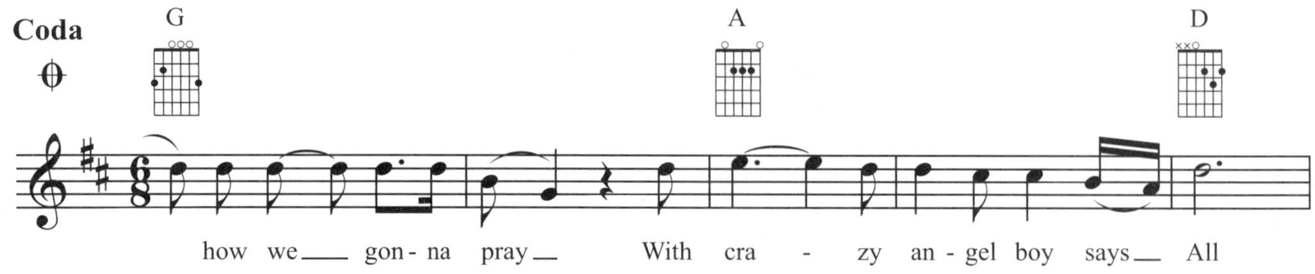
Coda
G
A
D
how we gon-na pray With cra - zy an-gel boy says All

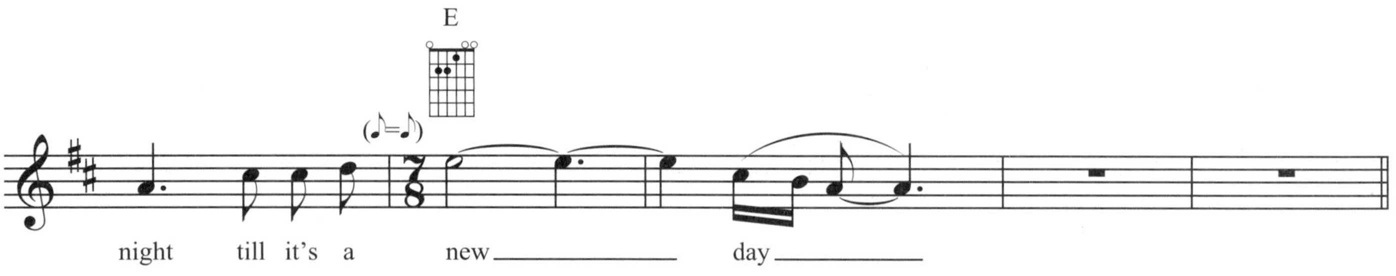
E
night till it's a new day

Peace-ful as a hur-ri-cane Peace-ful as a hur-ri-cane Peace-ful as a hur-ri-cane

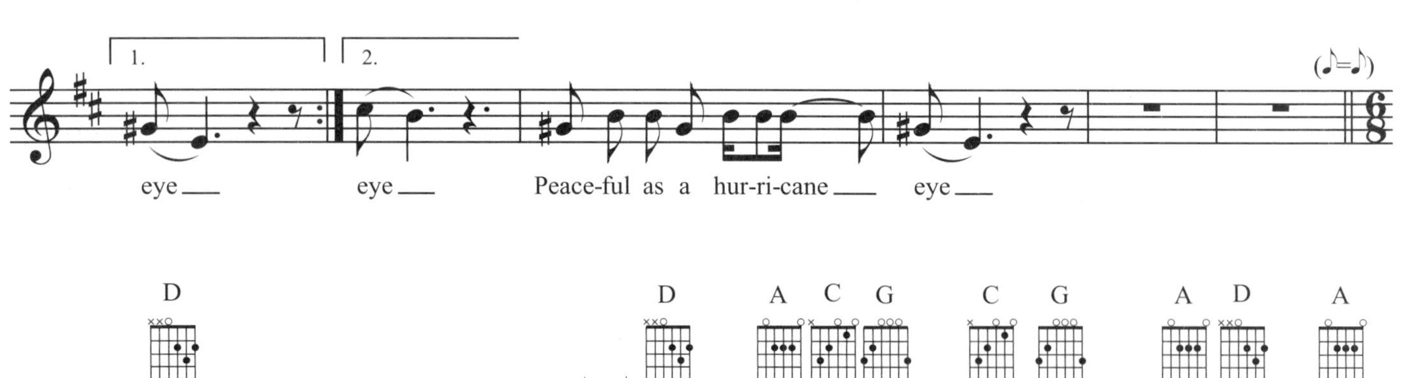
1.
2.
eye eye Peace-ful as a hur-ri-cane eye
D
D A C G C G A D A

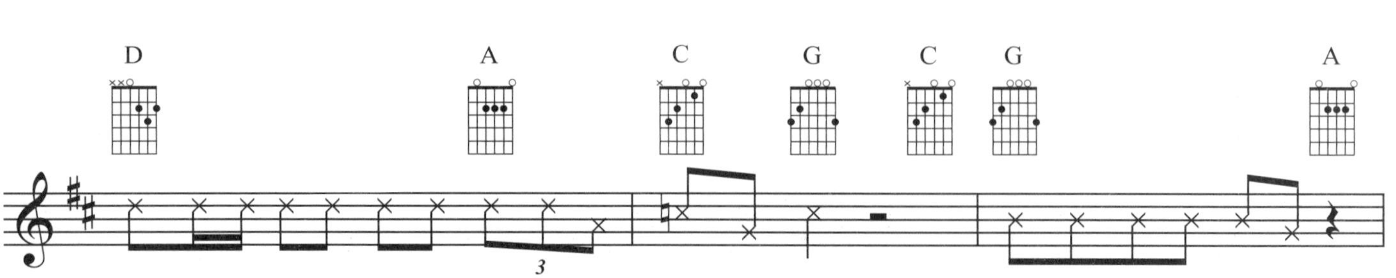
D A C G C G A
(spoken:) You want to be a lead-er You want to change the game? Turn your back on mon-ey,

D A D A C G C
walk a-way from fame? You want to be a mis-sion-ar-y, got that mis-sion-ar-y zeal? Let a
G A D A D A
strang-er change your life, how does that make you feel? You want to be a writ-er, but you don't know
C G C G A D A
how or when? Find a qui - et place, use a hum-ble pen. You wan - na
D A C G C G A
talk talk talk a-bout it All night squawk a-bout the o - cean and the at - mos-phere
D A D A C G C G A
Well, I've been a-way for a long time and it looks like I'll mess a -
D A D A C G C
round here And I'll be a - way for a long time So

2. A history of whispers
   A shadow of a horse
   Faces painted black in sorrow and remorse
   White cloud, black crow
   Crucifix and arrow
   The oldest silence speaks the loudest
   Under the deep green sea

Kathy's Song

Words and Music by Paul Simon

2.
A♭m
4fr.
D♭
G♭
C♭
C♭/G♭
To Eng - land where my heart lies.
D.S. al Coda
Coda
E♭m/G♭
And kiss you when you start your
day.
4.And a song I was writ - ing is left un - done
I don't know why I spend my time
B♭m/F
writ-ing songs I can't be - lieve

2. And from the shelter of my mind
Through the window of my eyes
I gaze beyond the rain-drenched streets
To England where my heart lies.

3. My mind's distracted and diffused
My thoughts are many miles away
They lie with you when you're asleep
And kiss you when you start your day.

5. And so you see I have come to doubt
All that I once held as true
I stand alone without beliefs
The only truth I know is you.

6. And as I watch the drops of rain
Weave their weary paths and die
I know that I am like the rain
There but for the grace of you go I.

I Am A Rock

Words and Music by Paul Simon

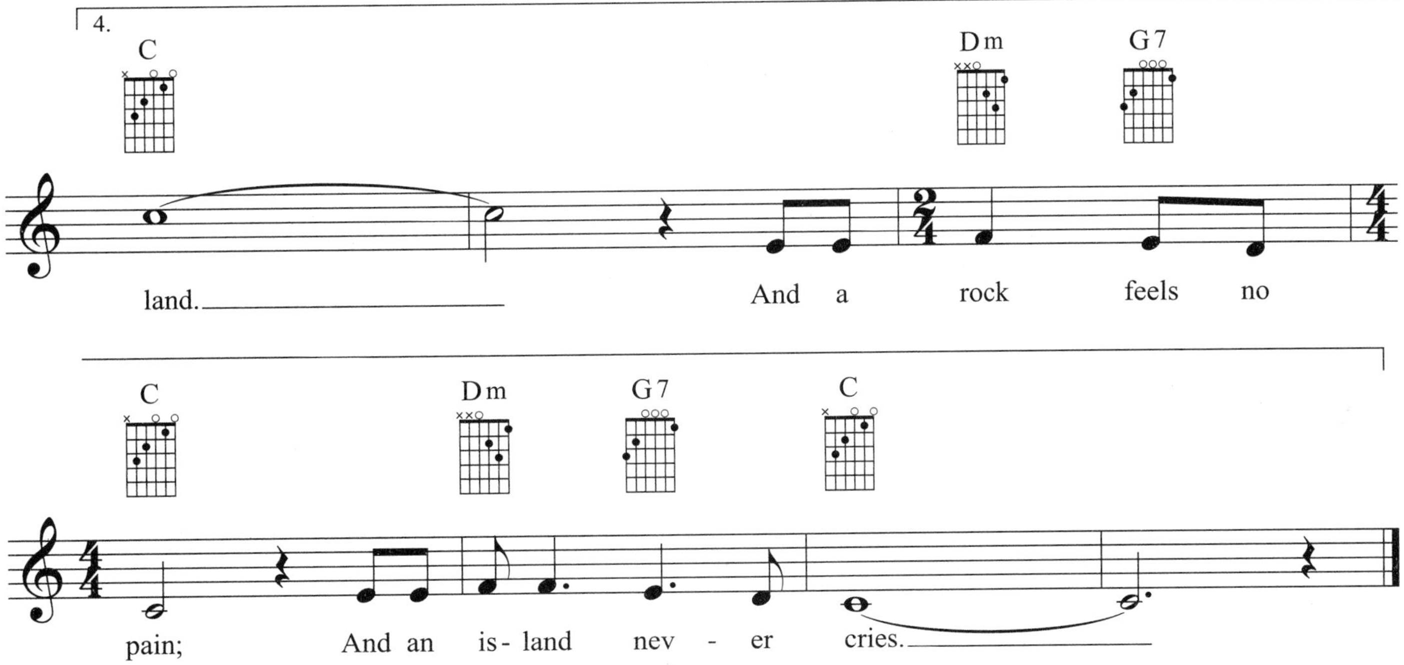

2. I've built walls,
A fortress deep and mighty,
That none may penetrate.
I have no need of friendship;
Friendship causes pain.
It's laughter and it's loving I disdain.
I am a rock,
I am an island.

3. Don't talk of love,
But I've heard the words before;
It's sleeping in my memory.
I won't disturb the slumber
Of feelings that have died.
If I never loved I never would have cried.
I am a rock,
I am an island.

4. I have my books
And my poetry to protect me;
I am shielded in my armor,
Hiding in my room,
Safe within my womb.
I touch no one and no one touches me.
I am a rock,
I am an island.

And a rock feels no pain;
And an island never cries.

I Know What I Know

Words by Paul Simon
Music by Paul Simon and General M.D. Shirinda

2. She said there's something about you
That really reminds me of money
She is the kind of a girl
Who could say things that
Weren't that funny
I said what does that mean
I really remind you of money
She said who am I
To blow against the wind

Chorus

3. She moved so easily
All I could think of was sunlight
I said aren't you the woman
Who was recently given a Fulbright
She said don't I know you
From the cinematographer's party
I said who am I
To blow against the wind

Chorus

Jonah

Words and Music by Paul Simon

Medium soft-rock beat

Amaj7
C♯7♯5
F♯m7
They say Jo - nah he was
Dmaj7
G♯m7♭5
C♯7♭9
swal - lowed by a whale
But I
Fmaj7
Fm7♭5
B♭7
E♭maj7
E♭7
say there's no truth to that tale
I know
A♭m7
D♭7
G♭maj7
Jo - nah he was swal - lowed by a song
1.
Bmaj7/B♭
E♭m
Fm/E♭
E♭m
Fm/E♭
2.
Bmaj7/B♭
E♭maj7
A♭maj7
Here's to all the boys who came a - long

2. No one lets their dreams be taken lightly
They hold them tightly
Warm against cold
One more year of traveling 'round this circuit
Then you can work it into gold

Kodachrome™

Words and Music by Paul Simon

With a moving beat

* "KODACHROME™" is a registered trademark for color film

A
C♯7
F♯7
Bm
E
chrome, They give us those nice bright col-ors, They give us the greens
A
D
B
E
of sum - mers, Makes you think all the world's a sun-ny
A
C♯7
F♯7
Bm
E
day. Oh yeah, I got a Ni - kon cam-'ra, I love to take a
A
D
B7
E
to Coda
pho - to - graph, So ma - ma, don't take my Ko - da - chrome a - way.
A
C♯m
4fr.
F♯m
B
If you took all
E
Emaj7
E7
A
the girls I knew when I was sin - gle
F♯m
B7
E
F♯m
B7
And brought them all to-geth - er for one night, I know they'd nev -

E
Emaj7
E7
A
- er match my sweet im - ag - i - na - tion,
F♯m
B7
E
E7
D.S. al Coda
And ev - 'ry-thing looks worse in black and white. Ko - da -
Coda
A
C♯m7
4fr.
F♯m
Ma - ma don't
A
C♯m7
F♯m
1., 2.
3.
take my Ko - da - chrome a - way.
Ma-ma don't
A
C♯m7
Ma-ma don't take my Ko - da - chrome, Ma-ma don't take my Ko - da - chrome,
F♯m
repeat and fade
Ma - ma don't take my Ko - da - chrome a - way.

Keep The Customer Satisfied

Words and Music by Paul Simon

E♭
Cm
E♭
one step a-head of the shoe shine, Two steps a-way from the
Cm
E♭
A♭
coun-ty line, Just trying to keep my cus-tom-ers sat-is-fied, sat-is-
1.
E♭
N.C.
2.
E♭
fied. 2.Dep-u-ty Sher-iff said to fied.
Whoa, whoa, whoa
E♭7
A♭7
E♭
Fm
whoa.
A♭
E♭
But it's the same old sto-ry Ev-'ry-where I

2. Deputy Sheriff said to me,
"Tell me what you come here for, boy.
You better get your bags and flee.
You're in trouble boy,
And you're heading into more."

Learn How To Fall

Words and Music by Paul Simon

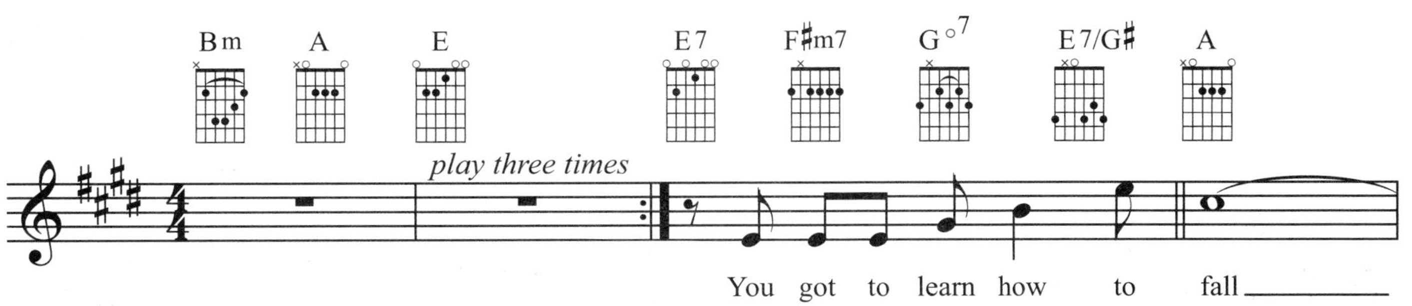

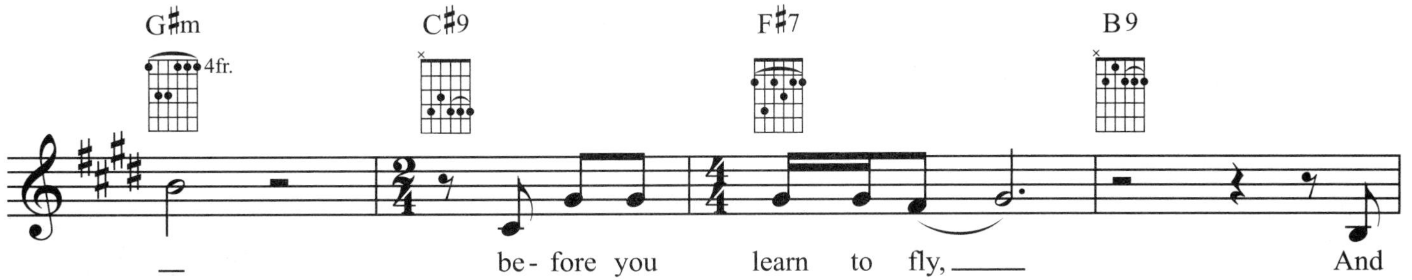

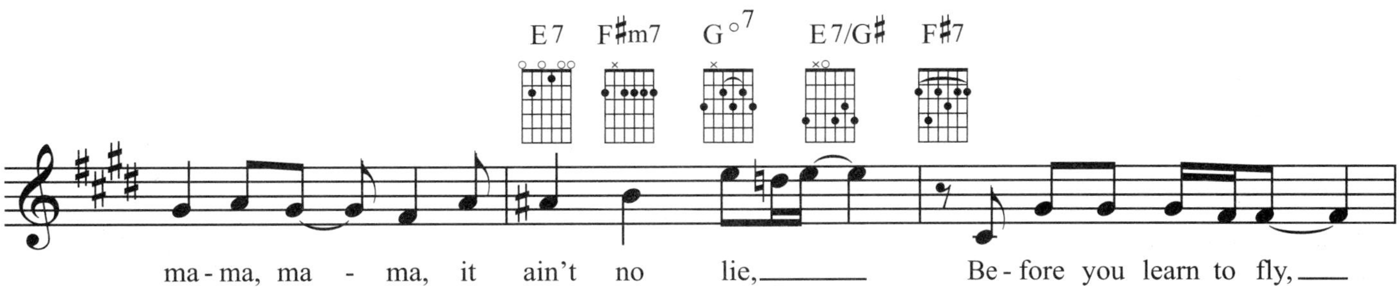

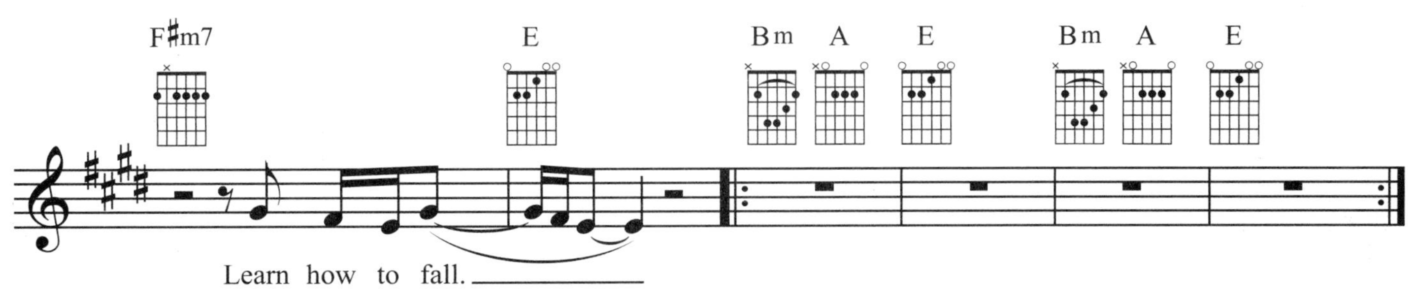

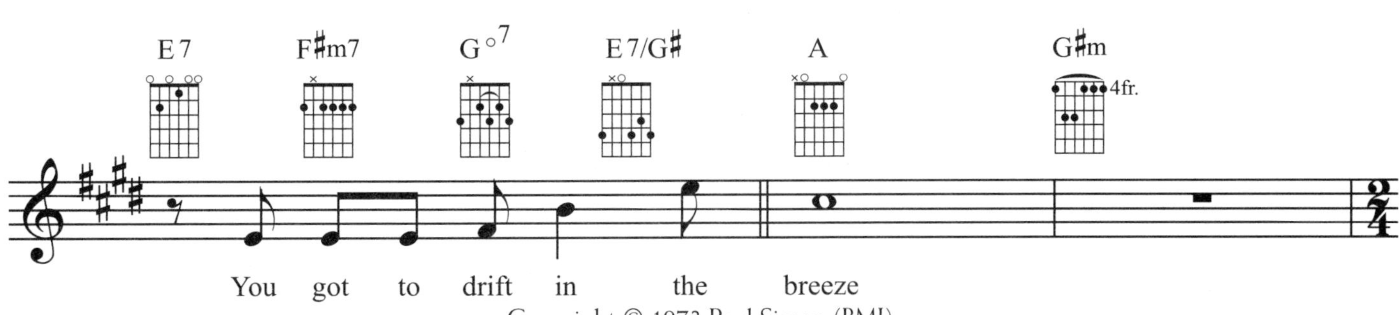

C♯9
F♯7
B9
Be- fore you set your sails,
Oh, yes, an
E7
F♯m7
G○7
E7/G♯
F♯7
oc-cu-pa - tion where the wind pre - vails.
Be- fore you set your sails,
F♯m7
E
Bm
A
E
Drift in the breeze.
Bm
A
E
Bm
A
Oh, and it's the same old sto - ry,
Ev-er since the world be-gan
E
Bm
A
E
Ev - ery - bod - y got the runs for glo - ry,
No - bod - y
Bm
A
E
Bm
A
stop and scru - ti - nize the plan.
No - bod - y stop and scru - ti - nize the plan.

E
Bm
A
E
Bm
A
E
No - bod-y stop and scru-ti-nize the plan.
E7
F♯m7
G°7
E7/G♯
A
G♯m
4fr.
You got to learn how to fall
C♯9
F♯7
B9
be-fore you learn to fly,
The tank towns, they
E7
F♯m7
G°7
E7/G♯
F♯7
tell no lie,
Be - fore you learn to fly,
F♯m7
E
Bm
A
E
repeat and fade
Learn how to fall.

Killer Wants To Go To College

Music by Paul Simon
Lyrics by Paul Simon and Derek Walcott

Moderate shuffle beat

D
E
A
mov - ie I got the style, I got the look.
A7
D7
This boy used to be on death - row Will his vi - o - lence re -
C♯m
4fr.
B7
turn? Will he call out to his moth - er,
E
"Ma-ma, you can watch me burn!" Kill - er wants to go to
A
F♯m
col - lege An - oth - er bull - shit de - gree
D
Tell the lit - tle town of New Paltz
E
A
D.C. al Fine
"You ain't got noth-in' to be scared a - bout with me"

Killer Wants To Go To College II

Music by Paul Simon
Lyrics by Paul Simon and Derek Walcott

F♯m
My life nev-er made much sense
I just wish that I could
D
E
A
hug you
You're my on - ly de - fense
A7
D
I don't un-der-stand your writ-ing
I could bare-ly sign my
C♯m
4fr.
B7
name
All I ev-er learned was fight-ing
E
But I'm not the on - ly one to blame
A
The streets were dark with dan - ger

F♯m
I have to stand up for my friends
D
In a land where I'm a strang - er
E
A
And the ha - tred nev-er ends
Kill - er wants to go on
F♯m
T. V.
D
E
A

Let Me Live In Your City

Words and Music by Paul Simon

Moderately slow

A/E Emaj7 Esus4 E7 A Am7 E9/G♯

F♯m7 G♯m7 C♯m Amaj7 B A/E Emaj7

1.You've got the cool wa - ter

Esus4 E7 A Am7 E9/G♯

when the fe - ver runs high,

F♯m7 G♯7 C♯m B/A

You've got the look of love - light in your eyes. And I was in

A/E Emaj7 Esus4 B♭7 A

cra - zy mo-tion 'til you calmed me down,

E F♯m7 B9sus4 B9 E

It took a lit-tle time, but you calmed me down.

B/A
A
E
E9
Whoa
Let me live in your city
A
E
F♯m7
B9sus4
B9
B/A
The river's so pretty,
the air is so fine
Let me a room where
A/E
G♯7
A7
C°7
C♯m
I can lay over
I'm just a traveler
eatin' up trav-'lin' time
Mm
F♯7
to Coda
I'm just a traveler
eatin' up my travelin' time
Emaj7
E sus4
E7
Am7
E9/G♯
G♯m7
Amaj7
B
1.
2.They've got a

2. They've got a wall in China
It's a thousand miles long
To keep out the foreigners they made it strong
And I've got a wall around me
That you can't even see
It took a little time
To get next to me

The Late Great Johnny Ace

Words and Music by Paul Simon
Coda by Philip Glass

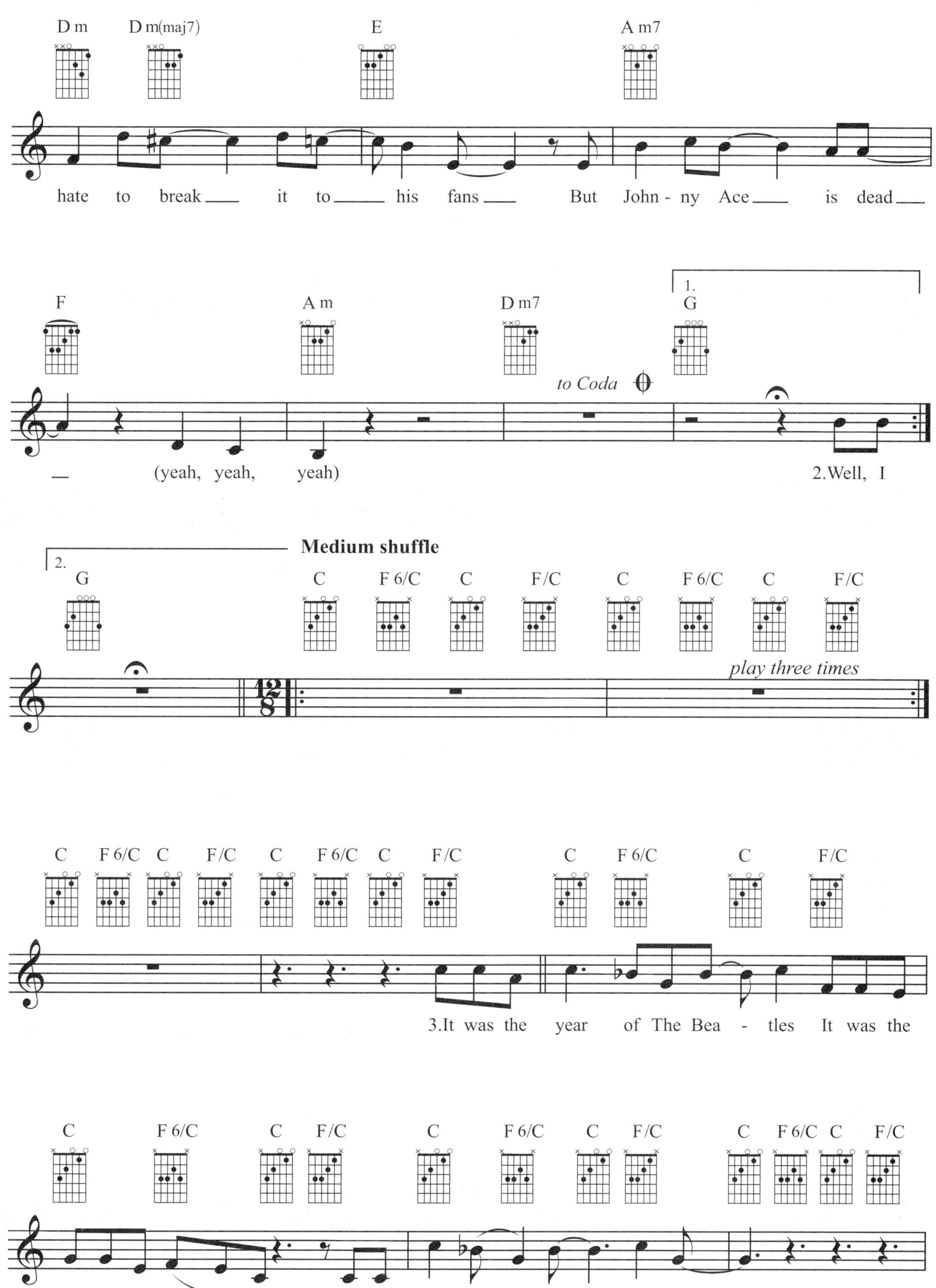

Dm
Dm(maj7)
E
Am7
hate to break it to his fans But John - ny Ace is dead
F
Am
Dm7
1.
G
to Coda
(yeah, yeah, yeah)
2.Well, I
2.
G
Medium shuffle
C
F 6/C
C
F/C
play three times
3.It was the year of The Bea - tles It was the
year of The Stones It was nine - teen six - ty - four

C F6/C C F/C C B♭/D Fm E♭
I was liv - ing in Lon - don With the girl
C B B♭ Am F♯°7 Fm7
from the sum - mer be - fore
G7♭9 3fr. C F6/C C F/C
It was the year of The Bea - tles It was the
C F6/C C F/C C F6/C C F/C C F6/C C F/C
year of The Stones A year af - ter J. F. K.
C F6/C C F/C C B♭/D Fm E♭ C B B♭ G
We were stay - ing up all night And giv-ing the days a - way

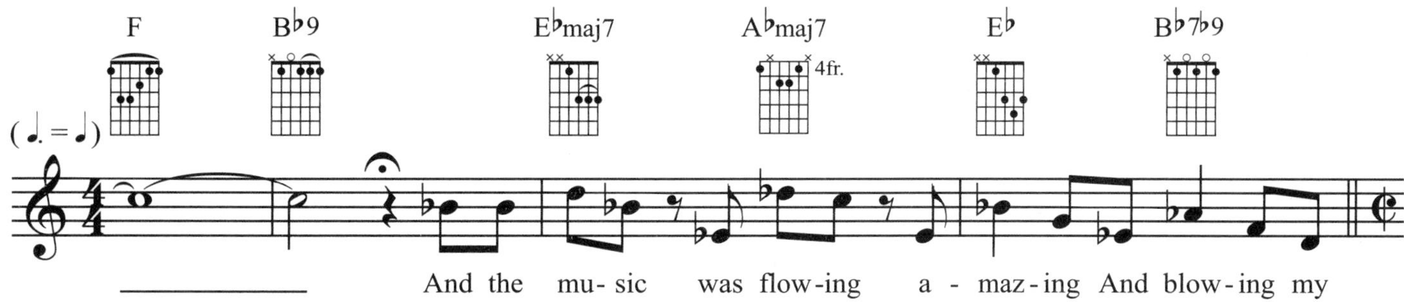

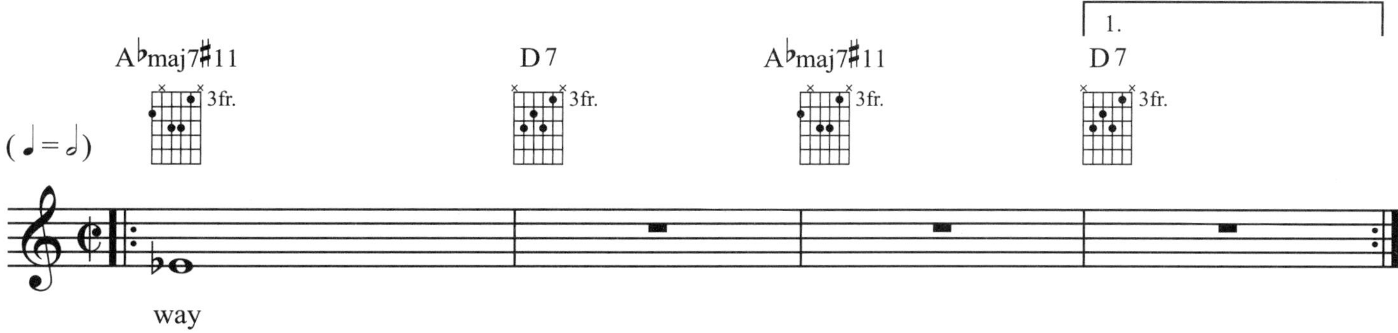

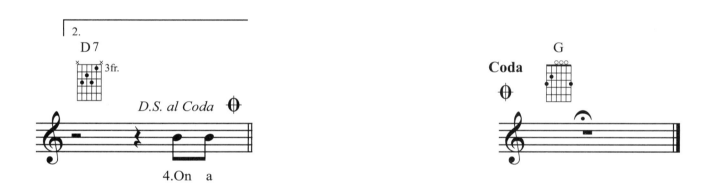

2. Well, I really wasn't
   Such a Johnny Ace fan
   But I felt bad all the same
   So I sent away for his photograph
   And I waited till it came
   It came all the way from Texas
   With a sad and simple face
   And they signed it on the bottom
   From the Late Great Johnny Ace, yeah, yeah, yeah

4. On a cold December evening
   I was walking through the Christmas tide
   When a stranger came up and asked me
   If I'd heard John Lennon had died
   And the two of us went to this bar
   And we stayed to close the place
   And every song we played
   Was for the Late Great Johnny Ace, yeah, yeah, yeah

Late In The Evening

Words and Music by Paul Simon

Brightly, in 2

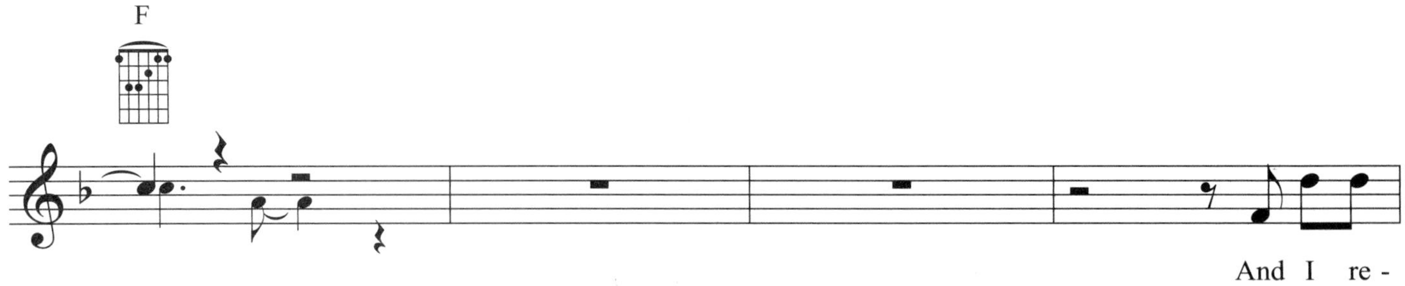

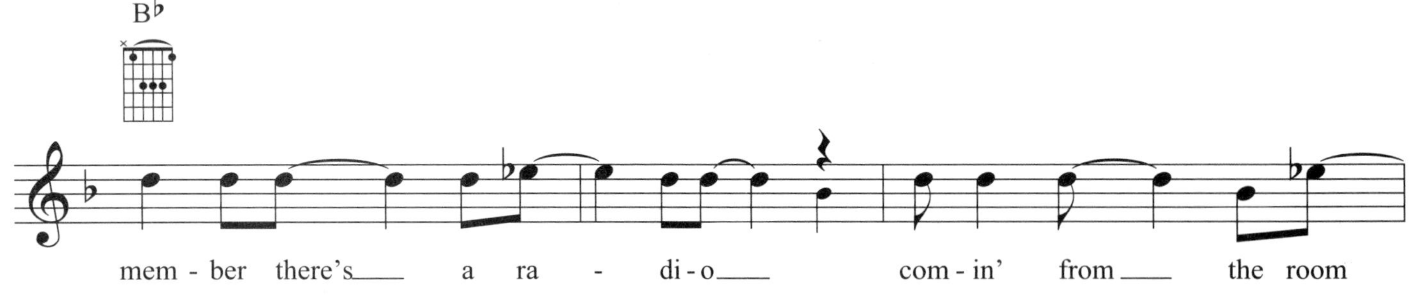

F
C
when it's late in the eve -
- ning
and the mu - sic's seep - ing through.
F
to Coda
1.
2.
3.
D.S. al Coda (instrumental)
2.The
3.Then I
Coda
B♭
4.The first thing I re - mem - ber when you came
in - to my life,
I said I'm gon - na get that girl no
F
mat - ter what I do.

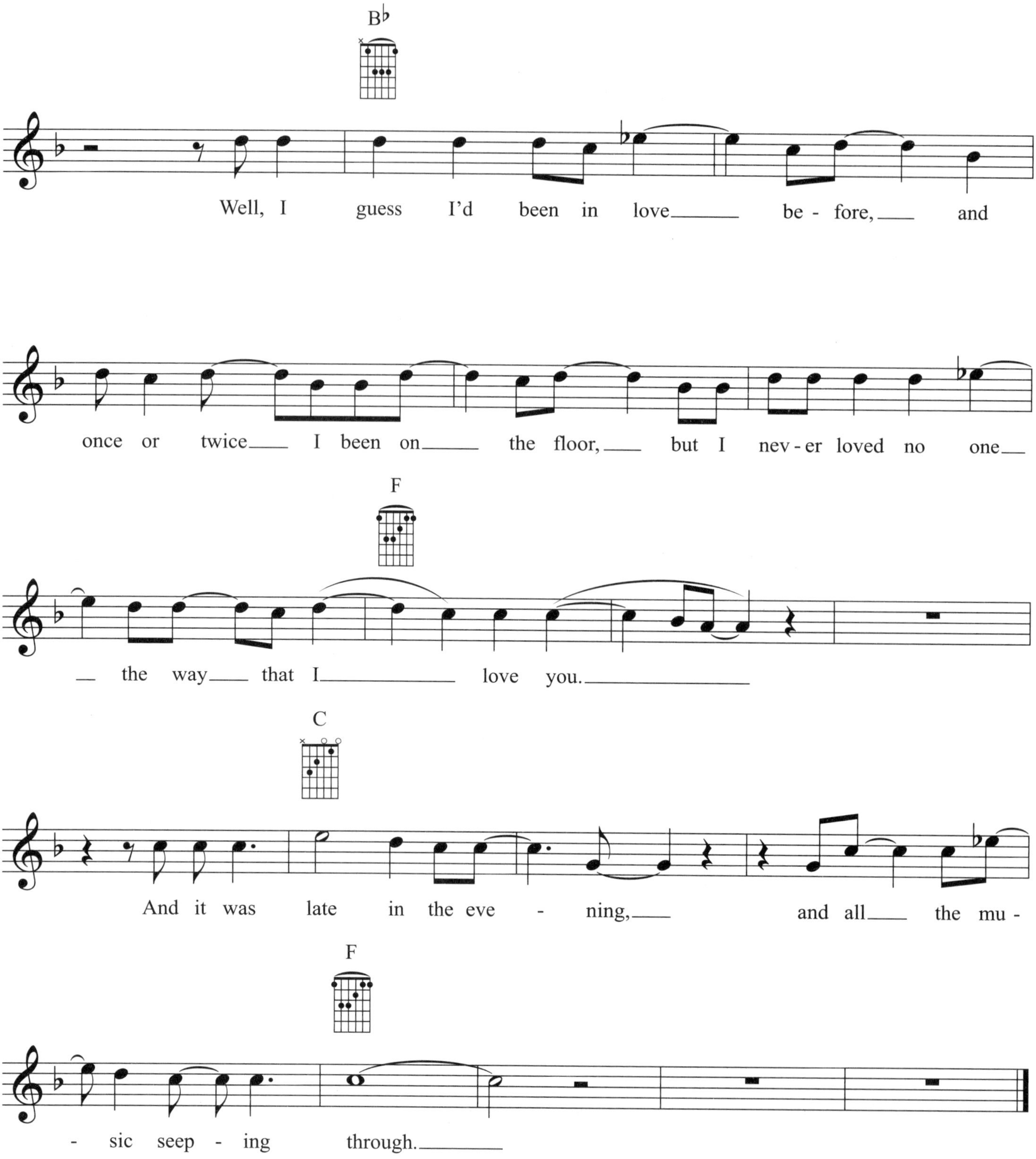

once or twice I been on the floor, but I nev - er loved no one

F

the way that I love you.

C

And it was late in the eve - ning, and all the mu -

F

- sic seep - ing through.

2. The next thing I remember
I was walking down the street
I'm feeling all right
I'm with my boys
I'm with my troops, yeah
And down along the avenue
Some guys were shootin' pool
And I heard the sound
Of a capella groups, yeah
Singing late in the evening
And all the girls out on the stoops, yeah

3. Then I learned to play some lead guitar
I was underage in this funky bar
And I stepped outside to smoke myself a "J"
And when I came back to the room
Everybody just seemed to move
And I turned my amp up loud and I began to play
And it was late in the evening
And I blew that room away

Look At That

Words and Music by Paul Simon

Em
G/A
know
I love you so
Look at
Dsus4
G
Bm/F♯
that Look at this Lov-ers merge and make a wish
They close their eyes
G/F
Em
Bm11
A7sus4
and now their dreams are leav-ing
And on the ho-ri-zon the
D
D7
G
ea - gle flies
Through clouds of fire
Swoop and
D
G
B7
glide
You can't be-lieve,
You can't de-
Em
G/A
Em9
5fr.
play four times
cide

D
C
D
G
D
C
D
Ask some-bod-y to love you
Takes a lot of nerve
Ask some-bod-y to love you
G
D
C
D
G
You got a lot of nerve
Ask some-bod-y to love you
Takes a lot of nerve
D
C
D
C
D
Ask some-bod-y to love you
Ma ma ma ma ma ma ma ma ma ma ma
C
D
C
D
Da da da da da da da da da da da
La la la la la la la la la la la la la la la la
D sus4
Oom ba pa doom Look at that Look at this This is near e-nough to bliss
G
B m/F♯
G/F
E m
B m11
Then o-ver the top we go and down Down to the bot-tom

G/A
D
D sus4
E m9
5fr.
play three times
If you're look-ing for wor-ries You got 'em
D
C
D
G
D
C
D
Ask some-bod-y to love you takes a lot of nerve Ask some-bod-y to love you You
got a lot of nerve
Deh deh deh deh deh deh deh deh deh deh deh deh deh deh deh deh
Guh guh guh guh guh guh guh guh guh guh guh guh guh guh guh guh
La la la la la la la la la la la la la la la la Oom ba pa doom Come a -
D sus4
G
wake, come a - live Come in sen - s'ry sur - vive
And hey,

D G

— and down the road we go — You might learn some- thing

B7 Em G/A

Yeah — you nev - er know — But an - y - way —

Em9 5fr.

— you got-ta go —

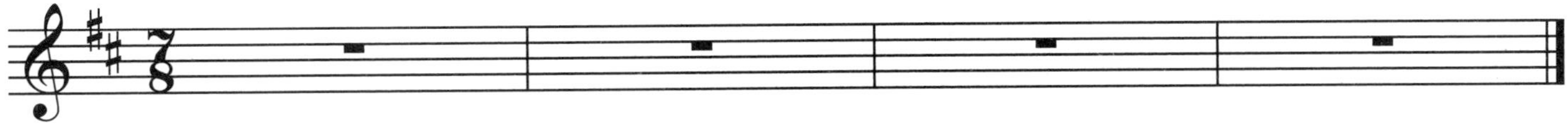

Leaves That Are Green

Words and Music by Paul Simon

B
B7
1.
2.
crum-ble in your hand.
2.Once my
E
F♯m
B
E
3.I threw a peb - ble in a brook And watched the
A
D
E
to Coda
rip - ples run a - way
And they
A
B
E
D
nev - er made a sound
And the leaves that are
A
B
E
green
turned to brown,
C♯m
4fr.
And they with-er with the wind,
B
B7
D.S. al Coda
And they crum-ble in your hand.

2. Once my heart was filled with the love of a girl.
   I held her close, but she faded in the night
   Like a poem I meant to write.
   And the leaves that are green turn to brown,
   And they wither with the wind,
   And they crumble in your hand.

3. I threw a pebble in a brook
   And watched the ripples run away
   And they never made a sound.
   And the leaves that are green turned to brown,
   And they wither with the wind,
   And they crumble in your hand.

4. Hello, Hello, Hello, Good-bye,
   Good-bye, Good-bye, Good-bye,
   That's all there is.
   And the leaves that are green turned to brown,
   And they wither with the wind,
   And they crumble in your hand.

Love

Words and Music by Paul Simon

F m7
E♭maj7
G 7♭9 /D
G
Like plants the med-i-cine is ev - 'ry-where
C
F
A m
F m
G 7
C
F
Love
Love
A m
F m
G 7
C
F
A m
F m
Love
1.We crave it so
C m
3fr.
F m
bad-ly Makes you wan-na laugh out loud when you re-ceive it And gob-ble it like
C m
3fr.
to Coda
B♭m
A♭
4fr.
can-dy We think it's eas-y Some-times it's eas-y
D♭
4fr.
E♭7
4fr.
A♭
4fr.
D♭
4fr.
E♭7
4fr.
But it's not eas-y You're gon-na break down and cry
A♭
4fr.
D♭
4fr.
E♭7
4fr.
A♭
4fr.
We're not im-por-tant We should be grate-ful

2. The price that we pay
When evil walks the planet
And love is crushed like clay

Long, Long Day

Words and Music by Paul Simon

1.
B♭13
6fr.
B°7
6fr.
Cm7
3fr.
It's been a long, long day.
G7♯5
3fr.
Cm
3fr.
B♭/C
G♭maj7
Good - night
D♭/A♭
4fr.
A♭m7
4fr.
D♭/A♭
4fr.
A♭m7
4fr.
A♭
4fr.
3
3
Good - - - - - night
E♭
3fr.
E♭7
Fm7
3fr.
E♭7/G
4fr.
My love
3
2.
G7♯5
3fr.
Cm
3fr.
B♭/C
G♭maj7
Good - night
D♭/A♭
4fr.
A♭m7
4fr.
D♭/A♭
4fr.
A♭m7
4fr.
A♭sus4
4fr.
A♭
4fr.
3
3
Good - - - - - night
My
3

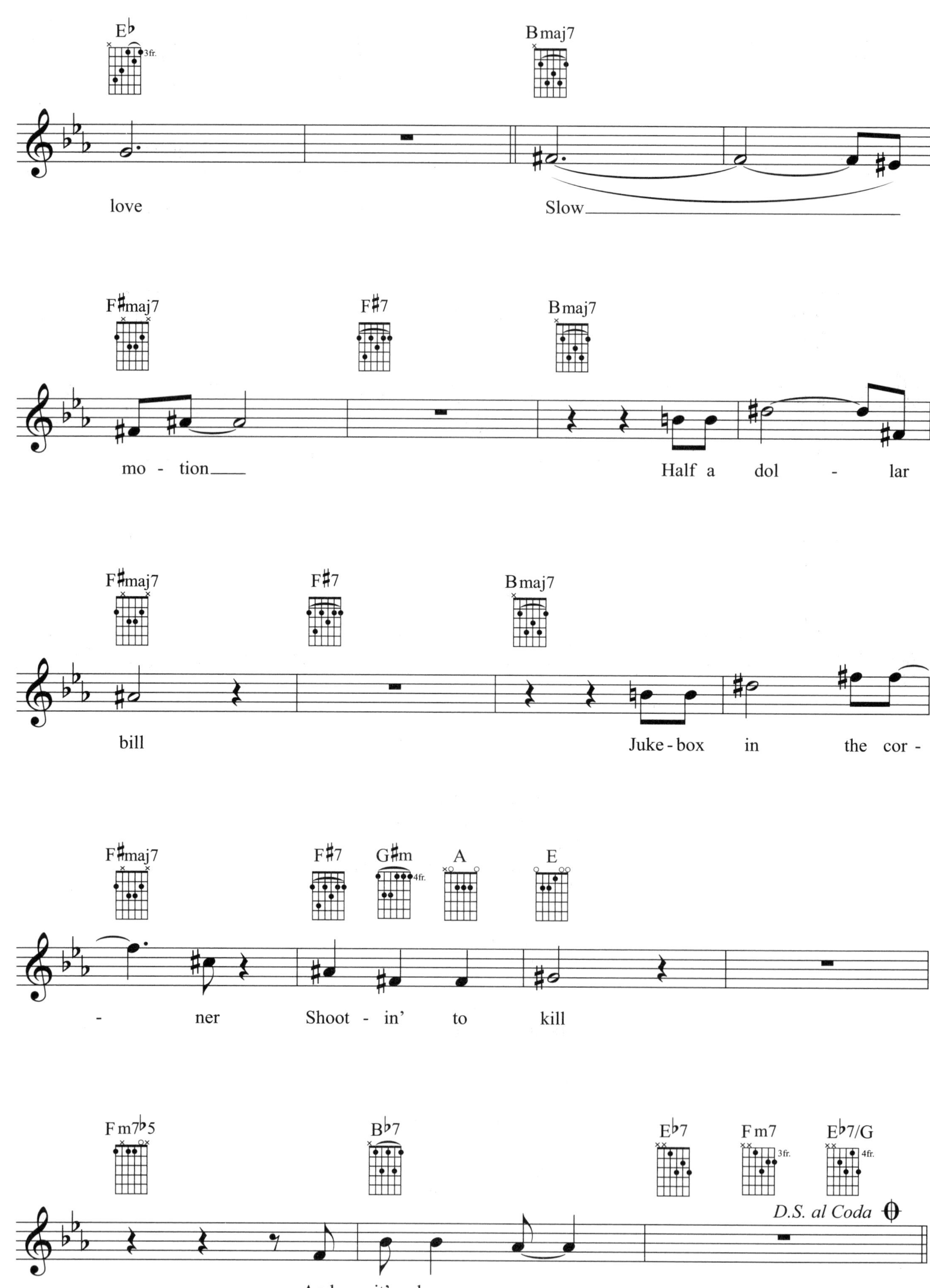
E♭
B maj7
love
Slow
F♯maj7
F♯7
B maj7
mo - tion
Half a dol - lar
F♯maj7
F♯7
B maj7
bill
Juke-box in the cor -
F♯maj7
F♯7
G♯m
A
E
- ner Shoot - in' to kill
Fm7♭5
B♭7
E♭7
Fm7
E♭7/G
D.S. al Coda
And it's been a

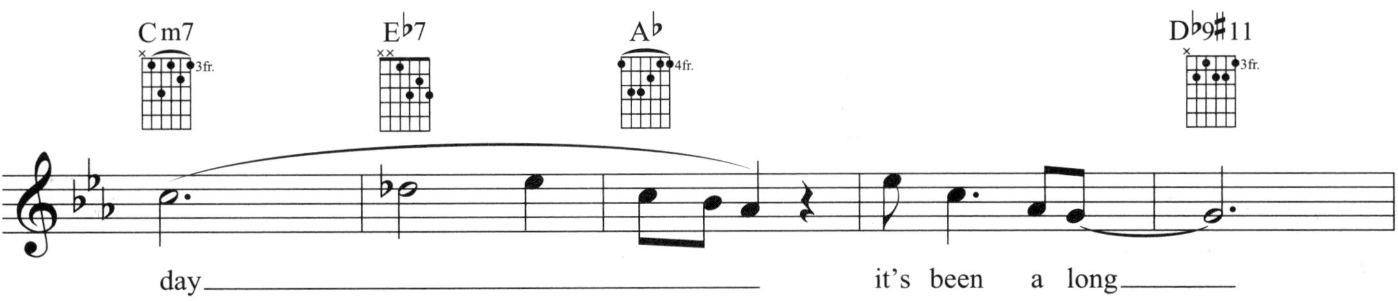

2. I sure been on this road
 Done nearly fourteen years
 Can't say my name's well known
 You don't see my face in *Rolling Stone*
 But I sure been on this road

 Slow motion
 Half a dollar bill
 Jukebox in the corner
 Shooting to kill
 And it's been a...

3. It's been a long, long day
 I sure could use a friend
 Don't know what else to say
 I hate to abuse an old cliché
 But it's been a long, long day
 It's been a long, long day

Loves Me Like A Rock

Words and Music by Paul Simon

C
F
C
G
She rocks me like the rock of ag - es and loves me.
She loves me, love me, love me, love me.
N.C.
2. When I was grown to be a
G
C
G
man, (Grown to be a man) and the dev - il would call my
C
G
C7
name, (Grown to be a man) I'd say, "Now who do,
G
C
who do you think you're fool - ing?" (Grown to be a
G
C
man) I'm a con - sum - mat - ed man, (Grown to be a
G
G7
C
man) I can snatch a lit - tle pu - ri - ty, My ma - ma loves

G
D
G
Em
— me, she loves — me. She get down on her knees and hug — me. Oh, she
C
G
F
C
loves me like a rock. She rocks me like the rock of ag - es and loves —
G
— me. — She love me, love me, love me, love me. —
G
C
3. And if I was the Pres - i - dent, (Was — the Pres - i -
G
C
dent) the min - ute the Con - gress call my name, (Was — the Pres - i -
G
C7
dent) I say, "Now who do, — who do you think you're fool -
G
C
G
ing?" I've got the Pres - i - den - tial
(Who do you think you're fool - ing?)

C G C
Seal, (Was the Pres - i - dent) I'm up on the pres - i - den - tial po - di - um.
G D
My ma - ma loves me, she loves me. She
G Em C G
get down on her knees and hug me. Oh, she loves me like a rock.
C F C G
She rocks me like the rock of ag - es and loves me.
She love me, love me, love me, love me. (Love me like a
repeat and fade
rock) She love me, love me, love me, love me. (Love me like a

Me And Julio Down By The Schoolyard

Words and Music by Paul Simon

A
ma-ma looked down and spit on the ground ev-'ry time my name gets-
D
E
men-tioned. The pa-pa said, "Oy, if I
A
get that boy I'm gon-na stick him in the house of de-ten-tion."
N.C.
D
A
Chorus
Well, I'm on my way, I don't know where I'm go-in',
D
A
B
E
I'm on my way, I'm tak-in' my time but I don't know where.
D
G
A
Good-bye to Ro-sie, the queen of Co-ro-na,
G
D
E
A
D
A
to Coda
See you, me and Ju-lio down by the school yard

E
A
G
D
E
A
D
A
See you, me and Ju - lio down by the school - yard.
E
D
A
3
(whistle solo)
D
A
B
E
D
G
A
A
G
D
E
A
D
A
E
A
G
D
E
A
D
A
E
D.S. al Coda
N.C.
2.Whoa in a

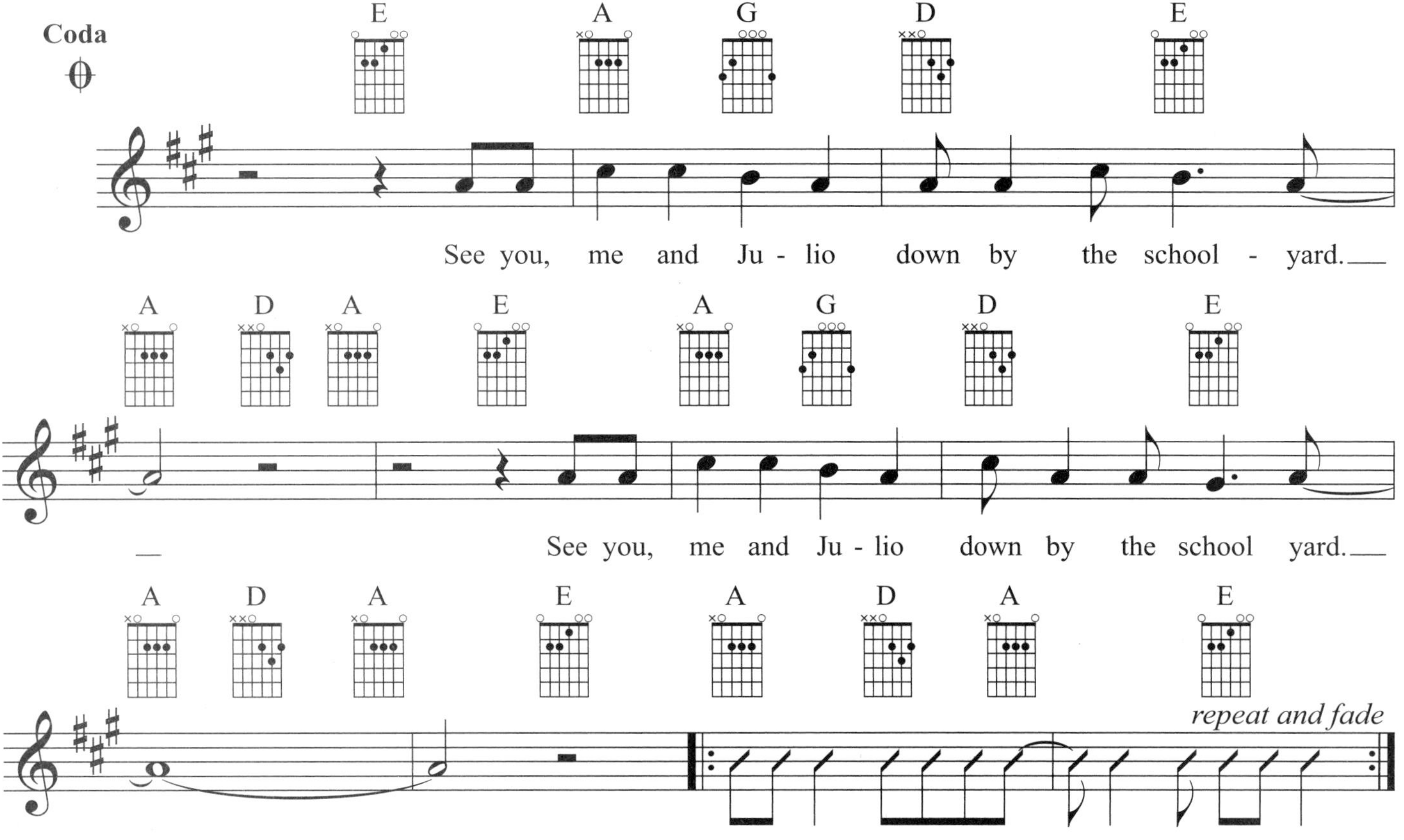

2. In a couple of days they come and take me away
But the press let the story leak
And when the radical priest
Come to get me released
We was all on the cover of *Newsweek*

Chorus:
And I'm on my way
I don't know where I'm going
I'm on my way
I'm taking my time
But I don't know where
Goodbye to Rosie the queen of Corona
See you, me and Julio
Down by the schoolyard
See you, me and Julio
Down by the schoolyard
Me and Julio down by the schoolyard

Mother And Child Reunion

Words and Music by Paul Simon

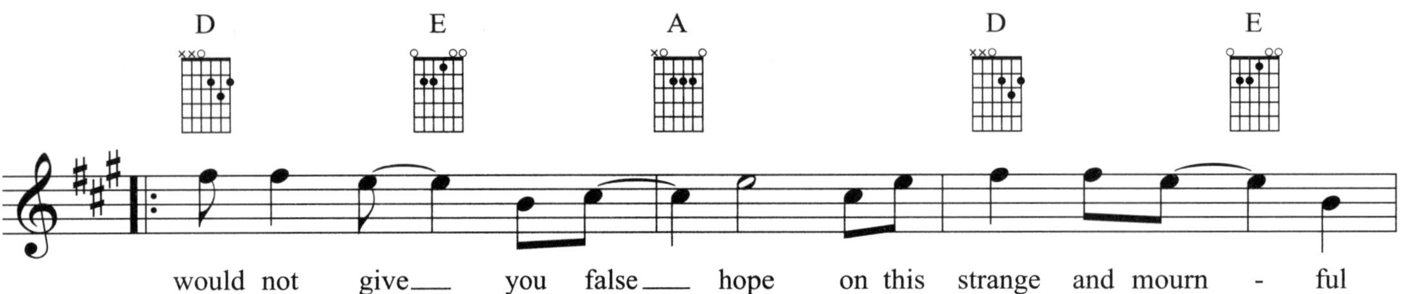

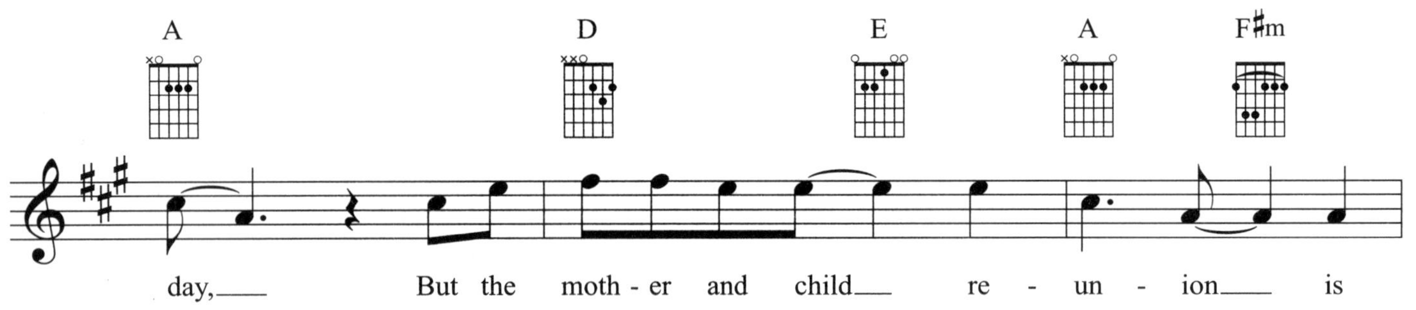

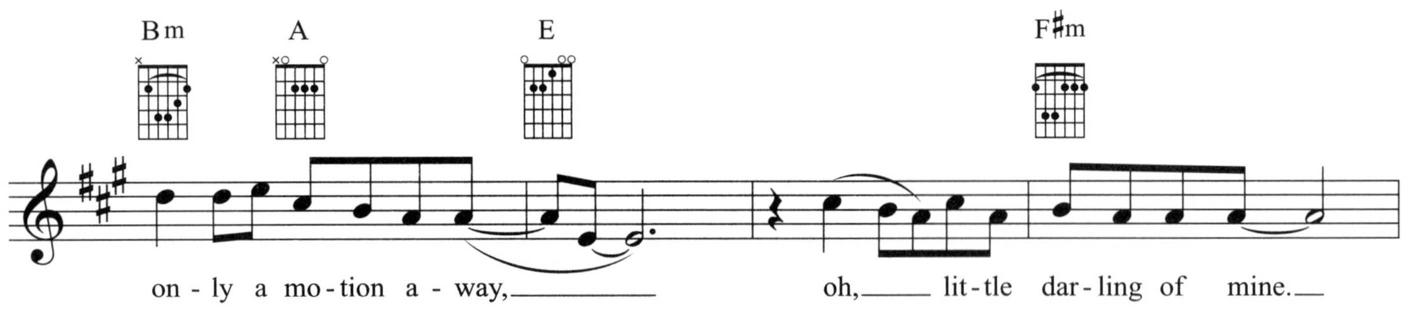

E
I know they say let it be,
But it just don't work

F♯m
D
out that way,
And the course of a life-time runs o-ver and

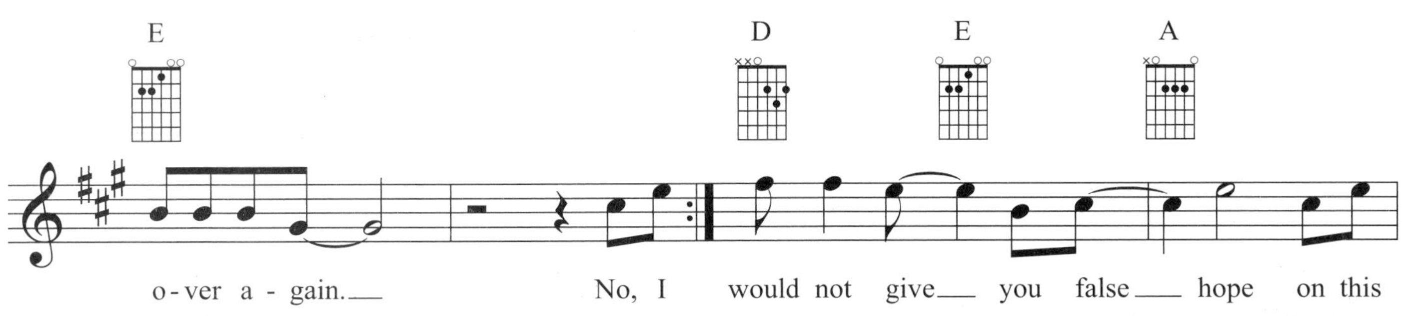
E
D
E
A
o-ver a-gain.
No, I would not give you false hope on this

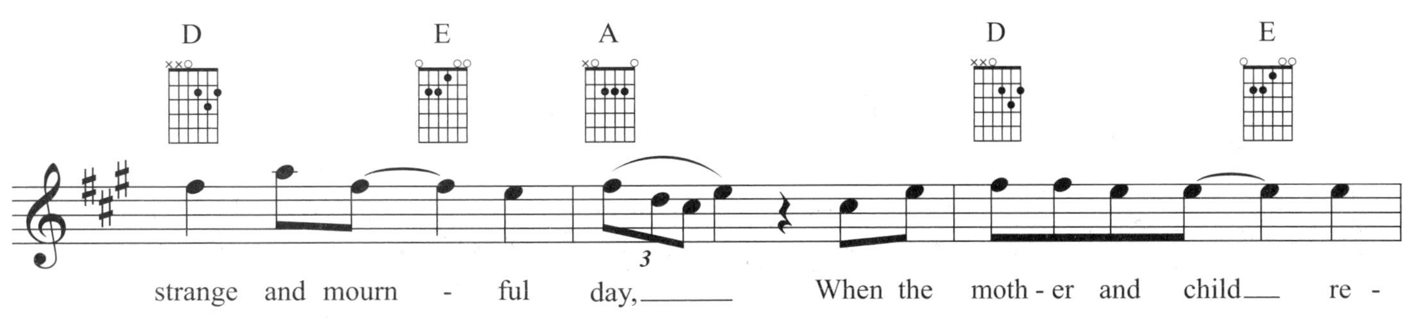
D
E
A
D
E
strange and mourn - ful day,
When the moth-er and child re -

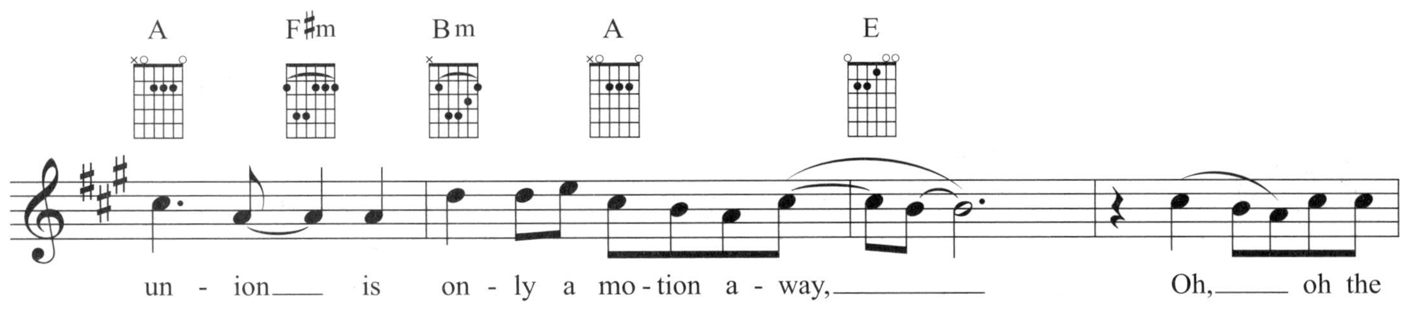
A
F♯m
Bm
A
E
un - ion is on - ly a mo-tion a - way,
Oh, oh the

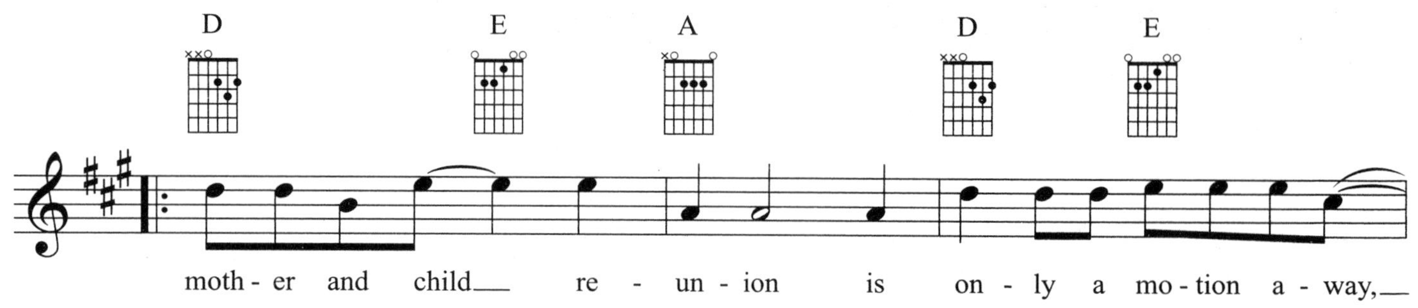

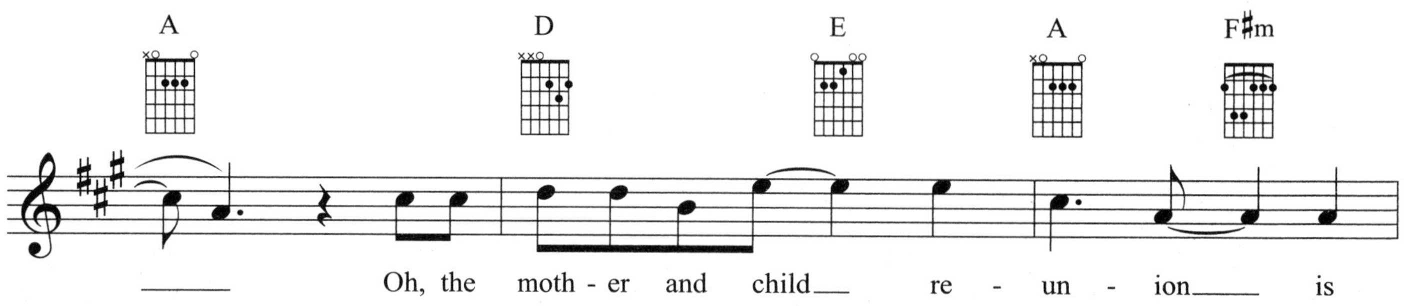

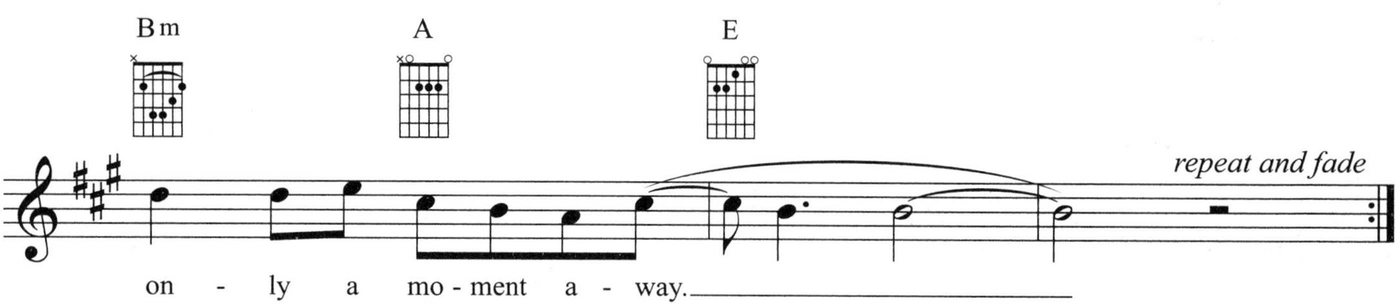

2. I just can't believe it's so,
and though it seems strange to say,
I never been laid so low
In such a mysterious way.
And the course of a lifetime runs
Over and over again.

A Most Peculiar Man

Words and Music by Paul Simon

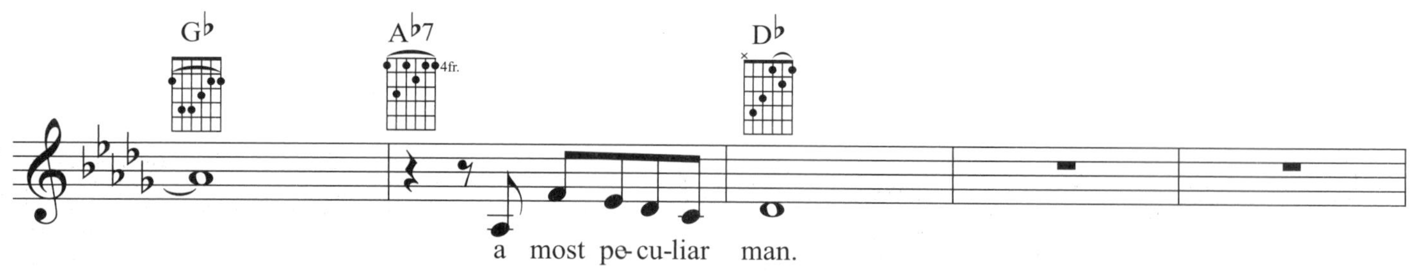

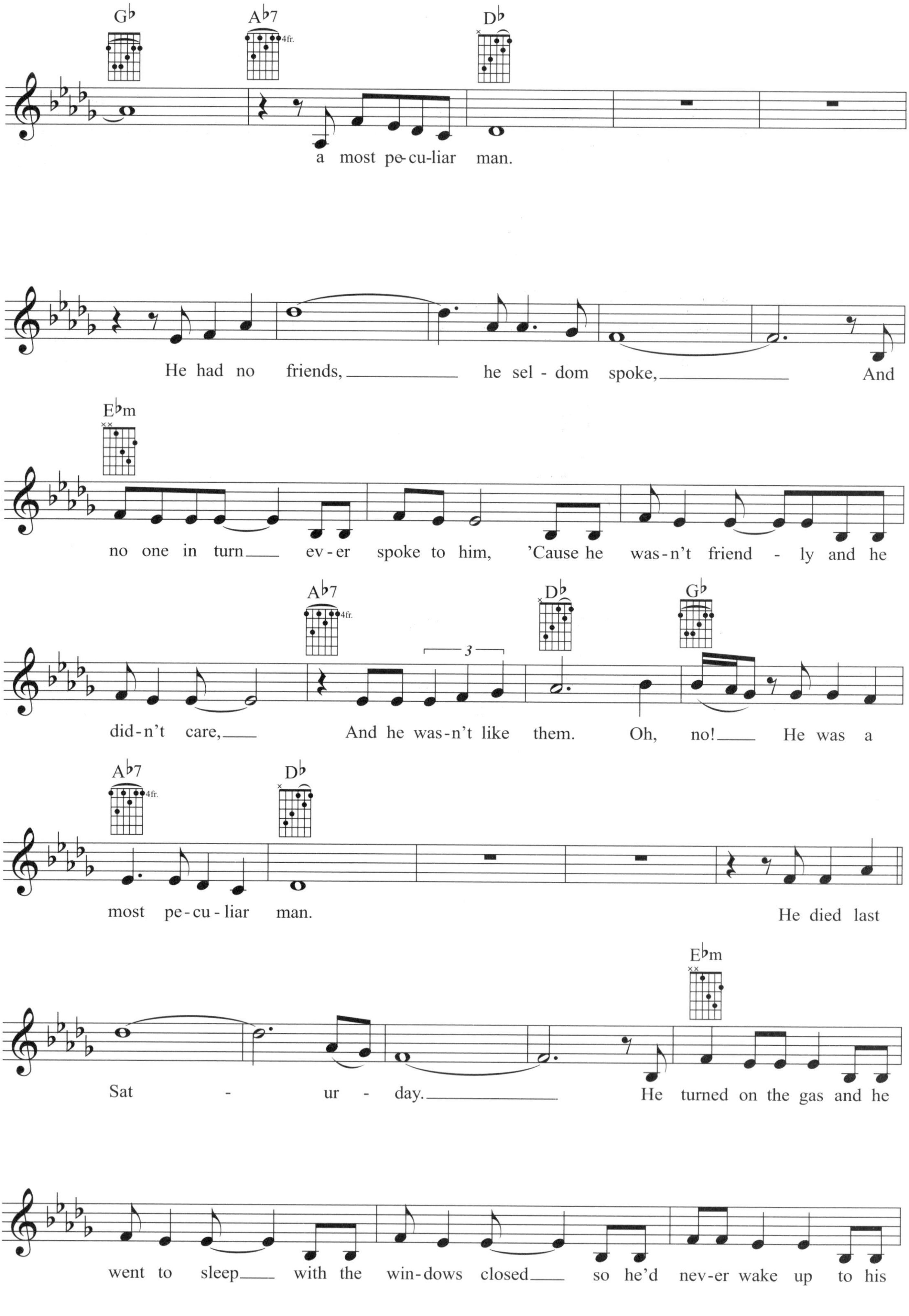

He had no friends, he sel - dom spoke, And

E♭m

no one in turn ev - er spoke to him, 'Cause he was - n't friend - ly and he

A♭7 4fr. D♭ G♭

3

did - n't care, And he was - n't like them. Oh, no! He was a

A♭7 4fr. D♭

most pe - cu - liar man. He died last

E♭m

Sat - ur - day. He turned on the gas and he

si - lent world and his ti - ny room; And Mis - sus Rior - don says he has a
A♭7
D♭
broth - er some - where Who should be no - ti - fied soon.
G♭
A♭7
D♭
And all the peo - ple said, "What a shame that he's
B♭m
G♭
A♭7
D♭
dead, But was - n't he a most pe - cu - liar man?"
4fr.

Night Game

Words and Music by Paul Simon

Bm7♭5
E
Am
F
num - ber was left on the ground Then the night turned
Am
B♭maj7
Gm
3fr.
cold Cold - er than the moon The stars were white as
Dm
Bmaj7
E
bones The sta - di - um was old Old - er than the
A7
D
A7
screams Old - er than the teams There were three men
Dmaj7
G
D7
G
E7
Bm
down And the sea - son lost And the tar - pau-lin was
Em6
B♭maj7
D
A7
Dmaj7
rolled Up - on the win - ter frost.

G D7/A G E7 F♯m Bm7 Bm7♭5 B°7
(instrumental solo)
Am F Am B♭maj7 Gm Dm
3fr.
Bmaj7 E A7
There were
D A7 Dmaj7 G D7 G E7 Bm
three men down And the sea - son lost And the tar-pau-lin was
Em6 B♭maj7 D A7/E Dmaj7
rolled Up - on the win - ter frost.
G D7/A G D7/A G D Em A D
rit.

Mrs. Robinson

Words and Music by Paul Simon

A
F♯m
A
And here's to you Mrs. Rob - in - son,
Je - sus loves you more
F♯m
D
E7
than you will know,
Whoa, whoa, whoa.
A
F♯m
A
God bless you, please, Mrs. Rob - in - son,
Heav-en holds a place
F♯m
D
Bm
for those who pray,
Hey, hey, hey.
F♯
to Coda
Hey, hey, hey.
F♯7
1.We'd like to know a lit - tle bit a - bout you for our files.

B7
We'd like to help you learn to help your - self.
E7
A
D
Bm
Look a-round you, all you see are sym-pa-thet - ic eyes,
F♯
E7
D.S. al Coda
Stroll a - round the grounds un - til you feel at home. And here's to you
Coda
F♯7
2.Hide it in a hid - ing place where no one ev - er goes,
B7
Put it in your pan - try with your cup - cakes.
E7
A
D
Bm
It's a lit - tle se - cret, just the Rob - in - son's af - fair.

F♯
E7
Most of all, you've got to hide it from the kids.
A
F♯m
Coo, coo, ca-choo, Mrs. Rob - in - son,
A
F♯m
D
Je - sus loves you more than you will know,
E7
A
Whoa, whoa, whoa. God bless you, please, Mrs. Rob -
F♯m
A
F♯m
D
- in - son, Heav - en holds a place for those who pray.
Bm
Hey, hey, hey. Hey, hey, hey.

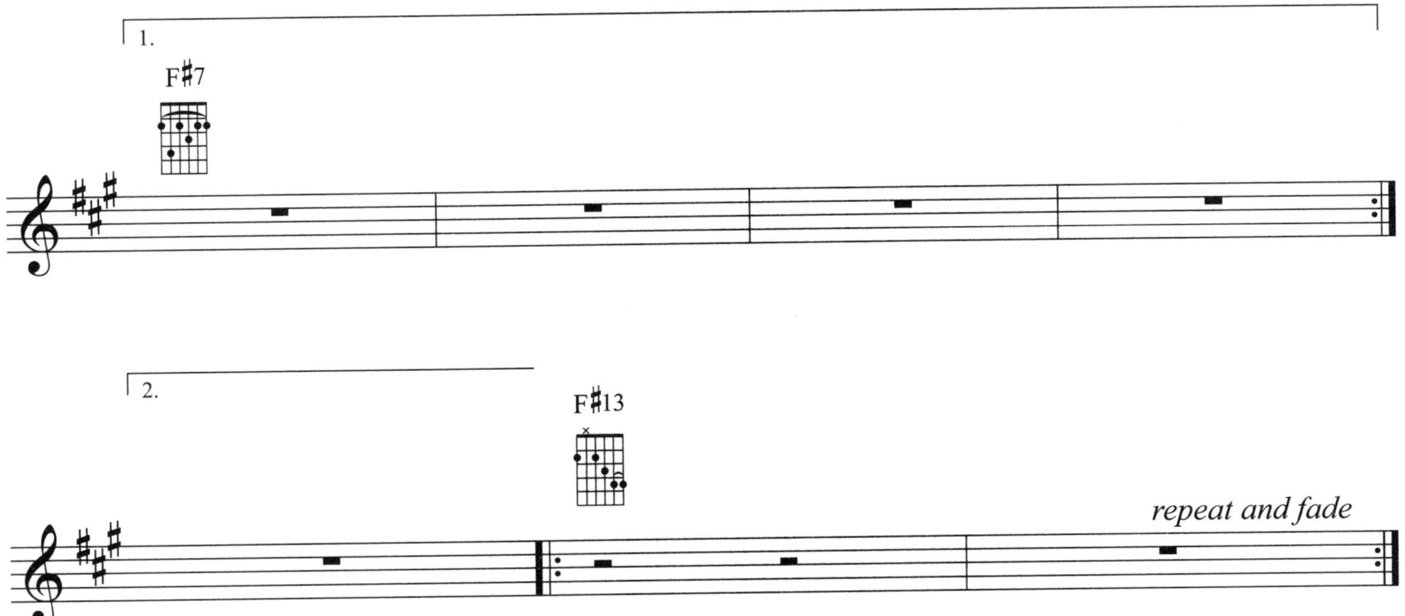

3. Sitting on a sofa on a Sunday afternoon,
Going to the candidates' debate,
Laugh about it,
Shout about it,
When you've got to choose,
Every way you look at it you lose.

Where have you gone, Joe DiMaggio?
A nation turns its lonely eyes to you.
Woo, woo, woo.
What's that you say, Mrs. Robinson?
"Joltin' Joe has left and gone away."
Hey, hey, hey. Hey, hey, hey.

My Little Town

Words and Music by Paul Simon

A/G♯
F♯m
Am6
Com- ing home af - ter school;
rid - ing my bike
D9
4fr.
G
E7
F
past the gates of the fac - to - ries;
B♭
F
F+
3
my mom doing the laun - dry,
hang - ing our
A/C♯
D
shirts in the dirt - y breeze.
And af - ter it
G
D
3
3
rains there's a rain - bow, and all of the col - ors are black.
It's
Em
D
G
3
3
not that the col - ors aren't there; it's just i - mag - i - na -

Dmaj7
E
Em7
3
tion they lack. Ev - 'ry-thing's the same back
A
D
G
D
G
in my lit-tle town.
Bm
A
D
G
D
G
D
C♯m7♭5
4fr.
Bm
Noth-ing but the dead and dy - ing back in my lit-tle town
D
C♯m7♭5
4fr.
Bm
noth-ing but the dead and dy - ing back in my lit-tle
A
F♯m
town.
In my lit-tle town

Am6
D9
4fr.
G
I nev-er meant noth - ing; I was just my fa - ther's son,
E7
F
B♭
F
B♭
mm.
Sav-ing my mon-ey,
dream-ing of
F
B♭
F
glo - ry;
twitch-ing like a fin - ger on the
F+
A
D
trig - ger of a gun!
Leav-ing noth -
D
C♯m7♭5
4fr.
Bm
- ing but the dead and dy - ing back in my lit-tle town,
D
C♯m7♭5
4fr.
Bm
repeat and fade
noth-ing but the dead and dy - ing back in my lit-tle town.
Noth

Nobody

Words and Music by Paul Simon

A♭
G m7
F 9
A♭/B♭
4fr.
3fr.
Who kissed my eyes and saw the scream Lying there No-
E♭7
A♭
1.
E♭
bod - y
Who is my rea - son to be
2.
E♭
D♭9♯11
C m7
B♭
No - bod - y but you, girl
Mmm,
No -
C m7
E♭9
5fr.
bod-y but you
No - bod - y in this whole
A♭
G♭
C♭
D♭
E♭7
to Coda
wide
world
No - bod - y
A♭7
E♭7
A♭7
E♭
D.S. (second ending) al Coda
Who makes the bed that can't be

C♭
Coda
G♭
C♭
G♭
D♭
4fr.
world
No- bod-y, girl
Oh
B♭/D
E♭
3fr.
F m/A♭
4fr.
Gm/B♭
6fr.
Fm/C
3fr.
E♭
3fr.
No - bod-y.
(guitar solo)
F m/A♭
4fr.
G m/B♭
6fr.
F m/C
3fr.
E♭
3fr.
E♭9
5fr.
A♭
4fr.
G m7
3fr.
F 9
A♭/B♭
4fr.
E♭7
4fr.
A♭
4fr.
E♭
3fr.
D♭9
3fr.
C m7
3fr.
B♭
(end solo)
No no no no - bod-y but you, yes.
No
C m7
3fr.
E♭9
5fr.
one but you.
No - bod - y in this

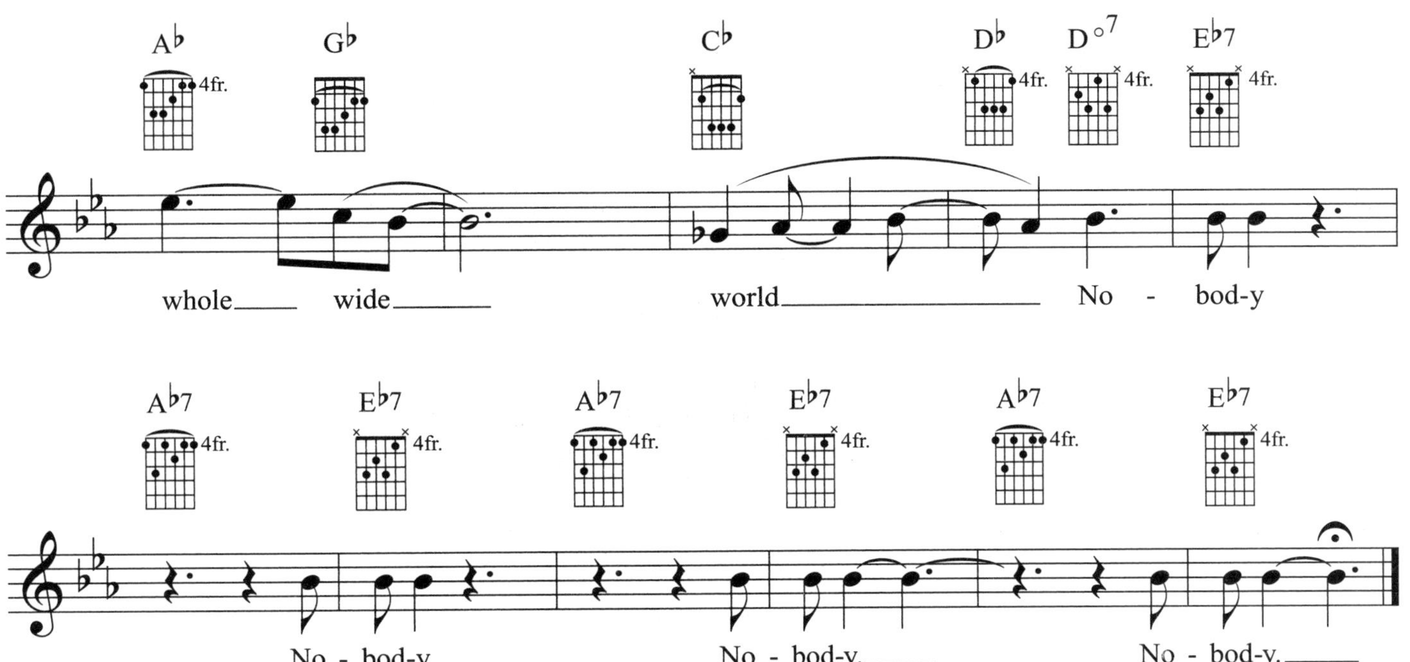

2. Who is my reason to begin
   Who plows the earth, who breaks the skin
   Who took my two hands and made them four
   Who is my heart, who is my door
   Nobody

   Nobody but you, girl
   Nobody but you
   Nobody in this whole wide world
   Nobody

3. Who makes the bed that can't be made
   Who is my mirror, who's my blade
   When I am rising like a flood
   Who feels the pounding in my blood
   Nobody

   Nobody but you
   Nobody but you
   Nobody in this whole wide world
   Nobody, girl
   Nobody

The Obvious Child

Words and Music by Paul Simon

Brightly, with a driving beat

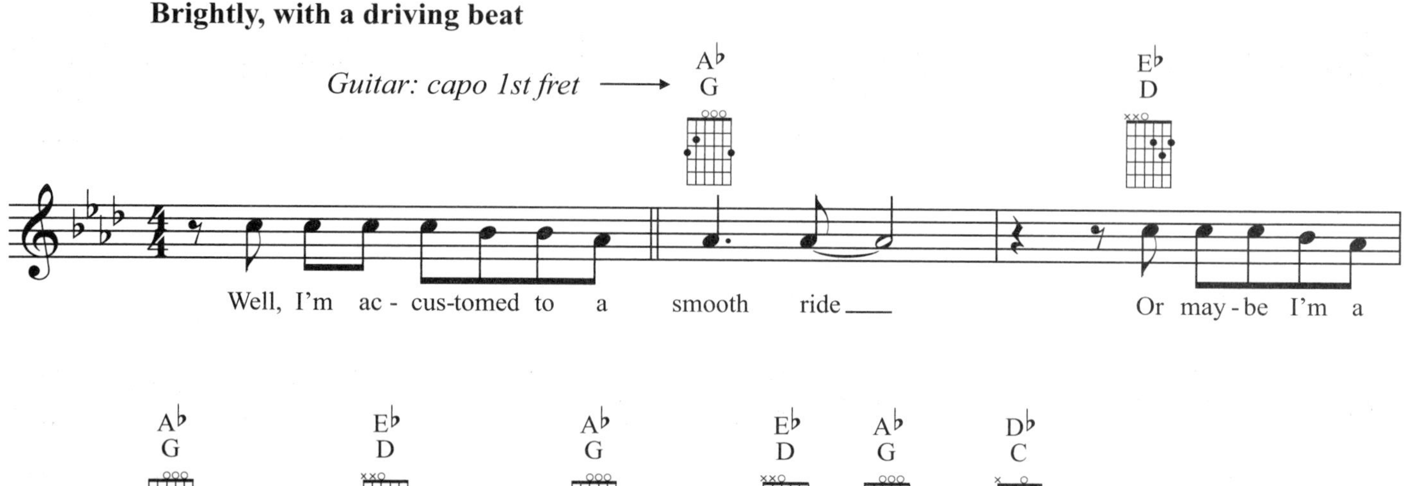

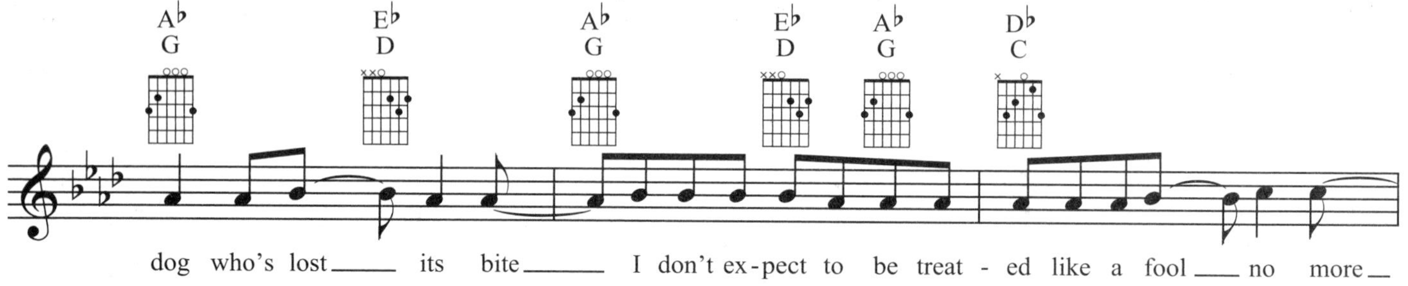

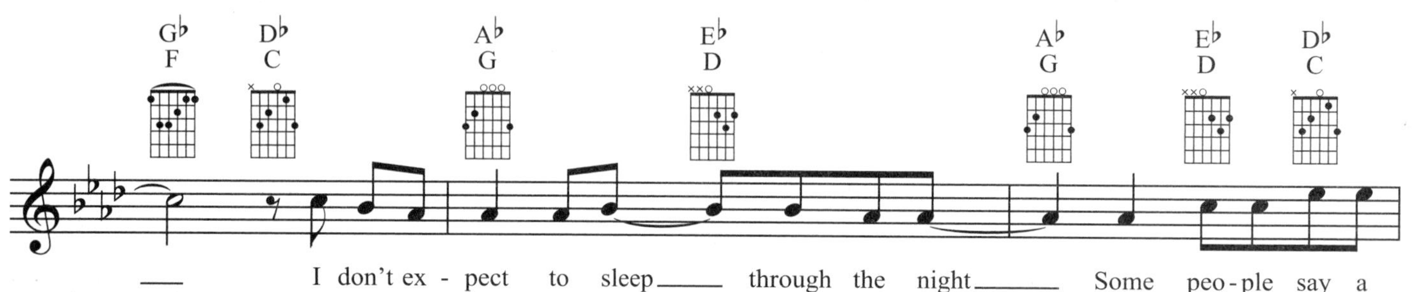

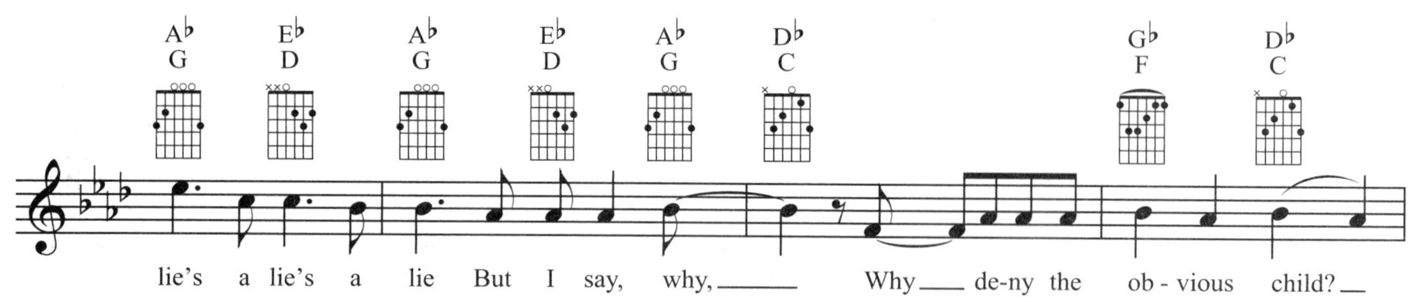

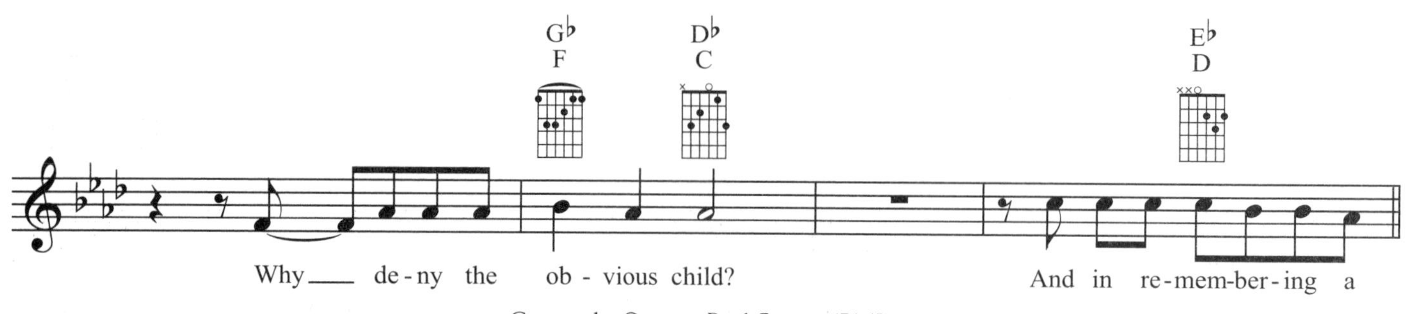

A♭ G
D♭ C
A♭ G
E♭ D
D♭ C
A♭ G
E♭ D
A♭ G
road sign I am re-mem-ber-ing a girl when I was young
D♭ C
G♭ F
D♭ C
A♭ G
E♭ D
And we said These songs are true
A♭ G
E♭ D
A♭ G
E♭ D
A♭ G
E♭ D
A♭ G
These days are ours These tears are free And hey
D♭ C
G♭ F
A♭ C
G♭ F
D♭ C
The cross is in the ball-park The cross is in the ball - park
E♭ D
D♭ C
We had a lot of fun We had a lot of mon-ey
A♭ G
E♭ D
D♭ C
We had a lit-tle son and we thought we'd call him Son-ny

E♭
D
A♭
G
D♭
C
E♭
D
Son-ny gets mar-ried and moves a-way
Son-ny has a ba-by and bills
A♭
G
D♭
C
E♭
D
A♭
G
D♭
C
E♭
D
to pay
Son-ny gets sun-ni-er Day by day by day by day
A♭
G
Doh doh
Doh doh
Doh doh
Doh doh
E♭
D
D♭
C
A♭
G
E♭
D
Well, I've been wak-ing up at sun-rise
I've been fol-low-ing the
A♭
G
E♭
D
A♭
G
E♭
D
A♭
G
D♭
C
G♭
F
D♭
C
light a-cross my room I watch the night re-ceive the room of my
A♭
G
E♭
D
A♭
G
E♭
D
D♭
C
A♭
G
E♭
D
A♭
G
E♭
D
A♭
G
day
Some peo-ple say the sky is just the sky
But I say

D♭ G♭ D♭ G♭ D♭ A♭
C F C F C G
Why de-ny the ob-vious child? Why de-ny the ob-vious child? (Mm,
D♭/A♭ A♭ D♭/A♭ A♭ D♭ A♭ E♭
C/G G C/G G C G D
mm, mm.) Son-ny sits by his win-dow and thinks
D♭ E♭ A♭ D♭ A♭ E♭ D♭
C D G C G D C
to him-self How it's strange that some rooms are like cag-es
E♭ A♭ D♭ A♭ E♭ D♭ E♭
D G C G D C D
Son-ny's year-book from high school Is down from the shelf And he
A♭ D♭ A♭ E♭ D♭ A♭ B♭m
G C G D C G Am
i-dly thumbs through the pag-es Some have died
A♭ D♭ A♭ E♭ A♭ E♭ A♭
G C G D G D G
Some have fled from them-selves Or strug-gled from here to get

E♭ D D♭ C A♭ G D♭ C A♭ G E♭ D
there Son-ny wan-ders be-yond his in-te-ri-or walls Runs his
A♭ G D♭ C A♭ G E♭ D D♭ C A♭ G E♭ D
hand through his thin-ning brown hair Well I'm ac-cus-tomed to a
A♭ G E♭ D B♭ A E♭ D
smooth-er ride Or may-be I'm a dog that's lost his bite
A♭ G E♭ D A♭ G D♭ C G♭ F D♭ C
I don't ex-pect to be treat-ed like a fool no more I don't ex-
A♭ G E♭ D A♭ G E♭ D D♭ C A♭ G E♭ D
pect to sleep the night Some peo-ple say a lie is just a lie
A♭ G E♭ D A♭ G E♭ C G♭ F D♭ C
But I say the cross is in the ball-park
G♭ F D♭ C
Why de-ny the ob-vious child?

Old

Words and Music by Paul Simon

Moderately fast

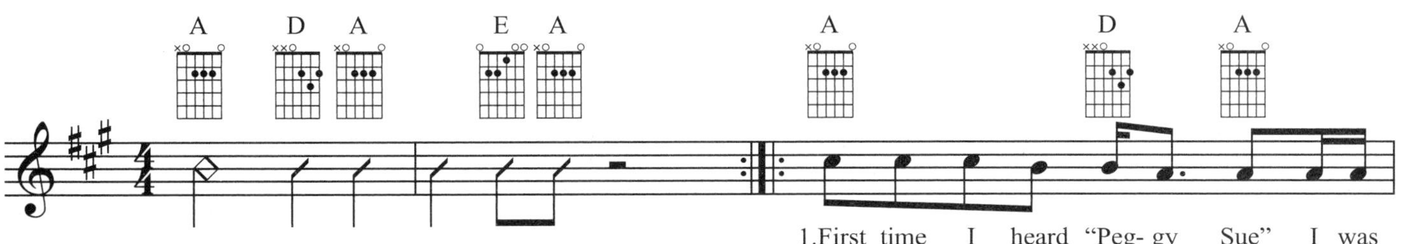

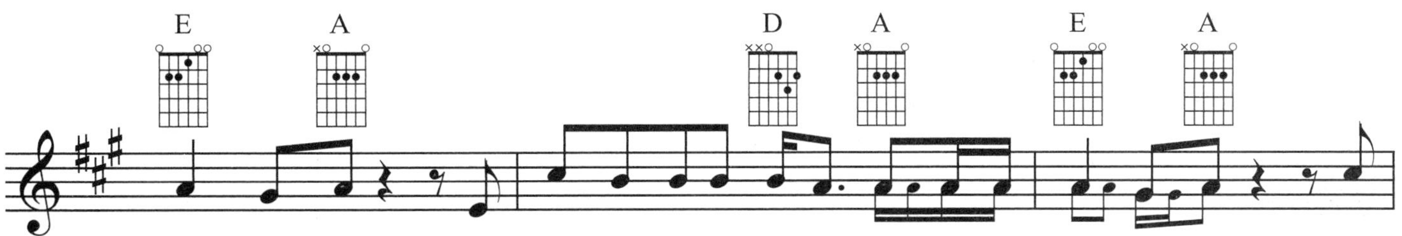

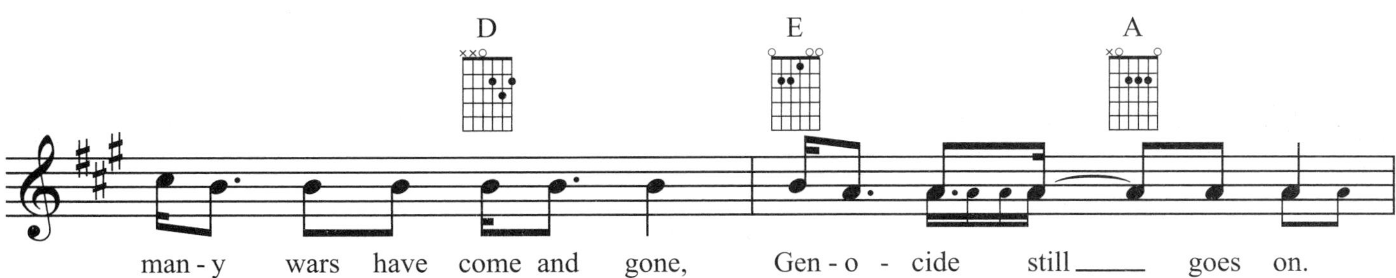

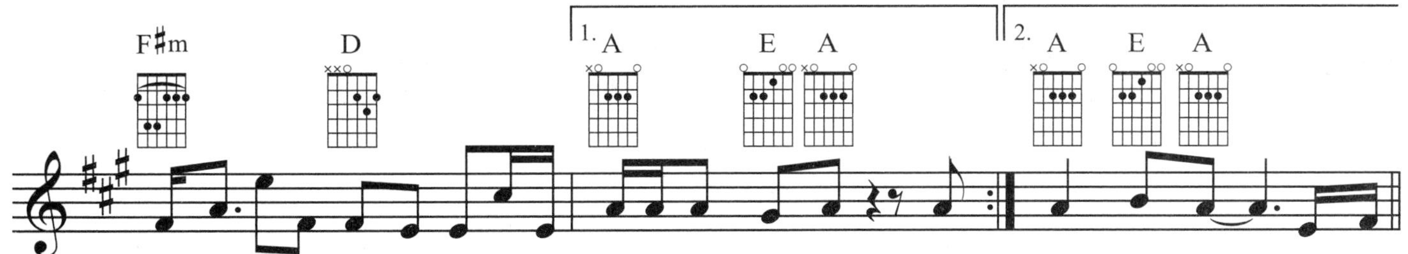

A D A A D A A D A D A D A
We
D A E A
cel - e - brate the birth of Je - sus on Christ-mas day, And
D A E A
Bud-dha found Nir - va - na a - long the Lo - tus Way. 'Bout
A D E A
fif - teen hun - dred years a - go the mes - sen - ger Mo - ham - med spoke And his
F♯m D A E A
wis - dom like a riv - er flowed Through hills of gold. Wis - dom is
D G C
old, The Ko - ran is old, The Bi - ble is old Great - est

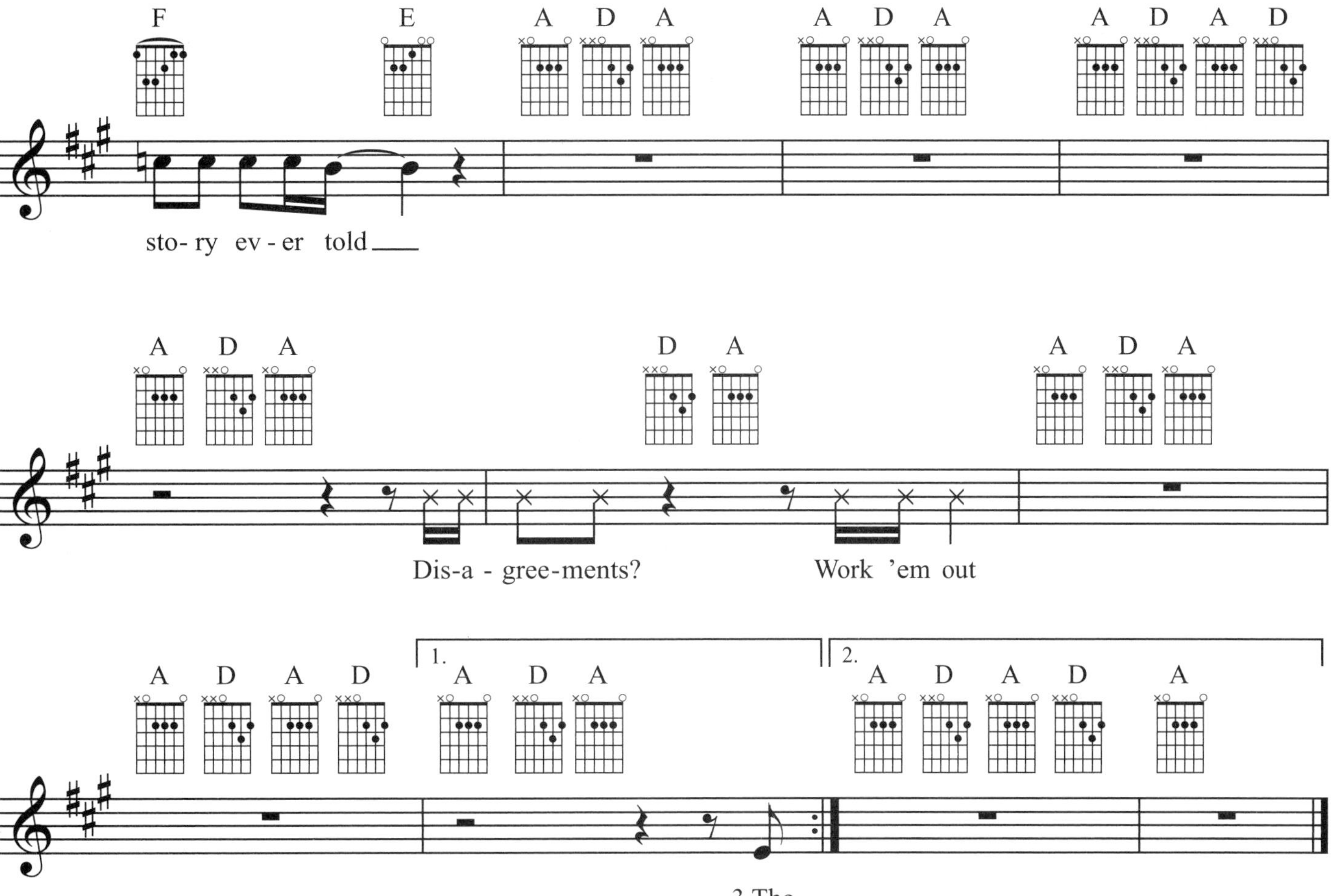

2. First time I smoked
guess what - paranoid.
First time I heard "Satisfaction"
I was young and unemployed.
Down the decades every year
Summer leaves and my birthday's here
And all my friends stand up and cheer
And say, "Man you're old."

3. The human race walked the Earth for 2.7 million
And we estimate the universe about 13-14 billion.
When all these numbers tumble into your imagination
Consider that the Lord was there before creation.
God is old,
We're not old.
God is old,
He made the mold.

Take your clothes off.
Adam and Eve.

Oh, Marion

Words and Music by Paul Simon

G♯m
G♯m/F♯
G♯m/F
E13
D♯7
The
(instrumental on D.S.)
boy's got a heart But it beats on the op-po-site side
It's a strange phe-nom-e-non The laws of na-ture de-fied
A♯○7
B
A
E
He said "It's a chance I had to take
So I shift - ed my heart for its safe - ty's sake"
D
D.S. al Coda
The boy's got a heart but it beats on His op-po-site
(end instrumental)

A♭
A♭/G
A♭/G♭
F m7
Oh, Mar - i - on, I think I'm in trou - ble here
A°7
B♭m7
B♭m7♭5
I should - 've be - lieved you When I heard you say -
E♭7
F m7
F♯°7
G m7
A♭
- ing it The on - ly time
C m7
D♭m7
B♭m7♭5
That love is an ea - sy game Is when two
B
F♯7
G°7
G♯m
G♯m/F♯
oth - er peo - ple Are play - ing it
G♯m/F
E 13
G♯m
G♯m/F♯
E 13
D♯7
to Coda
2.The

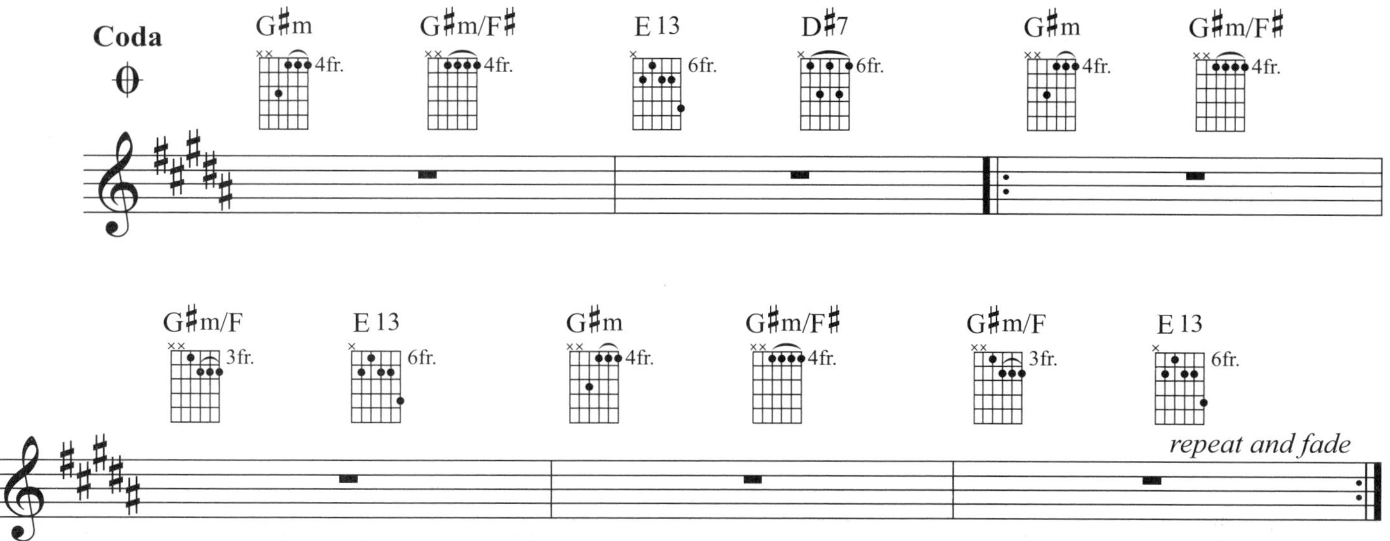

2. The boy's got a voice
But the voice is his natural disguise
Yes the boy's got a voice
But his words don't connect to his eyes
He says "Oh, but when I sing
I can hear the truth auditioning"
The boy's got a voice
but the voice is natural

Old Friends

Words and Music by Paul Simon

G♯m7 C♯m B A
Sift-ing through trees, set-tle like dust On the shoul-ders Of the
E6 F♯m7 B7 Emaj7
Old Friends. Can you i-mag-ine us Years from to-day,
A Am E F♯m7 B7 C♯m
Shar-ing a park bench qui-et-ly? How ter-ri-bly strange To be sev-en-ty.
Amaj7 Emaj7 F♯m7 B7 Amaj7 G♯m7 F♯m7 B7
Old Friends, mem-o-ry brush-es the same years. Si-lent-ly shar-ing the
E7 C♯m Amaj7 Emaj7 Amaj7 Emaj7 Amaj7 Emaj7
same fear...

One Man's Ceiling Is Another Man's Floor

Words and Music by Paul Simon

Moderately slow

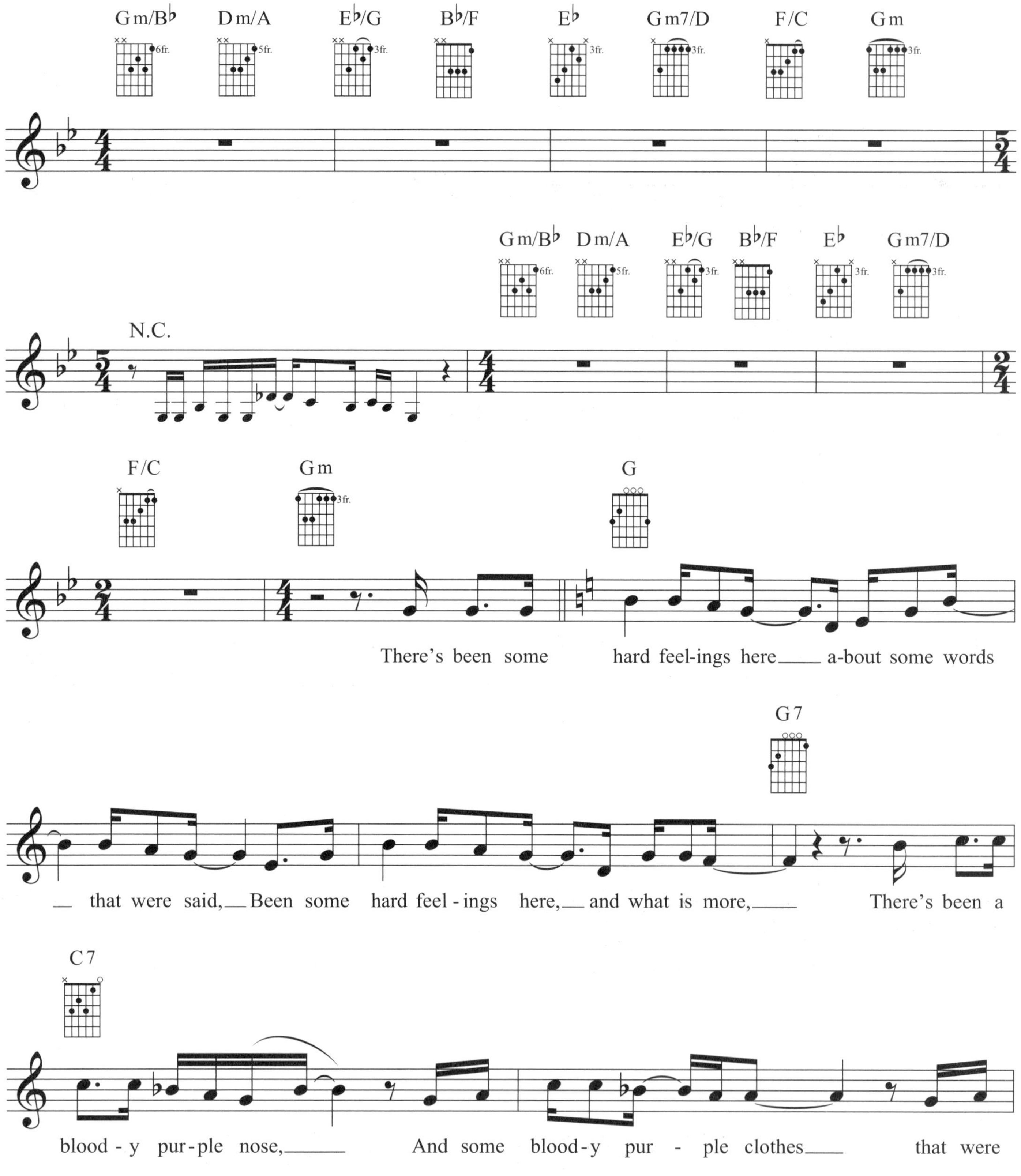

Gm/B♭ Dm/A E♭/G B♭/F E♭ Gm7/D F/C Gm

N.C. Gm/B♭ Dm/A E♭/G B♭/F E♭ Gm7/D

F/C Gm G

There's been some hard feel-ings here a-bout some words

G7

that were said, Been some hard feel-ings here, and what is more, There's been a

C7

blood-y pur-ple nose, And some blood-y pur-ple clothes that were

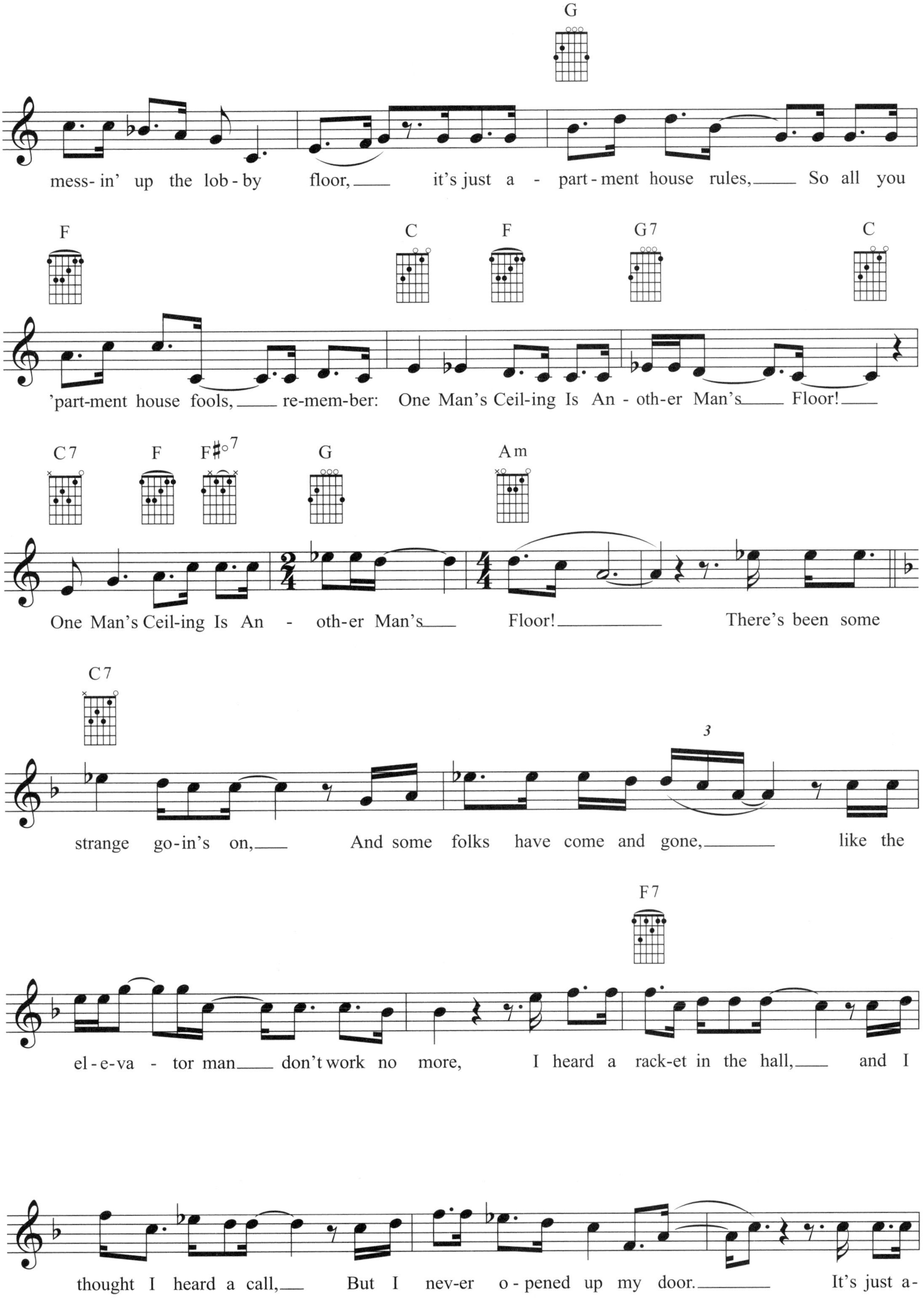

G
mess-in' up the lob-by floor, it's just a - part-ment house rules, So all you
F C F G7 C
'part-ment house fools, re-mem-ber: One Man's Ceil-ing Is An - oth-er Man's Floor!
C7 F F♯○7 G Am
One Man's Ceil-ing Is An - oth-er Man's Floor! There's been some
C7
3
strange go-in's on, And some folks have come and gone, like the
F7
el-e-va - tor man don't work no more, I heard a rack-et in the hall, and I
thought I heard a call, But I nev-er o-pened up my door. It's just a-

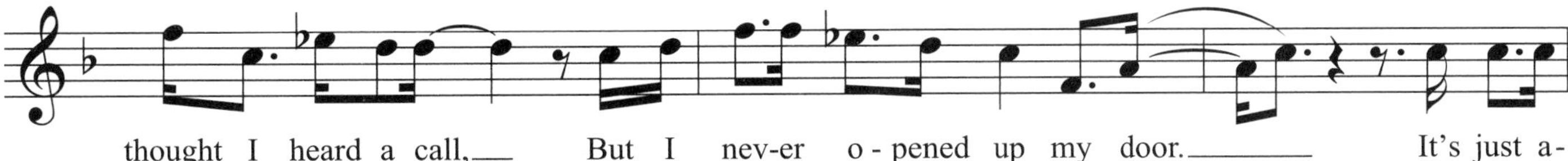

C
B♭
part - ment house sense, It's like a - part - ment house rents, re - mem - ber:
F
B♭
B°7
C7
F
One Man's Ceil - ing is An - oth - er Man's Floor!
F7
B♭
B°7
C
Dm
One Man's Ceil - ing Is An - oth - er Man's Floor!
Dm
A7
Dm
Gm7
There's an al - ley in the back of my build - ing where some
Dm
A7
Dm
A
Dm
A7
peo-ple con-gre - gate in shame. I was walk-ing with my dog, and the
Dm
G
F
A7
Dm
night was black with smog, When I thought I heard some-bod-y call my name.

F7
B♭7
(instrumental)
F
E♭
B♭
E♭
E°7
Ah. Re-mem - ber: One Man's Ceil - ing Is An-
F7
B♭
E♭
E°7
F
oth-er Man's Floor! One Man's Ceil-ing Is An - oth-er man's
Gm
Gm/B♭
Dm/A
E♭/G
B♭/F
floor!
E♭
Gm7/D
F/C
Gm
repeat and fade

Paranoia Blues

Words and Music by Paul Simon

Moderate country blues, with a beat

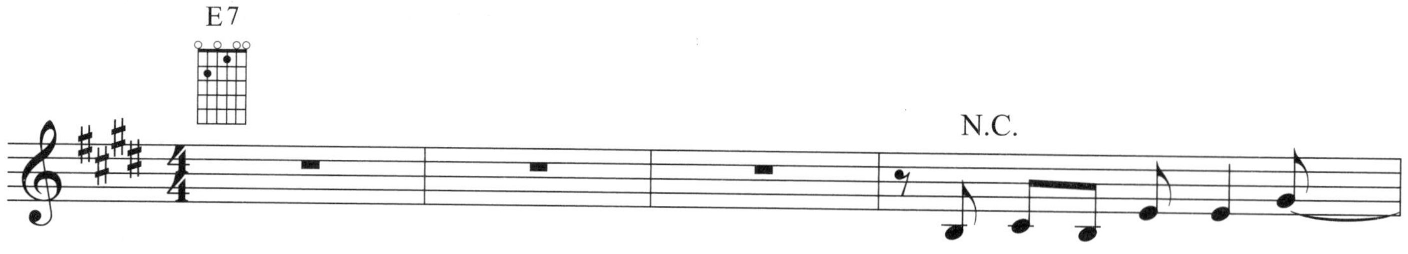

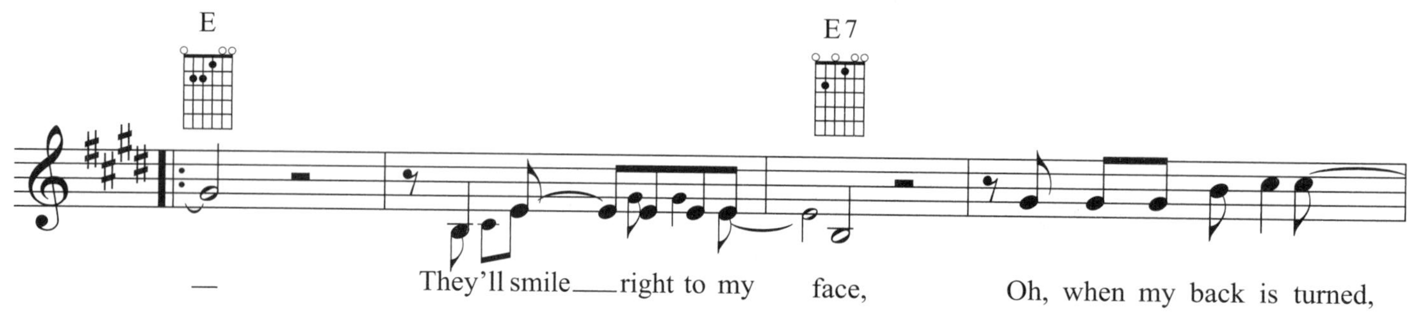

2.
F♯7 B7 E A
are you on? Whose side are you on? I got the Par-a-noi-a blues from
E
knock-in' a-round in New York Cit - y, Where they
A E
roll you for a nick-el, and they stick you for the ex-tra dime. An -
A E
- y way you choose, you're bound to lose in New York Cit - y, Oh,
A B7 E A B7
I just got out in the nick of time. Well, I just got out in the nick of time.
E N.C. E
Once I was down in Chi-na town, I was eat-in' some Lin's chow fun,
E7 A
I hap-pened to turn a - round,

Oh, no, no. There's

A E F♯7 B7

on-ly one thing I need to know: Whose side are you on? Whose side are you on?

E

Well, there's on - ly one thing I need

A F♯7 B7 E

to know: Whose side, whose side, whose side?

A E

repeat and fade

2. I fly into J.F.K.
My heart goes boom boom boom.
I know that customs man,
He's going to take me to that little room.
Oh, no, no. Oh, no, no.
There's only one thing I need to know:
Whose side are you on? Whose side are you on?

One-Trick Pony

Words and Music by Paul Simon

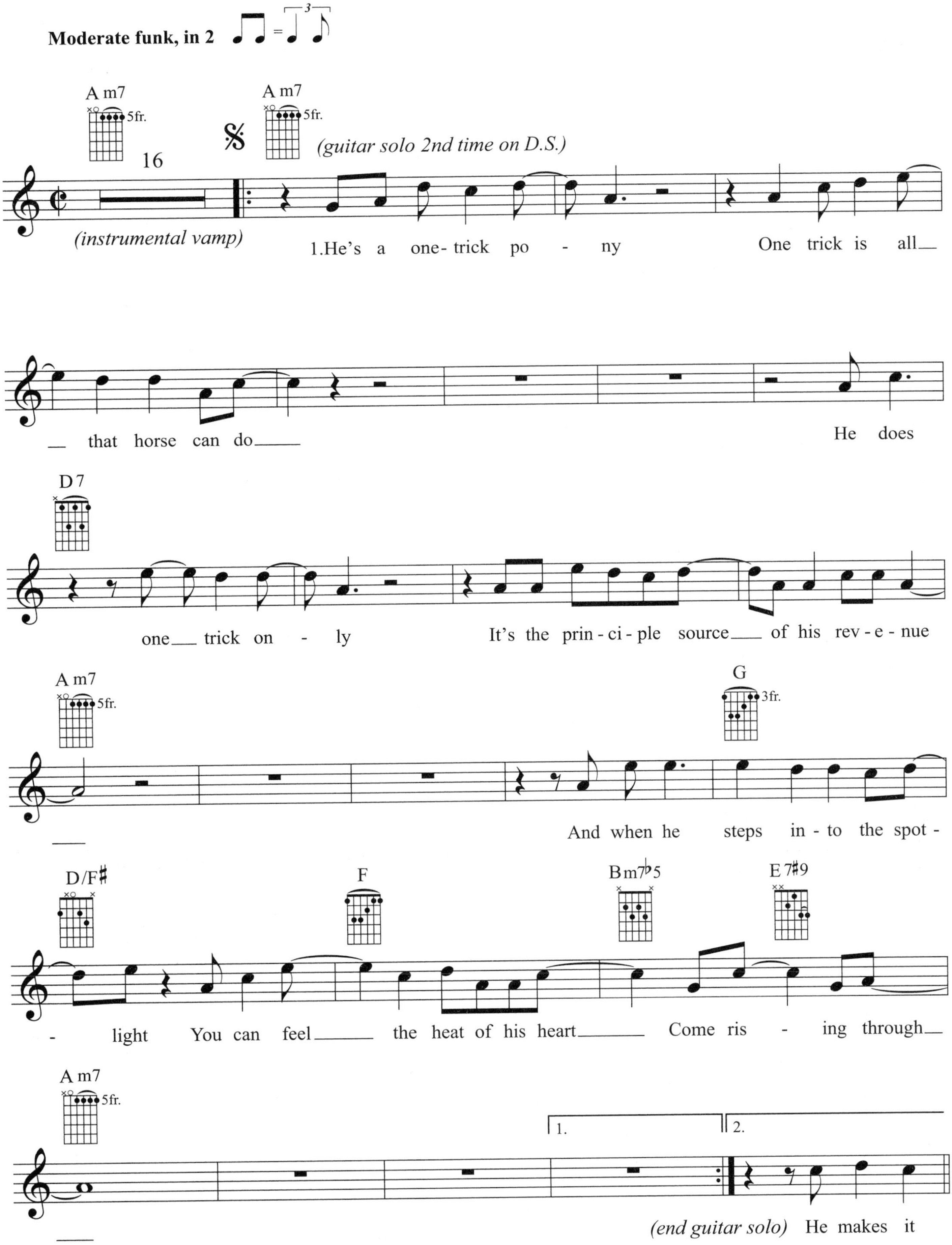

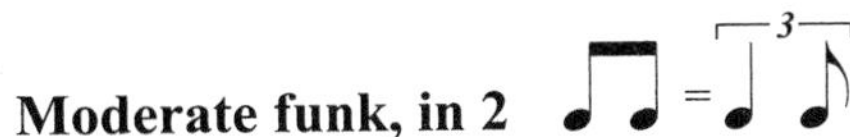

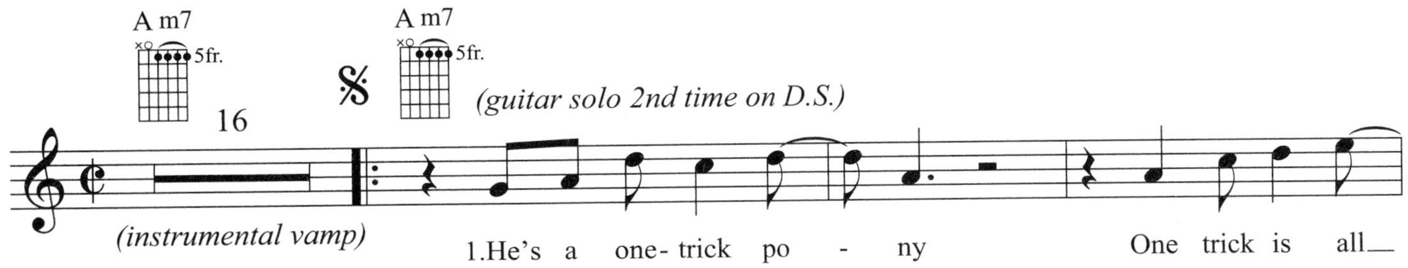

Moderate funk, in 2
Am7
5fr.
16
(instrumental vamp)
Am7
5fr.
(guitar solo 2nd time on D.S.)
1.He's a one-trick po - ny One trick is all
that horse can do
He does
D7
one trick on - ly It's the prin-ci-ple source of his rev-e-nue
Am7
5fr.
G
3fr.
And when he steps in-to the spot-
D/F♯
F
Bm7♭5
E7♯9
- light You can feel the heat of his heart Come ris - ing through
Am7
5fr.
1.
2.
(end guitar solo) He makes it

C
C 9
look so eas - y
He looks so clean
F
F♯○7
He moves like God's Im - mac - u - late ma - chine
C/G
E/G♯
He makes me think a - bout All these ex - tra moves I
A m
to Coda
make And all this herk - y - jerk - y mo - tion And the bag
C/B♭
5fr.
F
of tricks it takes To get me through my work - ing day
B♭9♯11
A m7
5fr.
D.S. al Coda (with repeats)
play three times
One-trick po - ny.
(guitar solo)

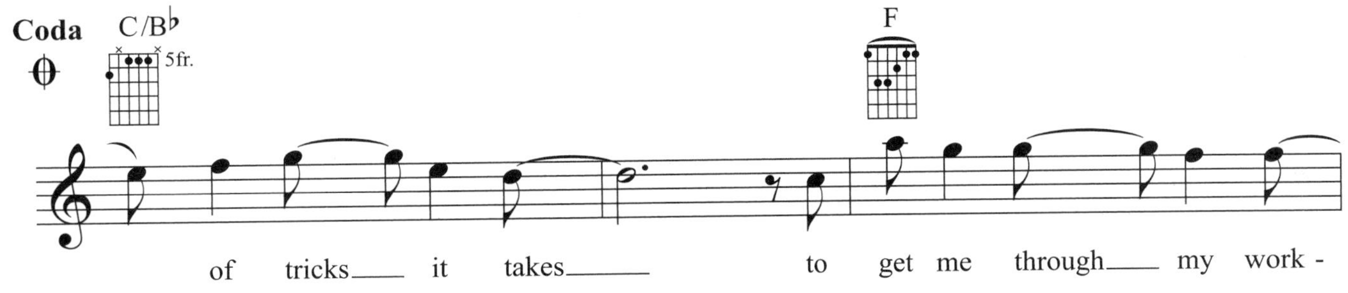

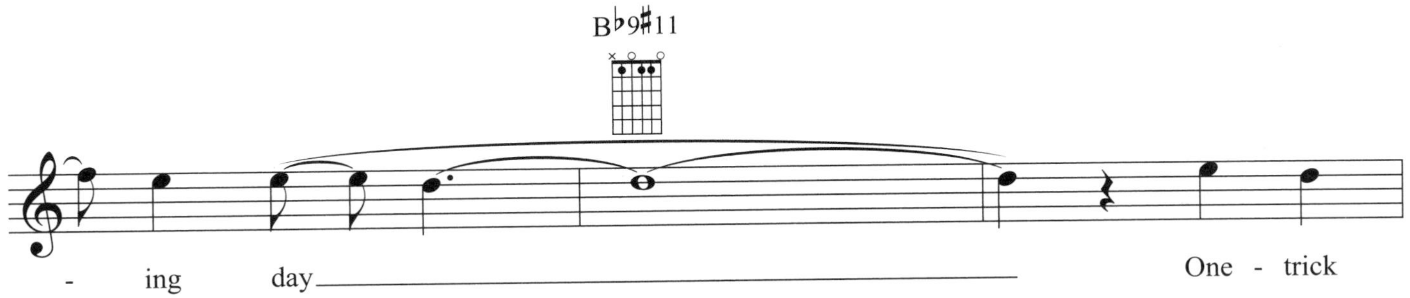

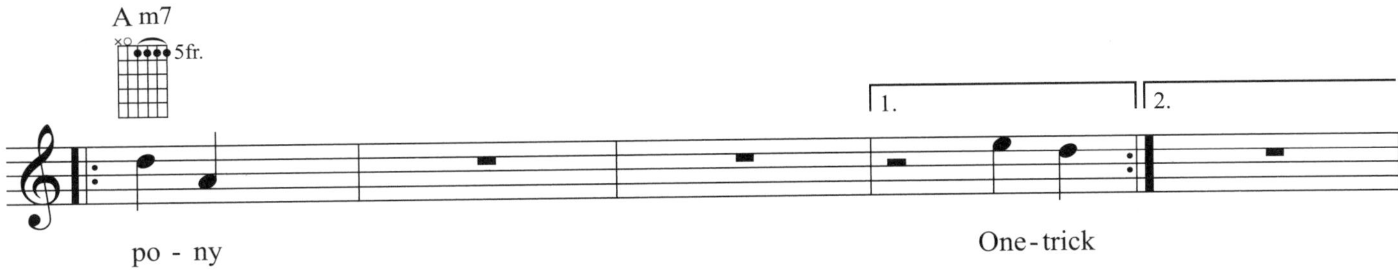

2. See how he dances
   See how he loops from side to side
   See how he prances
   The way his hooves just seem to glide
   He's just a one-trick pony (that's all he is)
   But he turns that trick with pride

3. He's a one-trick pony
   He either fails or he succeeds
   He gives his testimony
   Then he relaxes in the weeds
   He's got one trick to last a lifetime
   But that's all a pony needs
   (that's all he needs)

The Only Living Boy In New York

Words and Music by Paul Simon

Moderate, not too fast

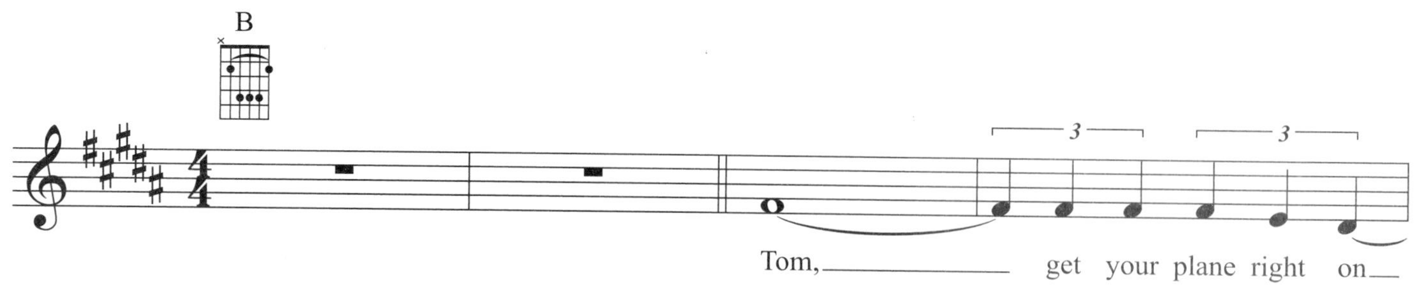

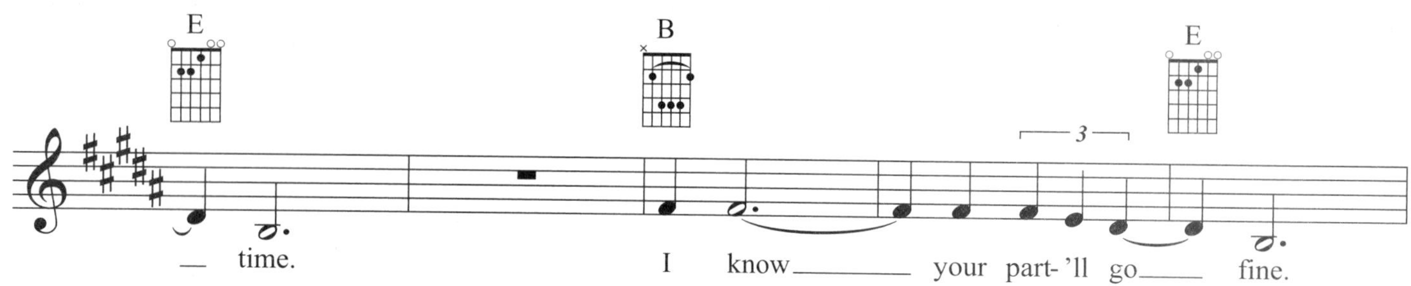

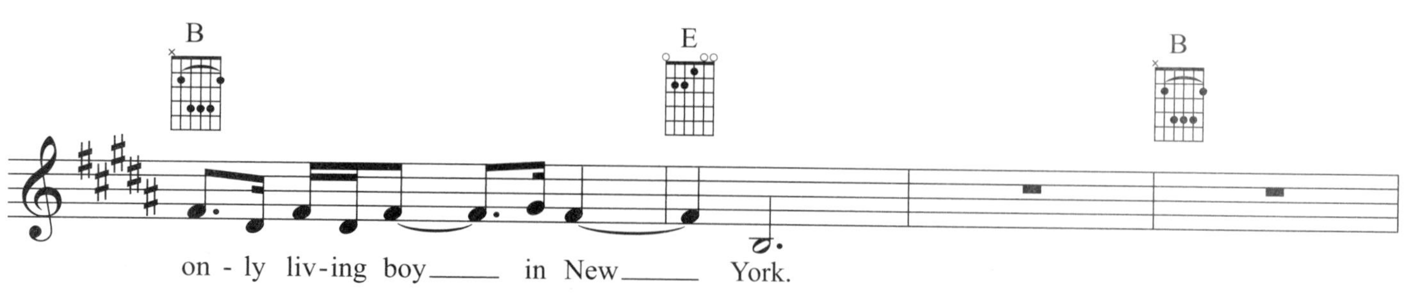

E
I get the news I need from the weath-er re-port.
B
E
I can gath-er all the news I need from the weath-er re-port.
B
E
E/D♯
C♯m7
C♯m7/B
Hey, I've got noth-ing to do to-day but smile.
F♯
E
Da-n-da-da-n-do-da-n-do-n here I am, The
B
E
G♯7
C♯m
on-ly liv-ing boy in New York.
Half of the time we're gone
F♯7
B
E
but we don't know where, And we don't know where.

B
E
Ah.
Ah.
B
E
B
Ah.
E
E/D♯
6fr.
C♯m7
4fr.
C♯m7/B
4fr.
F♯
Emaj7
Here I
B
E
G♯7
4fr.
C♯m
4fr.
am.
Half of the time we're gone
F♯7
B
E
but we don't know where, And we don't know where.
B
E
3
3
Tom, get your plane right on time.

B
E
I know that you've been ea-ger to fly now.
B
E
E/D♯
C♯m7
C♯m7
Hey let your hon-es-ty shine, shine, shine now,
F♯
Emaj7
E
do-da-n-do - da-n-do - da-n-do like it shines on me. The
B
E
on - ly liv-ing boy in New York. The
B
E
B
on-ly liv-ing boy in New York.
E
G♯7
C♯m
F♯7
B
E

A Poem On The Underground Wall

Words and Music by Paul Simon

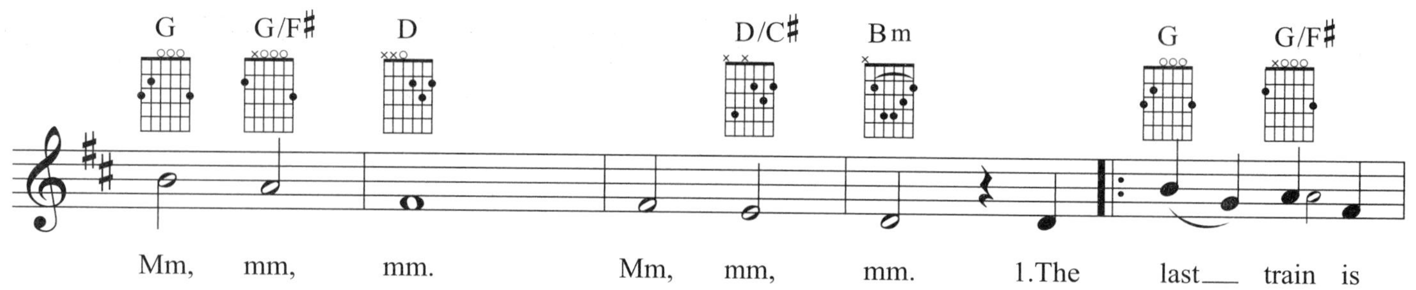

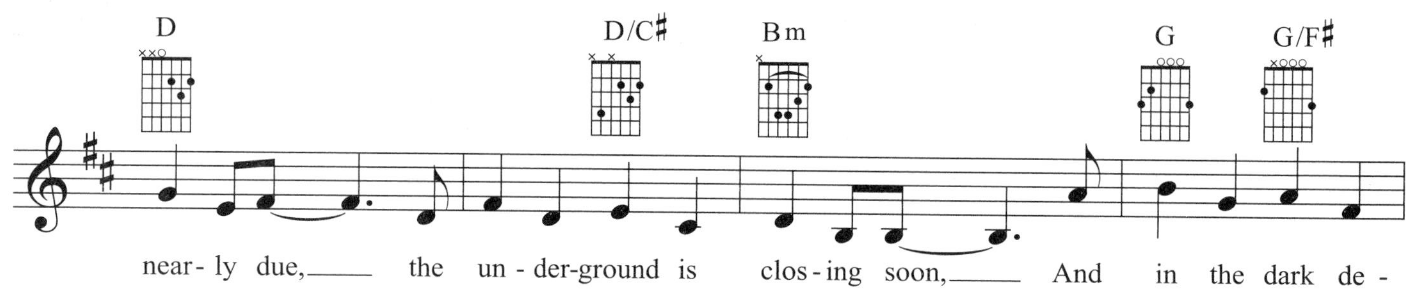

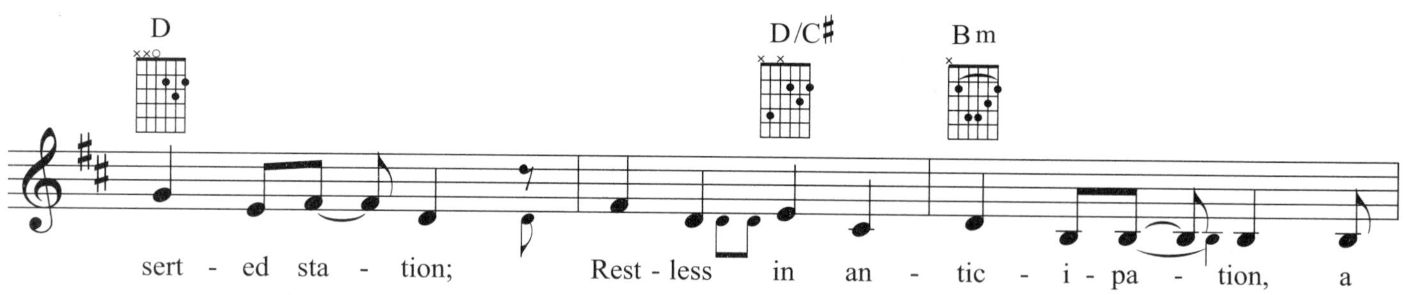

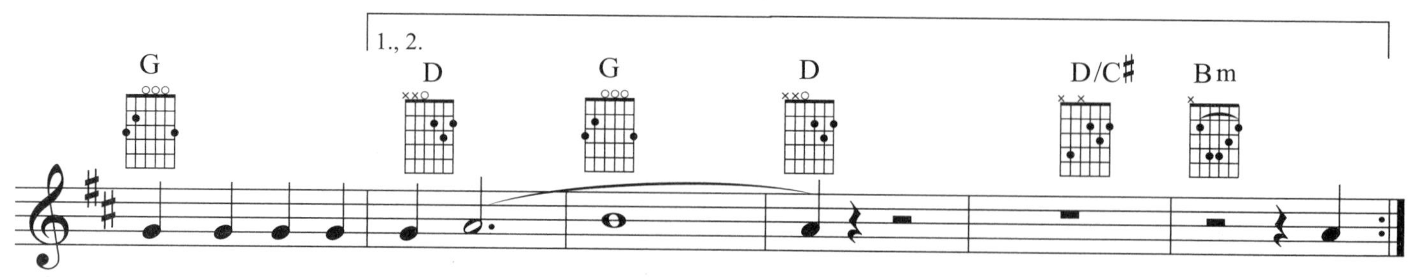

3.
D
Bm
shad - ows.
And the
Bm
train is gone sud - den - ly
on
A
wheels click - ing si - lent - ly
like a
G
Em
gen - tly tap - ping lit - a - ny,
And he
Bm
Em
G
holds his cray - on ro - sa - ry
tight - er in his
D
Bm
hand.
4.Now

2. His restless eyes leap and snatch,
at all that they can touch or catch,
And hidden deep within his pocket,
Safe within its silent socket,
He holds a colored crayon.

3. Now from the tunnel's stony womb,
the carriage rides to meet the groom,
and opens wide the welcome doors,
But he hesitates, then withdraws
Deeper in the shadows.

4. Now from his pocket quick he flashes,
the crayon on the wall he slashes,
deep upon the advertising,
a single-worded poem comprising
four letters.

5. And his heart is laughing, screaming, pounding,
The poem across the tracks resounding,
Shadowed by the exit light,
His legs take their ascending flight
To seek the breast of darkness and be
suckled by the night.

Overs

Words and Music by Paul Simon

Dmaj7
F♯7
It hard-ly mat-ters, we sleep sep-'rate-ly
G
Gm6
Dmaj7
F♯m/C♯
Bm
D/A
And drop a smile pass-in' in the hall But there's
G
D/F♯
A/C♯
Bm
E7/G♯
D
Bm7
no laughs left 'Cause we laughed them all And we laughed them-
G69
D
Em/D
F♯m/D
Em/D
all in a ver-y short time.
D
Em/D
F♯m/D
Em/D
D
Bm
is tap-ping on my fore-head
E7/G♯
G69
D
Bm
E7/G♯
G69
Hang-ing from my mir-ror Rat-tl-ing the

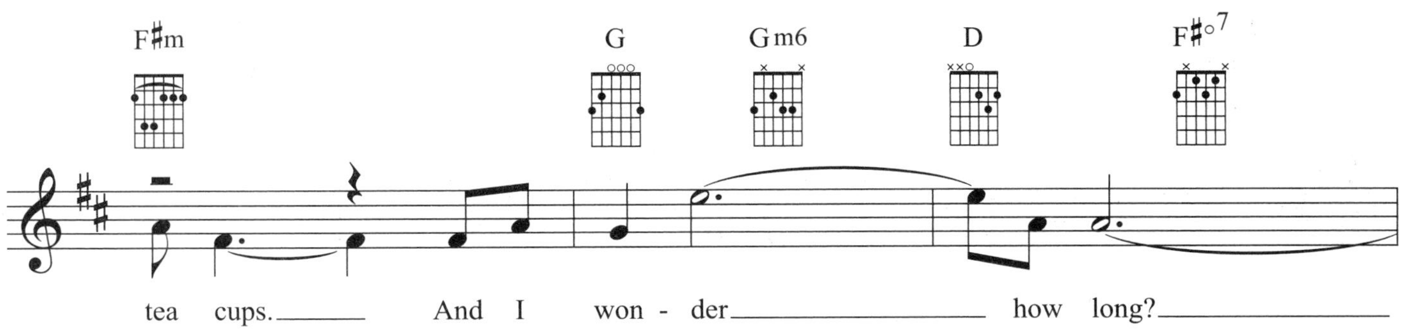
F♯m
G
Gm6
D
F♯°7
tea cups. And I won - der how long?

G
Gm6
Dmaj7
5fr.
Can I de - lay We're just a hab - it like sac - cha - rin

F♯7
G
Gm6
D
F♯m/C♯
Bm
D/A
3
And I'm ha - bit - u - al - ly feel - in' kind - a blue But

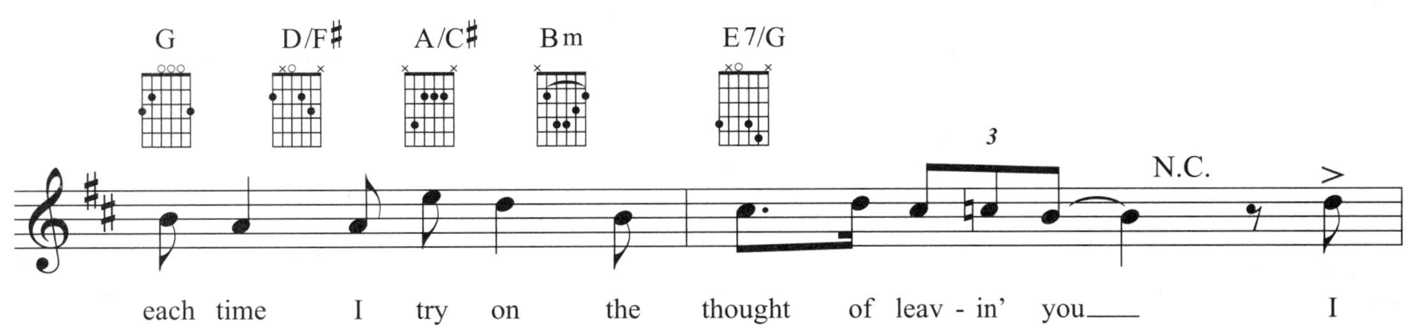
G
D/F♯
A/C♯
Bm
E7/G
3
N.C.
each time I try on the thought of leav - in' you I

stop! I stop and think it o - ver.

Papa Hobo

Words and Music by Paul Simon

G
G7
C
C♯°7
G
dressed like a school-boy, but I feel like a clown, It's a nat-'ral re-
E
C
G
B♭°7
D7/A
action I learned in this bas - ket-ball town.
G
G7
Am
G
Am
G
Am
C
F
Sweep up, I been sweep-in' up the tips I've made.
C
G/B
Am
I'm liv-in' - on Ga-tor-ade,

Am/E
G7
Plan - nin' my get a - way.
C
C/G
C7
De - troit, De - troit got a hell of a
F
C
hock - ey team, Got a left - hand - ed way of
E7/B
Am
Am/G
D/F♯
mak - in' a man sign up on that au - to - mo - tive dream, oh
G
G7
C7
C♯7
D
yeah, oh yeah, Oh, Pa - pa, Pa - pa Ho -

G G7 F B♭7 A7 A♭7 G
6fr. 5fr. 4fr.
bo, could you slip me a ride? Well, it's
F D/F♯ G7 C7 F
just af - ter break - fast, I'm on the road and the weath - er - man lied.
Dm/A B♭ Am B♭ Am Gm
3fr.
Oo ah
F D/F♯ G7 C7 F
Ba da doo wee doo ba. Oo ah. Oo, Oo,
D/F♯ G7 C7 F
oo. Oo wee oo. Oo wee oo. Ya.

Patterns

Words and Music by Paul Simon

2. Up a narrow flight of stairs
In a narrow little room,
As I lie upon my bed
In the early evening gloom.
Impaled on my wall
My eyes can dimly see
The pattern of my life
And the puzzle that is me.

3. From the moment of my birth
To the instant of my death,
There are patterns I must follow
Just as I must breathe each breath.
Like a rat in a maze
The path before me lies,
And the pattern never alters
Until the rat dies.

4. And the pattern still remains
On the wall where darkness fell,
And it's fitting that it should,
For in darkness I must dwell.
Like the color of my skin,
Or the day that I grow old,
My life is made of patterns
That can scarcely be controlled.

Peace Like A River

Words and Music by Paul Simon

Moderately, with a steady beat

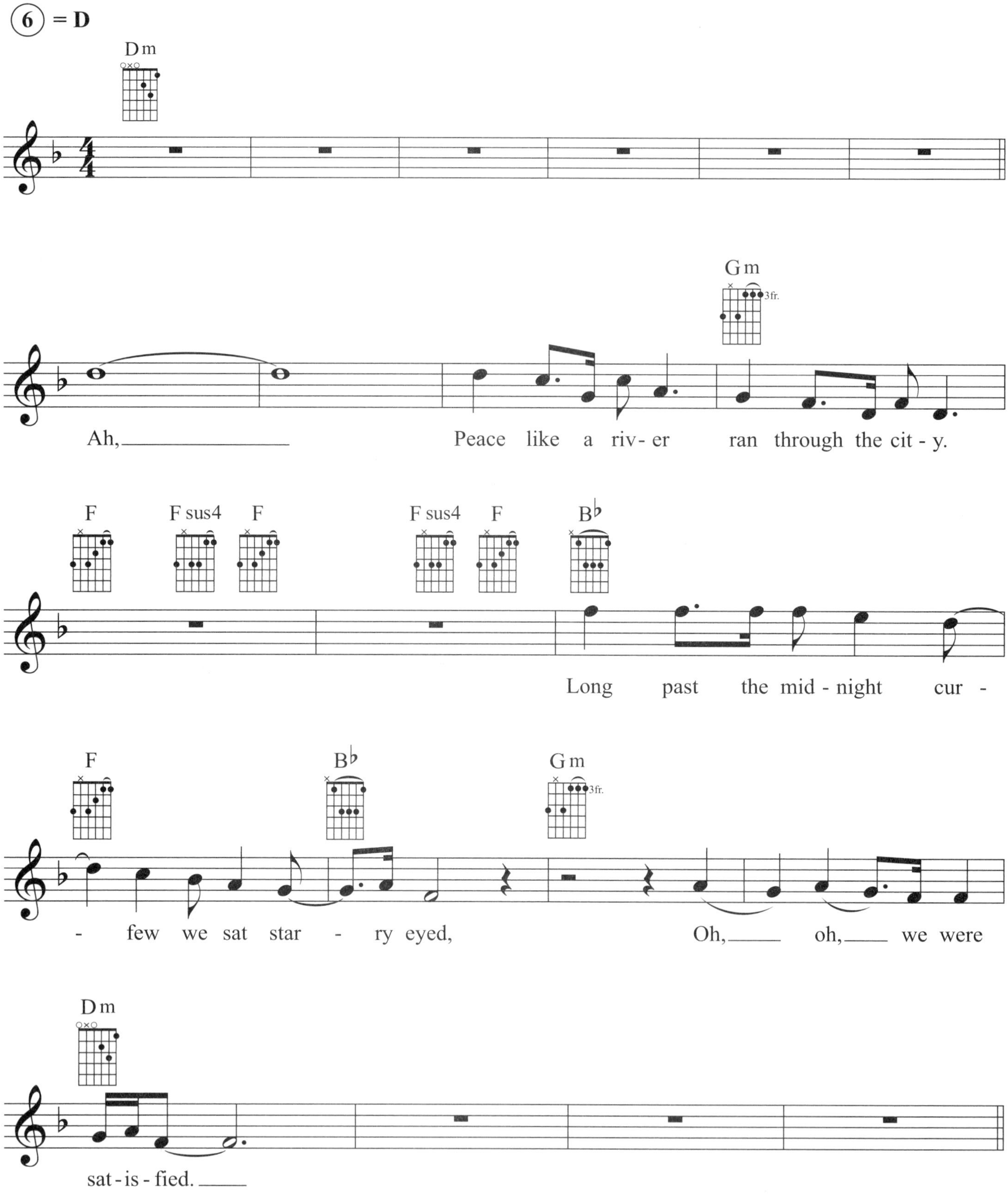

(6) = D

Dm

Gm

Ah, Peace like a riv - er ran through the cit - y.

F F sus4 F F sus4 F B♭

Long past the mid - night cur -

F B♭ Gm

- few we sat star - ry eyed, Oh, oh, we were

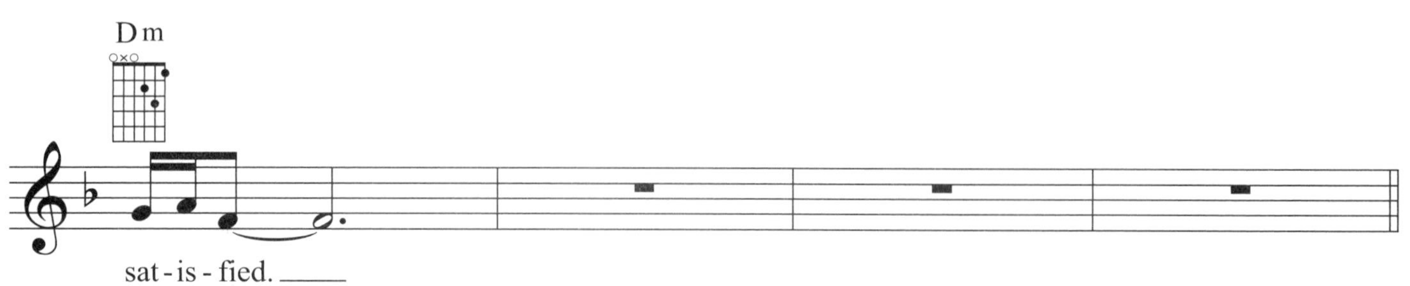

Oh, when I re-mem - ber mis - in - for - ma - tion fol -

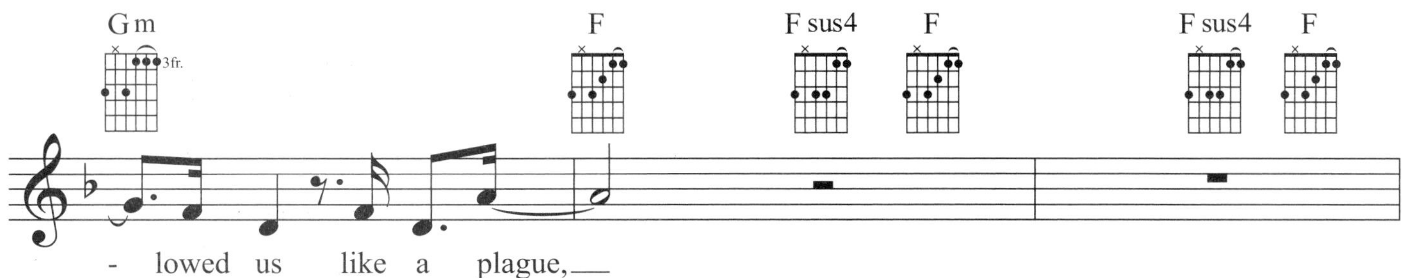
Gm
F
F sus4
F
F sus4
F
- lowed us like a plague,

B♭
F
B♭
No - bod - y knew from time to time if the plans were changed,

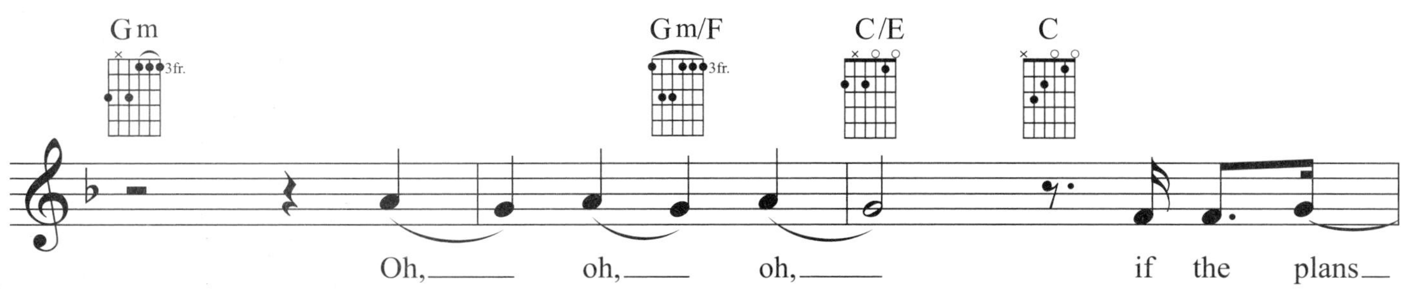
Gm
Gm/F
C/E
C
Oh, oh, oh, if the plans

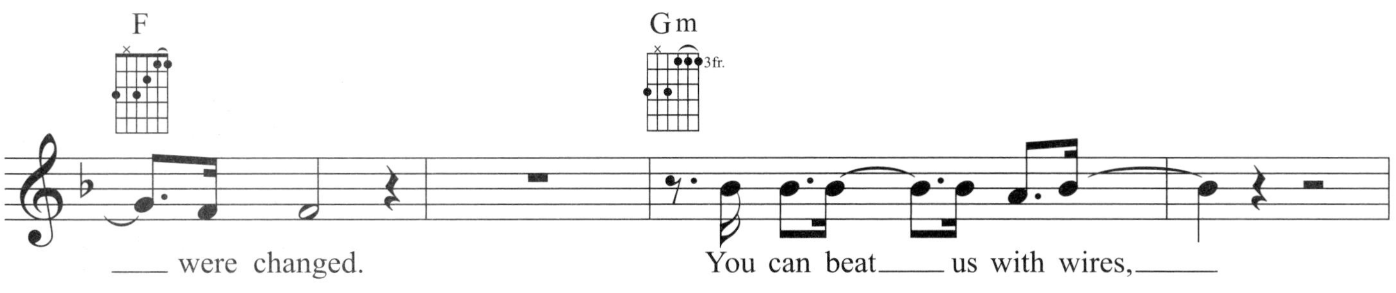
F
Gm
were changed.
You can beat us with wires,

Fmaj7
C
You can beat us with chain,
You can run lots of rules,
but you know you can't out-run the his-to-ry train
Dm
Gm
3fr.
F
I seen a glo-ri-ous day, ai ee
ee
C
Dm
Gm
3fr.
ee.
(instrumental)
Dm
Dm
Dm
Ah,

Gm
F
Four in the morn-in' I woke up from out of my dreams,
B♭
F
B♭
No-where to go but back to sleep, but I'm rec-on-ciled,
Gm
Gm/F
C/E
C
Oh, oh, oh, I'm gon-na be
Dm
Gm
Gm/F
C/E
C
up for a-while. Oh, oh, oh, I'm gon-na be
Dm
Gm
Gm/F
C/E
C
up for a - while. Oh, oh, oh, I'm gon-na be
Dm
Gm
Dm
repeat and fade
up for a - while.

Pigs, Sheep And Wolves

Words and Music by Paul Simon

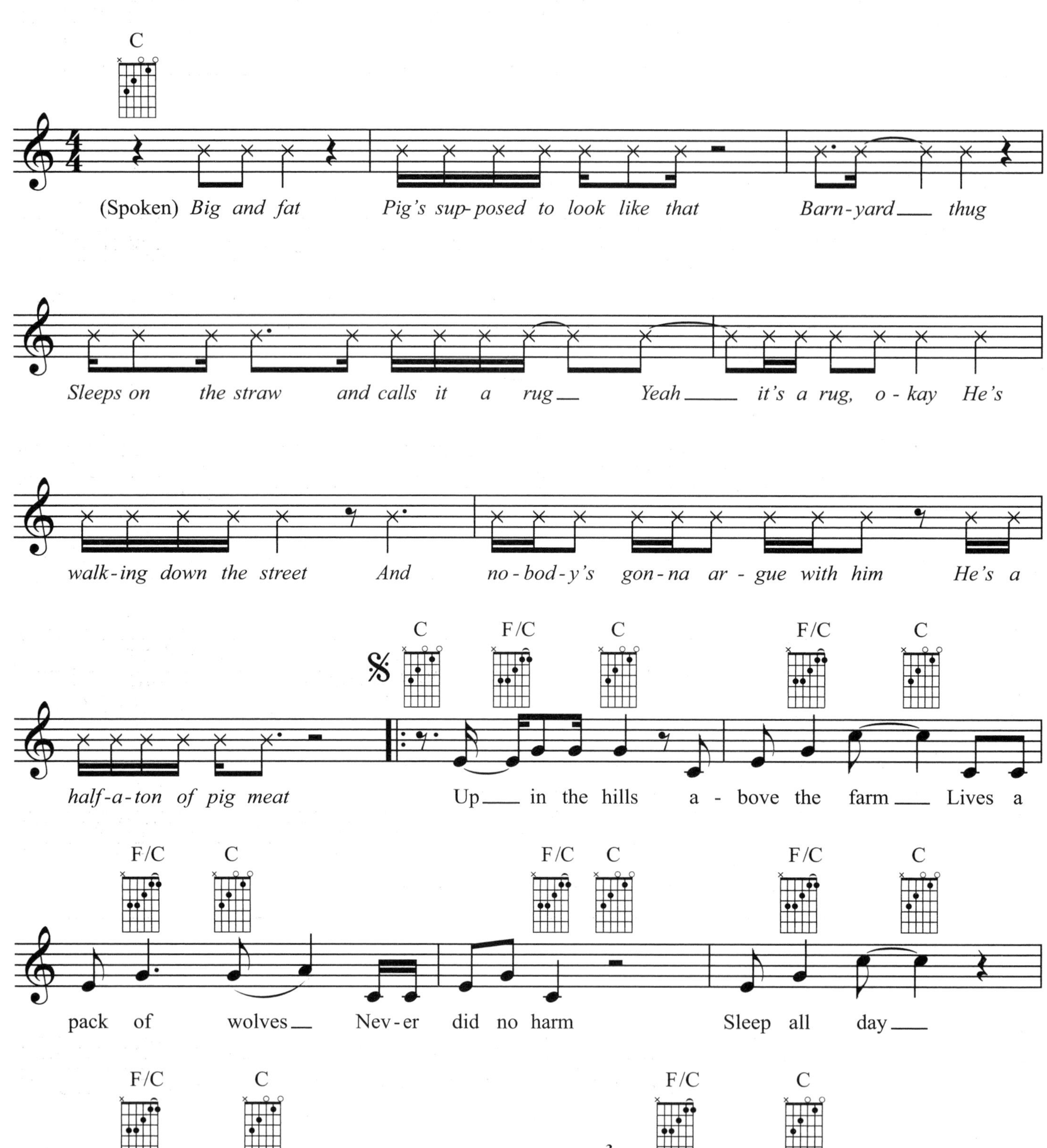

F/C
C
F
a car-ni-vore
Sheep in the mead-ow Nib-bl-ing on some clo-ver
C
F
to Coda
One of the sheep just wand-ers o-ver Sits by a rock Sep-a-rat-ed from the flock
1.
G
E7/G♯
Am
He's just sitting by a rock
(Spoken) Where'd he go?
I don't know Well he was here a min-ute a-go I don't know
3
Sheep's dead Got a gash as big as a wolf's head Oh, God
2.
C
F
Gov-er-nor says For-get it. It's a done deal It's e-lec-tion? I don't care, e-
C
lec-tion, give that wolf a le-thal in-jec-tion Let's get 'em let's get that wolf, Let's

F
get 'em let's get that wolf, let's get 'em Let's kill 'em, let's
G
E7/G♯
get 'em, Let's kill 'em, let's get 'em, kill 'em Let's get 'em let's kill 'em
A m
(Spoken) Whew, slow, here comes the med-i-a with their cam-er-a
ask-ing ev - 'ry bod-y's o - pin-ion 'Bout pigs, sheep and wolves
D.S. al Coda
Coda
C
(Spoken) An-i-mal be-hav-ior It's pigs, sheep and wolves
pigs, sheep and wolves pigs, sheep and wolves (Spoken) It's an - i-mal
be-hav - ior
It's pigs, sheep and wolves

2. (Spoken) *Big and fat*
Pig's supposed to look like that
Wallowing in lanolin
He's rubbing it into his pigskin
Police are going crazy
Sayin' let's get him
Let's get that wolf
Let's get him
Let's get that wolf
Let's get him
Let's kill him, let's get him
Let's kill him

Court-appointed lawyer wasn't very bright
Maybe he was bright
Maybe he just had a late night
Yeah it was just a late night
And he files some feeble appeal

3. (Spoken) *Big and fat*
Pig's supposed to laugh like that
This is hilarious
What a great time
I'm the pig who committed
The perfect crime

All around the world
France, Scandinavia
There's candle light vigils
Protesting this behavior
It's animal behavior

Animal behavior
It's pigs, sheep and wolves
Pigs, sheep and wolves
Pigs, sheep and wolves
It's animal behavior
It's pigs, sheep and wolves

Quality

Music by Paul Simon
Lyrics by Paul Simon and Derek Walcott

B♭
6fr.
E♭
6fr.
Slower
ty
I want to know
Are you my

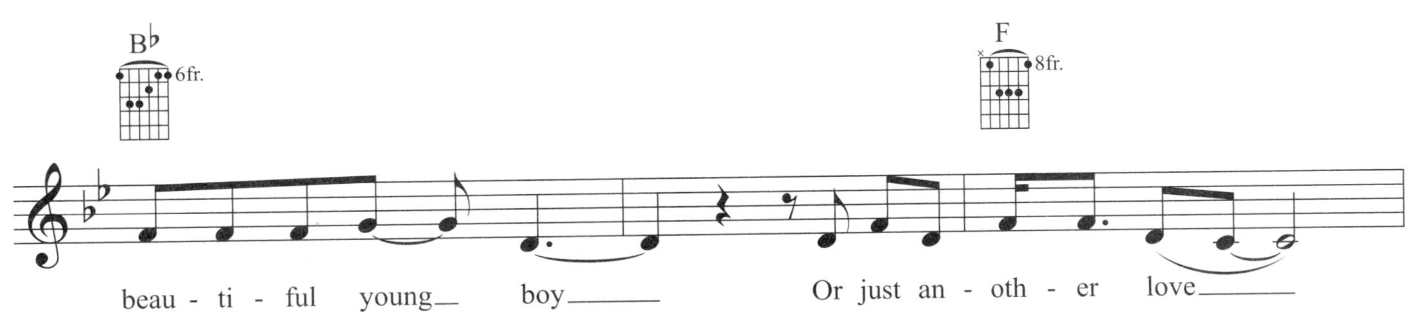
B♭
6fr.
F
8fr.
beau - ti - ful young boy
Or just an - oth - er love

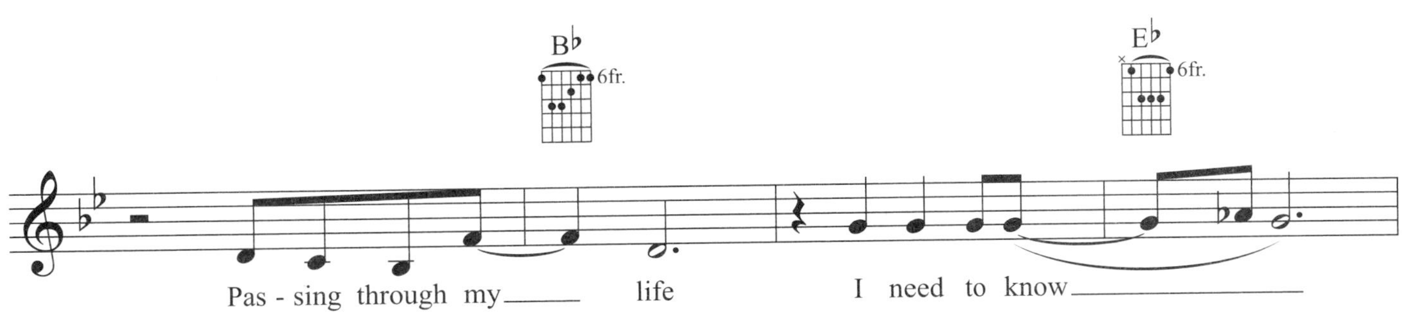
B♭
6fr.
E♭
6fr.
Pas - sing through my life
I need to know

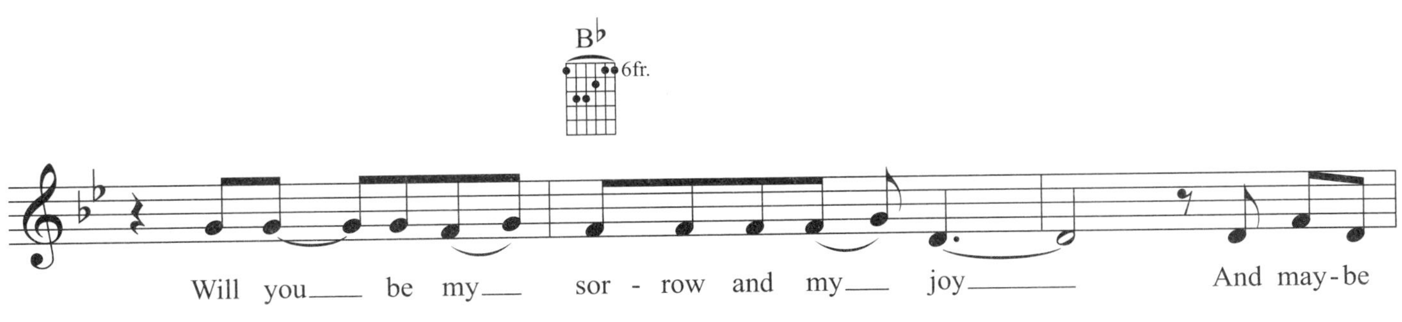
B♭
6fr.
Will you be my sor - row and my joy
And may-be

F
8fr.
B♭
6fr.
to Coda
one day soon
Will I be your wife.

Tempo I
N.C.
B♭
6fr.
E♭
6fr.
Come on ba - by, Let's rock some more
B♭
6fr.
I want to spend my sal - a - ry
The way you
F
8fr.
move
N.C.
It's got qual - i - ty
B♭
6fr.
E♭
6fr.
B♭
6fr.
(instrumental solo)
F
8fr.
B♭
6fr.

Zoom zoom zoom zoom
E♭
6fr.
B♭
6fr.
Ev - 'ry time they see me walk down the street They say Coñ - o that boy is
F
8fr.
fine The way he moves
B♭
6fr.
N.C.
Slower
D.S. al Coda
N.C.
Got qual - i - ty I want to know
Coda
B♭7
6fr.
E♭
6fr.
B♭
6fr.
Quie - ro sa - ber Quie - ro sa - ber
F
8fr.
B♭
6fr.
Na - die nun - ca sa - be En la vi - da

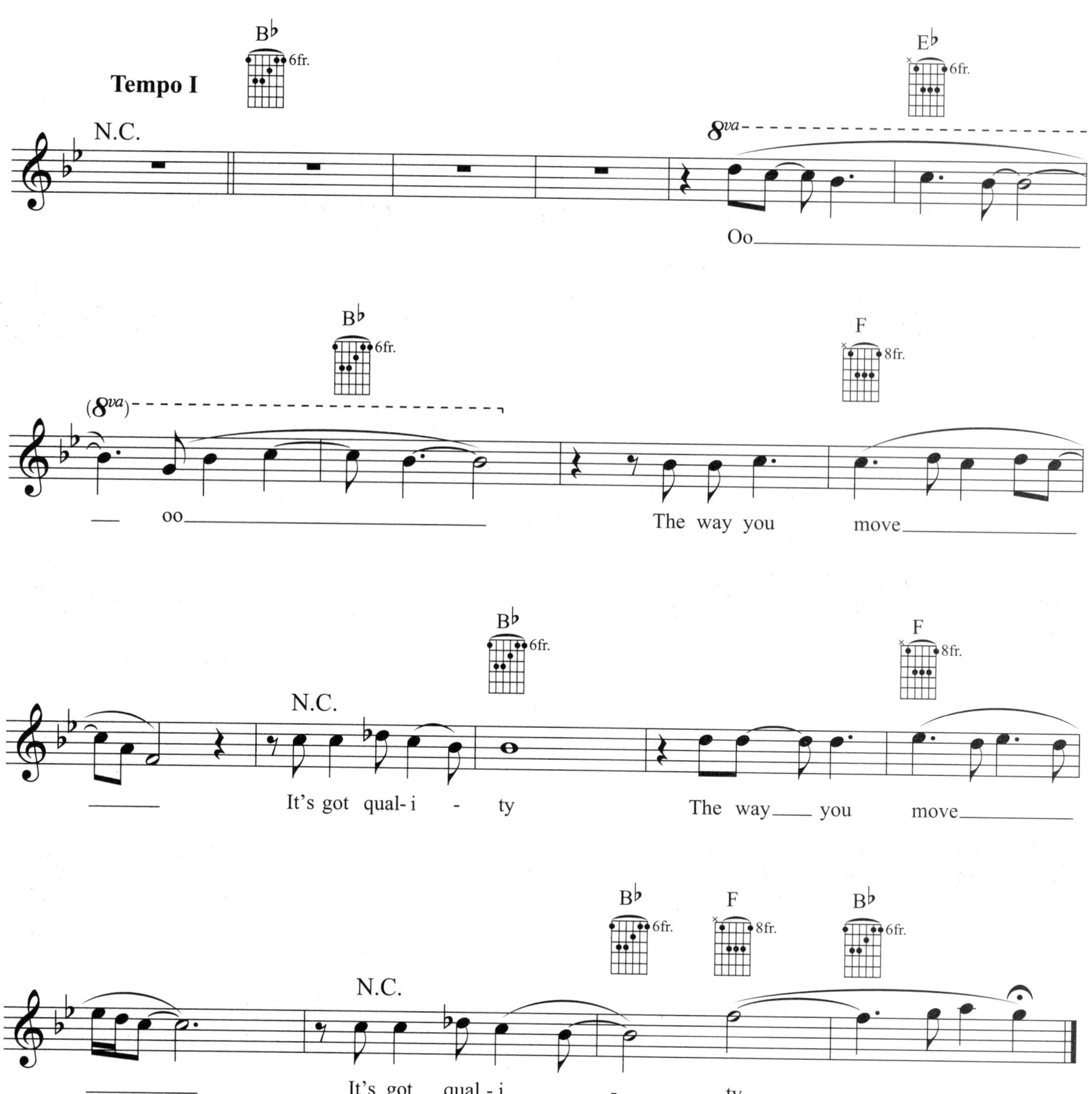

2. Come on baby now don't be shy
Step in the light so I can see
The way you move
It's got quality

Proof

Words and Music by Paul Simon

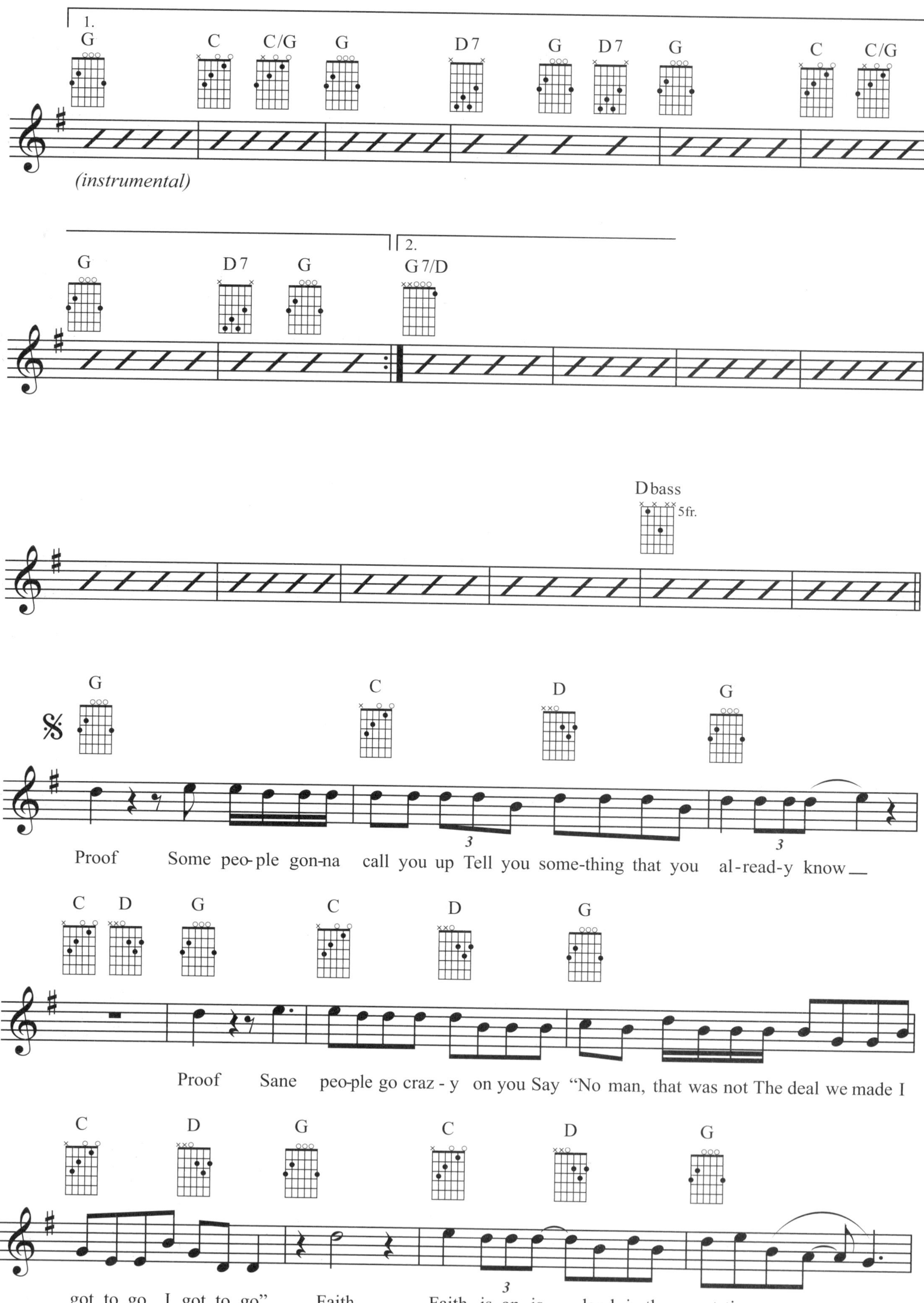
1.
G
C
C/G
G
D7
G
D7
G
C
C/G
(instrumental)
G
D7
G
2.
G7/D
Dbass
5fr.
G
C
D
G
Proof Some peo-ple gon-na call you up Tell you some-thing that you al-read-y know
C
D
G
C
D
G
Proof Sane peo-ple go craz - y on you Say "No man, that was not The deal we made I
C
D
G
C
D
G
got to go, I got to go" Faith Faith is an is - land in the set-ting sun

C D G C C G C D
But proof, yes
Proof is the bot-tom line for ev-ery-one
G C D G C D G C D
(He-lah wa-he-la a ton-ga he, he-la)
G C D G
My face, my race Don't mat-ter an-y-more My sex, my cheques
C D G C D Dbass
5fr.
D.S. al Coda
Ac-cep-ted at the door
Coda
G C D G C D G
Half-moon
C D G C D G
hid-ing in the clouds, my dar-ling And the sky is

C D G C D G
flecked with signs of hope Raise your wear - y
C D G C D
wings a - gainst the rain, my ba - by Wash your
G C D G C D D bass
5fr.
tan - gled curls with gam-bler's soap
G C D G
Proof Some peo-ple gon-na call you up Tell you some-thing that you al-read-y know
C D G C D G
Proof Sane peo-ple go craz - y on you Say "No man, that was not The deal we made I
C D G C D G
got to go, I got to go" Faith Faith is an is - land in the set-ting sun

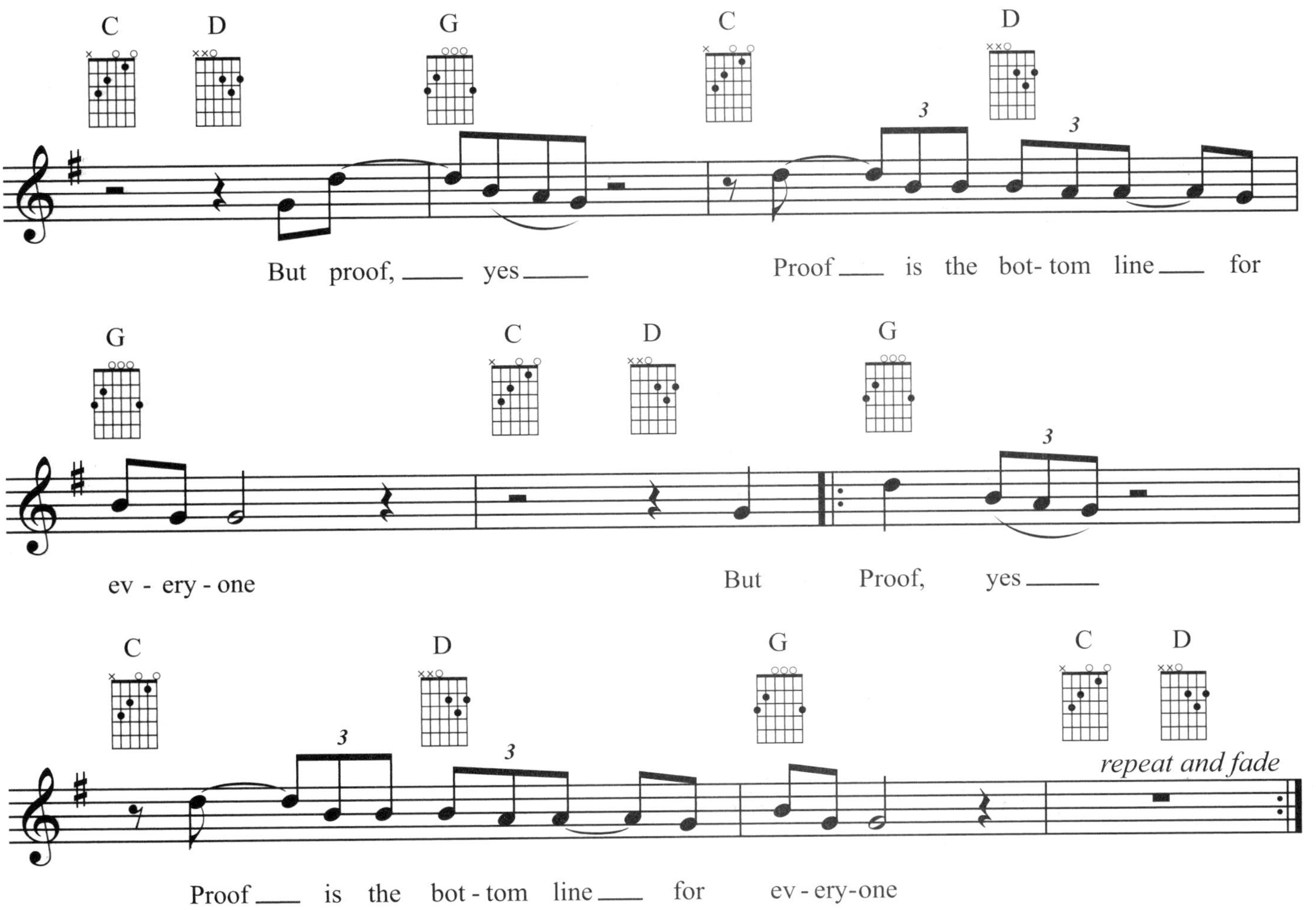

2. It's true the tools of love wear down.
   Time passes,
   A mind wanders.
   It seems mindless, but it does.
   Sometimes I see your face
   As if through reading glasses,
   And your smile seems softer than it was.

Punky's Dilemma

Words and Music by Paul Simon

Moderately

2. Wish I was an English muffin
'Bout to make the most out of a toaster
I'd ease myself down,
Comin' up brown.
I prefer boysenberry
More than any ordinary jam.
I'm a "Citizens for Boysenberry Jam" fan.

Quiet

Words and Music by Paul Simon

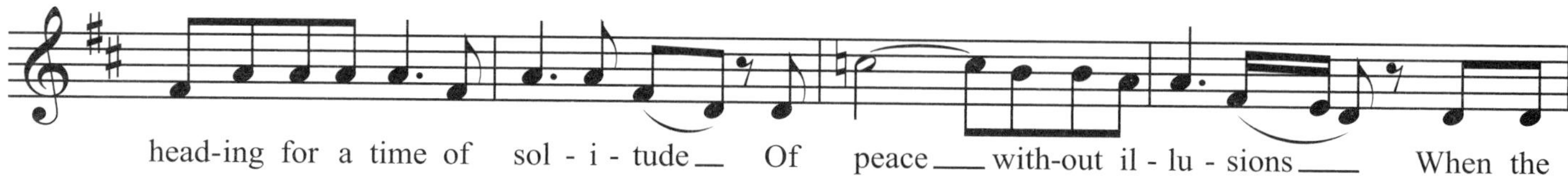

an - swer is you're not But who are they Or what is it that
eats at what you've got With the hun-ger of am - bi-tion For the
change in-side the purse? They are hand-cuffs on the soul,
my friends Hand-cuffs on the soul And
A/D
G/D
worse Now I'm
D
G/D
D
head-ing for a place of qui - et Where the sage and sweet grass grow By a
lake of sac - red wa - ter From the moun-tain's melt-ed snow

Red Rubber Ball

Words and Music by Paul Simon and Bruce Woodley

Moderately bright

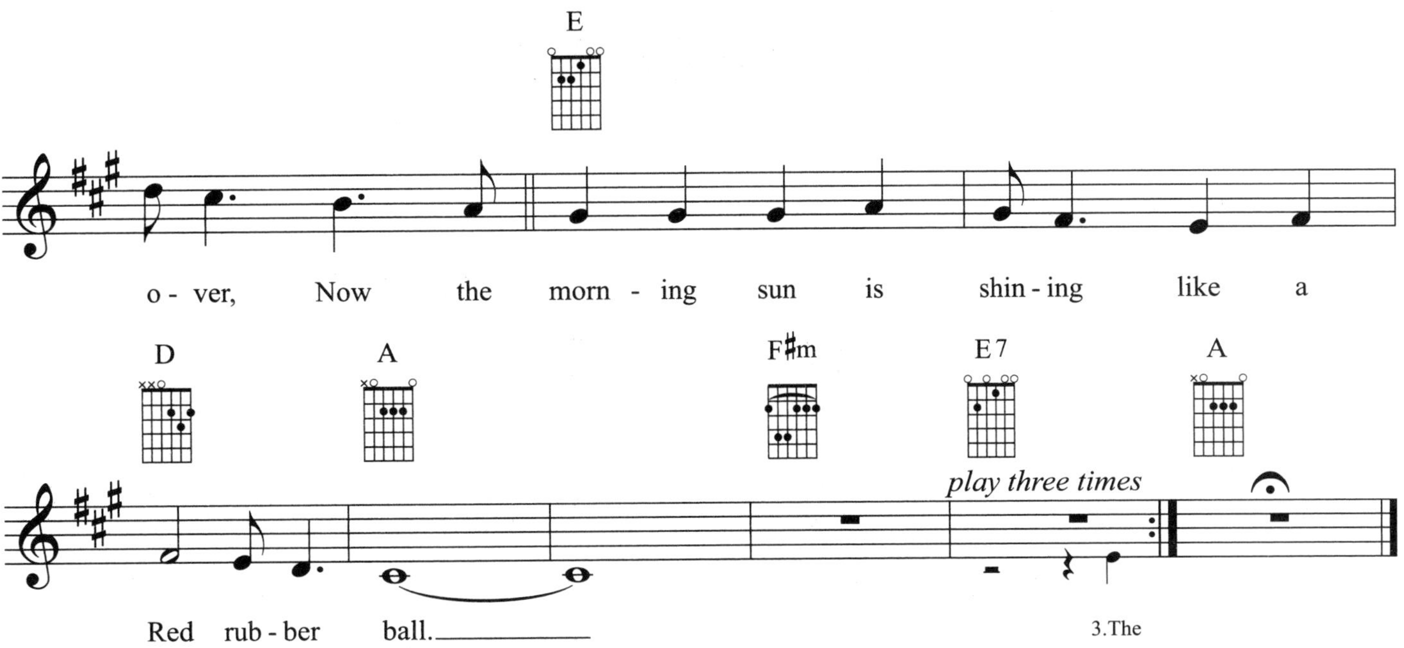

2. You never cared for secrets I'd confide.
   For you I'm just an ornament,
   Something for your pride.
   Always running, never caring,
   That's the life you live.
   Stolen minutes of your time
   Were all you had to give.

   Chorus

3. The story's in the past with nothing to recall.
   I've got my life to live and I
   Don't need you at all.
   The roller coaster ride we took is
   Nearly at an end.
   I bought my ticket with my tears,
   That's all I'm gonna spend.

   Chorus

Rene And Georgette Magritte With Their Dog After The War

Words and Music by Paul Simon

B9
E
G♯m7/D♯
C♯m7
E/B
Amaj7
4fr.
4fr.
Five Sat - ins The deep for-bid-den mu - sic They'd been long - ing for
F♯m6
B9
E
1.
Re - ne and Geor-gette Ma - gritte With their dog af-ter the war Re -
2.
F♯7
B
F♯/A♯
Amaj7
G♯m7
4fr.
4fr.
Side by side They fell a - sleep
A6
E/G♯
C°7
C♯m7
4fr.
4
Dec - ades glid - ing by like In - di - ans Time is cheap
A6
E/G♯
B7/F♯
E
F♯7
When they wake up they will find All their
B
F♯/A♯
Amaj7
G♯m7
4fr.
4fr.
4
per - son - al be - long - ings Have in - ter - twined

F♯m6
E bass
D bass
B bass
A bass
Oh___ Re - ne and Geor-gette Ma - gritte With their dog af-ter the
E
E bass
D♯bass
D bass
B bass
war Were din - ing with the pow-er e - lite And they looked in their
A maj7
F♯m6
bed - room drawer And what do you think They have
E 6/G♯
A 6
F♯7/A♯
4fr.
3
hid-den a-way In the cab - i-net cold of their hearts? The
G♯m
4fr.
D♯m
6fr.
E
freely
Pen - guins, the Moon - glows The Or - i - oles,___ and the
B
E
G♯m7/D♯
4fr.
C♯m7
4fr.
E/B
A maj7
a tempo
Five Sa - tins For__ now and ev - er af - ter___ As it was be - fore___

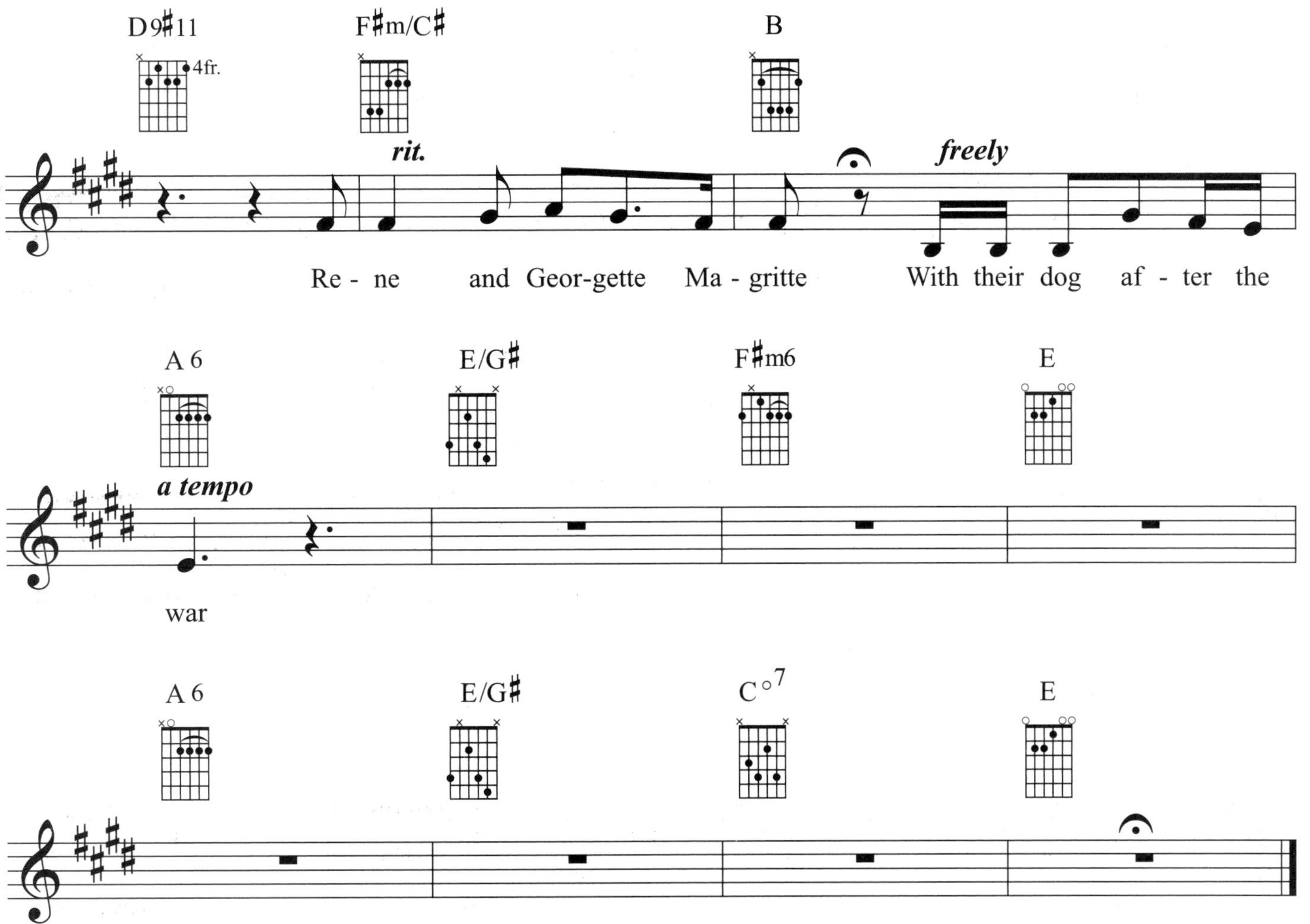

2. Rene and Georgette Magritte
With their dog after the war
Were strolling down Christopher Street
When they stopped in a men's store
With all of the mannequins dressed in the style
That brought tears to their immigrant eyes
Just like the Penguins
The Moonglows
The Orioles
and the Five Satins
The easy stream of laughter
Flowing through the air
Rene and Georgette Magritte
With their dog *après la guerre*

Save The Life Of My Child

Words and Music by Paul Simon

F C B♭/C G G6 G C/G G
must be high on some- thing," some-one said. Though it nev - er made The New York Times,
C/G G C F
In the Dai - ly News the cap - tion read "Save the life of my child!"
C F C
Cried the des-per-ate moth - er. Ah, ah, ah, ah.
1.- 3. 4.
G6 G C/G G C/G G C/G G G6 G C/G G
A pa - trol car pass-ing by
C/G G F C B♭/C G
halt - ed to a stop. Said Of - fi - cer Mac-Dou - gal in dis - may: "The
F C/G G C/G G C
force can't do a de-cent job 'Cause the kids got no res-pect for the law to - day."

F
C
G6
G
C/G
B♭/C
C7
repeat and fade
— "Save the life of my child!" — Cried the des-per-ate moth - er. —
— "What's be - com - ing of the chil - dren?" — Peo - ple ask - ing each oth -
- er. —
When dark-ness fell, ex-cite-ment kissed the
crowd and made them wild, in the at - mo - sphere of freak - y hol - i - day. When the
spot - light hit the boy — and the crowd be - gan to cheer, He flew a -
way. "Oh, my grace, I've got no hid - ing — place."

The Rhythm Of The Saints

Words and Music by Paul Simon

Moderately bright, with a steady beat

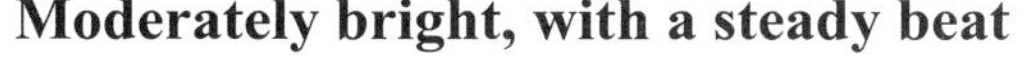

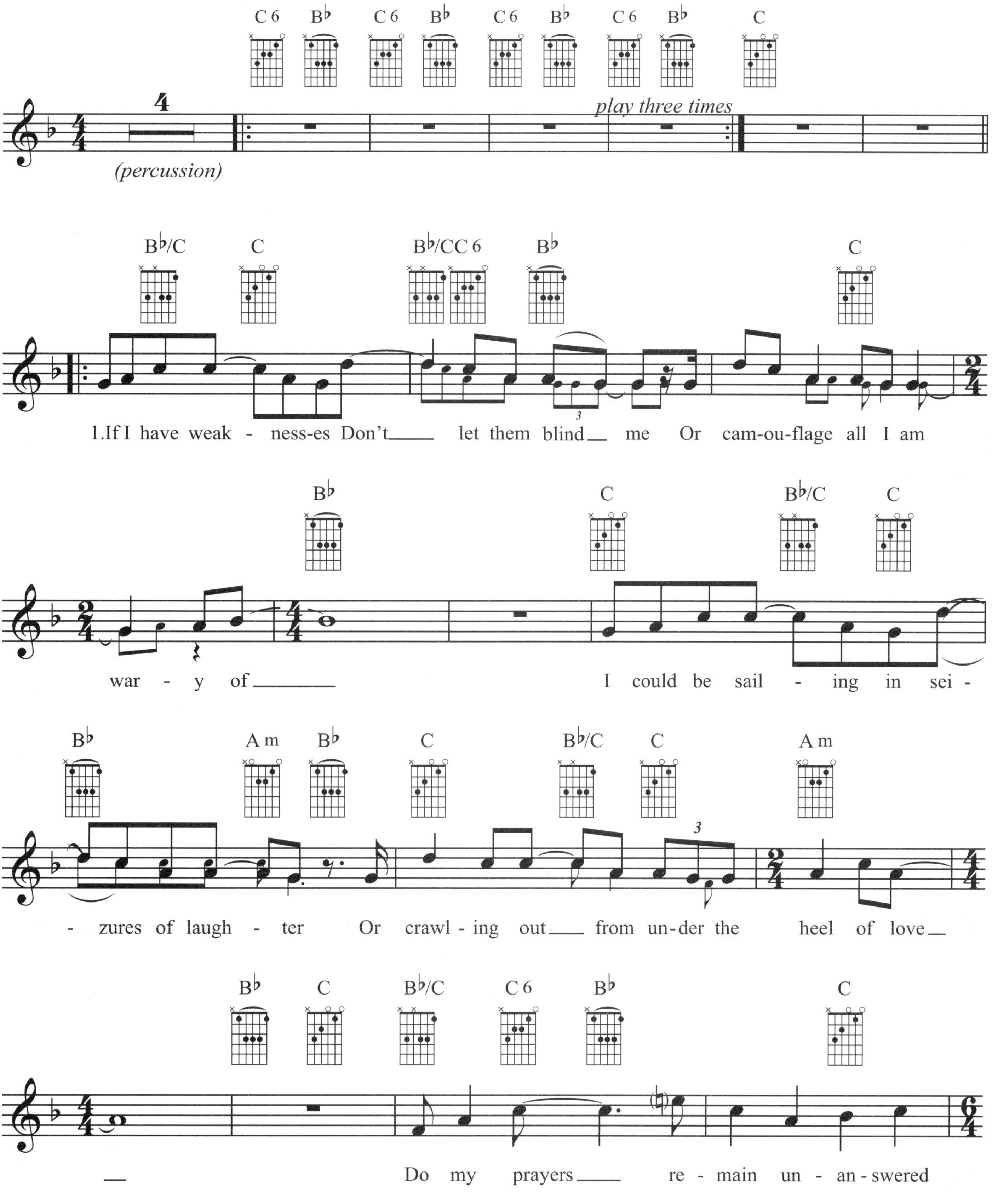

C 6 Bb C 6 Bb C 6 Bb C 6 Bb C
4
play three times
(percussion)
Bb/C C Bb/C C 6 Bb C
1.If I have weak - ness-es Don't let them blind me Or cam-ou-flage all I am
Bb C Bb/C C
war - y of I could be sail - ing in sei -
Bb A m Bb C Bb/C C A m
- zures of laugh - ter Or crawl - ing out from un-der the heel of love
Bb C Bb/C C 6 Bb C
Do my prayers re - main un - an - swered

B♭/C C B♭ C/B♭ B♭ C B♭/C C
Like a beg - gar at your sleeve O - lo - du - ma - re is smil -
B♭ A m/B♭ B♭ C B♭/C A m/B♭ C 6
- ing in heav - en Smil - ing in heav - en I do be - lieve
B♭ C 6 B♭ C 6 B♭
Reach in the dark - ness A reach in the dark
C 6 B♭ C 6 B♭ C 6 B♭
Reach in the dark-ness A reach in the dark To o - ver-come an ob-sta-cle or an
C 6 B♭ C 6 B♭ C 6 B♭
en - e-my To glide a-way from the ra - zor or a knife To
C 6 B♭ C 6 B♭ C 6 B♭
o - ver-come an ob-sta-cle or an en - e-my To dom-i-nate the im-pos-si-ble in your

2. Always a stranger when strange isn't fashionable,
And fashion is rich people waving at the door.
Or it's a dealer in drugs or in passion,
Lies of a nature we've heard before.
Do my prayers remain unanswered,
Like a beggar at your sleeve?
Babalu-aye spins on his crutches,
Says leave if you want,
If you want to leave.

Richard Cory

Words and Music by Paul Simon

Moderately

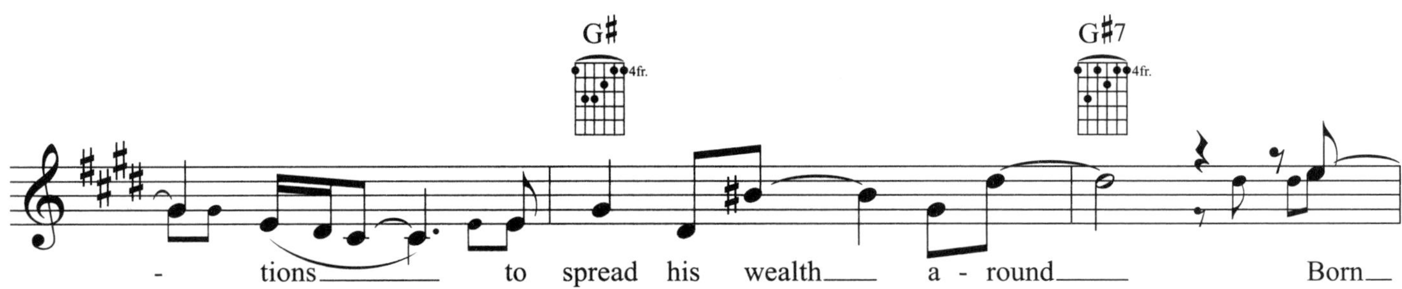

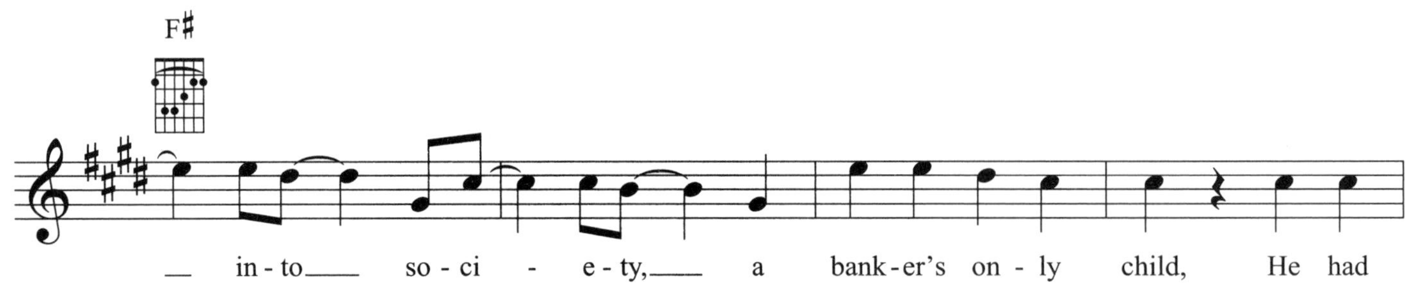

2. The papers print his picture almost everywhere he goes:
   Richard Cory at the opera, Richard Cory at a show.
   And the rumor of his parties and the orgies on his yacht!
   Oh, he surely must be happy with everything he's got.
   Chorus

3. He freely gave to charity, he had the common touch,
   And they were grateful for his patronage and thanked him very much,
   So my mind was filled with wonder when the evening headlines read:
   "Richard Cory went home last night and put a bullet through his head."
   Chorus

Run That Body Down

Words and Music by Paul Simon

Moderately slow shuffle

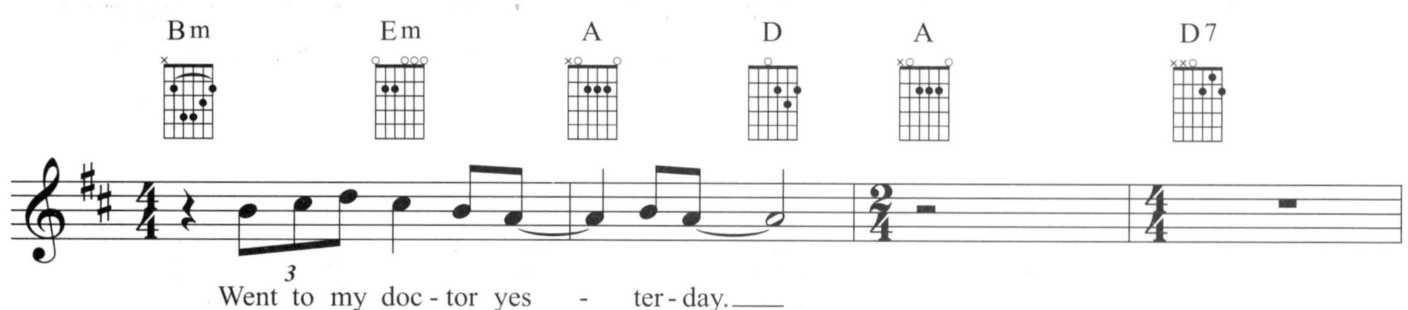

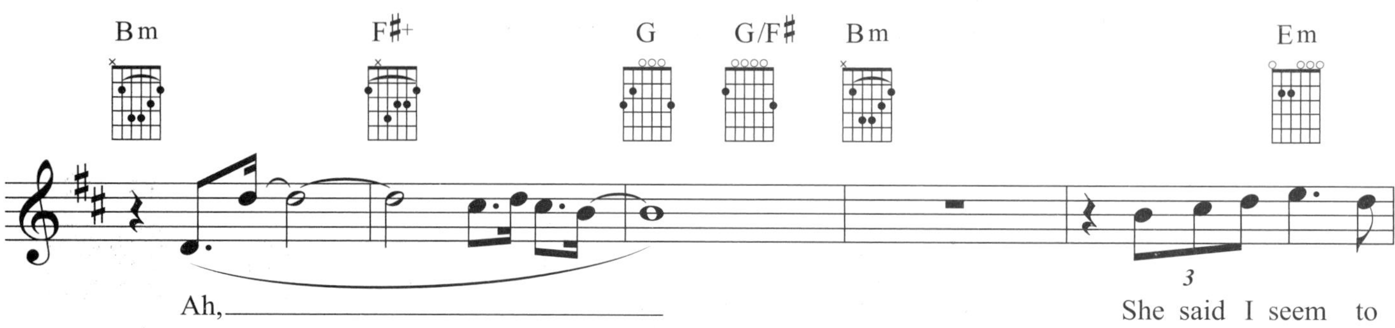

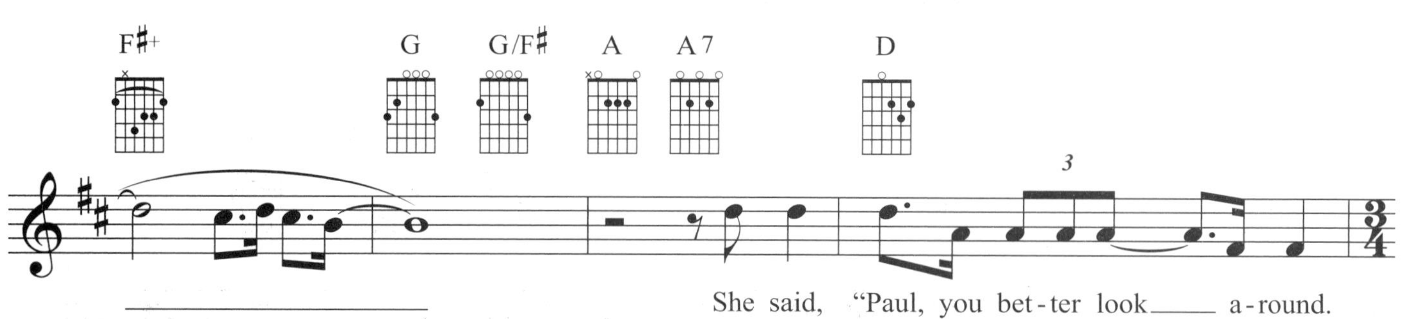

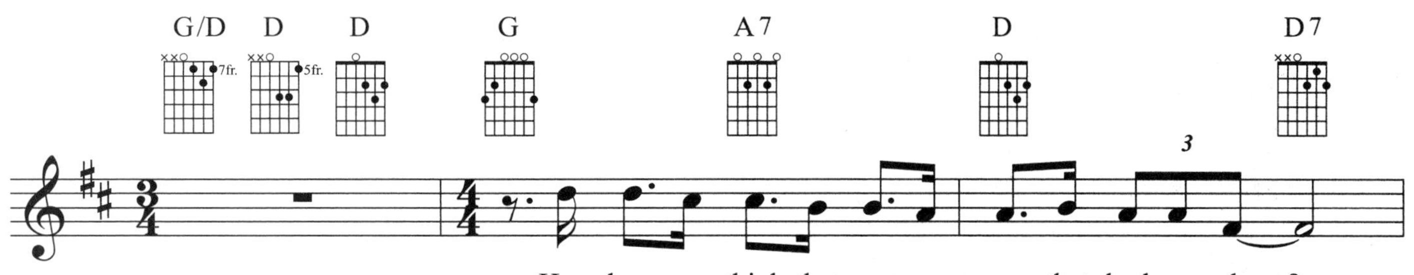
G/D D D G A7 D D7
7fr. 5fr.
How long you think that you can run that bod-y down?

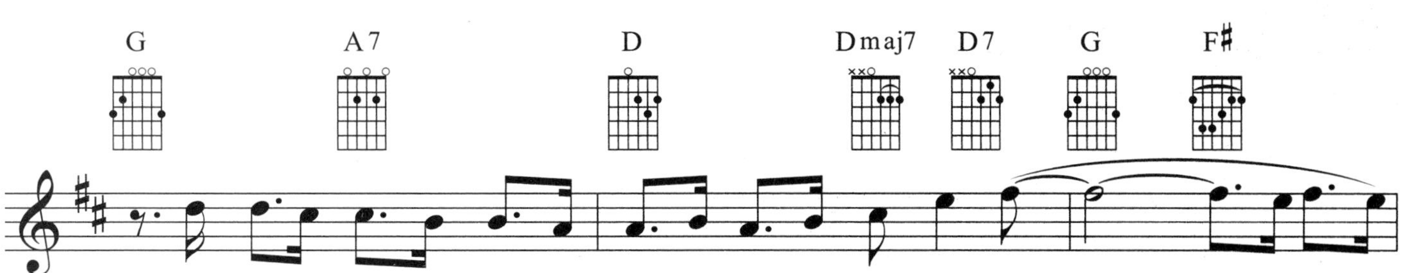
G A7 D Dmaj7 D7 G F♯
How man-y nights you think that you can do what you been do - - -

Bm Em A7 D Bm Em F♯+ F♯7
in'? Who, now, who you fool - in'?"

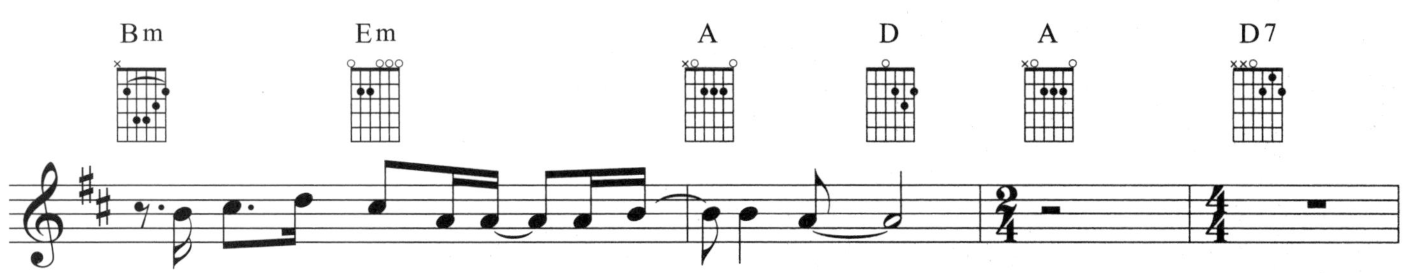
Bm Em A D A D7
I came back home and I went in - to bed.

Bm F♯+ G G/F♯ Bm
Ah, I was rest-in' my head.

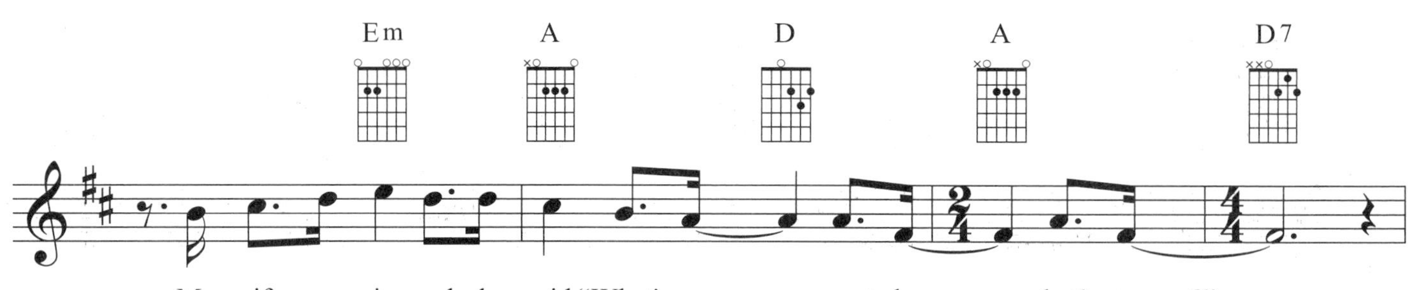
Em A D A D7
My wife came in and she said, "What's wrong, sweet boy, what's wrong?"

Bm F♯+ G G/F♯ A A7
Ah, I told her what's wrong. I said

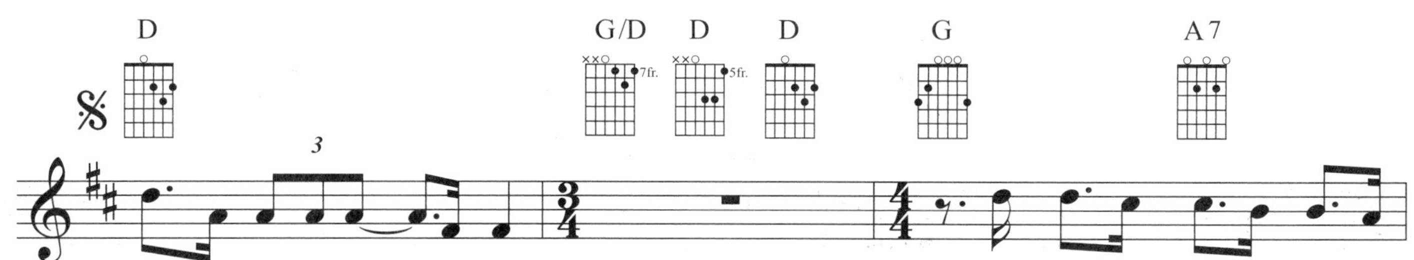
D G/D D D G A7
7fr. 5fr.
"Peg, you bet-ter look a-round. How long you think that you can

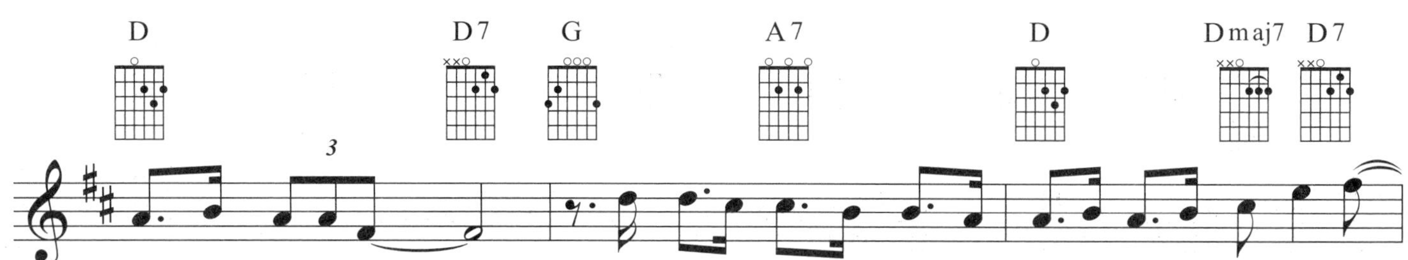
D D7 G A7 D Dmaj7 D7
run that bod-y down? How man-y nights you think that you can do what you been do -

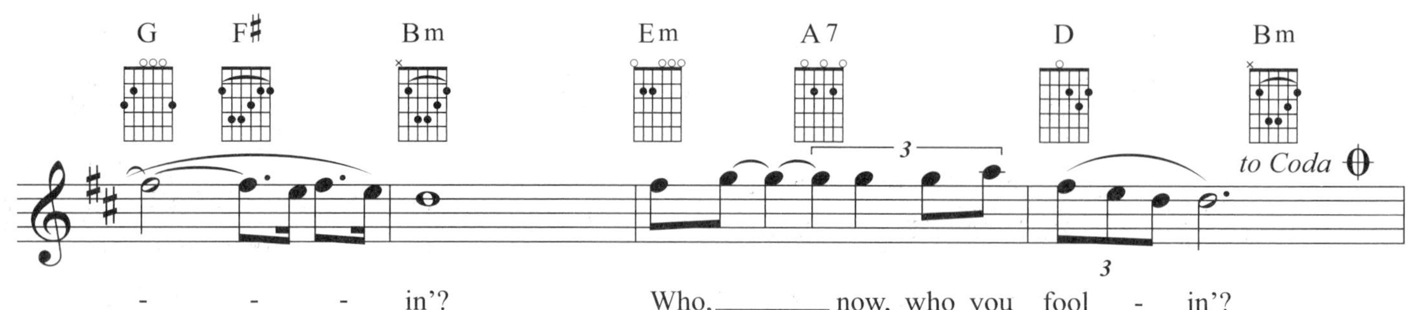
G F♯ Bm Em A7 D Bm
to Coda
- - - in'? Who, now, who you fool - in'?

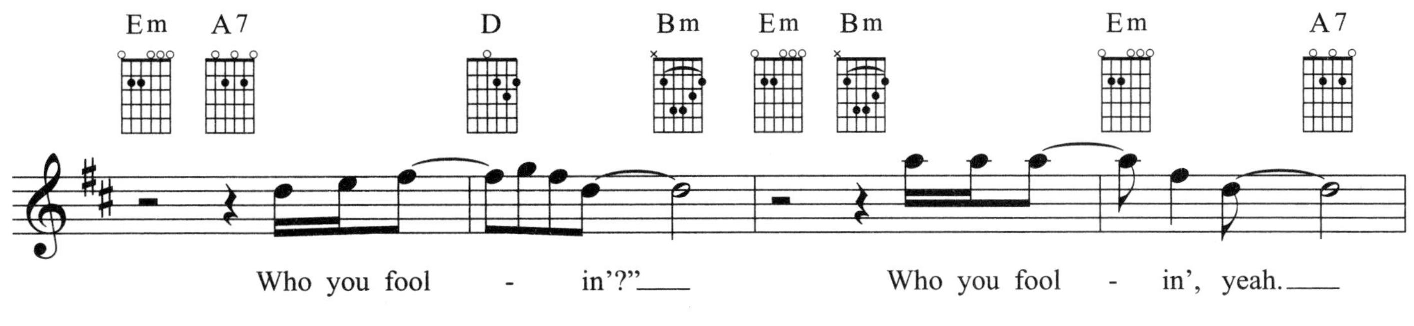
Em
A7
D
Bm
Em
Bm
Em
A7
Who you fool - in'?"
Who you fool - in', yeah.

Em
F♯
B
G♯m
4fr.
Ooh,
ah,
yeah, yeah, yeah,
3
yeah, yeah, yeah.

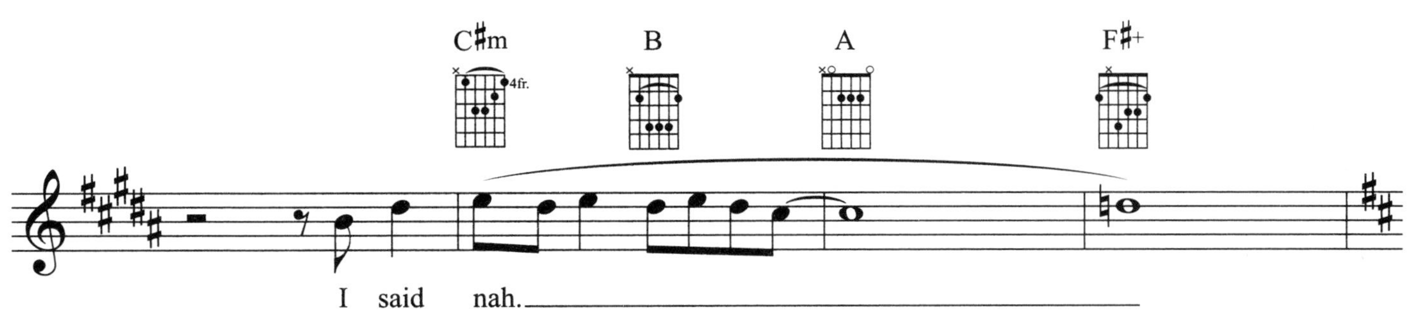
C♯m
4fr.
B
A
F♯+
I said nah.

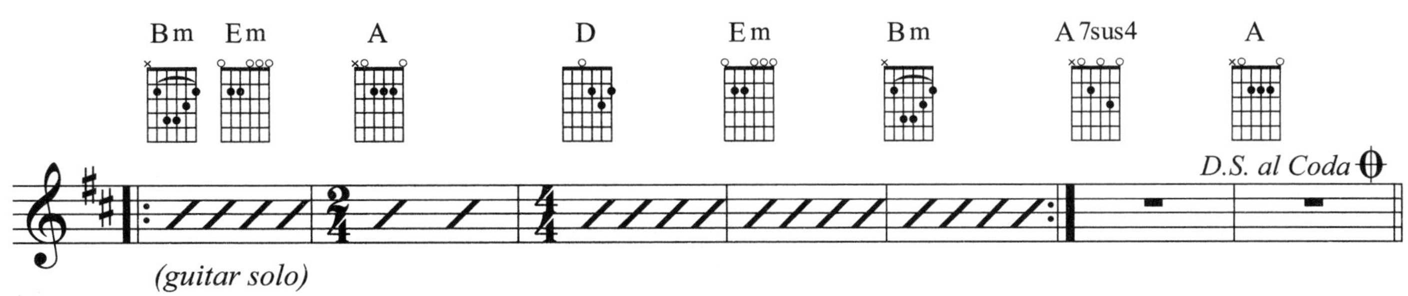
Bm
Em
A
D
Em
Bm
A7sus4
A
D.S. al Coda
(guitar solo)

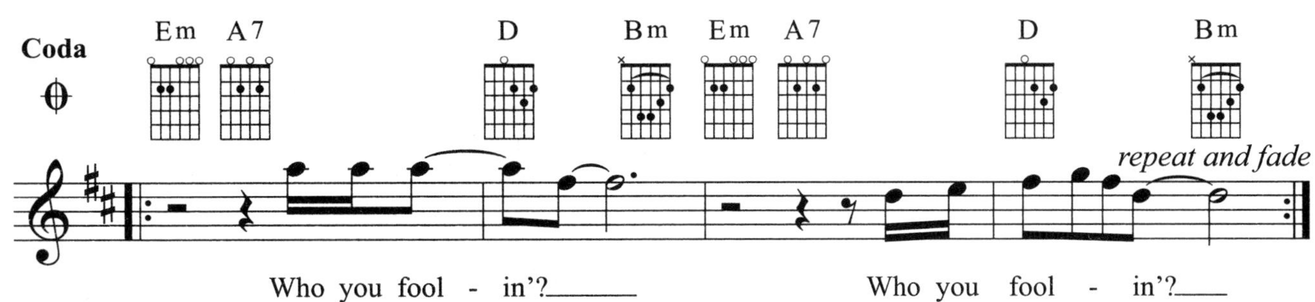
Coda
Em
A7
D
Bm
Em
A7
D
Bm
repeat and fade
Who you fool - in'?
Who you fool - in'?

Satin Summer Nights

Music by Paul Simon
Lyrics by Paul Simon and Derek Walcott

G
Am
G
Car-los and Yo-lan-da Danc - ing in the hall-way To an old mel-o-dy

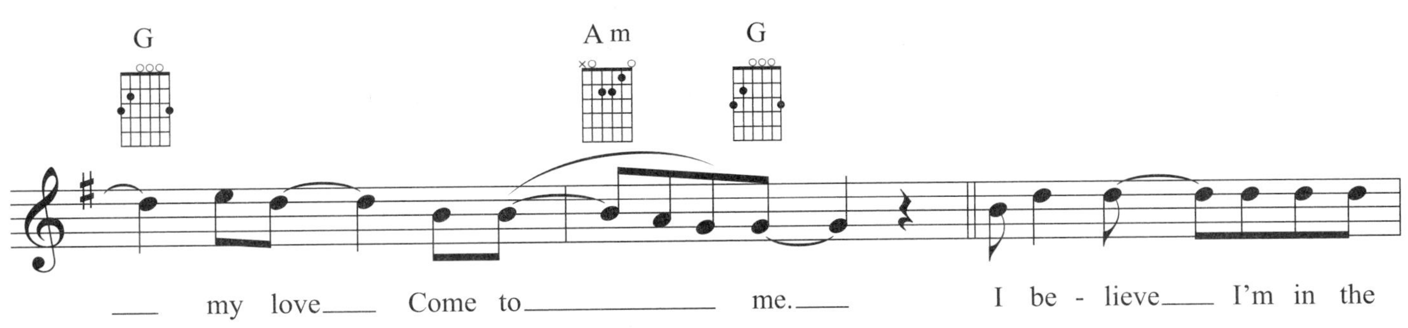
Am
G
D7
Span-ish eyes and soft brown curls My love,

G
Am
G
my love Come to me. I be-lieve I'm in the

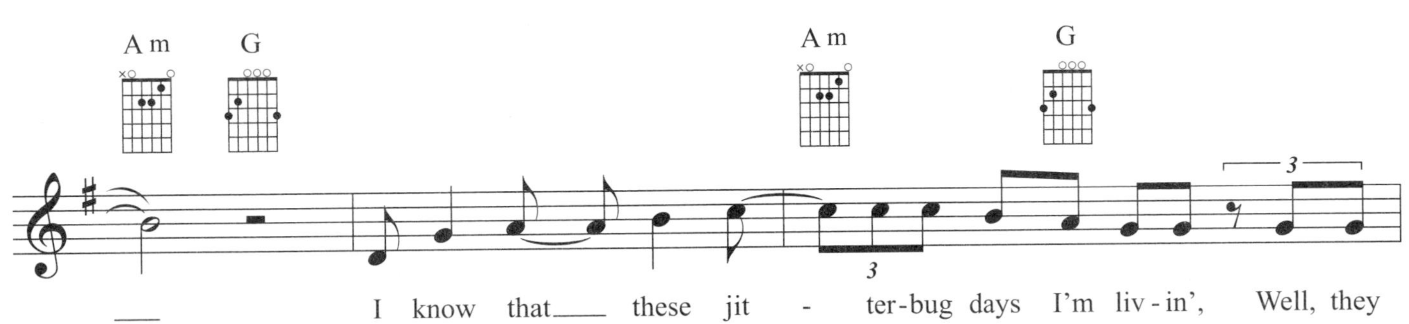
Am
G
pow-er of Saint Laz - a-rus. And he holds me in his sight
Am
G
Am
G
I know that these jit - ter-bug days I'm liv-in', Well, they

Am
G
C
won't last for all of us, But they'll last for a long sum-mer night.
C7
G
Oh - woh - oh
I can feel the fire
Am
G
Am
G
D7
in her eyes
To - night,
to - night
G
Am
G
Un-der sat-in sum-mer skies.
Am
G
G
Em
(instrumental solo)
Pum pum pum ba oo
Am
D7
Pum pum pum ba oo

G
Em
Ba-by, ba-by, ba - by Be my spe-cial one
Am
D7
I seen you move in from a - cross the street I like the way you walk I
G
Em
love the way you run Ba - by, ba - by, No more ba-by talk
Am
D7
Pa-pi, this ain't Ma - ya - güez This is the is-land of Nue -
G
- va York We'll go through the proj - ects,

Em
Am
Make-out on the roofs
Count the stars like sil - ver studs on my
D7
G
Mo - tor - cy - cle boots
Tengan cuidado con ese tipo. Ay verdad te digo, ese tipo es tan sucio. ¡Sucio!
Em
Pum pum pum ba oo
Am
D7
You wastin' your time, they don't know what I do. You little ghetto weeds . . . I feel like killin' you.
Pum pum pum ba oo
G
Em
Ba - nan - a - col - ored light - skinned spics,
You feel your peel so fine?
Am
I'm Her - nán - dez, The Um - brel - la Man,

D7
G
Your fu-ture's locked in mine.
The Chap-lains and The Gold - en Guin-eas
Em
The Red Wings and The Crowns,
Am
D7
The Might-y Mau Maus, Those Shines from Brook - lyn,
They want to cut The
G
Vam - pires down down
The Sav-age Skulls, The Ford-ham Bald - ies,
Em
Am
They'll treat you like you're piss
From the heart of the bar-ri-o, now my
D7
broth-er
We tell them moth - er fuck - ers suck on this.

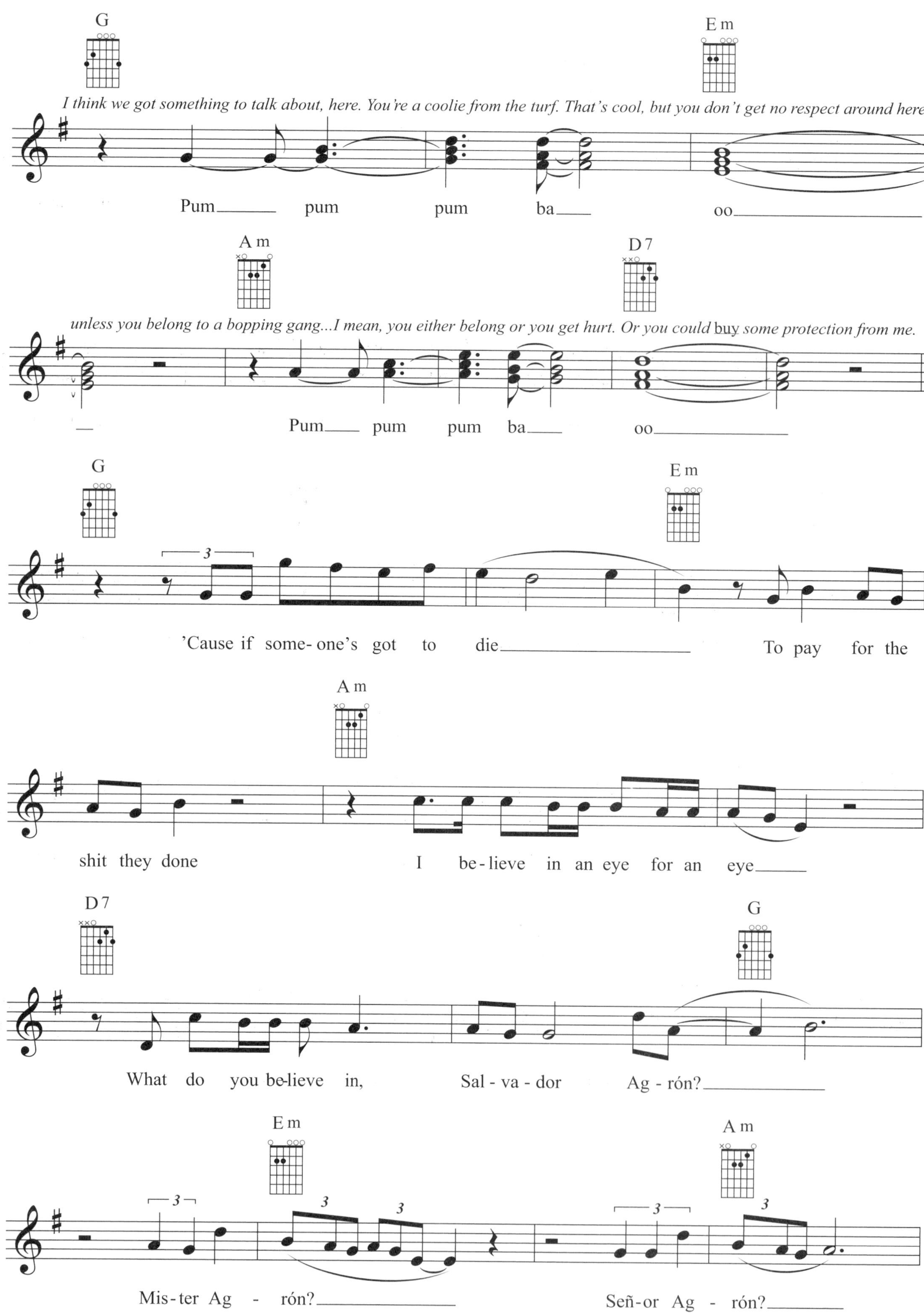
G
Em
I think we got something to talk about, here. You're a coolie from the turf. That's cool, but you don't get no respect around here
Pum pum pum ba oo
Am
D7
unless you belong to a bopping gang...I mean, you either belong or you get hurt. Or you could buy some protection from me.
Pum pum pum ba oo
G
Em
'Cause if some-one's got to die
To pay for the
Am
shit they done
I be-lieve in an eye for an eye
D7
G
What do you be-lieve in, Sal-va-dor Ag-rón?
Em
Am
Mis-ter Ag-rón?
Señ-or Ag-rón?

D7
I be - lieve
G
I'm in the pow - er of Saint Laz - a - rus And he
3
3
3
Em
Am
holds me in his sight
I be - lieve he watch - es
D7
ov - er us all Don't tear a - part This sat -
G
3
- in sum - mer night.

Scarborough Fair/Canticle

Arrangement and original counter melody by Paul Simon and Arthur Garfunkel

Em
D
Em
D
Em
On the side of a hill in the deep for - est
1.Tell her to make me a cam - bric shirt:
G
Em
G
A
Em
green.
Trac - ing of spar - row on
Pars - ley, sage, rose - mar - y and thyme.
G
F♯m
Em
snow-crest - ed brown.
Blan - kets and
With - out no seams nor nee - dle
D
Em
D
Em
D
Em
D
bed-clothes the child of the moun - tain.
work,
Then she'll be a true love of

1.
Em
Sleeps un - a - ware of the clar - i - on call.
mine.
2.
Em
mine.
3.
Em
D.S. al Coda
mine.
Coda
Em D Em D Em D Em
She once was a true love of mine.
rit.
G D Em

2. Tell her to find me an acre of land:
On the side of a hill a sprinkling of leaves.
Parsley, sage, rosemary and thyme;
Washes the grave with silvery tears.
Between the salt water and the sea strand,
A soldier cleans and polishes a gun.
Then she'll be a true love of mine.
Sleeps unaware of the clarion call.

3. Tell her to reap it with a sickle of leather:
War bellows blazing in scarlet battalions.
Parsley, sage, rosemary and thyme;
Generals order their soldiers to kill.
And gather it all in a bunch of heather,
And to fight for a cause they've
long ago forgotten.
Then she'll be a true love of mine.

Señorita With A Necklace Of Tears

Words and Music by Paul Simon

1.
G♯m
4fr.
B
A 6
C♯m
4fr.
B
E
That's the way it's al-ways been
And that's how I want it to be
2.
G♯m
4fr.
B
A 6
C♯m
4fr.
B
E
That's the way it's al-ways been that's the way I like it
A
E
Some peo-ple nev-er say no
Some peo-ple nev-er com - plain
A
Some folks have no i - de - a
And oth-ers will nev-er ex -
E
A
plain
That's the way it's al-ways been and that's the way I like it And
E
that's how I want it to be
That's the way it's al - ways been And

A
E
that's the way I like it And that's how I want it to be
A/C♯
E/B
E
A/C♯
E/B
E
D.S. al Coda
3.If I could
Coda
G♯m
B
A 6
C♯m
B
E
4fr.
4fr.
That's the way it's al-ways been
A
E
4.Some peo-ple al-ways want more Some peo-ple are what they lack
A
1.
E
Some folks o-pen a door Walk a-way and nev-er look back 5.And
2.
E
A
be That's the way it's al - ways been And that's the way I like it And

2. Nothing but good news
   There is a frog in South America
   Whose venom is a cure
   For all the suffering that mankind must endure
   More powerful than morphine
   And soothing as the rain
   A frog in South America
   Has the antidote for pain
   And that's the way it's always been
   And that's the way I like it

3. If I could play all the memories
   In the neck of my guitar
   I would write a song called
   "Señorita with a Necklace of Tears"
   And every tear a sin I'd committed
   All these many years
   That's who I was
   And that's the way it's always been

4. Some people always want more
   Some people are what they lack
   Some folks open a door
   Walk away and never look back

5. And I don't want to be a judge
   And I don't want to be a jury
   I know who I am
   Lord knows who I will be

Shelter Of Your Arms

Words and Music by Paul Simon

E♭/B♭
E♭9sus4
A♭
arms
In the palm of your em - brace
F♯
B
I could de - ny the ob - vi - ous
I could rest my
E
A
case and I don't rest my case for no one
If I'm not in the
E
A
A♯○7
A♭
mood to
When I'm in the mood I
try
C m7
Take a long look at these laugh lines
F m
C m
C
They go half - way 'round the block

E♭9sus4
A♭
D♭
In the shel - ter of your arms I stopped the clock
E♭
I stopped the clock I stopped the clock
E♭/G
D♭/F
E♭/B♭
I lived a year once in a ho-tel 'Cause I failed to re-de - sign
F♯
B
For a long time I was mis - er - a-ble Then I felt just
E
F♯m
G♯m
A
fine And now I feel so fine so of - ten I'm like a
A♯°7
text-book case Just a text-book case of Ah

Cm7
3fr.
Fm
In the na na of your arms
De de de da da da da
C
E♭9sus4
6fr.
A♭
4fr.
D♭
4fr.
A♭
4fr.
D♭
4fr.
Ah
do do do do do do
De da do da
Na na do da
A♭
4fr.
E♭
6fr.
D♭
4fr.
A♭
4fr.
G
Nu na na na
Na na na na na
C
G
C
G
na na na na na na na na
Na na na na na
C
Fm7
D♭/F
E♭/G
3fr.
na na na
Whoa
Whoa
A♭
4fr.
E♭/G
3fr.
D♭/F
E♭/G♭
3fr.
Wrap me Wrap me Wrap me do

E♭9sus4
A♭
In the shel-ter of your arms
F♯
B
5
I'm an ex - traor-di-nar-y in-di-vid-u-al
I won't do you no
E
F♯m
G♯m
A
E
harm I won't tell you no lies
Un-less you want me to
A
A♯○7
A♭
C m7
But if you want me to
I'll lie
Ly-ing in the shel-ter of your arms
F m
C
E♭9sus4
A♭
E♭
D♭
In the palm of your em-brace
Do ba do we oo ba
bo Bo bo
ba ba
A♭
D♭
A♭
E♭
D♭
A♭
rit.
Na na
nu na
Do de
do
Mm

She Moves On

Words and Music by Paul Simon

Moderately bright

B 7sus4 B m E m

8

Oo, oo.

B m

I feel good,

E m

It's a fine day, The way the sun hits off the run -

B m

- way. A cloud shifts, The plane lifts. She moves on.

But feel the bite, When-ev - er you be-lieve that You'll be lost and love will

Em
find you, When the road bends And the song ends. She moves
Bm
B 7sus4
on.
Bm
Em/B Bm
Em/B Bm
1. I know the
Bm
Em
rea- son I Feel so blessed: My heart still splash - es In - side my
chest, but she, She is like a top, She can - not
Bm
stop. She moves on.

A sym - pa - thet - ic strang - er Lights a
Em
can - dle in the mid - dle of the night.
Her voice cracks, She jumps back, But she moves
Bm
on.
She says, "Ooh my
Em
sto - ry - book lov - er, You have un - der - es - ti - mat - ed my pow -
Bm
- er As you short - ly will dis - cov - er." Then I

fall to my knees, Shake a rat - tle at the skies, And I'm a -

fraid that I'll be tak - en, A - ban - doned, for - sa - ken In her

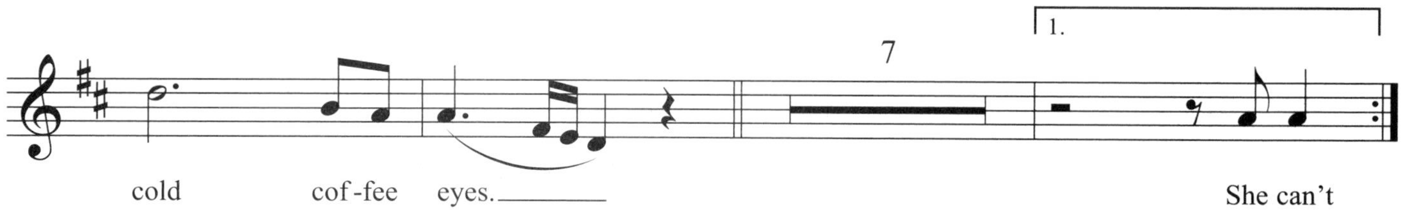
7
1.
cold cof-fee eyes.
She can't

2.
back But I feel good, It's a fine day, The way the
Em
sun hits off the run - way. A cloud shifts, The plane

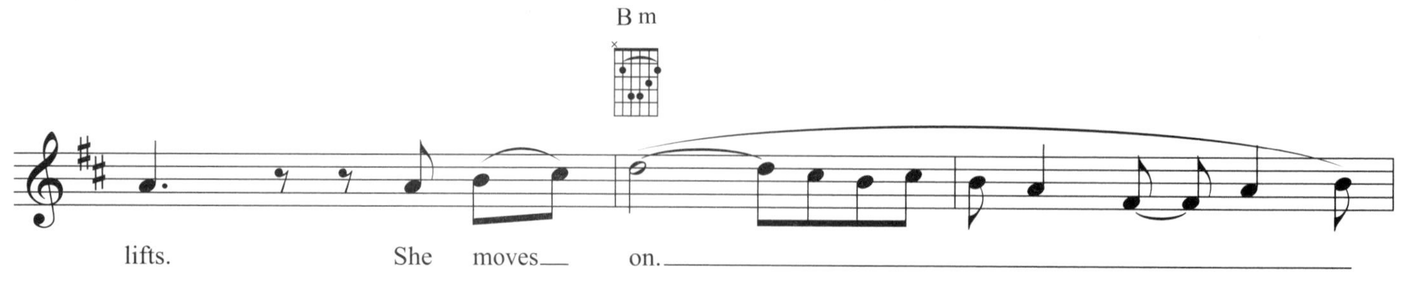
Bm
lifts. She moves on.

2. She can't sleep now, the moon is red.
She fights a fever, she burns in bed.
She needs to talk so we take a walk
Down in the maroon light.

She says, "Maybe these emotions are
As near to love as love will ever be."
So I agree.

The moon breaks.
She takes the corner, that's all she takes.
She moves on.

She says, "Ooh, my storybook lover,
You have underestimated my power
As you shortly will discover."

Then I fall to my knees,
I grow weak, I go slack,
As if she captured the breath of my
Voice in a bottle,
And I can't catch it back.

But I feel good, it's a fine day,
The way the sun hits off the runway.
A cloud shifts, the plane lifts.
She moves on.

A Simple Desultory Philippic
(Or How I Was Robert McNamara'd Into Submission)

Words and Music by Paul Simon

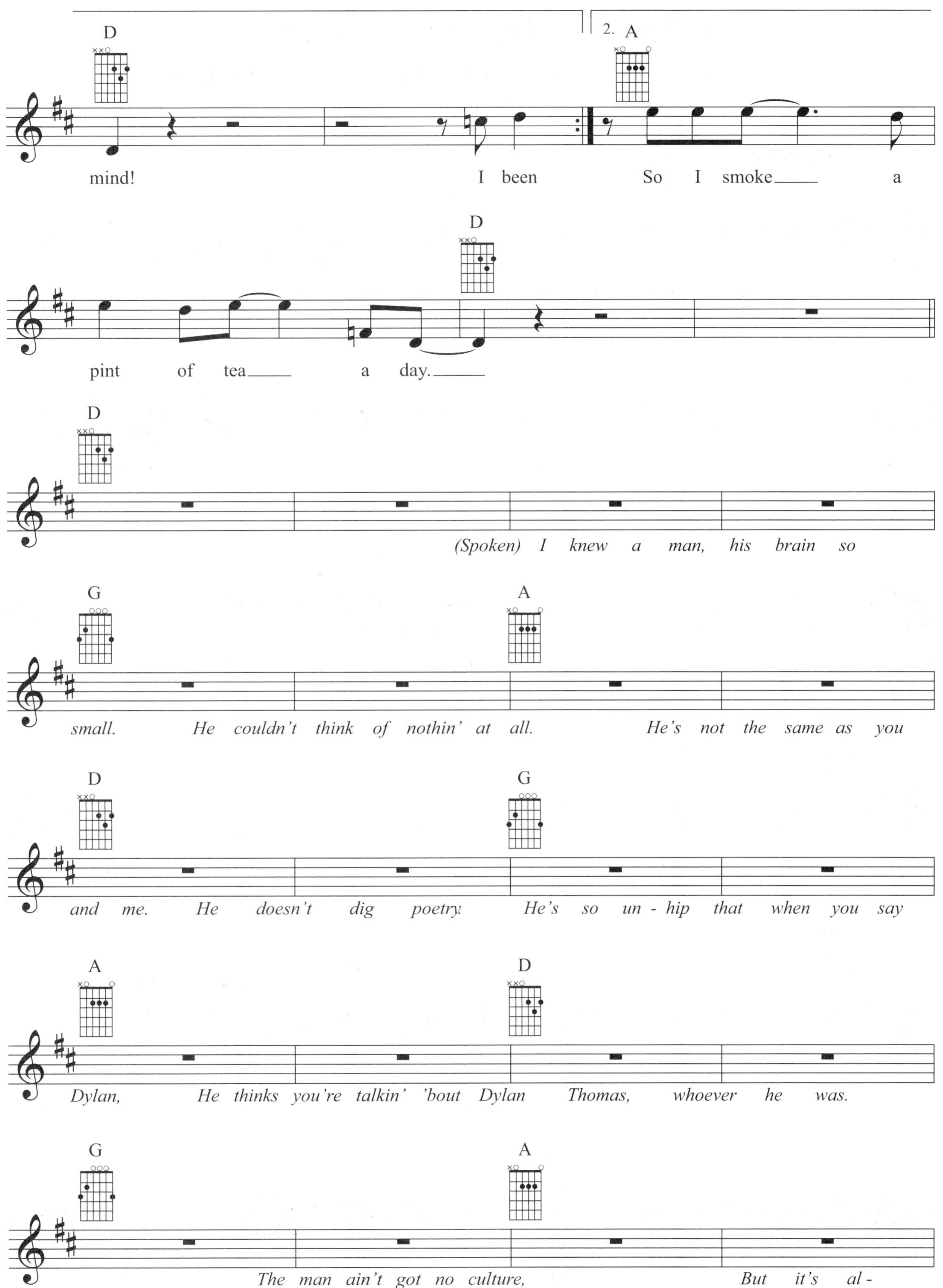
D
2. A
mind!
I been
So I smoke a
pint of tea a day.
D
(Spoken) I knew a man, his brain so
G
A
small. He couldn't think of nothin' at all. He's not the same as you
D
G
and me. He doesn't dig poetry. He's so un-hip that when you say
A
D
Dylan, He thinks you're talkin' 'bout Dylan Thomas, whoever he was.
G
A
The man ain't got no culture, But it's al-

2. I been Phil Spectored, resurrected.
I been Lou Adlered, Barry Sadlered.
Well, I paid all the dues I want to pay.
And I learned the truth from Lenny Bruce,
And all my wealth won't buy me health,
So I smoke a pint of tea a day.

Shoplifting Clothes

Music by Paul Simon
Lyrics by Paul Simon and Derek Walcott

Bright do-wop

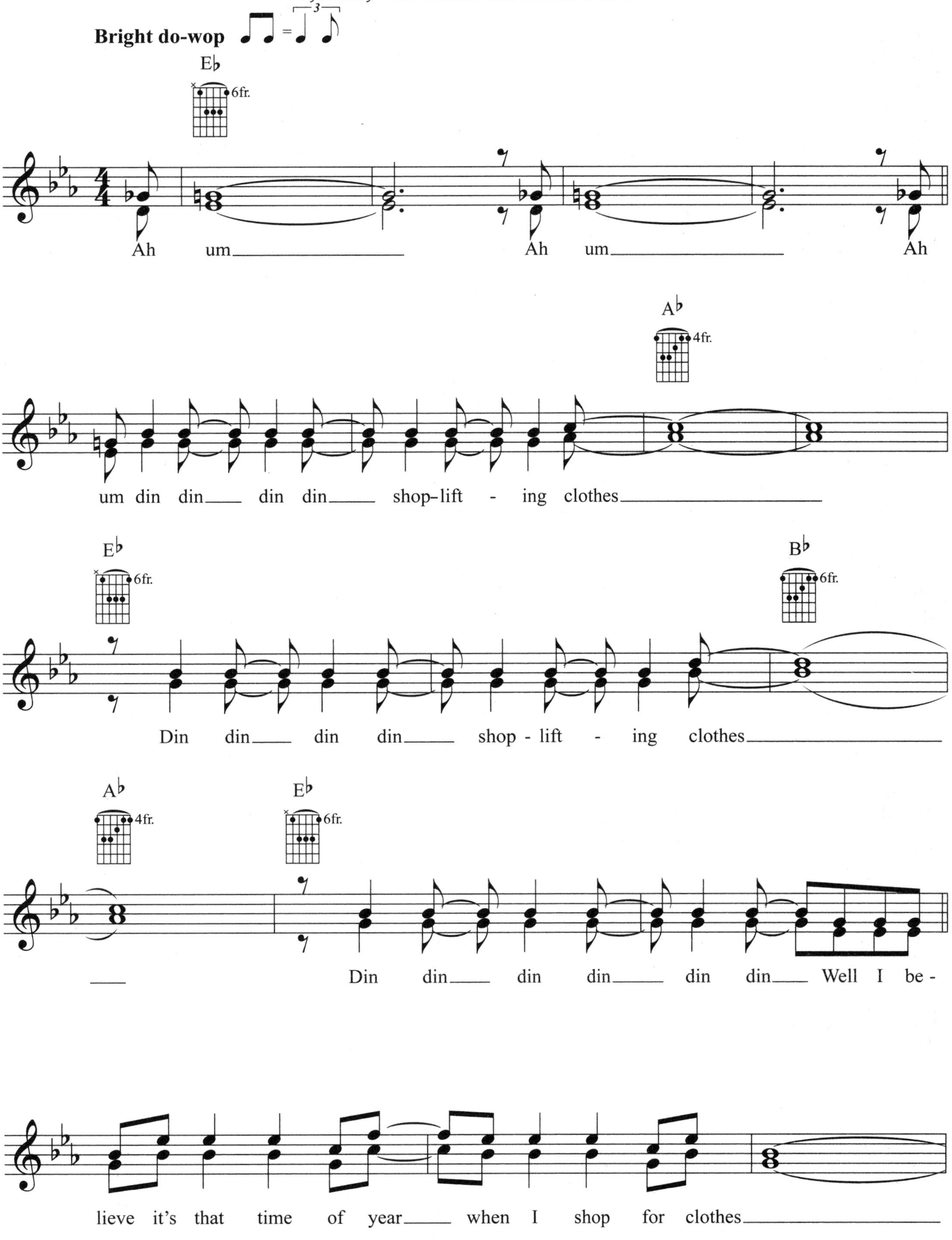

E♭
6fr.
Ah um Ah um Ah
A♭
4fr.
um din din din din shop-lift - ing clothes
E♭
6fr.
B♭
6fr.
Din din din din shop - lift - ing clothes
A♭
4fr.
E♭
6fr.
Din din din din din din Well I be -
lieve it's that time of year when I shop for clothes

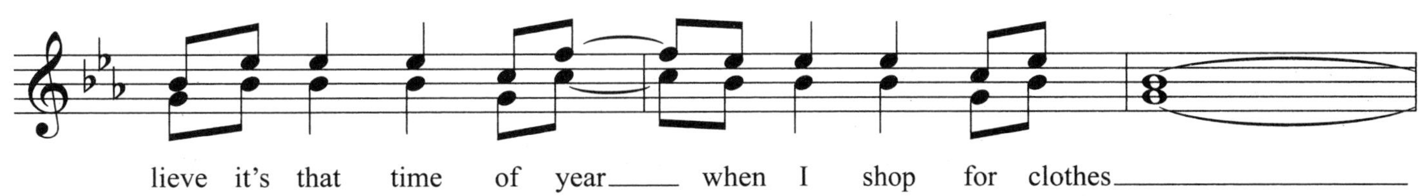

A♭
4fr.
E♭
6fr.
Well I be - lieve it's that time of year when I shop for clothes
B♭
6fr.
A♭
4fr.
E♭
6fr.
Tells you how far your hard - earned mon-ey goes
Ah um dit dit dit Ah um
A♭
4fr.
1. (Spoken) Come on in boys, get yourself a better view. Have a look around, see if anything appeals to you.
Oo Oo Oo
E♭
6fr.
B♭
6fr.
E♭
6fr.
1.
We got a sale right now, you buy one, you get two.
Oo Shop-lift - ing Oo Oo
2.
Well I be - lieve it's that time of year when I shop for clothes

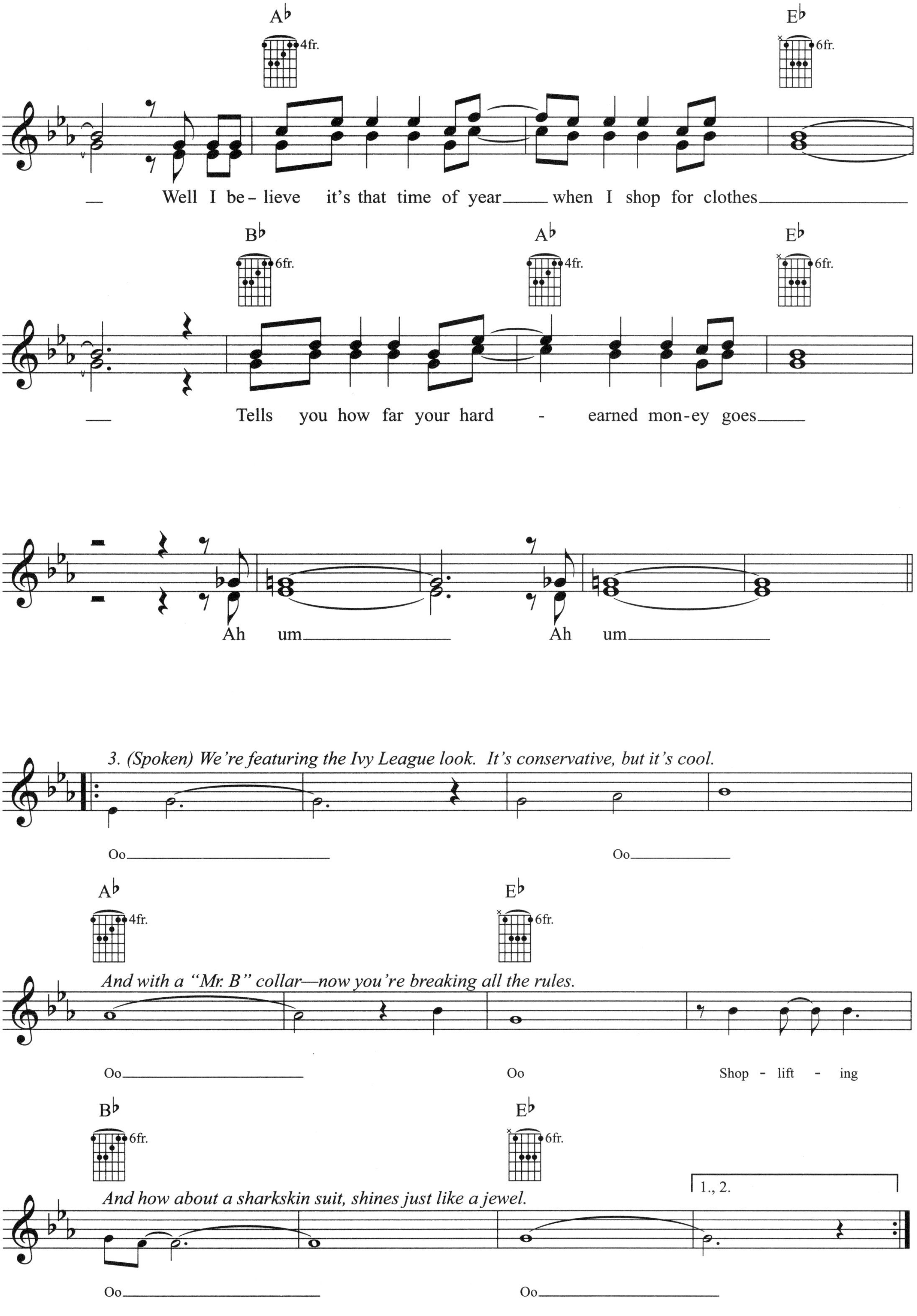

A♭
4fr.
E♭
6fr.
Well I be-lieve it's that time of year when I shop for clothes
B♭
6fr.
A♭
4fr.
E♭
6fr.
Tells you how far your hard - earned mon-ey goes
Ah um
Ah um
3. (Spoken) We're featuring the Ivy League look. It's conservative, but it's cool.
Oo
Oo
A♭
4fr.
E♭
6fr.
And with a "Mr. B" collar—now you're breaking all the rules.
Oo
Oo
Shop - lift - ing
B♭
6fr.
E♭
6fr.
And how about a sharkskin suit, shines just like a jewel.
1., 2.
Oo
Oo

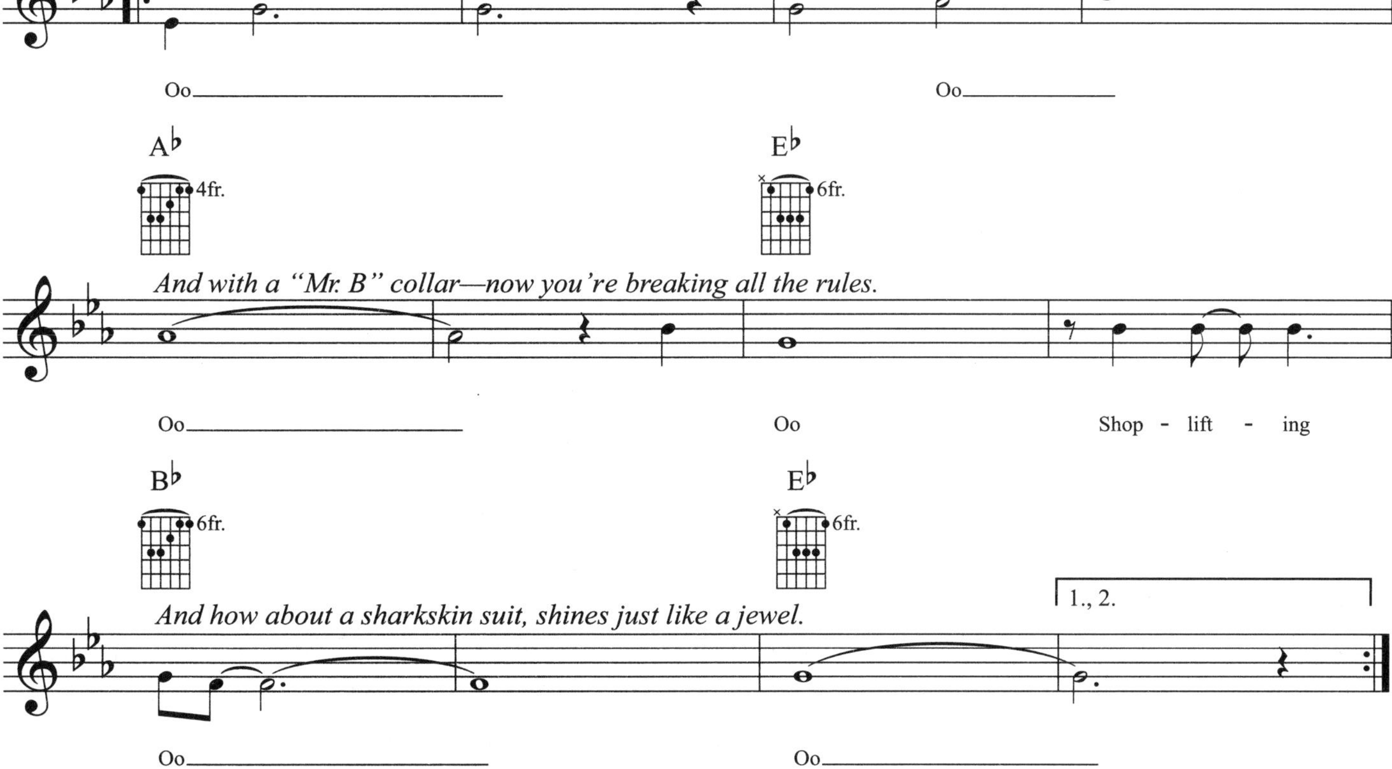

3.
Well I be - lieve it's that time of year when I shop for
A♭
4fr.
clothes
Well I be - lieve it's that time of year
when I shop for clothes
to Coda
B♭
6fr.
A♭
4fr.
E♭
6fr.
Tells you how far your hard - earned mon-ey goes
De de det de de det det de de de det De de det de de det
A♭
4fr.
det de de de det De de det de de det det de de de det

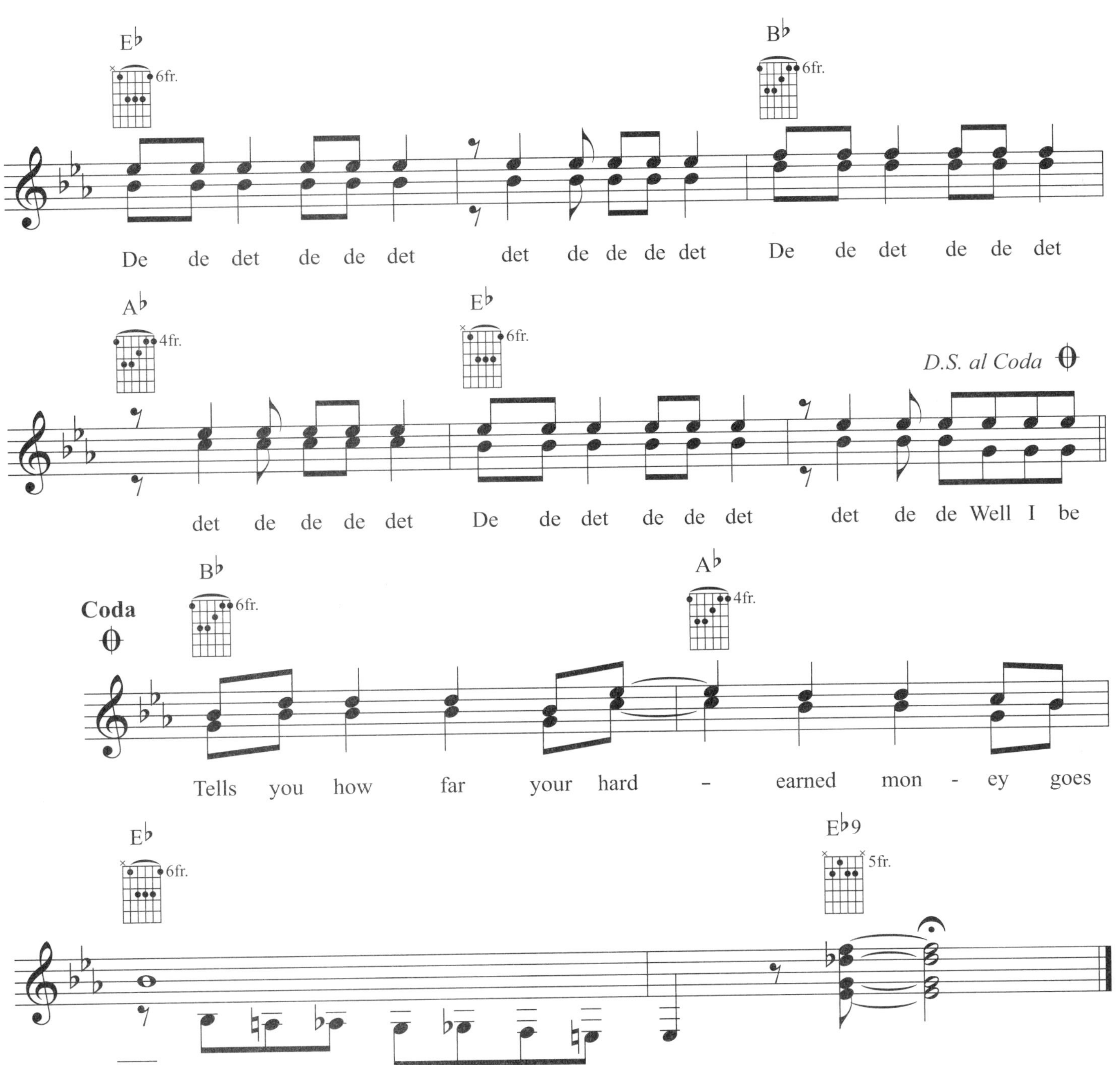

2. *(Spoken) Just look at the way that fabric drapes to your leg*
Now imagine that with a saddle stitch and a twelve-inch peg
Women see you comin', they're gonna get down
on their knees and beg

4. *(Spoken) If it's a hat you require, let me show you*
one of our stingy brims
Here, check yourself out in the mirror,
The shipment has just come in.
Man! That hat is you
That hat is him

5. *(Spoken) I'm sorry, my man, but the cape is not for sale*
I got a new shipment expected any day now
It's comin' in via the airmail
Yeah, this item gonna be very fashionable
come this fall

Silent Eyes

Words and Music by Paul Simon

E7
B
no one will com - fort her;
Je - ru - sa - lem
A7♯11
G♯m7
C♯m7
4fr.
weeps a - lone.
A
D7
F
She is sor - row,
sor - row;
F♯°7
G
C
G/B
A7sus4
she burns like a flame
A7
D
G
and she calls my name.
Mm.
D
G
Mm.

D
A
Gmaj7
3fr.
Bm
F♯m
Oh.
Bm
A
E
A
Mm.
Am7
5fr.
G/A
3fr.
Am
G
Si - lent eyes
Fmaj7
F7
C
B♭7♯11
5fr.
burn - ing in the des-ert sun
Am
C9
F
Fm
half-way to Je - ru - sa - lem.
B♭9
B♭m
And we shall all be called as wit-ness-es,

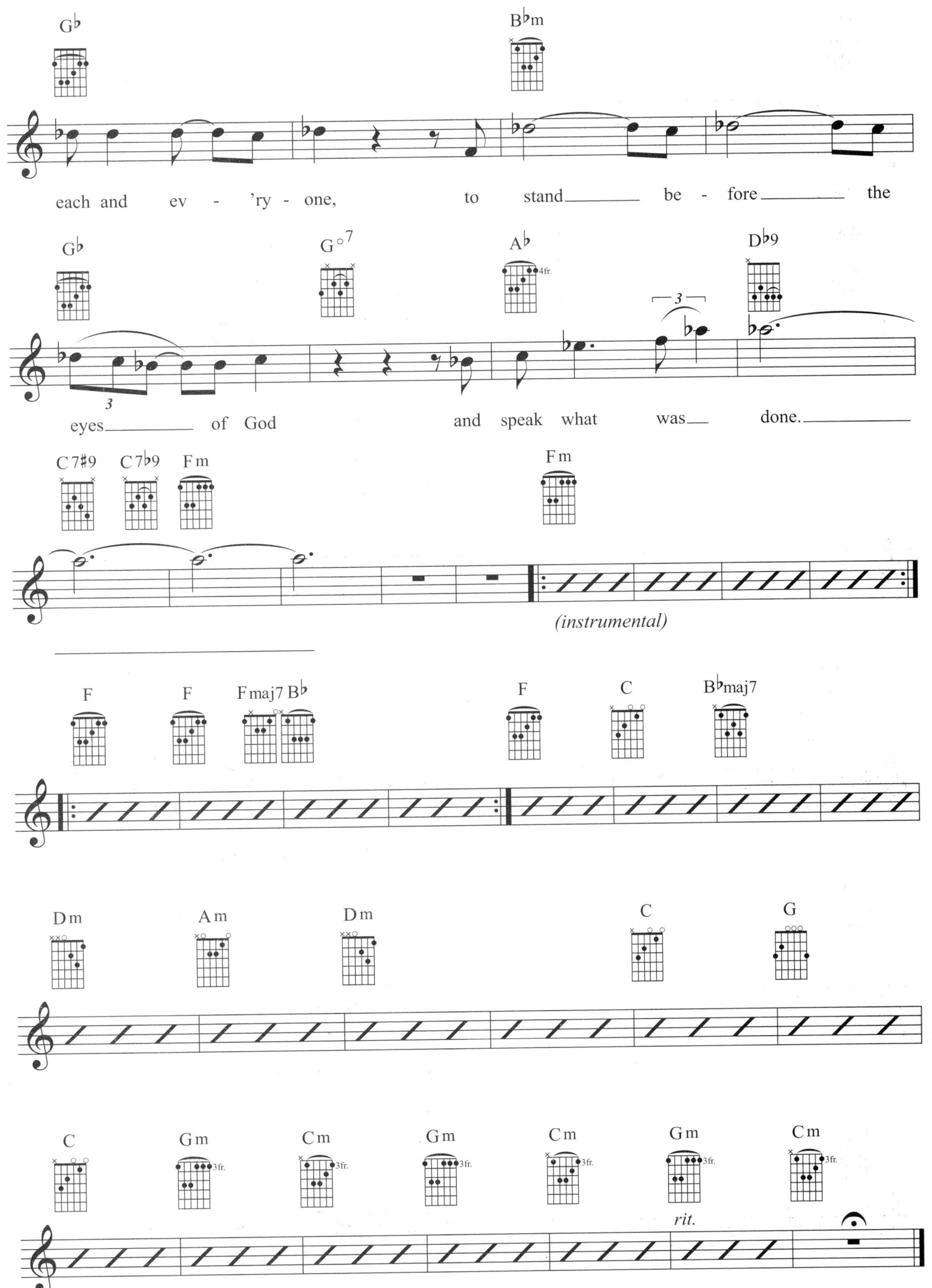
G♭
B♭m
each and ev - 'ry - one, to stand be - fore the
G♭
G○7
A♭
4fr.
D♭9
eyes of God and speak what was done.
C7♯9
C7♭9
Fm
Fm
(instrumental)
F
F
Fmaj7
B♭
F
C
B♭maj7
Dm
Am
Dm
C
G
C
Gm
3fr.
Cm
3fr.
Gm
3fr.
Cm
3fr.
Gm
3fr.
Cm
3fr.
rit.

Slip Slidin' Away

Words and Music by Paul Simon

A♭
Fm
lor - es, I live in fear. My love for
A♭
E♭
D♭
E♭
A♭
to Coda
you is so o-ver pow-'ring I'm a-fraid that I will dis-ap - pear.
1.
N.C.
2.
N.C.
A♭
Slip slid - in' a - Slip slid - in' a - way. slip slid - in' a-
Fm
A♭
E♭
way. You know the near - er your des-ti-na - tion the more
D♭
E♭
A♭
G♭
D♭
A♭
G♭
D♭
you're slip slid - in' a - way.

A♭
3.And I know a fa -
Fm
A♭
- ther
who had a son.
He longed to
D♭
E♭
D♭
D♭7
tell him all the rea - sons for the things he'd done.
He came a
A♭
Fm
long way
just to ex - plain.
He kissed his
A♭
E♭
D♭
E♭
A♭
boy as he lay sleep-ing, then he turned a-round and head-ed home a - gain.

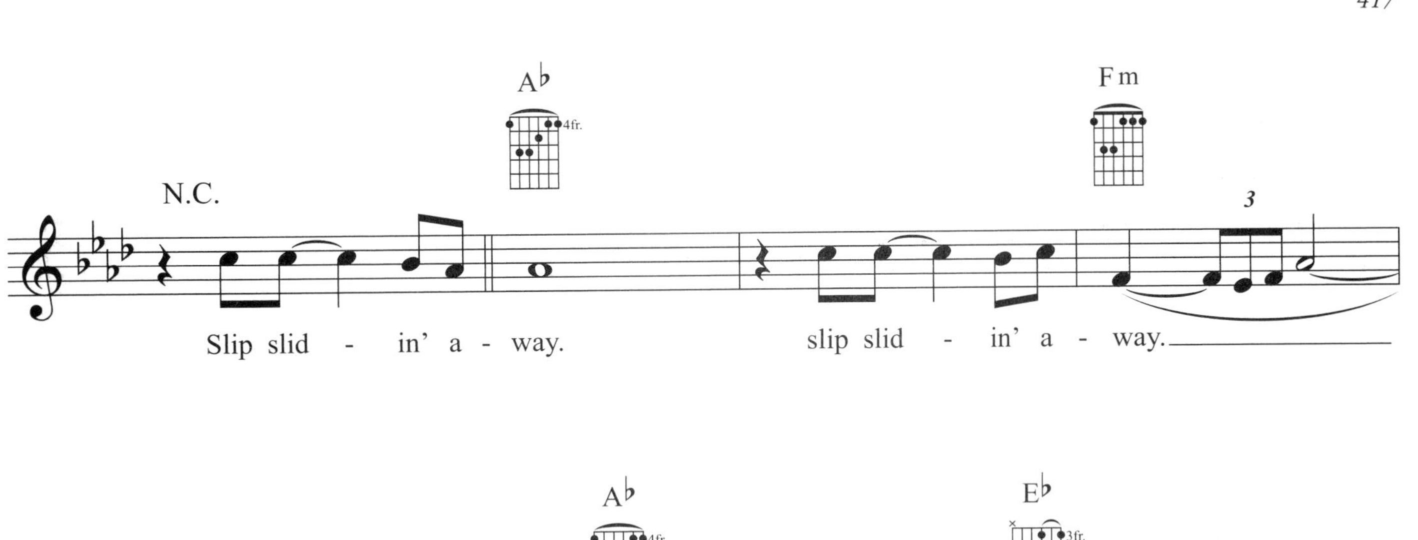
A♭
Fm
N.C.
3
Slip slid - in' a - way.
slip slid - in' a - way.

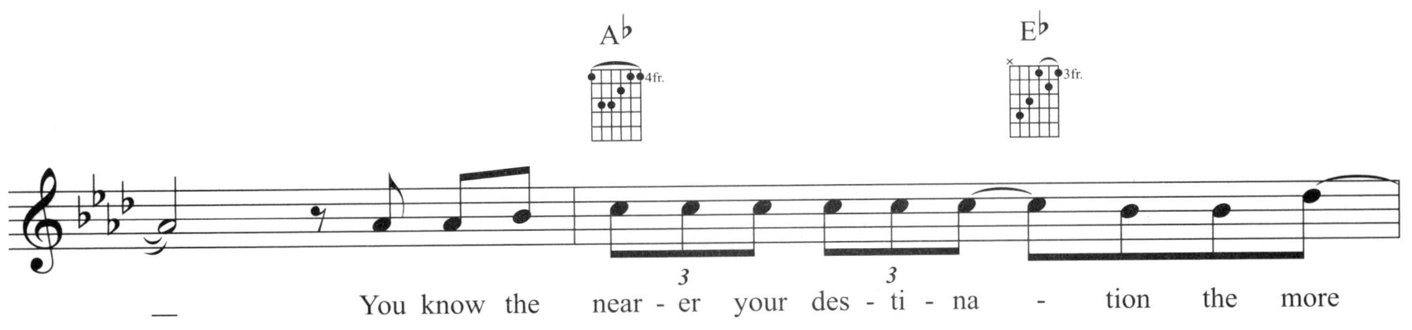
A♭
E♭
3
3
You know the near - er your des - ti - na - tion the more

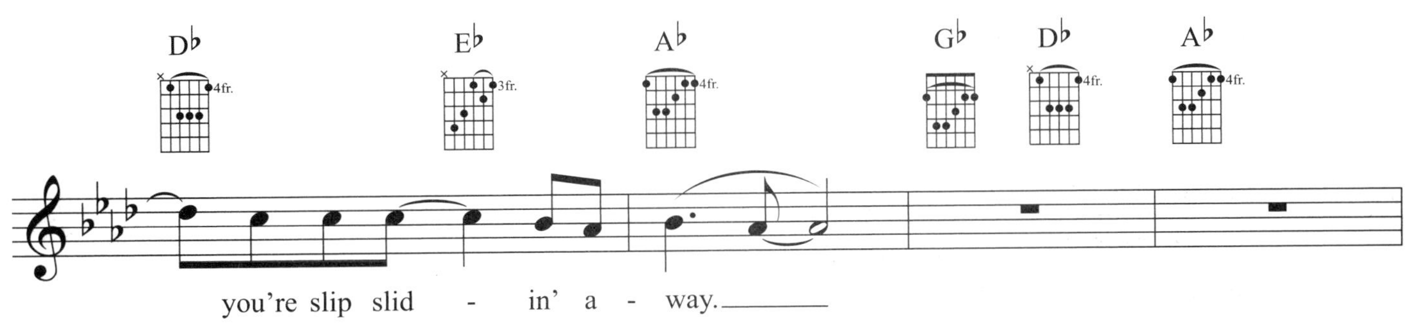
D♭
E♭
A♭
G♭
D♭
A♭
you're slip slid - in' a - way.

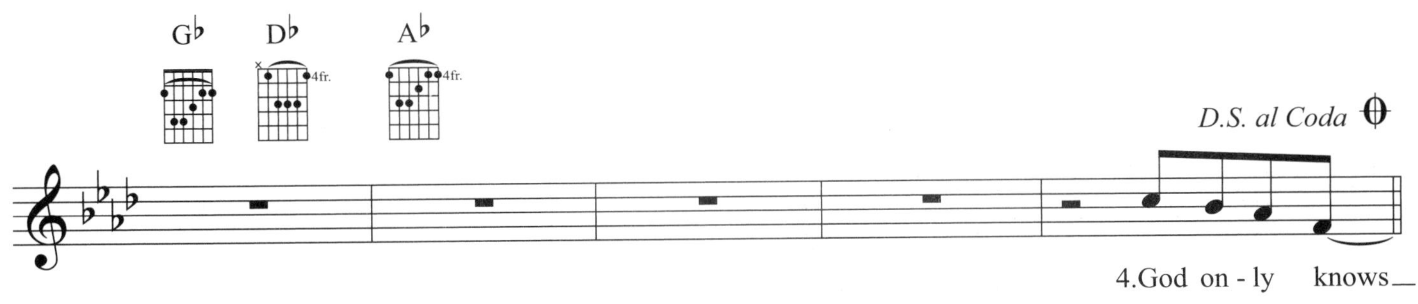
G♭
D♭
A♭
D.S. al Coda
4.God on - ly knows

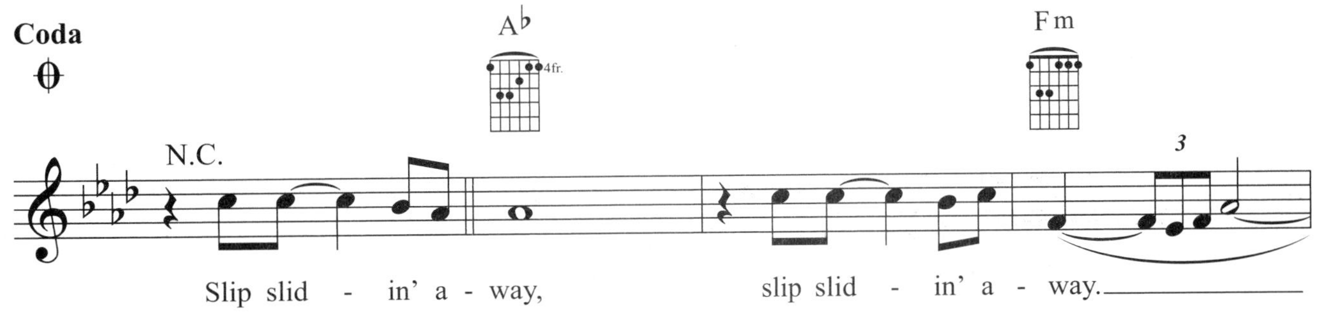
Coda
A♭
Fm
N.C.
3
Slip slid - in' a - way,
slip slid - in' a - way.

A♭
E♭
You know the near - er your des - ti - na - tion the more
D♭
E♭
A♭
you're slip slid - in' a - way.
Fm
Slip slid - in'- a - way.
You know the
A♭
E♭
D♭
E♭
near - er your des - ti - na - tion the more you're slip slid - in' a -
A♭
Fm
way.
Mm.
Mm,

2. I know a woman
Became a wife
These are the very words she uses
To describe her life
She said, a good day
Ain't got no rain
She said a bad day's when I lie in bed
And think of things that might've been

Slip slidin' away
Slip slidin' away
You know the nearer your destination
The more you're slip slidin' away

4. God only knows
God makes His plan
The information's unavailable
To the mortal man
We're workin' our jobs
Collect our pay
Believe we're gliding down the highway
When in fact we're slip slidin' away

Slip slidin' away
Slip slidin' away
You know the nearer your destination
The more you're slip slidin' away
Slip slidin' away
You know the nearer your destination
The more you're slip slidin' away

So Long, Frank Lloyd Wright

Words and Music by Paul Simon

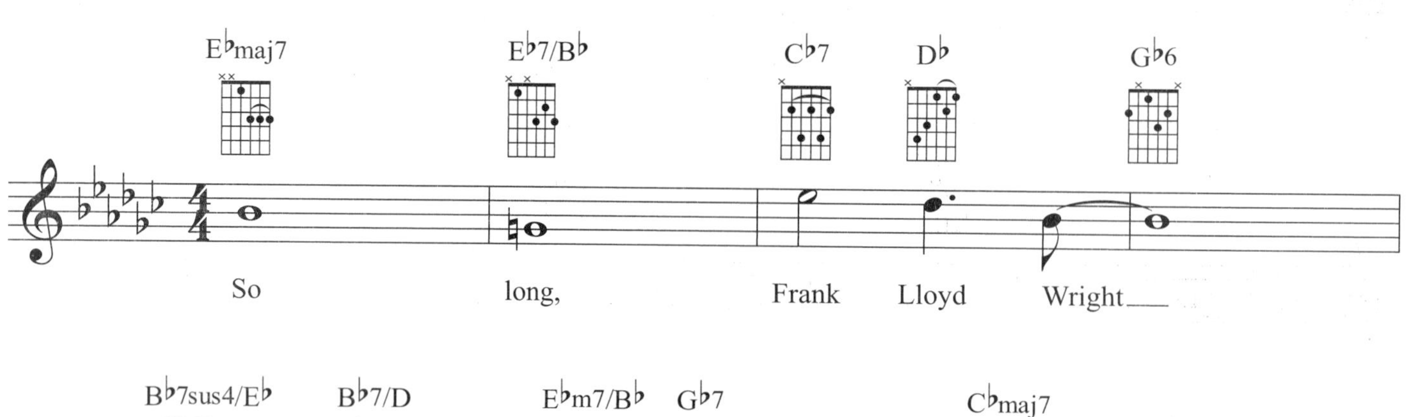

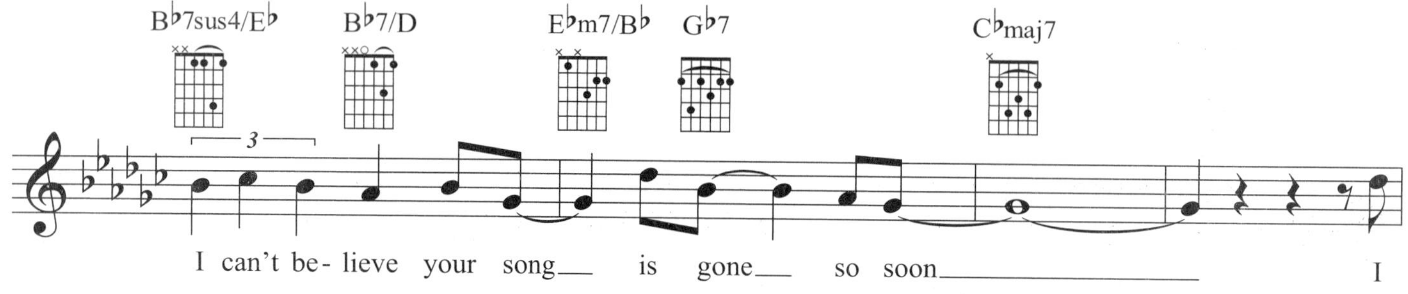

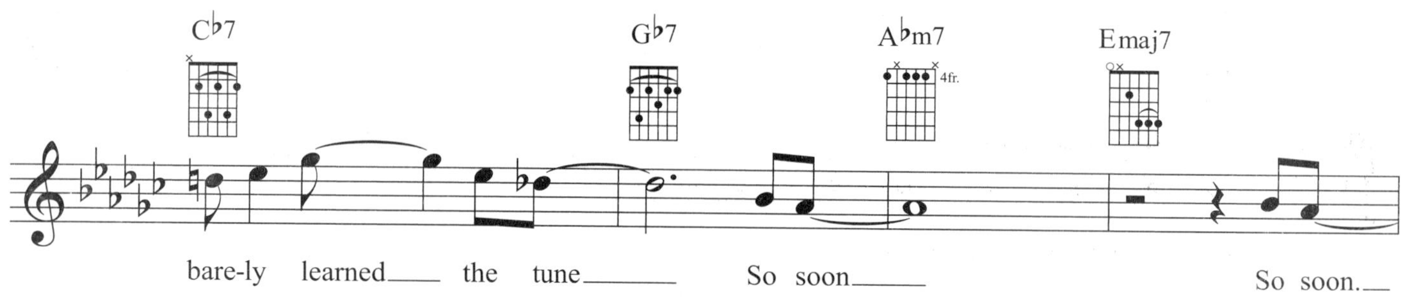

C♭7
G♭7
I nev-er laughed so long So long
A♭m7
A♭m(maj7)/G
G♭
G♭7
So long.
A♭m7
G♭maj7
Ar - chi - tects may come and Ar - chi - tects may go and nev -
D°
D♭7♭9
G♭maj7
B m7
E 7
B m7
- er change your point of view.
When I
B♭7
A maj7
G maj7
F♯7
B 7
E maj7
run dry I stop a - while and think of you.
(instrumental)
E 7/B
C 7
D
G 6
B 7sus4/E
B 7/D♯
E m7/B
G 7
C maj7
C 7
G 7
A m7

A♭7
Gmaj7
A♭m7
Ar- chi-tects may come and Ar -
G♭maj7
D°
D♭7♭9
G♭
- chi-tects may go and nev - er change your point of view.
Bm7
E7
Bm7
B♭7
Amaj7
Gmaj7
F♯7
B7
Emaj7
So
E7
C7
D
G6
B7sus4/E
B7/D♯
Long, Frank Lloyd Wright,
All of the nights we'd har -
Em7/B
G7
Cmaj7
C7
- mo - nize till dawn.
I nev-er laughed so long
G7
A7
A♭7
Gmaj7
A♭7
So long
So long
So long
A7
A♭7
Gmaj7
A♭7
repeat and fade
So long.
So long

Some Folks' Lives Roll Easy

Words and Music by Paul Simon

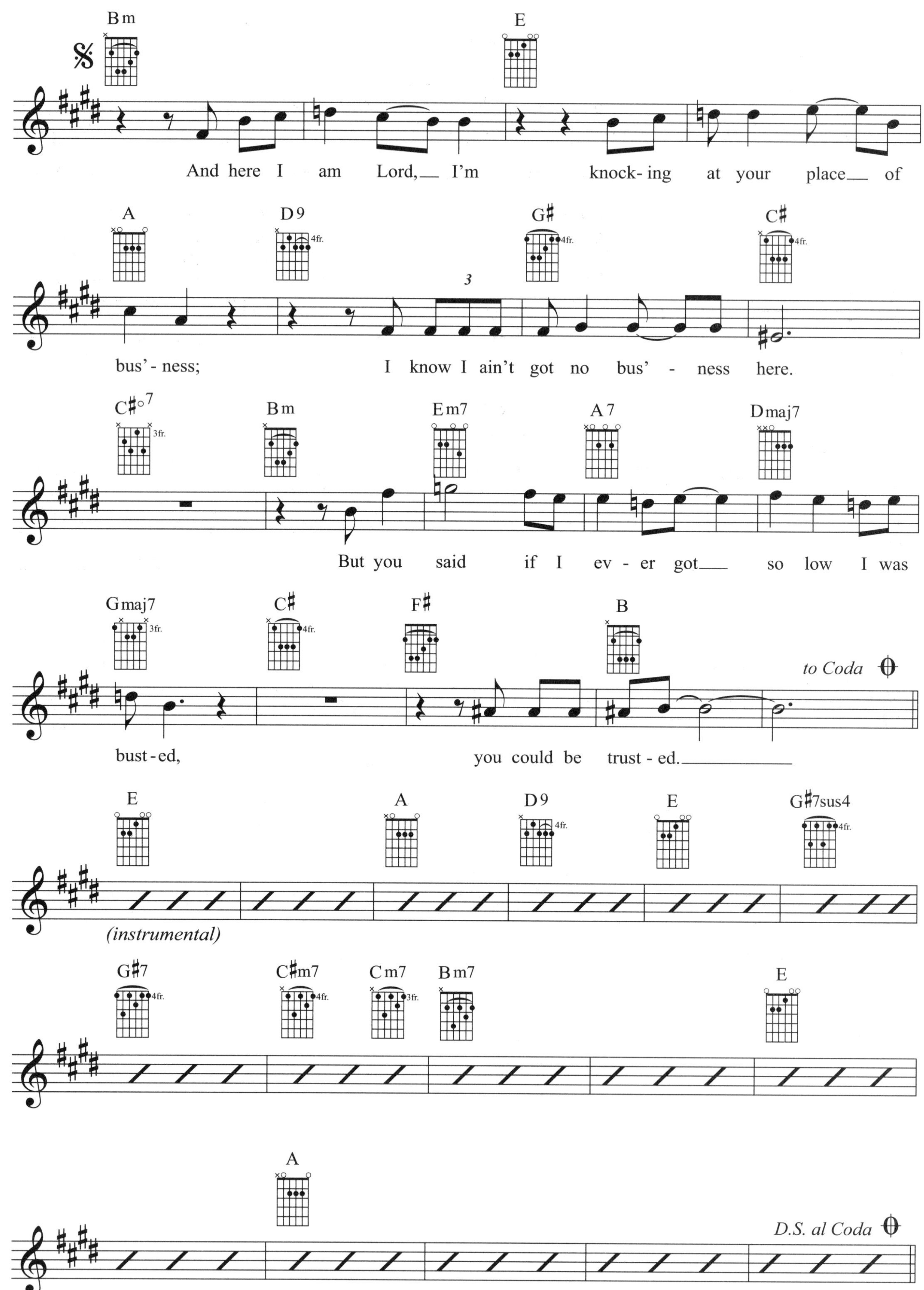
Bm
E
And here I am Lord, I'm knocking at your place of
A
D9
G♯
C♯
bus'-ness; I know I ain't got no bus' - ness here.
C♯○7
Bm
Em7
A7
Dmaj7
But you said if I ev - er got so low I was
Gmaj7
C♯
F♯
B
to Coda
bust-ed, you could be trust-ed.
E
A
D9
E
G♯7sus4
(instrumental)
G♯7
C♯m7
Cm7
Bm7
E
A
D.S. al Coda

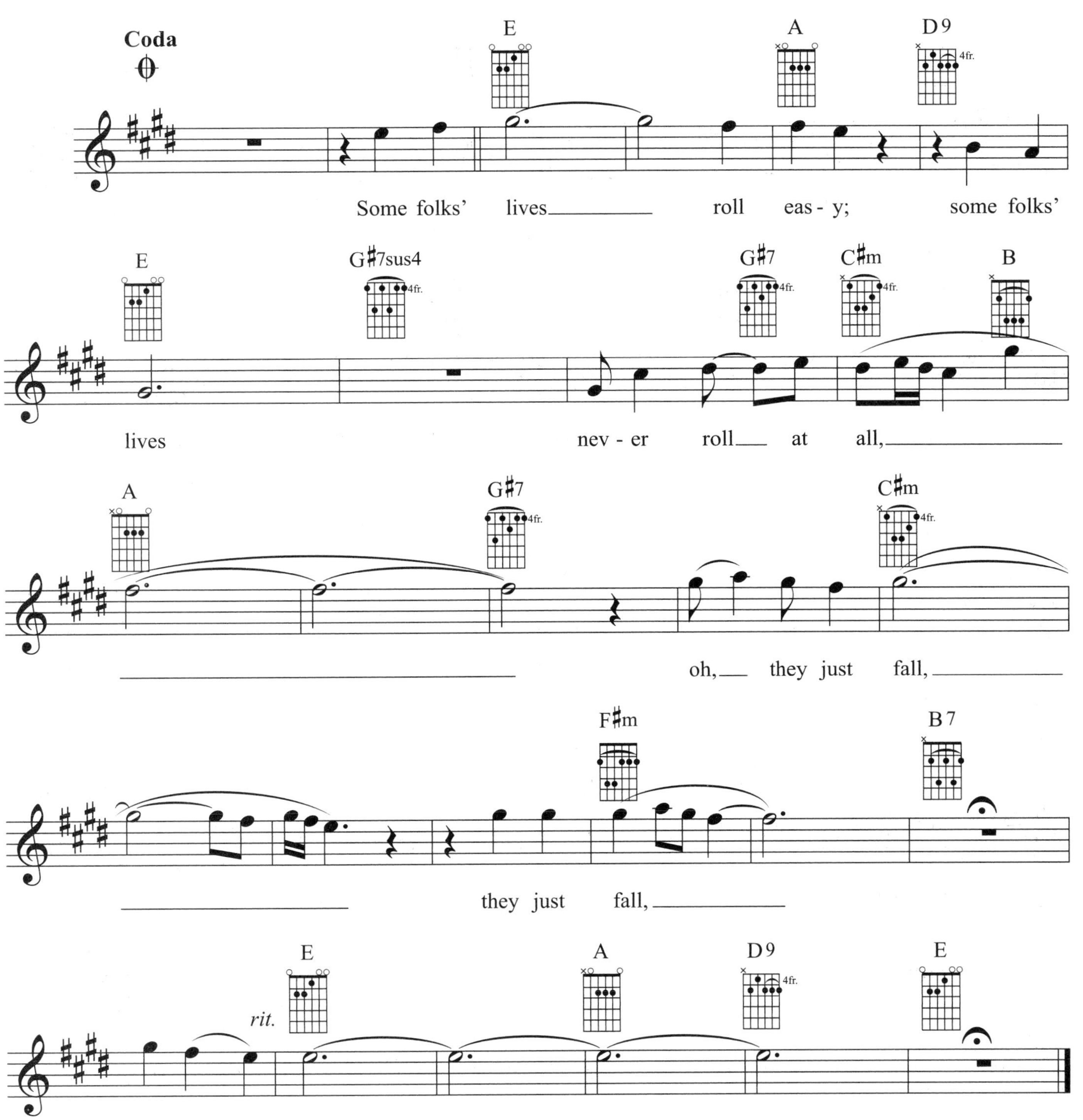
Coda
E
A
D9
4fr.
Some folks' lives roll eas - y; some folks'
E
G♯7sus4
G♯7
C♯m
B
lives nev - er roll at all,
A
G♯7
C♯m
oh, they just fall,
F♯m
B7
they just fall,
E
A
D9
E
rit.
some folks' lives.

Something So Right

Words and Music by Paul Simon

Moderately slow

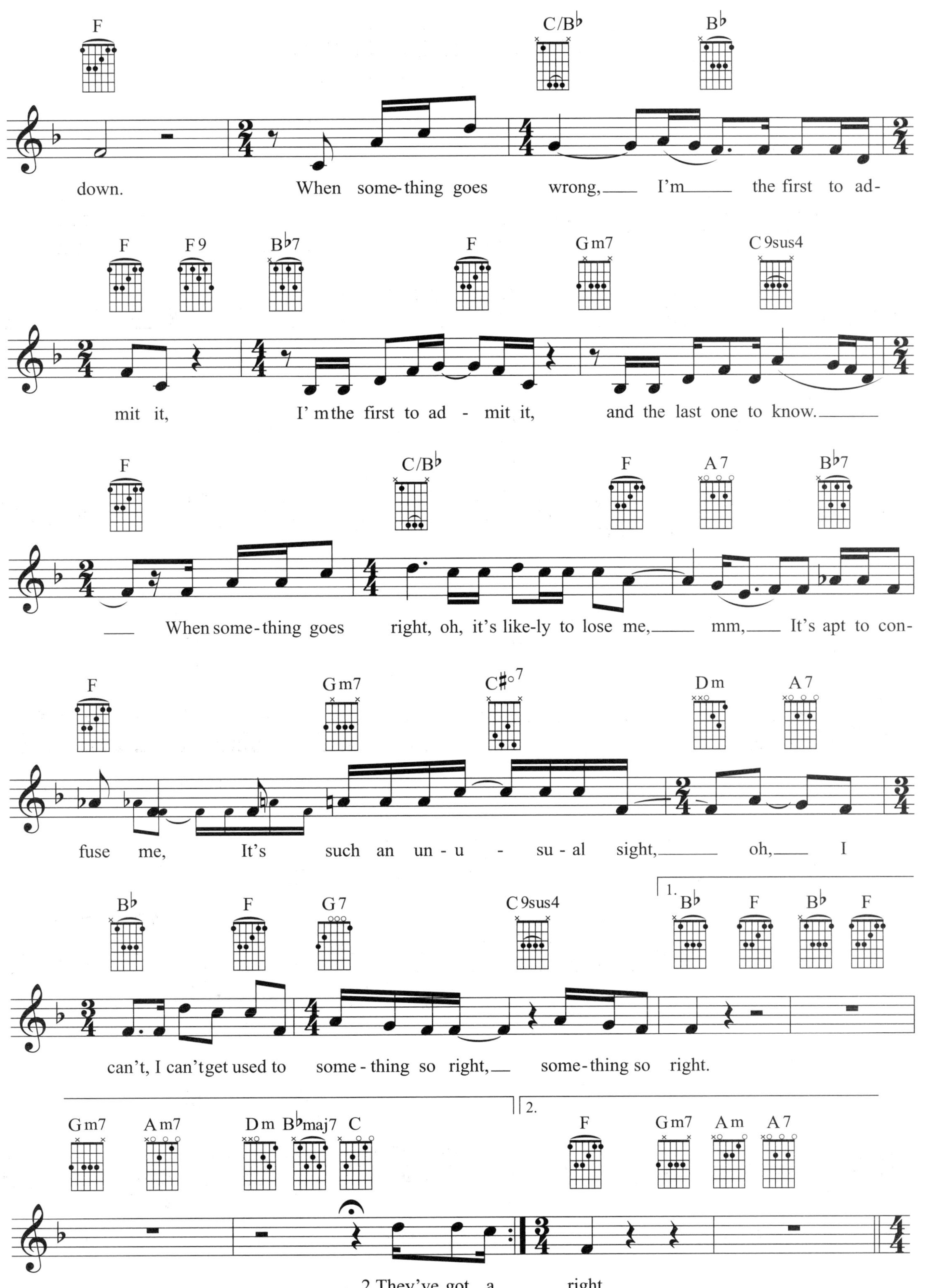
F
C/B♭
B♭
down.
When some-thing goes
wrong, I'm the first to ad-
F
F9
B♭7
F
Gm7
C9sus4
mit it,
I' m the first to ad - mit it,
and the last one to know.
F
C/B♭
F
A7
B♭7
When some-thing goes
right, oh, it's like-ly to lose me,
mm,
It's apt to con-
F
Gm7
C♯°7
Dm
A7
fuse me,
It's
such an un - u - su - al
sight,
oh,
I
B♭
F
G7
C9sus4
1.
B♭
F
B♭
F
can't, I can't get used to
some - thing so right,
some-thing so
right.
Gm7
Am7
Dm
B♭maj7
C
2.
F
Gm7
Am
A7
2. They've got a
right.

Dm
A
F7
Some peo-ple nev-er say the words, I love you, It's not their style to be so
B♭
A7
Dm
A
bold. Some peo - ple nev-er say those words, I love you, But like a
Dm
B♭
G7
C7sus4
C7
child they're long-ing to be told. Mm. When some-thing goes
F
C/B♭
B♭
F
F9
wrong, I'm the first to ad - mit it,
B♭7
F
Gm7
C9sus4
I'm the first to ad - mit it, and the last one to know.
F
C/B♭
F
When some - thing goes right, oh, it's like - ly to lose me,

2. They've got a wall in China,
It's a thousand miles long.
To keep out the foreigners,
They made it strong.
And I've got a wall around me
That you can't even see.
It took a little time
To get next to me.

Somewhere They Can't Find Me

Words and Music by Paul Simon

Moderately

2. Oh baby, you don't know what I've done,
   I've committed a crime, I've broken the law
   While you were here sleeping and just
   dreaming of me,
   I held up and robbed a liquor store.

   Chorus

3. Oh my life seems unreal, my crime an illusion,
   A scene badly written in which I must play.
   And though it puts me up tight to leave you,
   I know it's not right to leave you,
   When morning is just a few hours away.

   Chorus

Song About The Moon

Words and Music by Paul Simon

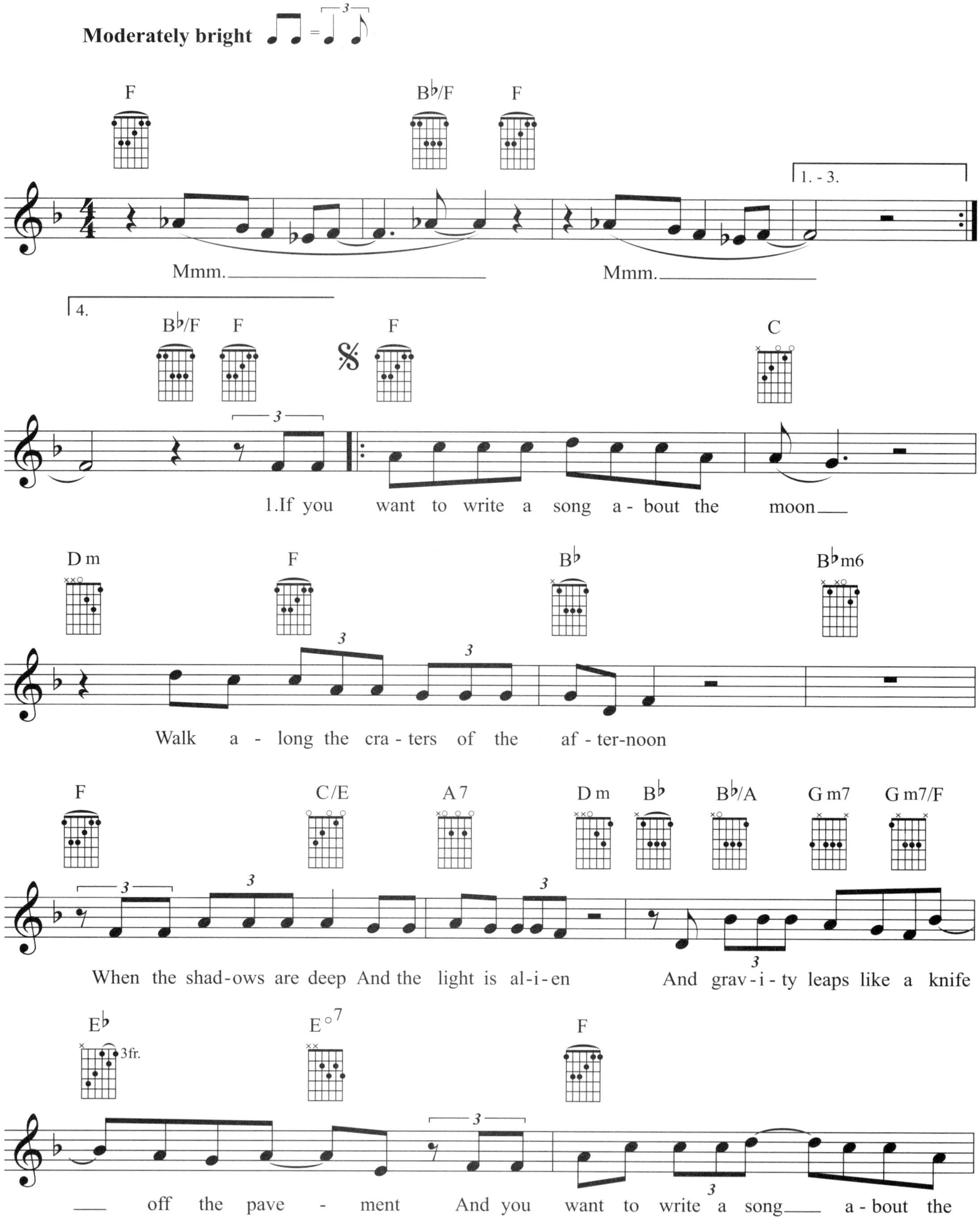

Moderately bright
F
B♭/F
F
1. - 3.
Mmm.
Mmm.
4.
B♭/F
F
F
C
1.If you want to write a song a - bout the moon
Dm
F
B♭
B♭m6
Walk a - long the cra - ters of the af - ter-noon
F
C/E
A7
Dm
B♭
B♭/A
Gm7
Gm7/F
When the shad-ows are deep And the light is al-i-en
And grav-i-ty leaps like a knife
E♭
3fr.
E°7
F
off the pave - ment And you want to write a song a - bout the

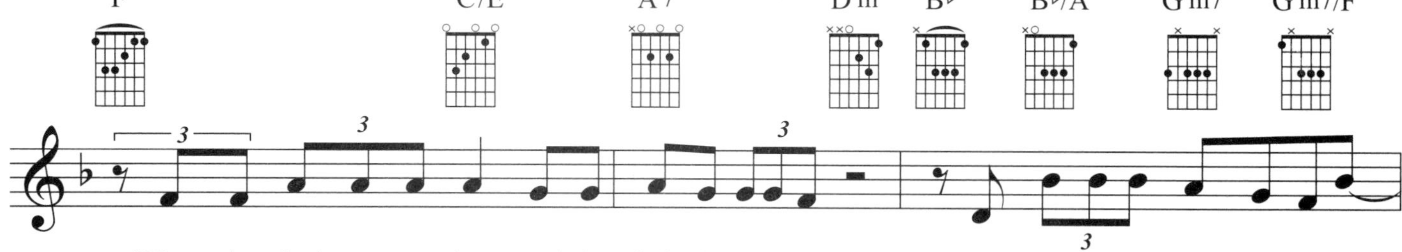

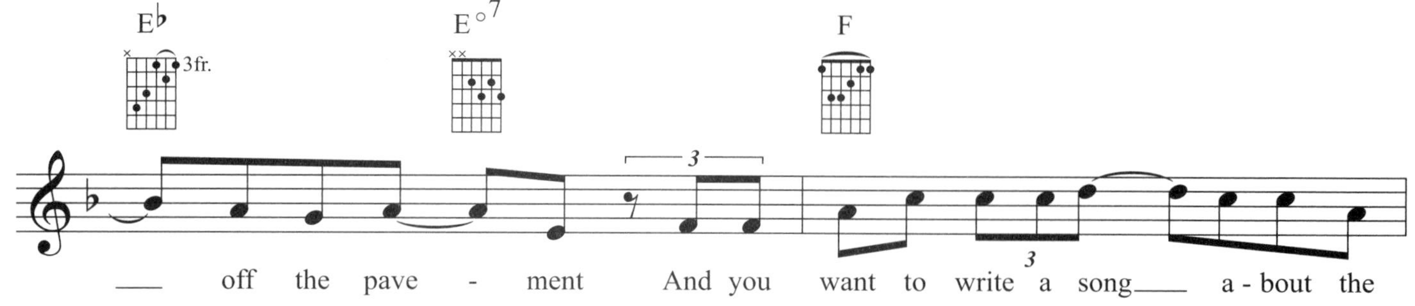

C
C♯°7
Dm7
F7
B♭
B°7
moon
You want to write a spir-i-tu-al tune
Then
F
Am/E
B♭maj7
F/A
G7
C7sus4
to Coda
nah nah nah nah nah nah yeah yeah
Pres - to! Song a-bout the moon
1.
F
B♭/F
F
B♭/F
F
Mmm.
Mmm.
2.If you
2.
F
B♭/B
F
B♭/F
F
Dm7
Fmaj7/C
3.The laugh - ing boy He
A♭maj7
4fr.
D7
Gm
3fr.
D7
Gm
3fr.
laughed so hard He fell down from his place

Dm7
Fmaj7/C
B♭maj7
A7
The laugh - ing girl She laughed so hard The
Dm
G9
C9
F
tears rolled down her face whoa. Hey Song - writ -
B♭/F
F
B♭/F
F
B♭/F
F
D.S. al Coda
- er: If you want to write a song a - bout a face
Coda
F
C
C♯°7
Dm
F7
B♭
B♭m
Oh, If you
F
C
C♯°7
want to write a song a - bout the moon You

2. If you want to write a song about the heart
Think about the moon before you start
Because the heart will howl
Like a dog in the moonlight
And the heart can explode
Like a pistol on a June night
So if you want to write a song about the heart
And its ever-longing for a counterpart
Write a song about the moon

4. Think about a photograph
That you really can't remember
But you can't erase
Wash your hands in dreams and lightning
Cut off your hair
And whatever is frightening
If you want to write a song
About a face
If you want to write a song about
The human race
Write a song about the moon
If you want to write a song about the moon
You want to write a spiritual tune
Then do it
Write a song about the moon

Song For The Asking

Words and Music by Paul Simon

St. Judy's Comet

Words and Music by Paul Simon

run come see St. Ju-dy's Com - et roll a-cross the skies, And leave a spray of dia-monds in its
Amaj7
Am6
E/G♯
F♯m
B
E
F♯m
wake. I long to see St. Ju-dy's Com-et spar-kle in your eyes when you a -
A
E9
Amaj7
wake, oh, when you wake, wake. Lit-tle boy, (lit-tle
Am6
E/G♯
E9
Amaj7
boy) Won't you lay your bod-y down? Lit-tle boy, (lit-tle
Am6
E/G♯
E9
G♯aug7
4fr.
G♯7
4fr.
boy) Won't you close your wea-ry eyes. Ain't noth-in' flash-in' but the
C♯m7
4fr.
Cm7
3fr.
Bm7
B♭m7
A
E9
to Coda
fire - flies.

Well, I sang it once, and I sang it twice, I'm goin' to
sing it three times more, I'm goin' to stay 'till your re - sis-tance is o - ver -
Amaj7
Am6
E/G♯
come, 'Cause if I can't sing my boy to sleep, well, it
F♯m
B
E
F♯m
A
E9
D.S. al Coda
makes your fa-mous dad-dy look so dumb, look so dumb. Won't you
Coda
Oo, lit-tle sleep-y boy, do you know what time it is? Well, the
Amaj7
Am6
E/G♯
hour of your bed-time's long been past, And though I know you're fight-in' it, I can
F♯m
B
E
F♯m
A
E9
repeat and fade
tell when you rub your eyes that you're fad-in' fast, oo, fad-in' fast.

The Sound Of Silence

Words and Music by Paul Simon

Moderately

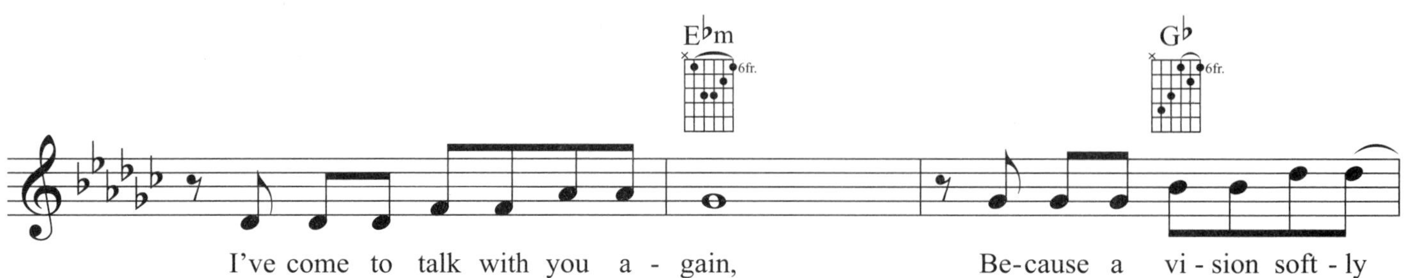

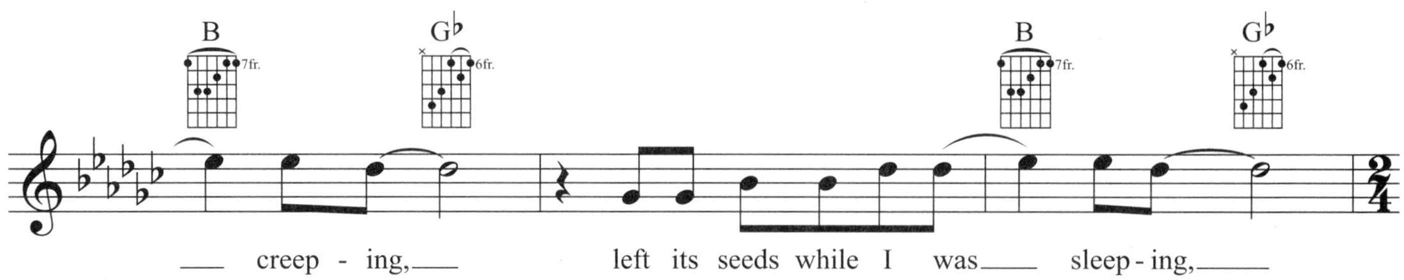

E♭m
6fr.
D♭
4fr.
In rest-less dreams I walked a - lone
nar-row streets of cob-ble-
E♭m
6fr.
G♭
6fr.
B
7fr.
G♭
6fr.
stone,
'Neath the ha - lo of a street lamp
B
7fr.
G♭
6fr.
I turned my col-lar to the cold and damp
When my
B
7fr.
G♭
6fr.
eyes were stabbed by the flash of a ne-on light that split the
E♭m
6fr.
G♭
6fr.
D♭
4fr.
E♭m
6fr.
night
and touched the sound of si-lence.
E♭m
6fr.
D♭
4fr.
And in the na-ked light I saw
Ten thou-sand peo-ple may-be

E♭m
G♭
B
G♭
more. Peo - ple talk - ing with out speak - ing,
B
G♭
B
Peo-ple hear-ing with-out list-'ning, Peo-ple writ-ing songs that
G♭
G♭
voi-ces nev-er share and no one dare dis - turb the
D♭
E♭m
E♭m
D♭
sound of si - lence. "Fools!" said I, "You do not know
E♭m
G♭
si-lence like a can-cer grows. Hear my words that I might
B
G♭
B
G♭
teach you, Take my arms that I might reach you."

B
G♭
E♭m
But my words like si-lent rain-drops fell, and
D♭
ech-oed in the wells of si-lence.
And the peo-ple bowed and
prayed to the ne-on god they made.
And the sign flashed out its
warn-ing,
In the words that it was form-ing,
And the signs said "The words of the proph-ets are writ-ten on the sub-way walls
and ten-e-ment halls"
And whis-per'd in the
rit.
sounds of si-lence.
7fr.
6fr.
4fr.

Sparrow

Words and Music by Paul Simon

2. Who will love a little Sparrow?
And who will speak a kindly word?
"Not I," said the swan,
"The entire idea is utterly absurd,
I'd be laughed at and scorned if the
other swans heard."

3. Who will take pity in his heart?
And who will feed a starving sparrow?
"Not I," said the golden wheat,
"I would if I could but I cannot I know.
I need all my grain to prosper and grow."

4. Who will love a little Sparrow?
Will no one write her eulogy?
"I will," said the earth,
"For all I've created returns unto me,
From dust were ye made and dust ye shall be."

Spirit Voices

Words and Music by Paul Simon
Portuguese lyrics by Milton Nascimento

G7
G/B
C
C/E
G/D
C
G7
G/B
And all of these spir - it voi - ces rule the night.
C
C/E
G/D
C
G/B
C
D
Em
By moon We walk To the bru - jo's door,
G/B
C
D
G
G/B
A - long a path of ri - ver stone. Wom - en with their nur -
C
D
Em
G/B
C
- sing chil - dren Seat - ed on the floor, We join the fe - vers And the
D
G
1.
D7omit3
G
D7omit3
G
D7omit3
brok - en bones.
G
D7omit3
G
D7omit3
G
D7omit3
G
D7omit3
G
D7omit3
G
2.
Em
D7/F♯
G
G/B
The Sau - da - coes! Da li -

C G/B C D Em D7/F♯ G G/B C G/B C
cen - ca um mo - men - to. Te lem - bro Quea - man - ha Se - ra tu - doou se - ra nao -
D Em D7/F♯ G G/B C G/B C D
- a De - pen - de co - ra - cao se - ra bre - veou se - ra gran - de De - pen - de
Em D7/F♯ G G/B C G/B C D Em D7/F♯ G
da pai - xao, Se - ra su - jo se - ra son - ho. Cui - da - do co - ra - cao,
G/B C G/B C D Em D7/F♯ G G/B
se - ra u - til se - ra tar - de sees - me - ra co - ra - cao, E con -
C G/B C D G7 C C/E G/D C
fi - a Na for - ca do a - man - ha.
G7 G/B C C/E G/D C G7 G/B
Lord of the earth - quake,
C C/E G/D C G7 C C/E
My trem - bling bed. The spi - der re - sumes the rhyth - m Of his gold - en

2. The candlelight flickers, the falcon calls,
A lime-green lizard scuttles down the cabin wall.
And all of these spirit voices
Sing rainwater, sea water,
River water, holy water,
Wrap this child in mercy - heal her,
Heaven's only daughter.
All of these spirit voices rule the night.
My hands were numb, my feet were lead,
I drank a cup of herbal brew.
Then the sweetness in the air,
Combined with the lightness in my head,
And I heard the jungle breathing in the bamboo.

Saudacoes *Greetings!*
Da licenca um momento *Excuse me, one moment*
Te lembro *I remind you*
Que amanha *That tomorrow*
Sera tudo ou sera naoa *It will be all or it will be nothing*
Depende, coracao *It depends, heart*
Sera breve ou sera grande *It will be brief or it will be great*
Depende da paixao *It depends on the passion*
Sera sujo, sera sonho *It will be dirty, it will be a dream*
Cuidado, coracao *Be careful, heart*
Sera util, sera tarde *It will be useful, it will be late*
Se esmera, coracao *Do your best, heart*
E confia *And have trust*
Na forca do amanha *In the power of tomorrow*

Still Crazy After All These Years

Words and Music by Paul Simon

G
C
G
G/B
C
2.I'm not the kind of man who tends to so-cial-ize
2.
F/G
Amaj7
years.
Four in the morn-ing;
E
Em7/B
G♯m7
C♯sus4
C♯7
crapped out, yawn-ing; long-ing my life a-
F♯maj7
Em7
B
C
B
C
way.
I'll nev-er wor-ry; why should
G
G7
C
Bm
C
I? It's all gon-na fade.
Bm
C
Bm
C
Bm

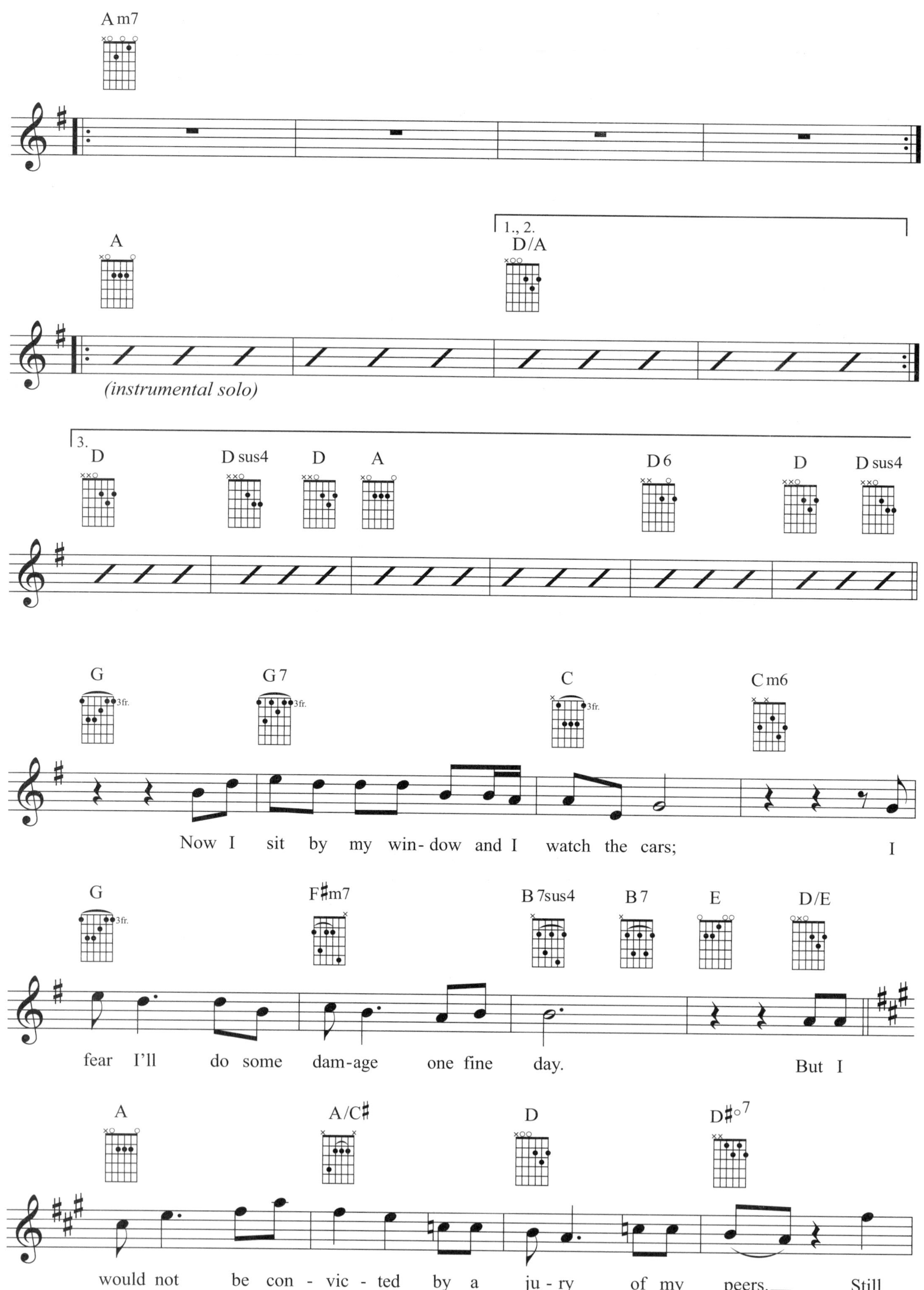
Am7
A
1., 2.
D/A
(instrumental solo)
3.
D
D sus4
D
A
D6
D
D sus4
G
G7
C
Cm6
Now I sit by my win- dow and I watch the cars; I
G
F♯m7
B7sus4
B7
E
D/E
fear I'll do some dam- age one fine day. But I
A
A/C♯
D
D♯°7
would not be con - vic - ted by a ju - ry of my peers. Still

2. I'm not the kind of man
Who tends to socialize
I seem to lean on
Old familiar ways
And I ain't no fool for love songs
That whisper in my ears
Still crazy after all these years
Oh, still crazy after all these years

The Teacher

Words and Music by Paul Simon

A♭maj7
4fr.
C7
Fm
B♭m
C
to Coda
dream - er of love sleeps on a quilt of stars
Fm
B♭m
D♭
C
Fm
B♭m
It's cold Some - times you can't
D♭
C
Fm
catch your breath It's cold
3
3
D.S. al Coda
3
Coda
Fm
B♭m
D♭
C
Fm
B♭m
D♭
C
Some-times we don't know who we are

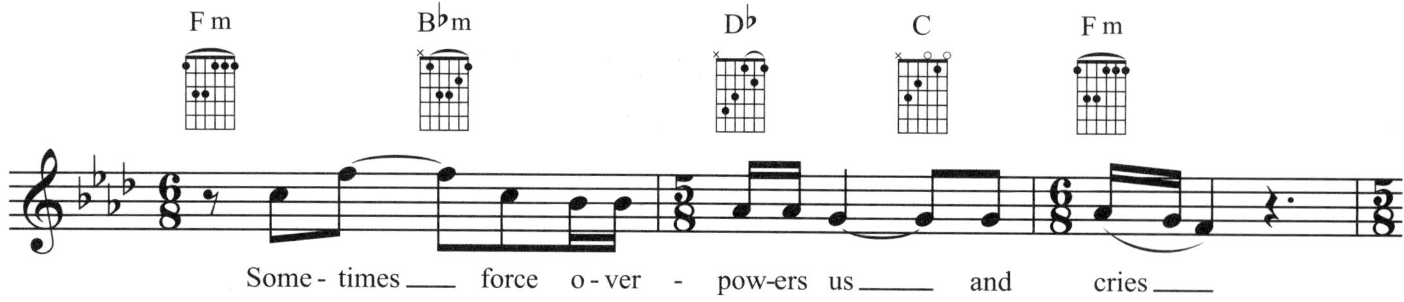

2. I was only a child of the city
   My parents were children of immigrant stock
   So we followed as followers go
   Over a mountain with a napkin of snow
   And ate the berries and roots
   That grow along the timberline

3. Time and abundance thickened his step
   So the teacher divided in two
   One half ate the forests and fields
   The other half sucked all the moisture from the clouds
   And we, we were amazed at the power of his appetite

Stranded In A Limousine

Words and Music by Paul Simon

Moderately fast, with a beat

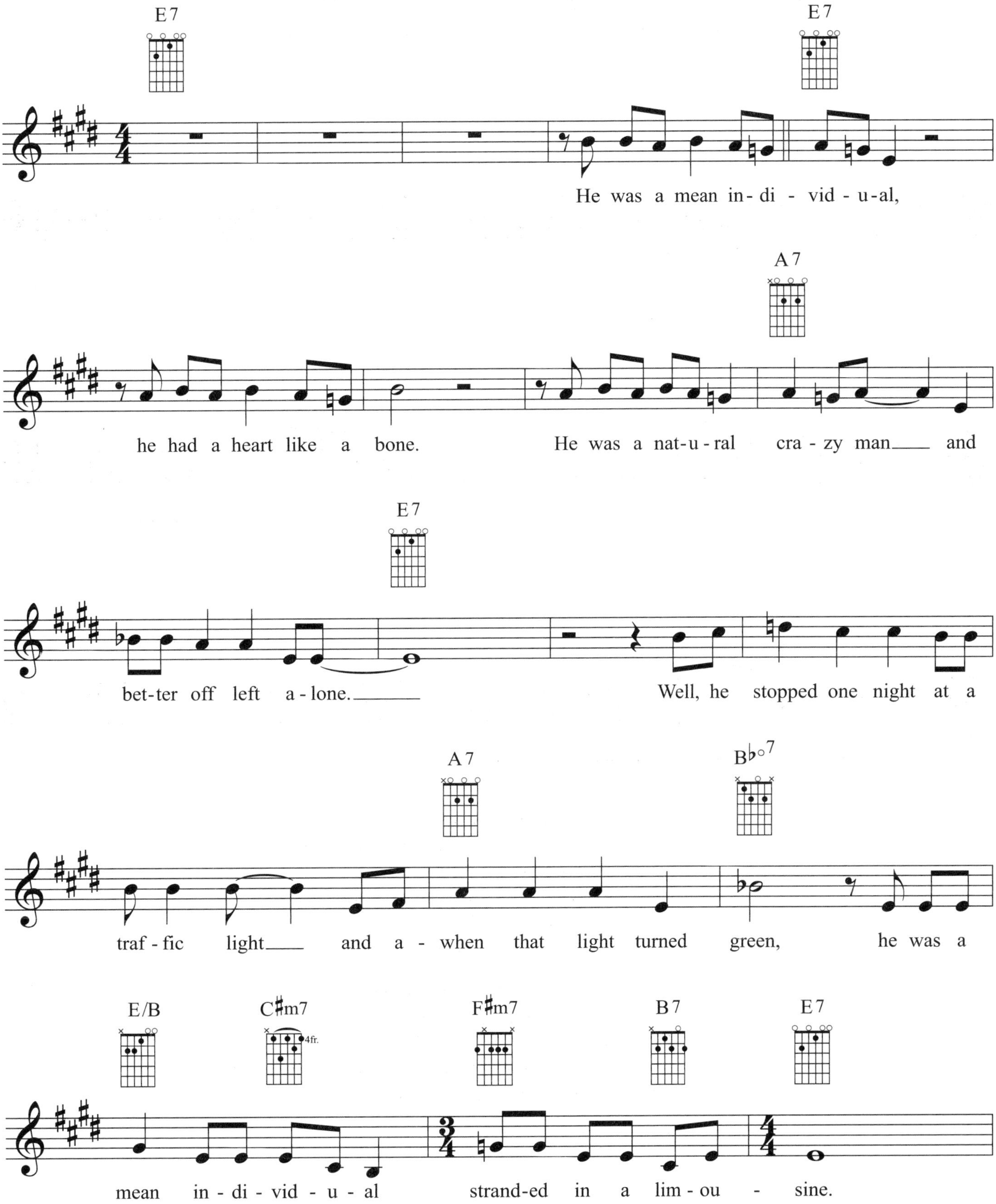

E7 E7

He was a mean in-di - vid - u-al,

A7

he had a heart like a bone. He was a nat-u-ral cra - zy man___ and

E7

bet-ter off left a - lone.___ Well, he stopped one night at a

A7 B♭°7

traf - fic light___ and a - when that light turned green, he was a

E/B C♯m7 F♯m7 B7 E7

mean in - di - vid - u - al strand-ed in a lim - ou - sine.

E7
N.C.
Hey, hey, hey, hey, all the chil-dren on the street.
A7
They come a - run - nin' out their front doors, run - nin' out their
E7
back doors flyin' on their feet. They said Ma - ma oh!
A7
Bb°7
E/B
C#m7
4fr.
Pa - pa oh! See what I have seen. There's a mean in - di - vid - u - al
F#m7
B7
E7
strand-ed in a lim - ou - sine. Then ev - 'ry bod - y came
A7
E7
run - nin', ev - 'ry-bod-y said Lord! Lord!

G°7
— Ev-'ry-bod-y was gun - nin', — they're gon-na div-vy up the
B7/F♯
B7
E7
re - ward. — And then a - wah, wah, wah, wah,
A7
B♭°7
wah, wah, wah, there's a si - ren a-flash - ing light, — but the
E/B
C♯m7
4fr.
F♯m7
B7
E7
to Coda
N.C.
mean in-di-vid - u-al had van-ished in the black of night. Hey, hey, hey,
E7
hey, they won-dered where to be - gin. 'Cause he left that
A7
E7
neigh-bor-hood just - like a rat - tle - snake sheds its skin. —

Well they searched the roofs, and they checked out the groups, and then
A7
Bb°7
E/B
C#m7
4fr.
pho - to - graphed the scene of the mean in-di - vid - u - al
F#m7
B7
E7
N.C.
strand - ed in a lim - ou - sine.
E7
A7
(instrumental)
E7
A7
Bb°7
E/B
C#m7
4fr.
F#m7
B7
E7
D.S. al Coda
Then ev - 'ry-bo-dy came

Coda
E7
E
C♯m7
4fr.
night.
The mean in - di - vid - u - al had
F♯m7
B7
E7
N.C.
van - ished in the black of night.
The
E
C♯m7
4fr.
F♯m7
B7
E7
mean in - di - vid - u - al had van - ished in the black of night.
N.C.
E7
repeat and fade

Sunday Afternoon

Music by Paul Simon
Lyrics by Paul Simon and Derek Walcott

Moderately

Dm Am E7 Am G7 C F

freely

E7 Am G/B C

a tempo

Sal - va - dor, the af - ter - noon

E7 Am B7

sun-light is fold - ing a - round us, The dish-es are done,

E Am G/B C E7

The build - ings here, tall as our moun - tains

Am B7 E

Slice through the win-dows and cut off the sun. On such

Am
E7
days I find I am long - ing for __ Puer - to Ri - co
Am
Am7
Dm
Though I __ nev - er would re - turn 'til you are free
Am
But when I hear the A - gui - nal - do my
E7
Am
G7
C
F
heart's a lit - tle light - er And we dance to - geth - er Au - re - a __ and
E
Am
3
me In my life I've been un - luck - y with two
E
Am
Dm
hus - bands Gum - er - sin - do liked his rum and wom - en friends

Am
E7
Then that hyp - o - crite who beat you and preached a - bout re-pen -
Am
G7
C
F
E
- tance Has gone, and so an - oth - er Sun - day ends
Am
E7
3
And to - mor-row is an - oth - er hard work - ing Mon-day
Am
Dm
I'm still hop - ing for the raise they prom - ised me
Am
E7
There's a job as op-er-a - tor I would not have to wait
Am
G7
C
F
E
poco rit.
for If I could speak the lan - guage eas - i - ly

Am
G/B
C
E7
a tempo
But I tell Au - re - a:
The bar-ri-o's bound - 'ries
Am
B7
are our own lit-tle na - tion
Some-times I hear you run up-
E
Am
G/B
C
stairs
And I view my light
with res - ig -
E7
Am
B7
na - tion
Keep your bi-ble near you
Time is an o - cean
E
Am
G/B
C
E7
rit.
a tempo
of end-less tears.
Mmm
mm
Am
B7
E7
Am
freely
mm
mm
mm

Ten Years

Words and Music by Paul Simon

B
E
G♯m
4fr.
Ten years come and gone so fast
I might as well been dream-ing
F♯
B
E
Sun - ny days have burned a path
G♯m
F♯
G♯m
to Coda
3
a - cross an-other - er sea - son
A for - tune ris -
D♯7
6fr.
G♯m
F♯
E
- es to the sky
B
E
G♯m
1.
F♯
Ten years come and gone so fast
You are
2.
F♯
B
E
G♯m
F♯
B
(guitar solo)

2. You are driving down an empty road
Beside a shady river
When the sky turns dark as stone
The trees begin to shiver
The grace of God is nigh

Ten years come and gone
and that Flash has never been forgotten
Sunny days have burned a path
Across another season
How do the powerless survive?

Ten years come and gone so fast

3. And if you look into your future life
Ten years from this question
Do you imagine a familiar light
burning in the distance?
The love that never dies

Ten years come and gone so fast
I might as well have been dreaming
Sunny days have burned a path
Across another season…

Ten years come and gone so fast…
Sunny days have burned a path…

Take Me To The Mardi Gras

Words and Music by Paul Simon

Bm
You can le-gal-ize your laws, you can wear your sum-mer clothes in the New Or-
3
A
A7
D
leans.
And I will lay my bur-den down,
Rest my head up-on that shore,
And when I wear that star-ry
C
Em
E7
crown,
I won't be want-ing an-y more.
A
N.C.
Take your bur-dens to the Mar-di Gras,
Let the mu-sic wash your
E7
soul,
You can min-gle in the street, You can

A
jin- gle in the beat of the jel- ly roll.
Tum-ba, tum-ba, tum-ba,
E7
Mar - di Gras,
Tum - ba, tum - ba, tum - ba day,
A
Hey,
hey.
E7
(instrumental)
Bm
A
repeat and fade

Tenderness

Words and Music by Paul Simon

F♯m7
C♯9
D9
C♯9
A
D
E
You and me, we're such good friends.
What's your hur - ry?
A
C♯7
B7
F♯m7
C♯9
D9
C♯9
A
C♯7/G♯
You and me could make a - mends.
I'm not wor - ried,
Bm7
G13
C9
F7
E7
I'm not wor - ried.
Oh, hon - es - ty,
oh, hon - es -
Am
C7
F
F♯°7
ty, ooh, it's such a waste of en - er - gy.
No, you don't have to
C/G
G7
C
A7
lie to me, just give me some ten-der - ness be-neath your hon-es - ty.
You don't have to
D7
G7
C
Am7
Fm/C
G7
lie to me, just give me some ten-der - ness.
C
C7
F
F♯°7
C
C/G
G7
C
E♭
B♭
C
rit.

That Was Your Mother

Words and Music by Paul Simon

Brightly, in 2

F C

(accordian solo)

F

1.A long time a-

F

go, yeah Be-fore you was born dude When I was still

C F

sin-gle And life was great I held this job as a trav-el-ing

C F

sales-man That kept me mov-ing from state to state

F
Well, I'm stand-ing on the cor-ner of La - fa - yette State of Lou-i - si-an -
C
F
- a Won-dering where a cit-y boy could go To
get a lit-tle con - ver-sa - tion Drink a lit-tle red wine
C
F
to Coda
Catch a lit-tle bit of those Ca-jun girls Danc-ing to Zy-de-co
1.
F
(sax solo - play three times)
C
F
(third time:) 2.A - long come a

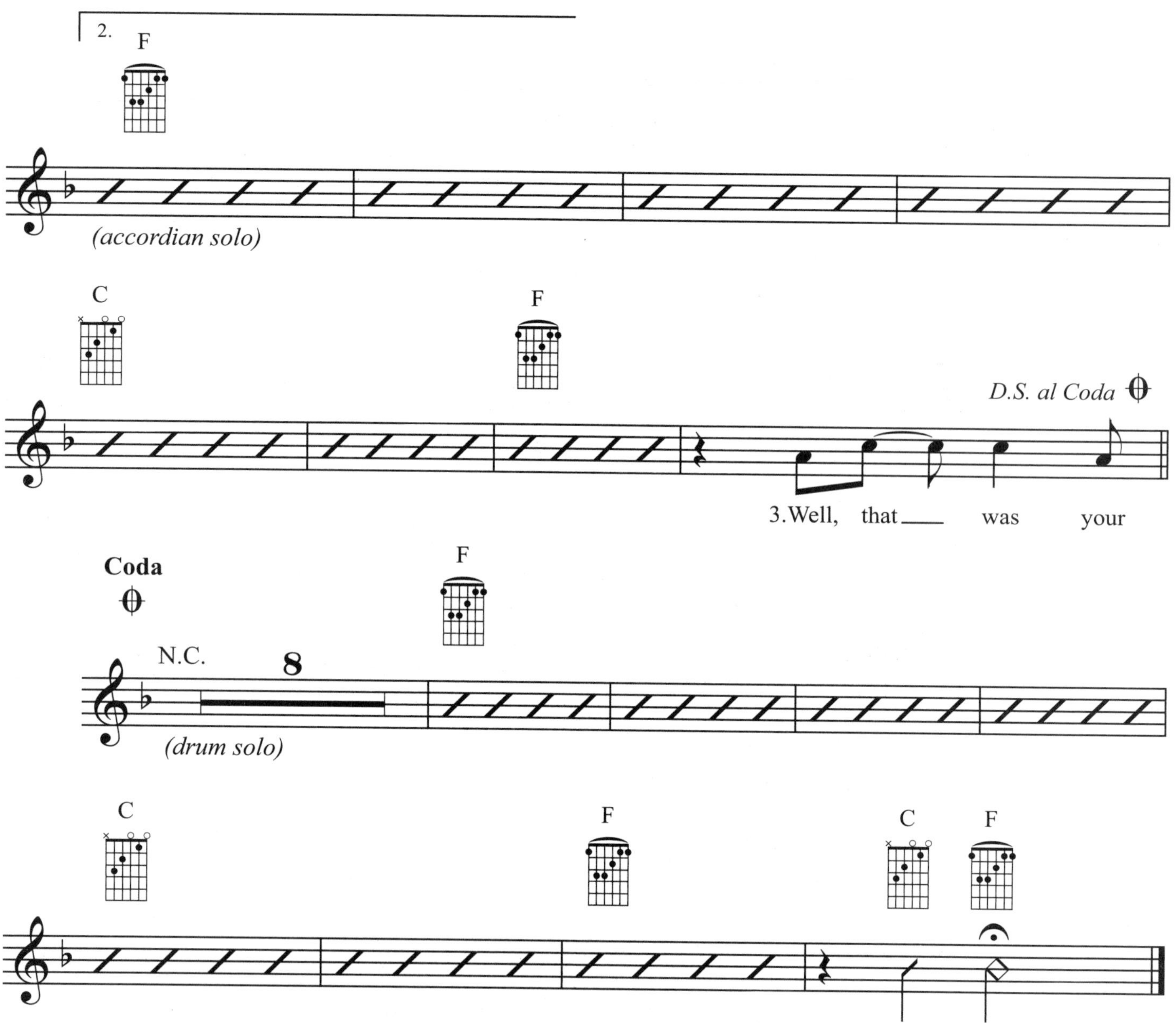

2. Along come a young girl
She's pretty as a prayer book
Sweet as an apple on Christmas day
I said good gracious can this be my luck
If that's my prayer book
Lord let us pray

Well, I'm standing on the corner of Lafayette
State of Louisiana
Wondering what a city boy could do
To get her in a conversation
Drink a little red wine
Dance to the music of Clifton Chenier
The King of the Bayou

3. Well, that was your mother
And that was your father
Before you was born dude
When life was great
You are the burden of my generation
I sure do love you
But let's get that straight

Well, I'm standing on the corner of Lafayette
Across the street from The Public
Heading down to the Lone Star Cafe
Maybe get a little conversation
Drink a little red wine
Standing in the shadow of Clifton Chenier
Dancing the night away

That's Where I Belong

Words and Music by Paul Simon

E♭
D
A♭
G
C m
B m
gin-ning.
The way you turn
And catch me with your eye
I
B♭
A
E♭
D
A♭
G
B♭
A
C m
B m
A♭
G
B♭
A
That's where I be - long.
C m
B m
A♭
G
E♭
D
When I see you smil - ing,
When I hear you sing - ing.
Lav-en-der and
B♭7
A 7
E♭
D
A♭
G
ros - es,
Ev-'ry end-ing a be - gin-ning.
That's the way it is, I don't know
C m
B m
B♭
A
E♭
D
why.
I
But that's where I be - long
D♭
C

A♭
G
A spin-y lit-tle is-land man Plays a jin-gling
E♭
D
B♭7
A7
ban - jo. He's walk-ing down a dirt road, Car-ry-ing his
E♭
D
A♭
G
ra - di-o To a riv - er where the wa - ter meets the
Cm
Bm
B♭
A
sky. I That's where I
E♭
D
A♭
G
B♭
A
Cm
Bm
A♭
G
B♭
A
Cm
Bm
be-long.

That's Why God Made The Movies

Words and Music by Paul Simon

Moderate blues

A7
7fr.
E7
7fr.
A7
7fr.
E7
7fr.
Well I laid a - round in my swad-dling
B7♯5
7fr.
Gmaj7
5fr.
C♯m7♭5
4fr.
Cmaj7
3fr.
F♯
clothes Un-til the doc - tor came and turned out the light
Then I
G♯m
4fr.
F♯m7♭5
9fr.
Em7
7fr.
D
5fr.
Bm7
packed my bag And my name - tag And
E
7fr.
D♯m7♭5
6fr.
D7
5fr.
C♯7
4fr.
F♯7
stole a-way in - to the night Hop - ing things would work out right
E7
7fr.
E
F♯m7
E/G♯
That's why God made the mov - ies
Say you will, say you
A
5fr.
G♯m7
4fr.
F♯m7
Emaj7
will Say you'll take me to your lov - ing breast

F♯m7
Say you'll nour - ish me with your ten - der - ness
B 9
C♯m
B
E
F♯m7
E/G♯
The way the la-dies some-times do
Say you won't, say you
A
G♯m
F♯m7
Emaj7
won't
Say you won't leave me for no oth - er man
F♯m7
E
B 7/D♯
Say you'll love me just the way I am, mm.
B
E 7
Say you will, ba-by, now.
Say you will, just say you will.
A 7
E 7
A 7
E 7
1.-3.
A 7
Say you will.
(instrumental solo)

4.
A7
7fr.
E7
7fr.
B7♯5
7fr.
When I was born my moth- er died She said
Gmaj7
5fr.
C♯m7♭5
4fr.
Cmaj7
3fr.
F♯
G♯m
4fr.
bye - bye ba - by, bye - bye And since that day
F♯m7♭5
9fr.
Em7
7fr.
D
5fr.
Bm7
I've paid my way The no-
E
7fr.
D♯m7♭5
6fr.
D7
5fr.
C♯7
4fr.
F♯7
to - ri - ous boy of the wild A - dop - ted by the wolves when he was a child
B
N.C.
B
N.C.
B
N.C.
That's why God. That's why God. That's why God made the
E7
7fr.
A7
7fr.
repeat and fade
mov - ies

Train In The Distance

Words and Music by Paul Simon

A♭
G m7
E♭
D♭/E♭
drew
Ev - 'ry - bod - y loves the
A♭/E♭
E♭m7
sound of a train in the dis - tance
Ev - 'ry - bo - dy thinks it's true
E♭
D♭/E♭
A♭/E♭
1.
E♭m7
Ev - 'ry - bod - y loves the sound of a train in the dis - tance
Ev - 'ry - bo - dy thinks it's
E♭
D♭/E♭
A♭/E♭
E♭m7
true
2.
E♭
D♭maj9
Ev - 'ry - bo - dy thinks it's true
Two dis - ap - point - ed be -
C m7
B○7
E♭/B♭
A7♯11
liev - ers
Two peo - ple play - ing the game

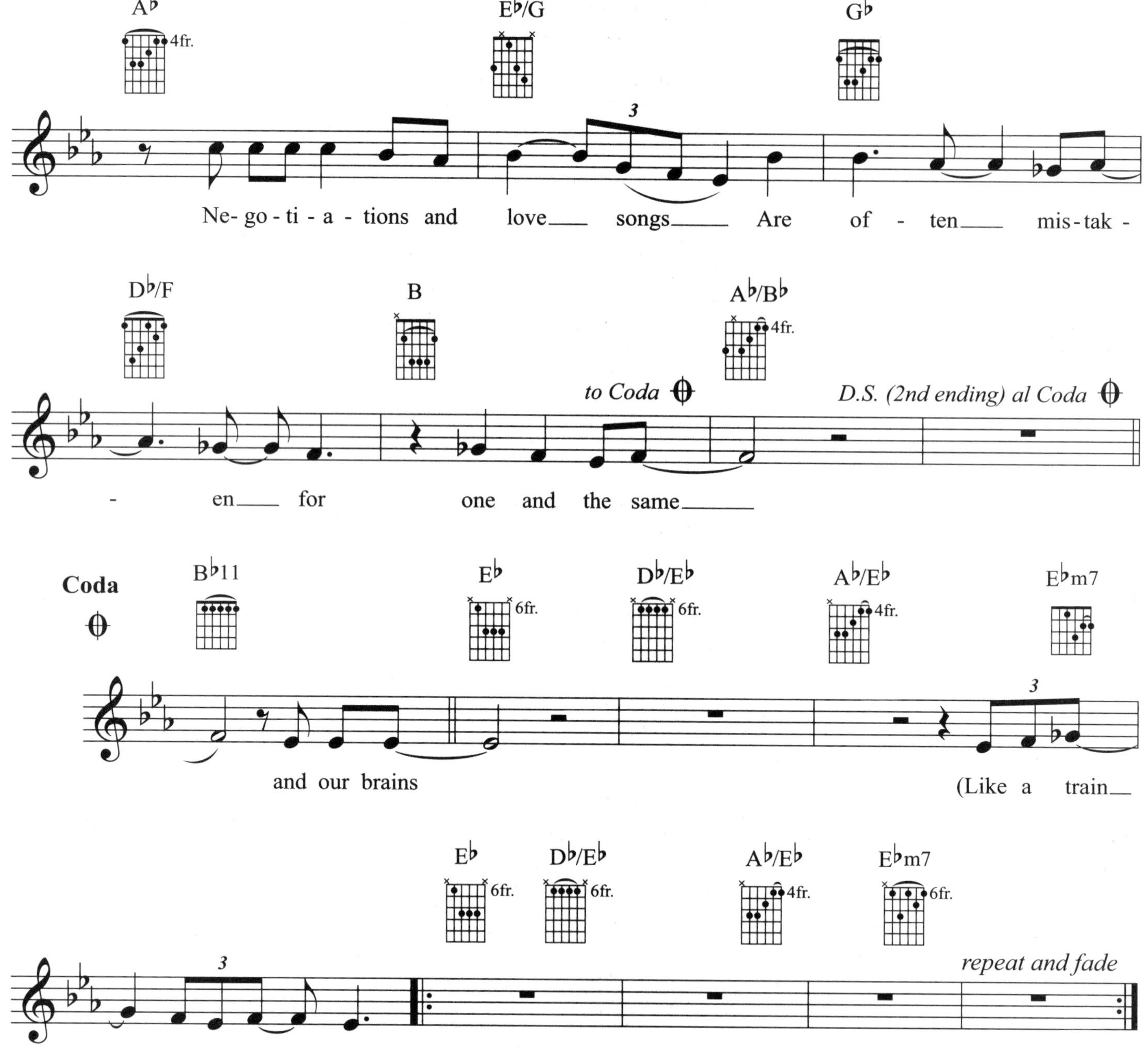

2. Well eventually the boy and the girl get married
Sure enough they have a son
And though they both were occupied
With the child she carried
Disagreements had begun
And in a while they just fell apart
It wasn't hard to do
Everybody loves the sound of a train in the distance
Everybody thinks it's true
Everybody loves the sound of a train in the distance
Everybody thinks it's true

Two disappointed believers
Two people playing the game
Negotiations and love songs
Are often mistaken for one and the same

4. Now the man and the woman remain in contact
Let us say it's for the child
With disagreements about the meaning
Of a marriage contract
Conversations hard and wild
But from time to time he makes her laugh
She cooks a meal or two
Everybody loves the sound of a train in the distance
Everybody thinks it's true
Everybody loves the sound of a train in the distance
Everybody thinks it's true

What is the point of this story
What information pertains
The thought that life could be better
Is woven indelibly
Into our hearts and our brains

Thelma

Words and Music by Paul Simon

F
C9sus4
F
All for the taste of your sweet love Thel-ma
If the heart is an o-pen
Gm
3fr.
F
mem - o - ry book That was the chance I took but the more I searched, the
C
F
Dm
C
more I shook for Thel-ma
3
Last night I slept on a rent-ed pil-low
B♭
C
Dm
A sil-ver moon a-bove my head
A thirs-ty dream-less sleep re-
C
B♭
C
leased me
And I reached for the phone by the side of the bed
F/C
C9sus4
F/C
C9sus4
F

Gm
3fr.
F
Now the first time that I saw you I thought "She's beau-ti-ful, but she's too
C
F
young to be caught" Peo-ple a-ware of my his-to-ry
C
F
Try-ing to steer you a-way from me I left a mes-sage at your ho-tel
C
F
don't let man-age-ment poi-son the well I will need you, feed you, siege you, plead with
C9sus4
F
C9sus4
F
you All for the taste of your sweet love, Thel-ma

Dm
C
B♭
C
The phone is ring-ing and I re-al-ize we're time zones and o-ceans a-
Dm
C
part words I speak in the mid-dle of my night
B♭
C
F
fall on your yes-ter-day scars If the sun don't shine, if the wind don't break if your
C
F
C
F
clock don't jump off the wall Thel-ma, my dar-ling, I will cush-ion your fall I will
Gm
3fr.
F
need you, feed you, siege you, plead with you Got the taste of your sweet love, Thel-ma
C9sus4
F
C
3
I am on-ly a man who skirt-ed the edge of des-pair for a

F
C 9sus4
F
long time now, and I don't care
D m
C
I watch you sleep-ing in the hos - pi - tal bed
B♭
C
D m
The ba - by curled up in a ball
Win - ter sun - light hits the
C
B♭
fam - i - ly tree
And ev - ery - thing else be - comes
C
F
C 9sus4
F
noth - ing at all

Think Too Much (a)

Words and Music by Paul Simon

Moderately bright

A D A D A D A D A D

A D A D 1. A D 2. A D

1.They say that the

A D A D A D A D

left side of the brain ___ con- trols ___ the right ___ They say that the

A D A D A D A D

right side Has to work ___ hard all ___ night May-be I

C♯m F♯m C♯m F♯m C♯m F♯m C♯m F♯m

think too ___ much for my ___ own good ___ Some peo - ple say ___

Bm
7fr.
C♯m
9fr.
so
Oth-er peo-ple say
No
no
The
fact
is
you
Bm
7fr.
to Coda
E
7fr.
N.C.
don't
think
as
much as
you
could
hmmm
A(bass)
I
had
a
child
-
hood
that
was
mer -
-
ci
-
ful
-
ly
brief
I
grew
up
in
a
C♯(bass)
state
of
dis
-
be
-
lief
I
start-ed
to
think
too
Bm7
much
when
I
was
twelve
go-ing
on
thir
-
teen

C♯m7
4fr.
B m7
Me and girls from St. Au-gus-tine
Up in the mez-za-nine
E
7fr.
A
5fr.
E
7fr.
N.C.
3
Think-ing about God, yeah.
May-be I think too much
F♯m
9fr.
May-be I think too much
May-be I
E
7fr.
F♯m
9fr.
think too much
May-be I think too much
A D A D A D A D
5fr.
N.C.
A D A D A D A D
5fr.
D.S. al Coda
2.Have you ev-er ex-

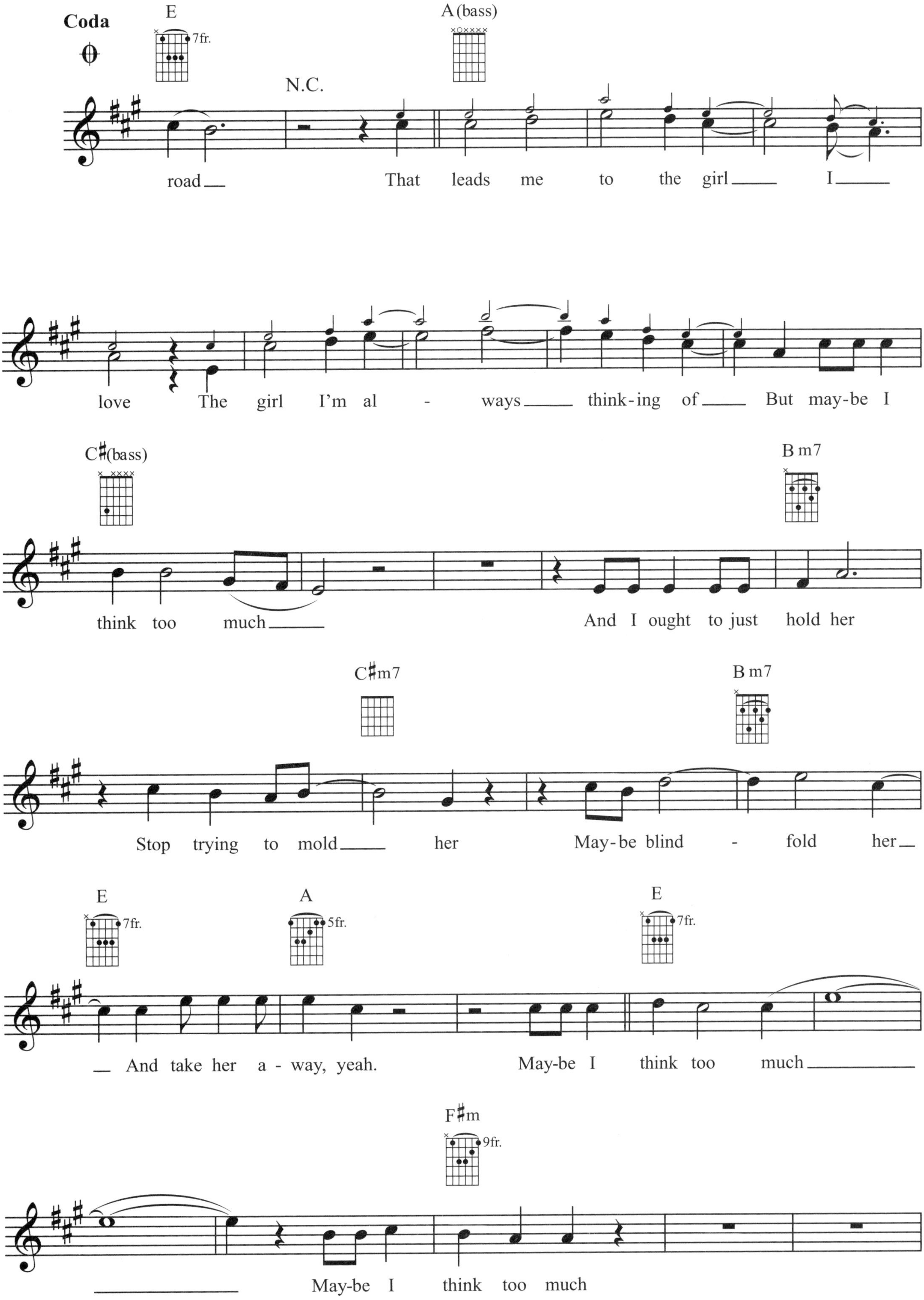

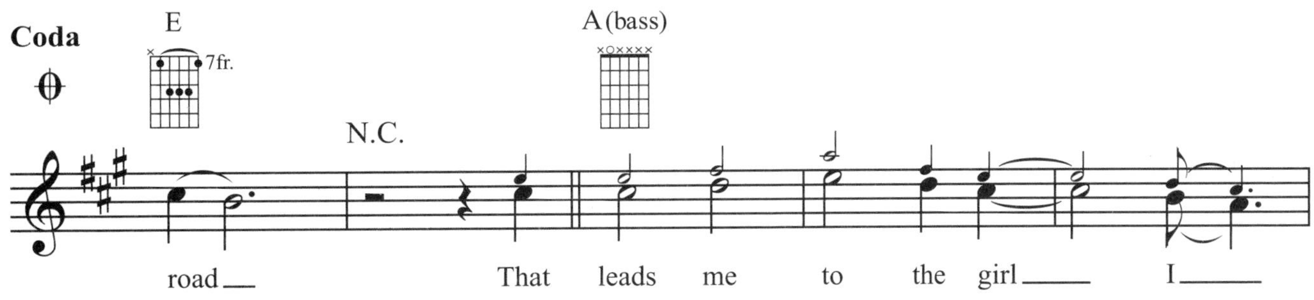

love The girl I'm al - ways think-ing of But may-be I

C♯(bass) B m7

think too much And I ought to just hold her

C♯m7 B m7

Stop trying to mold her May-be blind - fold her

E 7fr. A 5fr. E 7fr.

And take her a - way, yeah. May-be I think too much

F♯m 9fr.

May-be I think too much

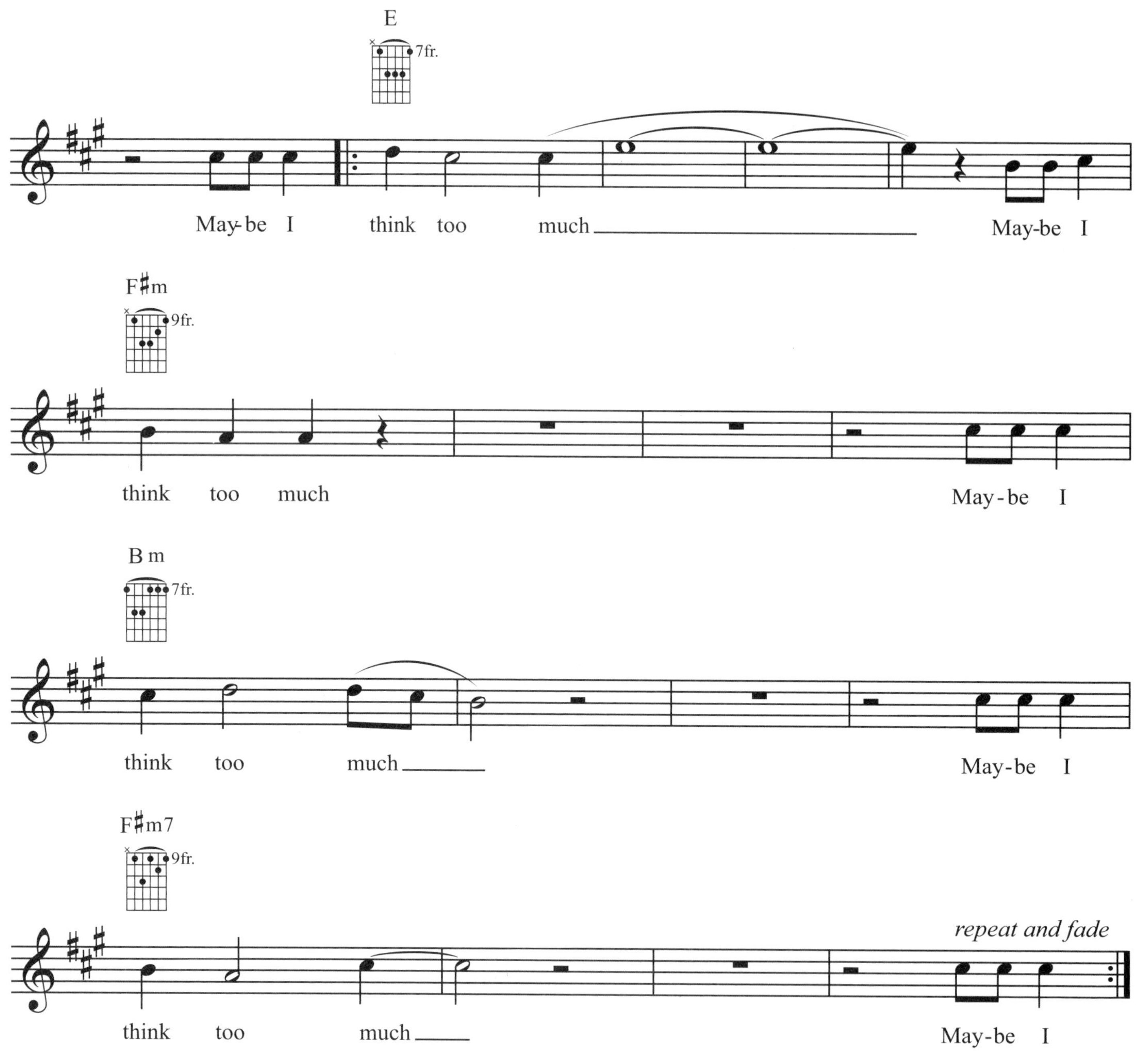

2. Have you ever experienced a period of grace
When your brain just takes a seat behind your face
And the world begins The Elephant Dance
Everything's funny
Everyone's sunny
You take out your money
And walk down the road
That leads me to the girl I love
The girl I'm always thinking of
But maybe I think too much
And I ought to just hold her
Stop trying to mold her
Maybe blindfold her
And take her away

Think Too Much (b)

Words and Music by Paul Simon

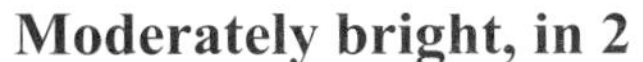

A
And they sat a - mong our pho - to-graphs
F♯m
A
Ex-am-ined ev - ery one
And in the end
F♯m
we com - pro - mised
And met the mor -
A
- ning sun
May-be I think
too much
May-be I think too much
F♯m
1.
May-be I think too much
May-be I think too much

2. They say the left side of the brain
Dominates the right
And the right side has to labor
Through the long and speechless night
And in the night
My father came to me
And held me to his chest
He said there's not much more that you can do
Go on and get some rest
And I said yeah

Time Is An Ocean

Music by Paul Simon
Lyrics by Paul Simon and Derek Walcott

Em
Gadd9
C♯m7♭5
4fr.
F♯7
stum-bled through silv - 'ry wa - ter to my sav - ior, my Sal - va -
Bm
Gadd9
Dadd9
2fr.
Gadd9
dor! It took me four years to learn I was in pris - on
Aadd9
Bm7
Em7
not in church. And two more to be-gin the
C♯m7♭5
4fr.
F♯7
Bm
Em
book of my soul's search. Time is an o - cean
F♯7
Bm
of end - less tears A wild boy from the
Em
F♯7
Bm
streets of El Bar - rio An or - phan from the hills of Ma - ya - güez

A
Bm
G
And when I wrote my sto - ry The words flew from
A
Bm
the page And my soul in sol - i - tar - y Es -
Gmaj7
A
Bm
Em
caped its i - ron cage. Time is an o - cean
C♯m7♭5
4fr.
F♯7
Bm
Em
Gmaj7
A
of end - less tears
Gadd9
Em
Gadd9
C♯m7♭5
4fr.
F♯7
Bm
Em
Gadd9
A
Gmaj7
3
Ma - ma, I got your let - ter to - day

Em
Gadd9
C♯m7♭5
4fr.
F♯7
Bm7
The next time that you write I'll be trans - ferred far a - way.
Gadd9
Dadd9
2fr.
Gmaj7
I'm leav - ing Green - ha - ven's tow - ers of stone
A
Bm7
Em7
Where the Lat - in pop - u - la - tion will
C♯m7♭5
4fr.
F♯7
Bm
Em
soon be mi - nus one.
Time is an o - cean
F♯7
Bm
of end - less tears.
I know how hard
Em
F♯7
Bm
it's been for you these man - y years,

Aadd9 Bm Gmaj7 A
You say the A - gui-nal - do makes you dream of home
Bm Gmaj7 A
Where once we strolled the beach at El Mal - e - con
Bm Em7 C♯m7♭5 4fr. F♯7 Bm7
Go back don't you wor-ry, I am your grown - up son.
1. 2.
Em11 5fr. Em
N. C.
The pol -
Gmaj7 A Gadd9
- i - tics of pris - on are a mir - ror of the street.
Em Gadd9 C♯m7♭5 4fr.
The poor en - dure op - pres - sion The po - lice

F♯7
Bm
Em
— con - trol — the state. —
Cor -
Gadd9
A
Gmaj7
rec - tion - al fa - cil - i - ty
That's what they call this place
Em
Gadd9
C♯m7♭5
4fr.
F♯7
Bm7
But look a-round and you — will see
The pol - i - tics — of race. —
Gadd9
Dmaj7
A for - est and a pris - on —
Where the
Gmaj7
A
Bm
snow and guards — are white —
If you want to — keep your
Em7
C♯m7♭5
4fr.
F♯7
Bm7
san - i - ty
You'll teach your - self — to write. —

Bm
Em
F♯7
You were a child of six - teen With a twelve - year - old
Bm
Em
mind You came here numb and bat-tered By the
F♯7
Bm
Bm7
streets I left be - hind I'll take the e - vil in
Em
F♯7
Bm
me And turn it in - to good, Though all your in - sti-
Em
F♯7
Bm
tu - tions Nev - er thought I could
Aadd9
Bm
Gmaj7
A
So now I'll turn to say good - bye

Bm
Gmaj7
A
I'll keep your im-age in my eye
Bm
Gmaj7
A
I turn a-round to say good-bye
Bm
Gmaj7
A
I'll keep your im-age with me till the day I die
Bm
Em
F♯7
Bm
Em
Time is an o-cean
F♯7
Bm
Em
Gmaj7
A
Gadd9
of end-less tears
Em
Gadd9
C♯m7♭5
F♯7
Bm

Under African Skies

Words and Music by Paul Simon

Moderately fast 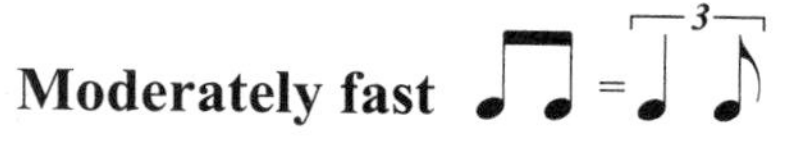

E♭ 6fr. A♭ 4fr. E♭/B♭ 6fr. B♭ 6fr. E♭ 6fr. A♭ 4fr. E♭/B♭ 6fr. B♭ 6fr.

play three times

𝄋

E♭ 6fr. A♭ 4fr. E♭/B♭ 6fr. B♭ 6fr. E♭ 6fr. A♭ 4fr. E♭/B♭ 6fr. B♭ 6fr.

1.Jo - seph's face was black as__ night The

E♭ 6fr. A♭ 4fr. E♭/B♭ 6fr. B♭ 6fr. E♭ 6fr. A♭ 4fr. E♭/B♭ 6fr. B♭ 6fr.

pale yel-low moon__ shone in his eyes His

E♭ 6fr. A♭ 4fr. E♭/B♭ 6fr. B♭ 6fr. E♭ 6fr. A♭ 4fr. E♭/B♭ 6fr. B♭ 6fr.

path was marked By the stars in the South-ern Hem - i - sphere And he

E♭ 6fr. A♭ 4fr. E♭/B♭ 6fr. B♭ 6fr. E♭ 6fr. A♭ 4fr. E♭/B♭ 6fr. B♭ 6fr.

to Coda 𝄌

walked his days Un-der Af - ri - can skies

E♭
A♭
E♭/B♭
B♭
6fr.
4fr.
This is the sto-ry of how we be-gin to re-mem - ber
This is the pow-er-ful pul - sing of love in the vein
Af-ter the dream of fall - ing and call - ing your name out
These are the roots of rhy-thm And the roots of rhy-thm re-main
1.
2.In

2. In early memory
   Mission music
   Was ringing 'round my nursery door
   I said take this child, Lord
   From Tucson, Arizona
   Give her the wings to fly through harmony
   And she won't bother you no more

Trailways Bus

Music by Paul Simon
Lyrics by Paul Simon and Derek Walcott

Am
E
The far - mer sleeps a - gainst his wife
Am
G
C
Em
He won - ders what their life must be
Am
G
A Trail - ways bus is head - ing south
F
B7
E
In - to Wash - ing - ton, D. C.
A
A
moth - er and child, the ba - by may - be two months old
B
E
Pre - pare them - selves for sleep and feed - ing.

A
B
E
Am
E
Am
G
C
Em
Am
G
F
C
G
D
The shad - ow of the Cap - i - tol dome slides a - cross his face
And his heart is rac - ing with the urge to free - dom.
The fa - ther mo - tion - less as stone,
A shep - herd rest - ing with his flock,
The Trail - ways bus is turn - ing west,
Dal - las vi - a Lit - tle Rock.

G
Bm
O my dar-ling, dar - ling Sal The des-ert moon is my
A
D
G
wit - ness. I've no mon - ey to come East, But I
Bm
A
know you'll soon be here We
D
G
pull in-to down - town Dal - las by the side of the Grass - y Knoll Where the
A
D
lead-er fell and a town was bro-ken. A-
G
way from the feel and flow of life for so man-y years He hears

A
D
D7
mu - sic play - ing and Span - ish spo - ken
G
D
A
D
(instrumental solo)
1.
D7
2.
D
E
The bor-der pa-trol out-side of Tuc - son
A
B
board-ed the bus An-y a - li-ens here? You bet-ter
E
check with us, How 'bout you son? You look like you got
A
B
E
Span-ish blood. Do you 'Ha-bla In-gles,' am I un-der-stood?

Am
E
Yes, I am an a - li - en, from Mars.
Am
G
C
Em
I come to earth from out - er space.
Am
G
And if I trav-eled my whole life
F
C
G
You guys would still be on my case
F
C
F
G
You guys would still be on my case
F
C
F
G
F
C
F
G

F
Am
G
But he can't leave his fears___ be - hind,
C
He re - calls each fa - tal thrust
The screams car - ried by___ the wind,
Phan-tom fig - ures in the dust
Phan-tom fig - ures in the
dust
Phan - tom fig - ures in the
rit.
dust.

Wednesday Morning, 3 A.M.

Words and Music by Paul Simon

Moderately bright

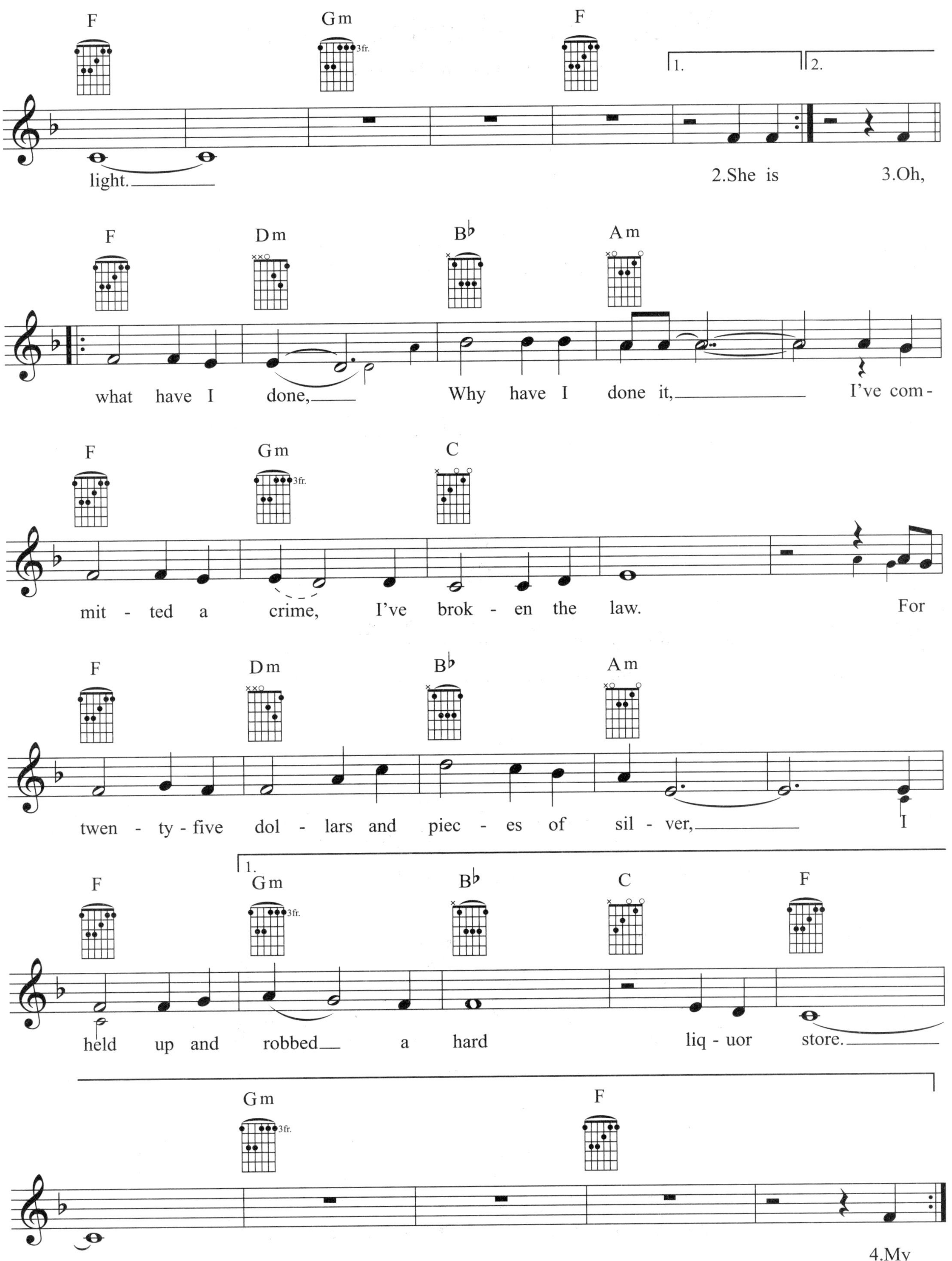
F
Gm
3fr.
1.
2.
light.
2.She is
3.Oh,
F
Dm
B♭
Am
what have I done,
Why have I done it,
I've com-
F
Gm
C
mit - ted a crime,
I've brok - en the law.
For
F
Dm
B♭
Am
twen - ty - five dol - lars and piec - es of sil - ver,
I
1.
F
Gm
B♭
C
F
held up and robbed a hard liq - uor store.
Gm
F
4.My

2. She is soft, she is warm,
But my heart remains heavy,
And I watch as her breasts
Gently rise, gently fall,
For I know with the first light of dawn
I'll be leaving,
And tonight will be
All I have left to recall.

3. Oh, what have I done,
Why have I done it,
I've committed a crime,
I've broken the law.
For twenty-five dollars
And pieces of silver
I held up and robbed
A hard liquor store.

4. My life seems unreal,
My crime an illusion,
A scene badly written
In which I must play.
Yet I know as I gaze
At my young love beside me,
The morning is just a few hours away.

The Vampires

Music by Paul Simon
Lyrics by Paul Simon and Derek Walcott

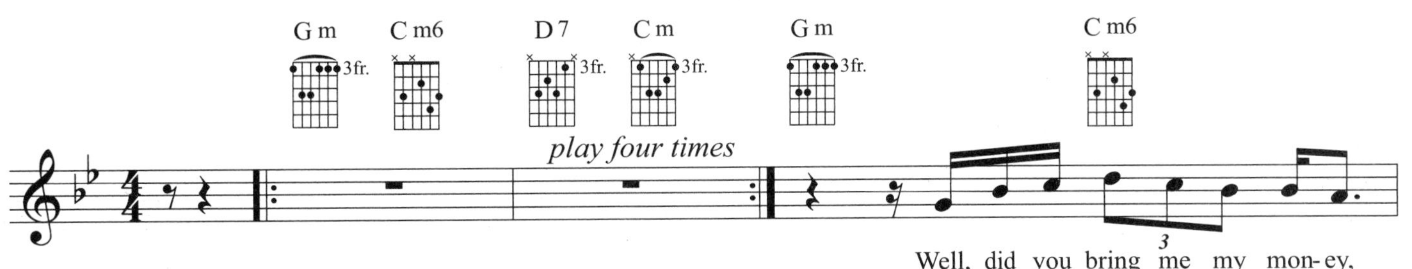

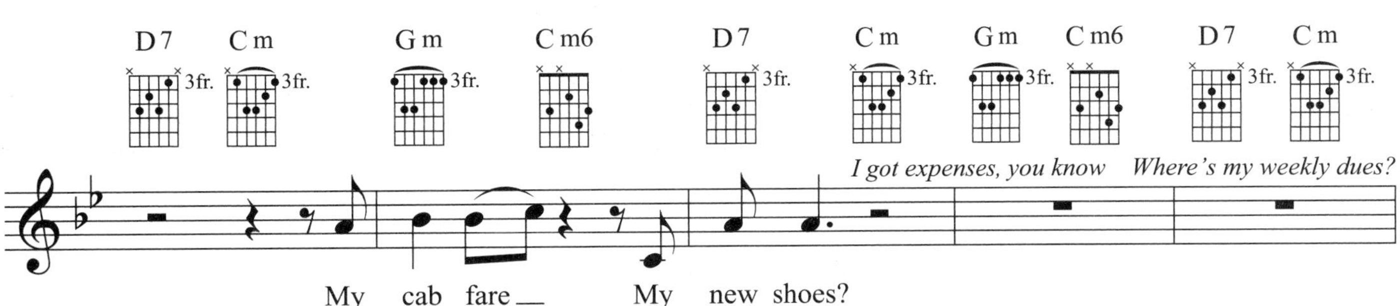

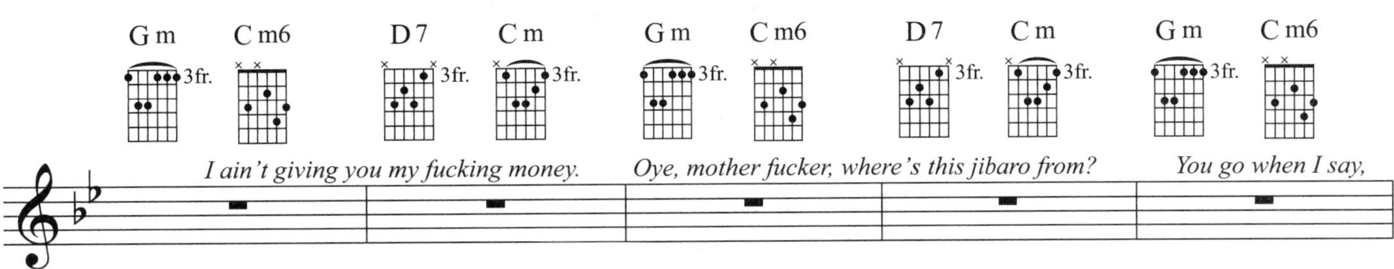

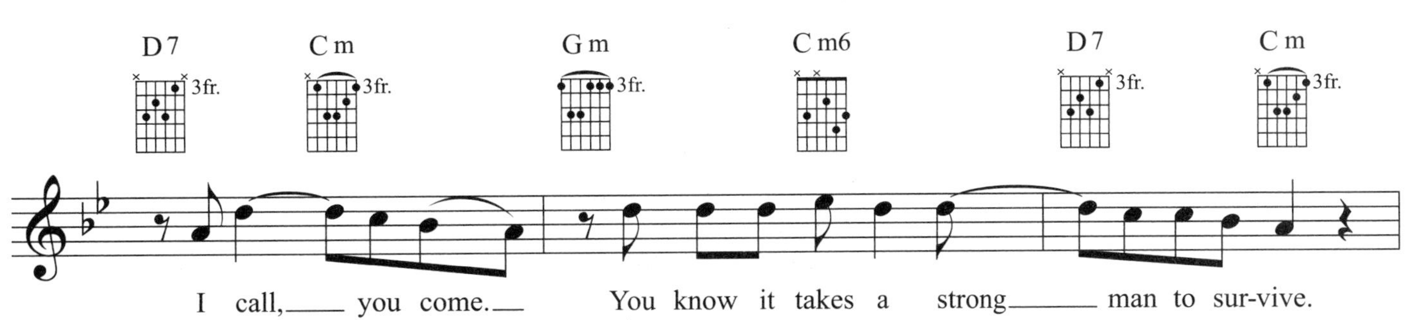

Gm Cm6 D7 Cm Gm Cm6 D7 Cm
It ain't no ac-ci-dent that you're still a - live. We stand for the neigh-bor-hood
Gm Cm6 D7 Cm Gm Cm6
He still lives with his mami, but he sneaks down, A coolie in the shadow of the playground. You want to fight for your people,
D7 Cm Gm Cm6 D7 Cm
don't you, Sal?
Well, yeah, if I got to.
Oh, you got to.
Gm Cm6 D7 Cm Gm Cm6
Come here, I want to show you something.
This is the cave of The Vam -
D7 Cm Gm Cm6 D7 Cm Gm Cm6
pires, Count Drac-u-la's cas - tle, The ver-y sight could turn
D7 Cm Gm Cm6 D7 Cm Gm Cm6
a white man grey. Made in the shade,
3fr.

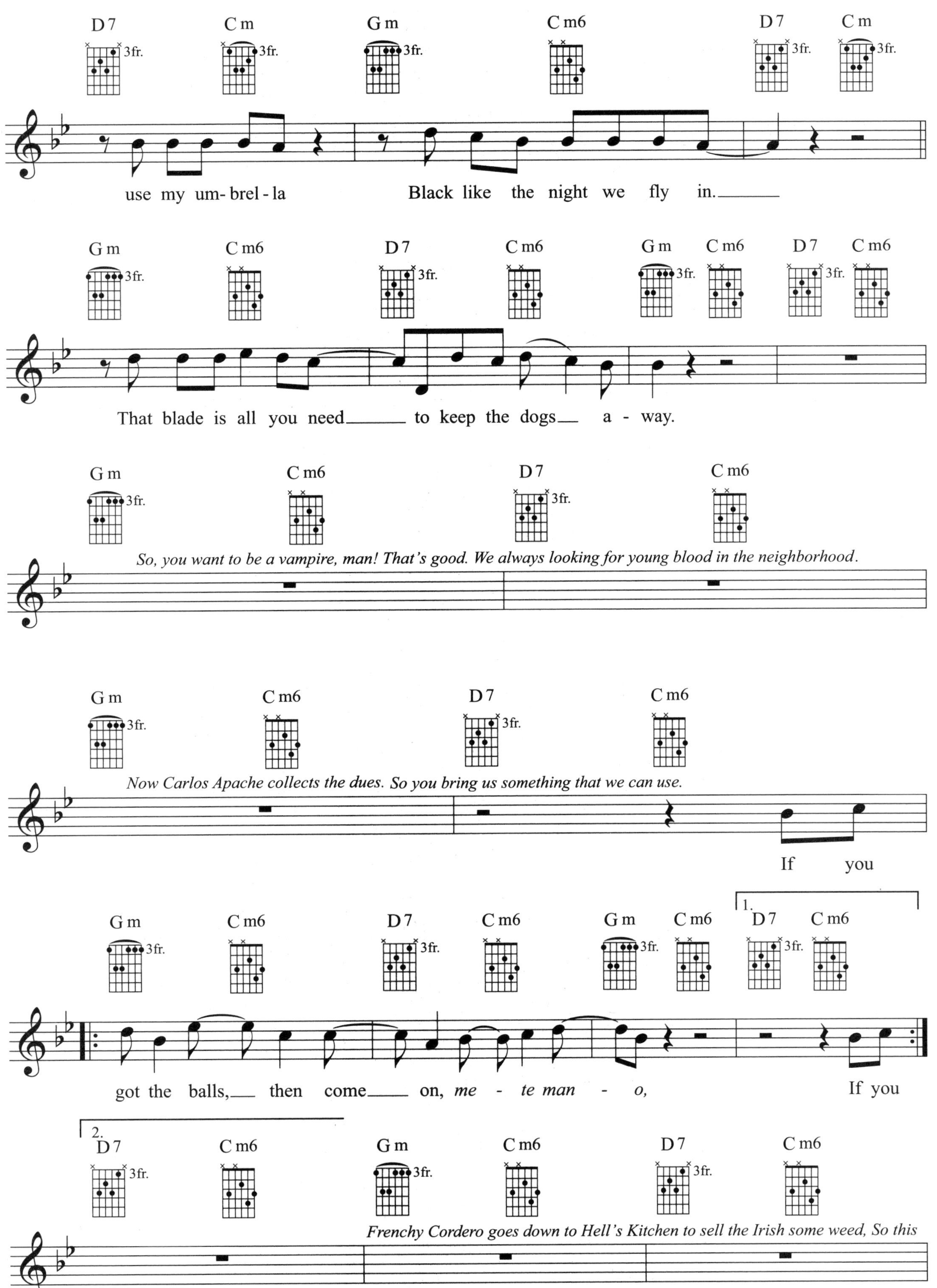
D7
Cm
Gm
Cm6
D7
Cm
3fr.
use my um- brel - la
Black like the night we fly in.
Gm
Cm6
D7
Cm6
Gm
Cm6
D7
Cm6
That blade is all you need to keep the dogs a - way.
Gm
Cm6
D7
Cm6
So, you want to be a vampire, man! That's good. We always looking for young blood in the neighborhood.
Gm
Cm6
D7
Cm6
Now Carlos Apache collects the dues. So you bring us something that we can use.
If you
Gm
Cm6
D7
Cm6
Gm
Cm6
1.
D7
Cm6
got the balls, then come on, me - te man - o,
If you
2.
D7
Cm6
Gm
Cm6
D7
Cm6
Frenchy Cordero goes down to Hell's Kitchen to sell the Irish some weed, So this

Gm
Cm6
D7
Cm6
Gm
Cm6
3fr.
Paddy boy's mother on the stoop starts bitchin' 'Bout spics is a mongrel breed. Now here comes her son, He looks like a ton
of corned beef Floating in beer.
He says:
"Fuck- ing Puer - to Ri - can dope
deal-ing punk Get your shit-brown ass out of here."
We stand for the neigh - bor - hood.
So the shanty-town Irish they kicked his ass good. Fractured his collar bone.
Coño, all I was thinking is,

D7
Cm6
Gm
Cm6
3fr.
'What home of the brave? This is a fucking war zone!'
If you got the balls, then come
on, me - te ma - no,
If you got co - jo - nes, come
on, me - te ma - no
- no
1.
2.
Gm
Bb13
A7#9
Ab13
Gm6
6fr.
5fr.
4fr.
(instrumental solo)
repeat ad lib
N. C.
D7
Cm
D
D/C
play three times

You Can Call Me Al

Words and Music by Paul Simon

Moderately

F C B♭ F C F C B♭ C F

F C F Gm 3fr. F C

1.A man ___ walks down the street ___ He says Why am I soft in the mid-dle now

F C F Gm 3fr. F C F

Why am I soft in the mid-dle The rest of my life is so hard

C F Gm 3fr. F C

I need a pho-to op-por-tu-ni-ty I want a shot at re-demp-tion

F C F Gm 3fr. F C

Don't want to end up a car - toon In a car - toon ___ grave - yard

F Gm 3fr. C F

Bone dig-ger Bone dig-ger Dogs in the moon - light ___ Far a-way in my

Gm
3fr.
C
F
well - lit door
Mis-ter Beer bel-ly Beer bel-ly
Get these mutts a-way from me
I don't find this stuff a - mus - ing an - y - more
B♭
If you'll be my bod-y - guard
I can be your long lost pal
to Coda
I can call you Bet-ty
And Bet-ty when you call me You can
1.
call me Al
2.
call me Al
call me Al
play four times then D.C. al Coda
(instrumental)

2. A man walks down the street
He says why am I short of attention
Got a short little span of attention
And wo my nights are so long
Where's my wife and family
What if I die here
Who'll be my role model
Now that my role model is
Gone Gone
He ducked back down the alley
With some roly-poly little bat-faced girl
All along along
There were incidents and accidents
There were hints and allegations

3. A man walks down the street
It's a street in a strange world
Maybe it's the Third World
Maybe it's his first time around
He doesn't speak the language
He holds no currency
He is a foreign man
He is surrounded by the sound
The sound
Cattle in the marketplace
Scatterlings and orphanages
He looks around, around
He sees angels in the architecture
Spinning in infinity
He says Amen! And Hallelujah!

Virgil

Music by Paul Simon
Lyrics by Paul Simon and Derek Walcott

Dm
(instrumental solo on D. S.)
Since he's been here he's fol-lowed ev-'ry rule Well I told you
A
Dm
3
my po - si-tion The law says he's got the right to go
G
A
G
F
Dm
D♯bass
to school, We a - bide by the court's de - ci - sion
Ebass
Fbass
F♯bass
G
(end instrumental solo)
1.I got a Win-ches - ter two-for-ty-three
D
I like that gun for deer
G
Up-state No - vem-ber when the air is free

2. There ain't no way that punk gets his degree
And hides behind the Constitution
No way in hell that smart-ass spic goes free
Not while I'm in this institution

You Don't Know Where Your Interest Lies

Words and Music by Paul Simon

Dm
C
B♭
you don't know where your in - ter - est lies.
Gm7 Am B♭ Am C♯°7 Dm E°7
3fr.
to Coda
No, you don't know where your in - ter - est
A
Dm
Dm
lies.
You're just a game that I like
C Dm C Dm B♭
to play, You may think that we're friends all right, but
Dm C B♭
I won't let friend - ship get in my way, No,
Gm7 Am B♭ Am C♯°7 Dm Dsus2
3fr.
I won't let friend - ship get in my way.

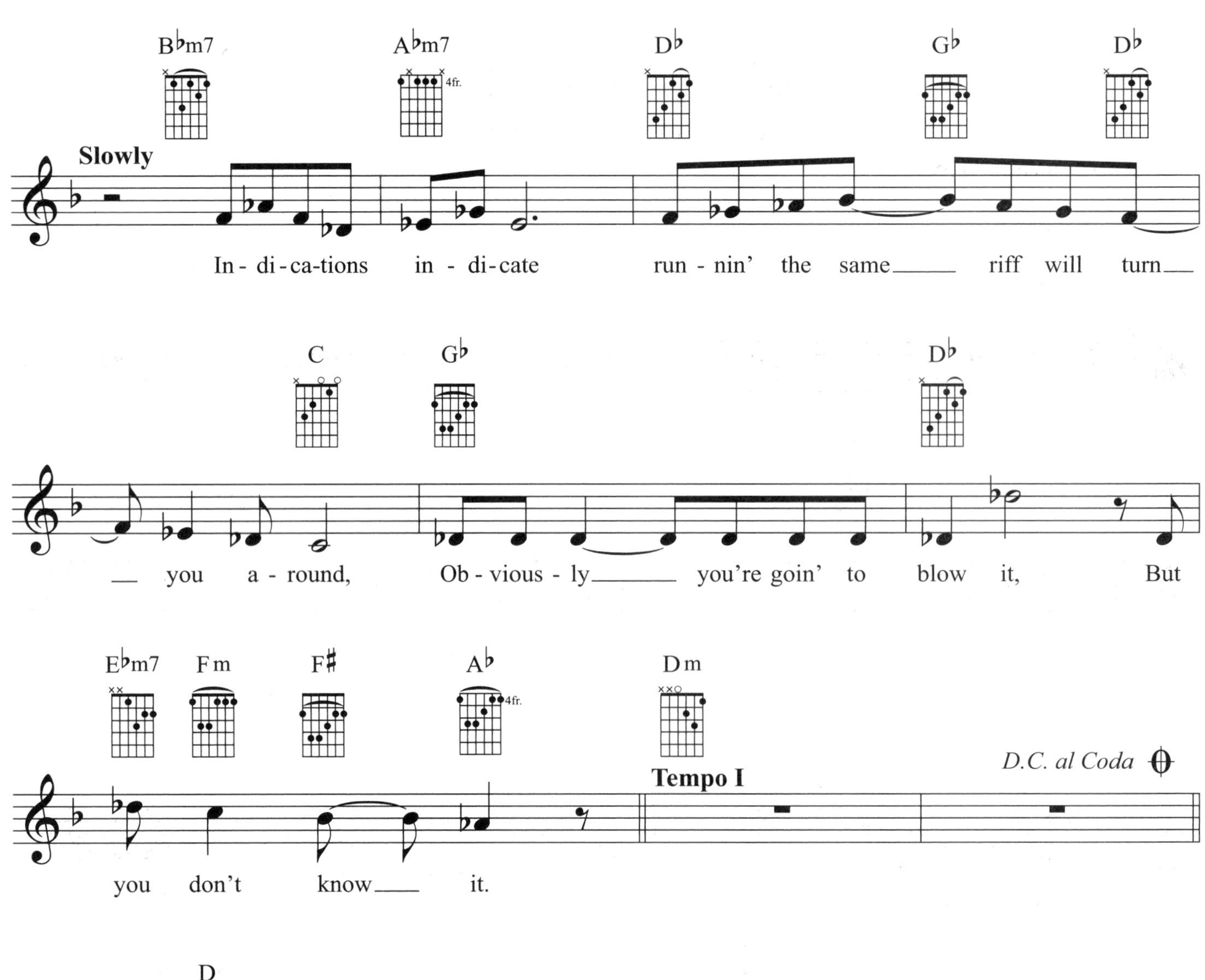
B♭m7
A♭m7
D♭
G♭
D♭
Slowly
In - di - ca-tions in - di - cate run - nin' the same riff will turn
C
G♭
D♭
you a - round, Ob - vious - ly you're goin' to blow it, But
E♭m7
Fm
F♯
A♭
Dm
Tempo I
D.C. al Coda
you don't know it.
Coda
D
lies.

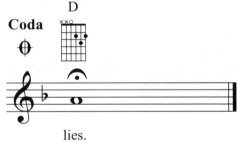

Was A Sunny Day

Words and Music by Paul Simon

Medium calypso

C7 G D7

G N.C. C7

Was a sun - ny day,

G D7

Not a cloud was in the sky, Not a neg - a - tive word was heard

Em G C7

from the peo - ples pass - ing by. 'Twas a sun - ny day,

G

All the bird - ies in the trees, And the ra - di - o's sing -

D7 G

- ing song, All the fav - 'rite mel - o - dies. 1.He was a Na -

Am
D
G
E
- vy man
sta- tioned in New - port News,
She was a high - school queen with noth - ing real - ly left
C
C7
— to lose.
She was a high - school queen with noth -
ing real - ly left to lose.
Was a sun - ny day,
D7
Not a cloud was in the sky,
Not a neg - a - tive word was heard
Em
from the peo - ples pass - ing by.
'Twas a sun - ny day,
All the bird - ies in the trees,
And the ra - di - o's sing - ing song,

2. Her name was Lorelei,
She was his only girl.
She called him "Speedoo,"
But his Christian name was Mister Earl.
She called him "Speedoo,"
But his Christian name was Mister Earl.

We've Got A Groovy Thing Goin'

Words and Music by Paul Simon

Moderately fast

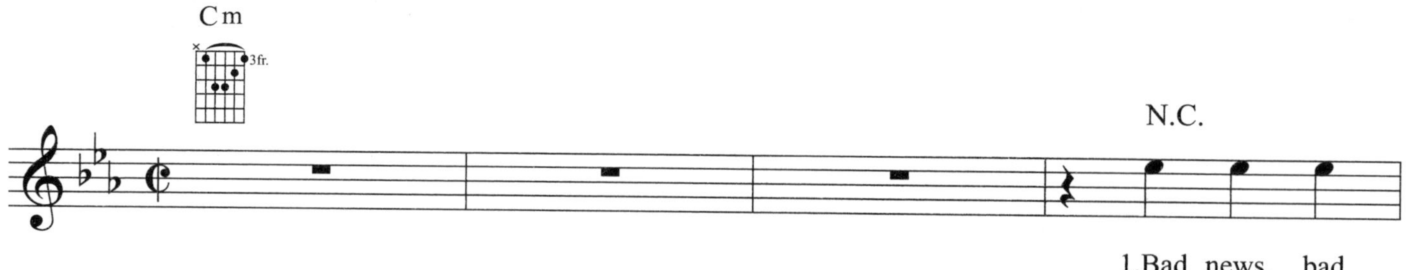

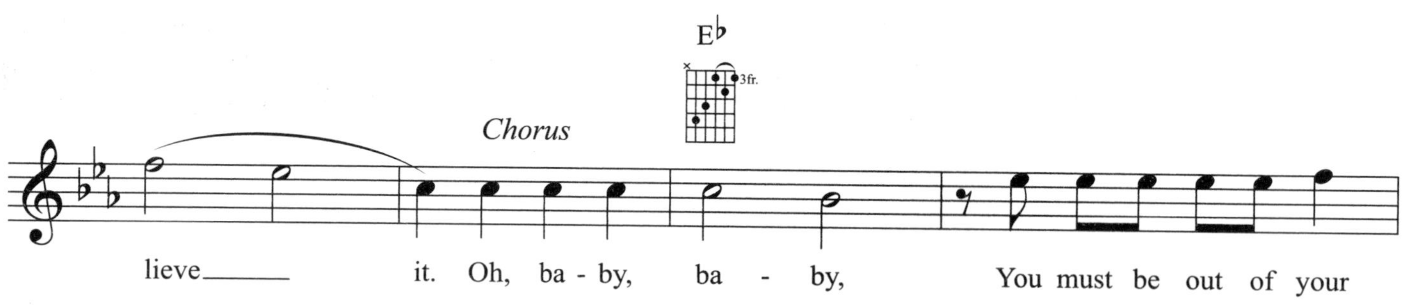

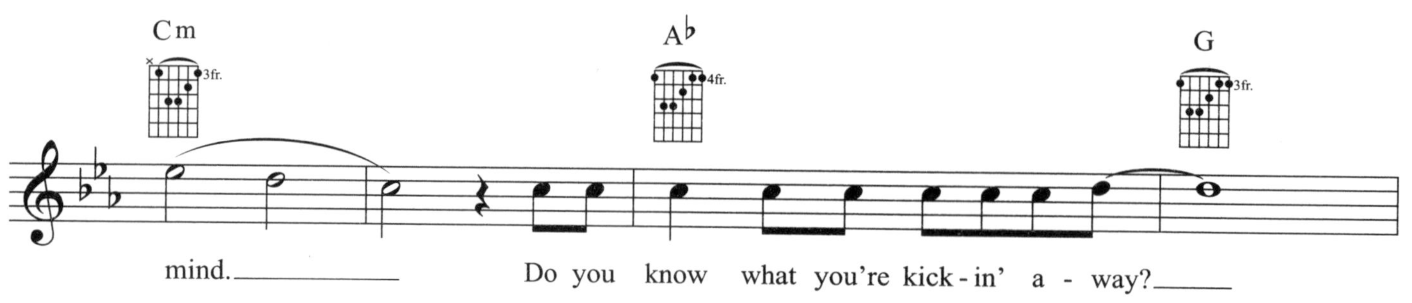

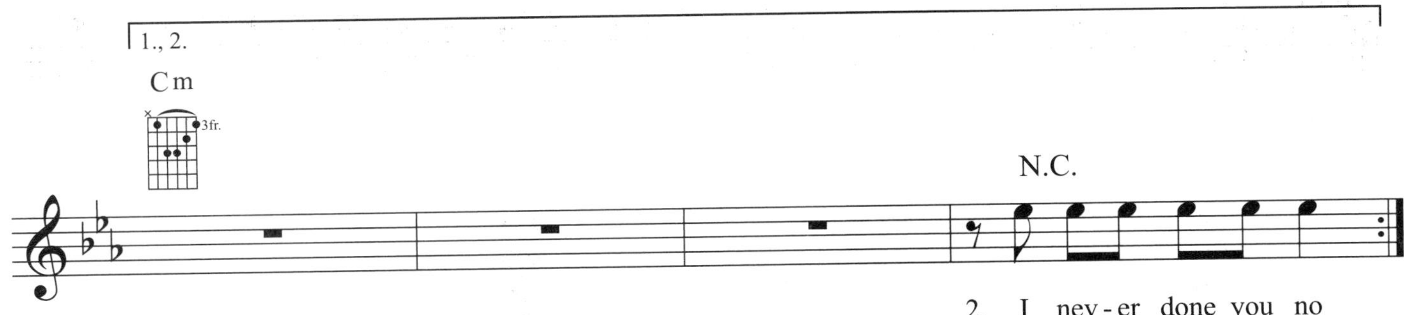

2. I never done you no wrong,
I never hit you when you're down,
I always gave you good loving,
I never ran around,
I never ran around.

Chorus

3. There's something you ought to know
If you're fixing to go,
I can't make it without you;
No no no no, no, no, no, no,
No no no no, no, no, no.

Chorus

When Numbers Get Serious

Words and Music by Paul Simon

Moderately bright

N.C. D G/D D

1.I have a num-ber in my ___ head Though I don't know why it's

G C/G G C/G G Am D G

there When num-bers get se - ri-ous

Em D/F♯ D

You see their shape eve-ry-where ___ Di-vi-ding and mul -

G Bm7/F♯ Em C/E

- ti-plying Ex-chang-ing with ease When times ___ are mys-te -

G Am/C D *to Coda* G C/G G

- ri-ous Se-ri-ous num - bers are ea - ger to please ___

F♯7
B
Take my ad-dress Take my phone
Call me if you can
Here's my ad-dress Here's my phone
Please don't give it to some mad - man
Hey hey,
whoa whoa
it's a com-pli-cat-ed life
Num-bers swirl - ing thick and cu-ri-ous You can
Em7
C/E
D/F♯
cut them with a knife
You can cut them with a knife
G
C/G
1.
2.
2.Two times two is twen -
D.S. al Coda
3.So wrap me Wrap me Wrap

Coda
G
C/E
D7/F♯
G
When times are mys - te - ri-ous Se-ri-ous num - bers will al - ways be heard
Triplet feel
C/E
D7/F♯
G
C/G
G
E♭/G
B♭
A♭
And af-ter all is said and done
And the num-bers all come home The four rolls in - to three
Gm
Fm7
E♭
E♭9
A♭
the three turns in - to two
the two be - comes a One
Gm
Fm7
E♭

2. Two times two is twenty-two
Four times four is forty-four
When numbers get serious
They leave a mark on your door
Urgent. Urgent.
A telephone is ringing in the hallways
When times are mysterious
Serious numbers will speak to us always
That is why a man with numbers
Can put your mind at ease
We've got numbers by the trillions
Here and overseas
Hey hey, whoa whoa
Look at the stink about Japan
All those numbers waiting patiently
Don't you understand?
Don't you understand?

3. So wrap me
Wrap me
Wrap me do
In the shelter of your arms
I am ever your volunteer
I won't do you any harm
I will love innumerably
You can count on my word
When times are mysterious
Serious numbers
Will always be heard
When times are mysterious
Serious numbers will always be heard
And after all is said and done
And the numbers all come home
The four rolls into three
The three turns into two
And the two becomes a
One

Why Don't You Write Me?

Words and Music by Paul Simon

Moderate, with a strong beat

F7
8fr.
— And I know — I got to be there.
(yeah)
B♭7
6fr.
Cm
3fr.
May-be I'm lost, — But I can't — make the cost — Of the air - fare. — (oo) —
Gm
3fr.
E♭
6fr.
A♭
4fr.
Tell me why —
Tell me why —
B♭
6fr.
E♭
6fr.
E♭7
6fr.
A♭7
4fr.
E♭7
6fr.
E♭
6fr.
Why don't you write — me? A let - ter would bright - en my lone -

F7
8fr.
B♭7
6fr.
- li - est eve - ning.
Mail it to - day___ if it's on -
Cm
3fr.
Gm
3fr.
- ly to say___ that you're leav - ing me.___ (Oo)___
E♭
6fr.
A♭7
4fr.
E♭7
6fr.
(Falsetto:) (la, la,___ la)
A♭7
4fr.
E♭7
6fr.
A♭7
4fr.
Mon - day morn - ing, sit-ting in the sun Hop - ing and wish-ing for the mail___ to come.
E♭
6fr.
E♭7
6fr.
Tues - day, nev - er got a word, mmm.___

A♭7
4fr.
Wednes - day, Thurs - day, ain't no sign, Drank a half a bot - tle of i - o - dine.
E♭
6fr.
E♭7
6fr.
A♭
4fr.
Fri - day, woe is me I'm gon - na hang my bod - y from the high - est tree.
E♭
6fr.
E♭7
6fr.
A♭
4fr.
(Falsetto:) Why don't you write me?
Why don't you write me?
A♭7
4fr.
E♭
6fr.
E♭7
6fr.
Why don't you write me?
Why don't you write

You're Kind

Words and Music by Paul Simon

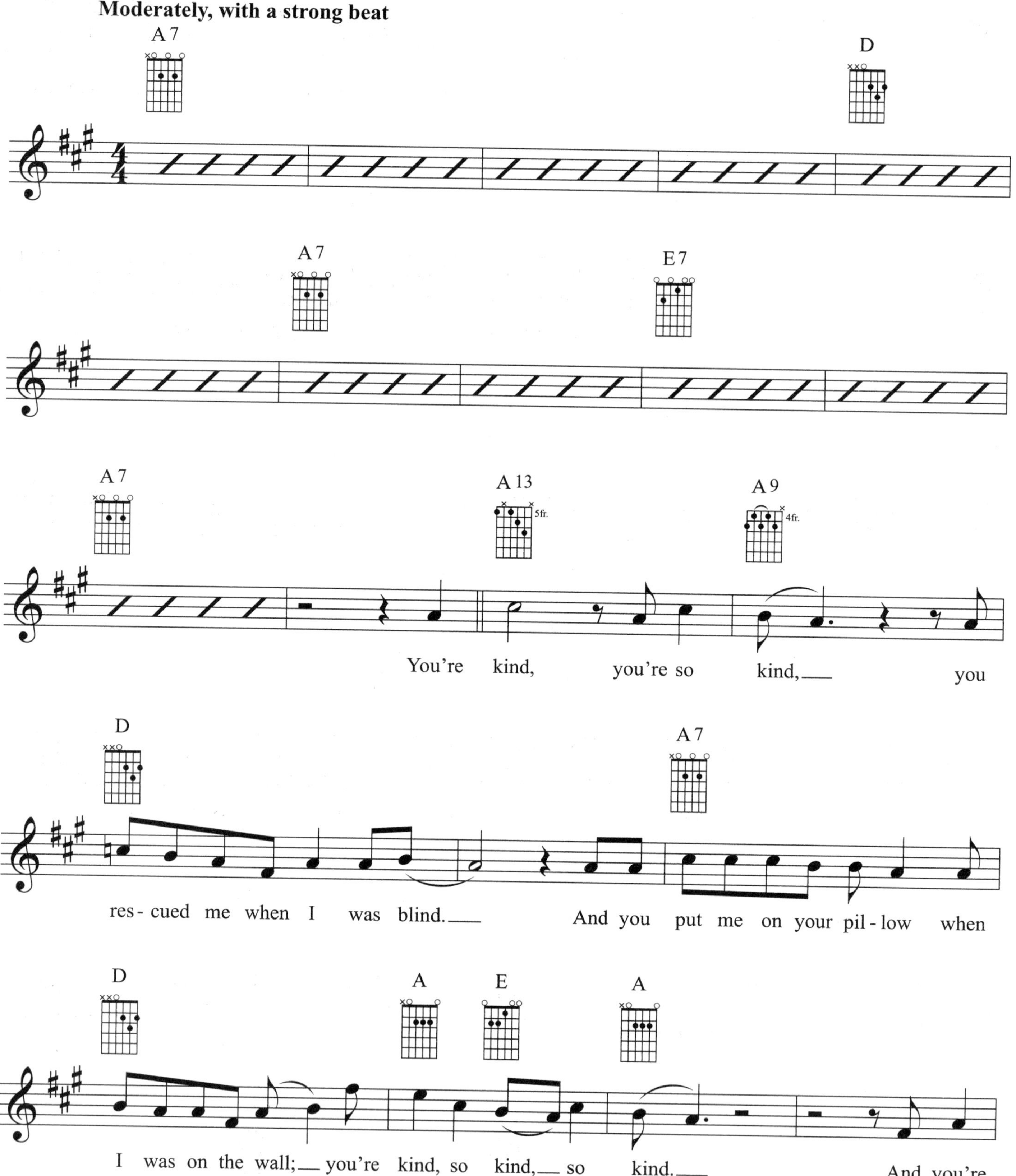

A 13
A 9
D
good, you're so good; you in-tro-duced me to your neigh-bor-
A
D
hood. Seems like I ain't nev-er had so man-y friends be-fore; that's be-
A
E
A
cause you're good, you're so good.
B maj7
E
Why you don't treat me like the oth-er hu-mans do is just a
A 13
E
B maj7
mys-ter-y to me. It gets me ag-i-tat-ed
E
A 9
F♯7
when I think that you're gon-na love me now in-def-i-nite-ly So good-

B
A9
4fr.
E
bye, good - bye, I'm gon-na leave you now and here's the rea - son
B9
why: I like to sleep with the win - dow o - pen and you
E
B
F♯
keep the win - dow closed. So good - bye, good - bye, good
B
E7
B9
B7
to Coda
bye. Oh, oh, oh, oh, oh,
E7
B9
B7
E7
oh, oh, oh,
B9
B7
F♯13
F♯7
D.S. al Coda
So good-

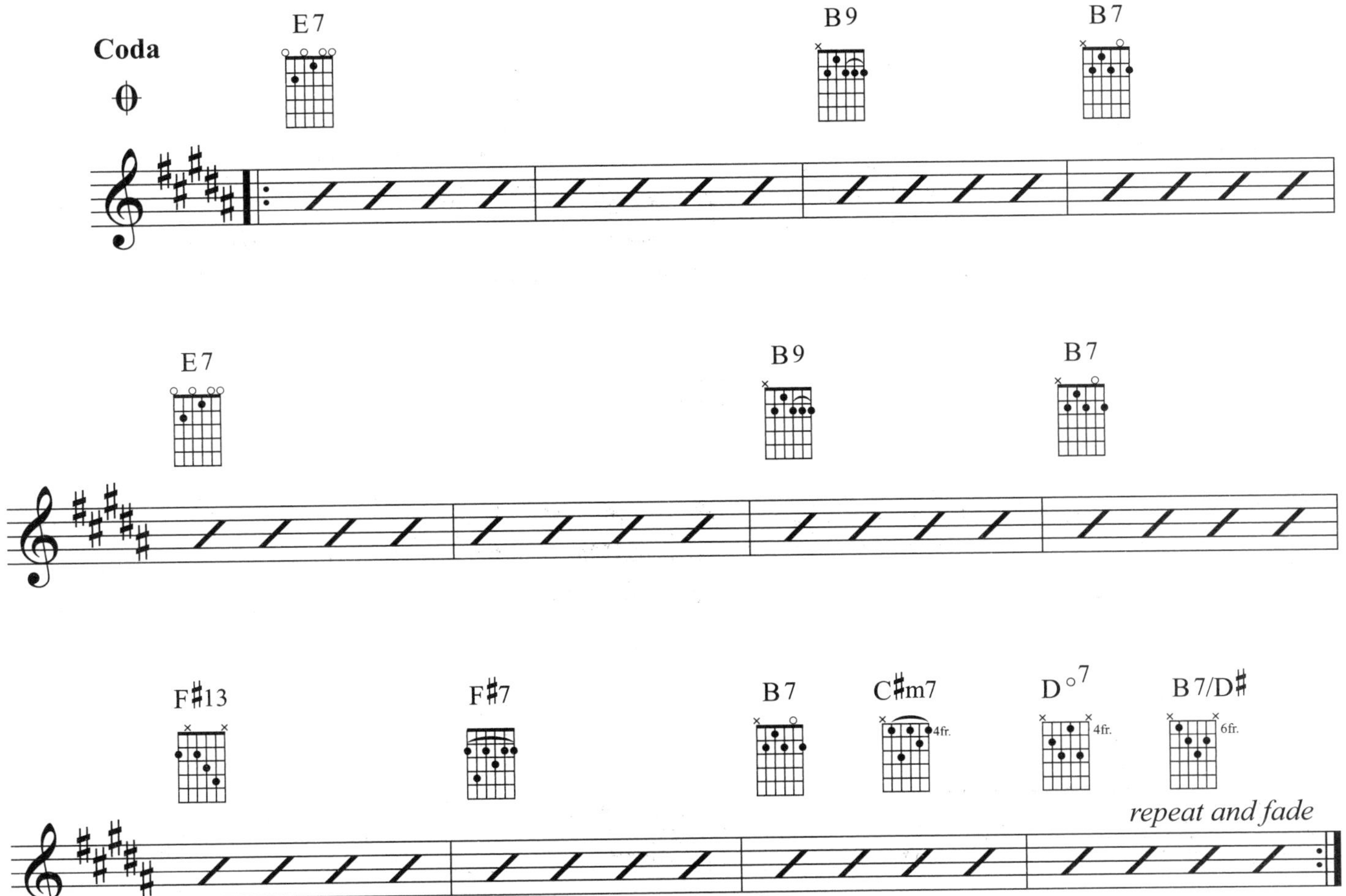
Coda
E7
B9
B7
E7
B9
B7
F♯13
F♯7
B7
C♯m7
4fr.
D°7
4fr.
B7/D♯
6fr.
repeat and fade

You're The One

Words and Music by Paul Simon

B♭m
6fr.
F
5fr.
Take its temp-'ra-ture ev - 'ry hour Ner-vous when you own it Ner - vous when it's gone
E♭
B♭/D
B♭
C
F
5fr.
Fmaj7
5fr.
What do you think has been go - ing on For
Gm7
8fr.
B♭m
6fr.
F
5fr.
N.C.
so long?
You
are the air In-
side my chest
F
5fr.
Chorus
You're the one You broke my heart You

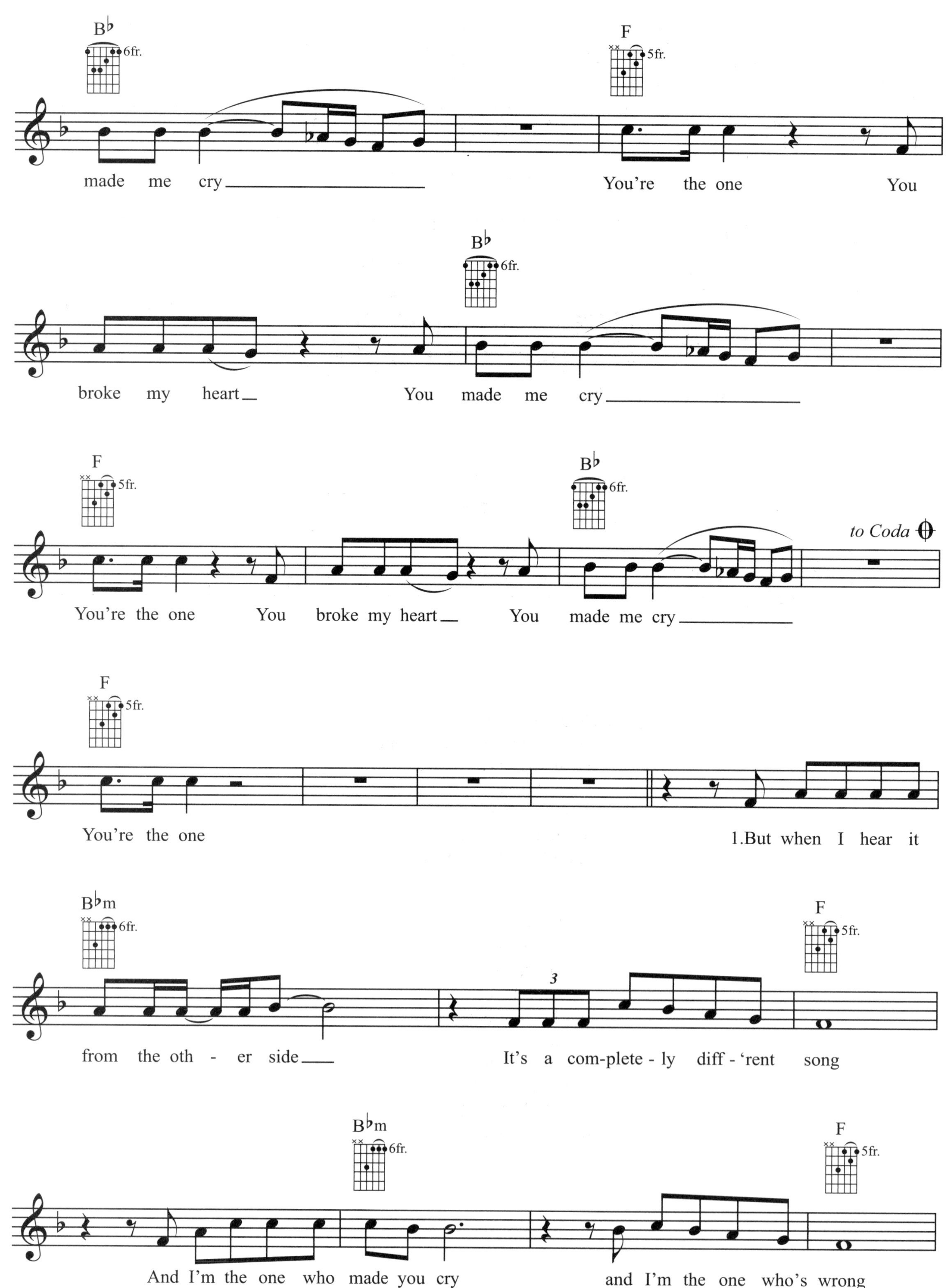
B♭
6fr.
F
5fr.
made me cry
You're the one You
broke my heart
You made me cry
You're the one You
broke my heart
You made me cry
to Coda
You're the one
1.But when I hear it
B♭m
from the oth - er side
It's a com-plete - ly diff - 'rent song
And I'm the one who made you cry
and I'm the one who's wrong

2. Nature gives us shapeless shapes
Clouds and waves and flame
But human expectation
Is that love remains the same
And when it doesn't
We point our fingers
And blame blame blame

Chorus:
You're the one
You broke my heart
You made me cry
And I'm the one
I broke your heart
I made you cry
And you're the one
You broke my heart
You made me cry
We're the ones